Integrating South and East Asia

Integrating South and East Asia

Economics of Regional Cooperation and Development

Edited by
Jayant Menon
and
T.N. Srinivasan

Copublication of the Asian Development Bank
and Oxford University Press India

50 YEARS ADB

OXFORD
UNIVERSITY PRESS

OXFORD
UNIVERSITY PRESS

Oxford University Press is a department of the University of Oxford. It furthers the University's objective of excellence in research, scholarship, and education by publishing worldwide. Oxford is a registered trademark of Oxford University Press in the UK and in certain other countries.

Published in India by
Oxford University Press
2/11 Ground Floor, Ansari Road, Daryaganj, New Delhi 110 002, India

6 ADB Avenue, Mandaluyong City
1550 Metro Manila, Philippines
Tel +63 2 632 4444
Fax +63 2 636 2444
www.adb.org

First Edition published in 2018

ISBN-13: 978-0-19-947412-7
ISBN-10: 0-19-947412-5

Typeset in Dante MT Std 10.5/13
by Excellent Laser Typesetters, Pitampura, Delhi 110 034
Printed in India by Rakmo Press, New Delhi 110 020

Note: In this publication, '$' refers to US dollar, unless stated otherwise. The maps in this volume do not claim to represent the authenticate domestic or international boundaries of nations. They are not to scale and are provided for illustrative purposes only.

Contents

Tables, Figures, and Boxes

Tables

Figures

Boxes

Foreword

From the late 1940s up until the early 1990s, the economic trajectories of East and South Asia could not have looked more different. The postcolonial period saw most of East Asia rebuilding regional ties and embracing outward-looking economic policies. There were some stragglers in the subregion—the Mekong countries and the People's Republic of China only began market-based reforms in the late 1980s—but these countries managed to adopt outward-oriented and market-friendly reforms in a relatively short period of time. Whereas East Asia began to look ever outwards, for about four decades, South Asia chose to focus inwards, relying on central planning and import-substituting industrialization for growth. To protect local industries, South Asia adopted stringent regulations and erected trade and investment barriers, but these did little to develop the manufacturing sector. Meanwhile, decades of central planning led to serious fiscal imbalances and an increasingly inefficient public sector. Thus, while East Asian economies flourished with openness, South Asian economies floundered in isolation.

South Asia had a number of short-lived attempts at liberalization between the 1960s and mid-1980s. But the gradual process of reform and liberalization in the subregion only took off in the 1990s, triggered by growing macroeconomic imbalances and the worldwide transformation of centrally planned economies into market economies. The transition towards a more open and market-based system has allowed South Asia to reinvent itself as one of the most dynamic subregions in the world. Over the next 2 years, South Asia is projected to grow at a faster pace than East Asia. The 'Asian Development Outlook 2017' of the Asian Development Bank forecasts growth in the subregion to accelerate to 7.0 per cent in 2017 and 7.2 per cent in 2018, after a slight drop to 6.7 per cent in 2016.

Greater openness has also led to growing economic ties between South and East Asia. East Asia's share in South Asia's trade has grown from 22 per cent in 1990 to 28 per cent in 2014, and while South Asia's share in East Asia's trade remains small, it has nonetheless increased from 3 per cent to 6 per cent during the same period. With the Doha Development Round stalled, both subregions are now looking at free trade agreements as a means of pursuing integration. As of February 2016, there were six plurilateral and 12 bilateral FTAs involving South and East Asian countries, at various stages of completion.

Despite these notable gains, however, the trade and investment stories of these two subregions continue to remain vastly different. Barriers to trade and investment remain high in South Asia compared to East Asia. South Asia's borders remain thick, trade within the subregion is still one of the lowest in the world, and protectionist domestic policies continue to distort factor and commodities markets. Clearly, greater liberalization and more ambitious domestic policy reform will be necessary to increase trade and investment linkages and further open up opportunities for South Asia to promote labour-intensive manufacturing; participate in regional production networks; and transition to higher value-added activities.

This volume examines how greater integration between South and East Asia can help spur further growth in trade and investment in both subregions, with a focus on the challenges that South Asia continues to face. But this volume also emphasizes that regional cooperation will not amount to much, if it is not complemented by a much wider set of domestic structural reforms. Ultimately, true progress must still come from within the countries themselves.

Yasuyuki Sawada
Chief Economist and Director General
Economic Research and Regional Cooperation Department
Asian Development Bank

Abbreviations*

ABB	ASEA Brown Boveri
ABS	acrylonitrile-butadiene-styrene
ABTC	Australian Business Travel Card
ACT	Agreement on Textiles and Clothing
AD	anti-dumping
ADB	Asian Development Bank
ADBI	Asian Development Bank Institute
ADF	Augmented Dickey and Fuller
AEC	ASEAN Economic Community
AFAS	ASEAN Framework Agreement on Services
AIC	Akaikie Information Criterion
AIFTA	ASEAN–India Free Trade Area
AIMT	Asian Institute of Management and Technology
AIOE	All India Organisation of Employers
APEC	Asia-Pacific Economic Cooperation
APTA	Asia-Pacific Trade Agreement
ASEAN	Association of Southeast Asian Nations
BCCT	Brandix College of Clothing Technology
BCIM	Bangladesh–China–India–Myanmar
BCTI	Brandix Clothing Training Institution
BEC	broad economic categories

* The list consolidates abbreviations used in the book. There might be instances of duplication of an abbreviation by virtue of a difference in its full form. Readers are recommended to refer to the list contextually.

BHEL	Bharat Heavy Electricals Limited
BIAC	Brandix India Apparel City
BIMSTEC	Bay of Bengal Initiative for Multi-Sectoral Technical and Economic Co-operation
BIPA	Bilateral Investment Promotion and Protection Agreement
BOI	Board of Investment
BoT	Bank of Thailand
BPCB	bare printed circuit board
BTA	bilateral trade agreement
BTG	boiler turbine generator
BTIA	Broad-based Trade and Investment Agreement
BTO	build-transfer-operate
BV	business visitor
CAD	computer aided design
CADP	Comprehensive Asia Development Plan
CAM	computer aided manufacturing
CBSL	Central Bank of Sri Lanka
CEAMA	Consumer Electronics and Appliances Manufacturers Association
CECA	Comprehensive Economic Cooperation Agreement
CENVAT	central value added tax
CEPA	Comprehensive Economic Partnership Agreement
CEPEA	Comprehensive Economic Partnership for East Asia
CEPII	the French Centre d'Etudes Prospectives et d'Informations Internationales
CGE	computable general equilibrium
CII	Confederation of Indian Industry
CLMV	Cambodia, Lao PDR, Myanmar, and Viet Nam
CMT	cut, make, and trim
CPC	Central Product Classification
CRGO	cold-rolled grain-oriented steel
CSO	Central Statistics Office
CSR	corporate social responsibility
CSS	contractual service suppliers

CST	central sales tax
CTS	consolidated tariff schedules
CVD	countervailing duties
DDT	dichlorodiphenyltrichloroethane / dividend distribution tax
DIPP	Department of Industrial Policy and Promotion
DMIC	Delhi Mumbai Industrial Corridor
DTAA	Double Taxation Avoidance Agreement
EDB	Export Development Board
EDI	electronic data interchange
EFTA	European Free Trade Association
ELCINA	Electronic Industries Association of India
ENT	economic needs test
EPZ	export processing zone
ERIA	Economic Research Institute for ASEAN and East Asia
ERP	enterprise resource planning
EU	European Union
EVA	economic value added
EVI	economic vulnerability indicator
EXPY	export substitution
FDA	Food and Drug Administration
FDI	foreign direct investment
FERA	Foreign Exchange Regulation Act
FICCI	Federation of Indian Chambers of Commerce and Industry
FIE	foreign invested enterprises
FIPB	Foreign Investment Promotion Board
FISME	Federation of Indian Micro and Small & Medium Enterprises
FPD	flat panel display
FSMP	Financial Sector Master Plan
FTA	free trade agreement
FTZ	Free Trade Zone
GAAR	General Anti-Avoidance Rules
GATS	General Agreement on Trade in Services
GATT	General Agreement on Tariffs and Trade

GCC	Gulf Cooperation Council
GCEC	Greater Colombo Economic Commission
GDP	gross domestic product
GEP	Globalisation and Economic Policy
GII	global innovation index
GLI	Grubel-Lloyd Index
GM	General Motors
GNI	gross national income
GSP	generalized system of preferences
GST	goods and services tax
GVC	global value chain
HAI	human assets index
HMR	head motion regression/Helpman, Melitz, and Rubinstein
HO theory	Hecksher-Ohlin theory
HS level	harmonized standard level
HSHT	high skill and high technology
HTDZ	High Technology Development Zone
HVM	high value manufacturing
ICD	Inland Clearance Depots
ICRIER	Indian Council for Research on International Economic Relations
ICT	information and communication technology/ intra-corporate transferees
IDB	integrated data base
IDE	Institute of Developing Economies
IIT	intra-industry trade
ILO	International Labour Organization
IMF	International Monetary Fund
IMO	Institute of Marketecology
IMTTH	India–Myanmar–Thailand Trilateral Highway
IP	independent professionals
IPoA	Istanbul Programme of Action
ISIC	International Standard of Industrial Classification
IT	information technology
ITA	International Technology Agreement
ITeS	information technology enabled services
JAAF	Joint Apparel Association Forum

JNPT	Jawahar National Port Trust
KGEPZ	export processing zone in Koggala
KIEP	Korea Institute for International Economic Policy
KORUS	Korea Free Trade Agreement
LARR	Land Acquisition, Rehabilitation and Resettlement
LCD	liquid crystal display
LDC	least developed country
LED	light-emitting diode
LEED	Leadership in Energy and Environmental Design
LPI	logistics performance index
LSP	logistics service provider
MAT	minimum alternate tax
MFA	Multi-Fibre Agreement
MFN	most favoured nation
MIEC	Mekong–India Economic Corridor
MIMT	Institute of Management and Technology
MITI	Ministry of International Trade and Industry
MNC	multinational corporation
MRA	mutual recognition agreement
MRTP	Monopolies and Restrictive Trade Practices
MSME	Ministry of Micro, Small and Medium Enterprises
MUL	Maruti Udyog Limited
NAFTA	North American Free Trade Agreement
NASSCOM	National Association of Software and Services Companies
NBER	National Bureau of Economic Research
NCLAT	National Company Law Appellate Tribunal
NCLT	National Company Law Tribunal
NIE	newly industrializing economy
NIMZ	national investment and manufacturing zones
NMCC	National Manufacturing Competitive Council
NML	National Metallurgical Laboratory
NMP	National Manufacturing Policy
NRI	non-resident Indian
NTB	non-tariff barrier
NTM	non-tariff measure
OBM	original brand manufacturing
ODM	original design manufacturing

OECD	Organisation for Economic Co-operation and Development
OEM	original equipment manufacturing
OLS	ordinary least square
OPC	Open Port City
PCBA	printed circuit board assembly
POSCO	Pohang Iron and Steel Company
PPP	public-private partnership
PRC	People's Republic of China
PTA	plurilateral free trade agreement
P&C	parts and components
RBI	Reserve Bank of India
RCA	revealed comparative advantage
RCEP	Regional Comprehensive Economic Partnership
RCI	regional cooperation and integration
RINL	Rashtriya Ispat Nigam Limited
RMS	risk management system
ROO	rules of origin
SAARC	South Asian Association for Regional Cooperation
SAFTA	South Asia Free Trade Agreement
SAP	Systems, Applications, and Products
SATIS	SAARC Agreement on Trade in Services
SEZ	Special Economic Zone
SGS	Société Générale de Surveillance
SIPA	Software Industry Promotion Agency
SITC	Standard International Trade Classification
SME	small and medium-sized enterprise
SOE	state-owned enterprises
TAR	Trans-Asian Railway
TEFTA	Thailand–European Free Trade Association
TIEP	Temporary Import for Export Processing
TIG	trade in goods
TiVA	Trade in Value Added
TPP	Trans-Pacific Partnership
TUSFTA	Thailand–US Free Trade Agreement
TVS	TV Sundaram
UAE	United Arab Emirates

UK	United Kingdom
UN	United Nations
UNCTAD	United Nations Conference on Trade and Development
UNESCAP	United Nations Economic and Social Commission for Asia and the Pacific
UNIDO	United Nations Industrial Development Organization
US	United States
USAID	United States Agency for International Development
USITC	United States International Trade Commission
VAR	vector autoregression
VAT	value added tax
WDI	World Development Indicators
WIOD	World Input-Output Database
WITS	World Integrated Trade Solutions
WTO	World Trade Organization

T.N. SRINIVASAN AND JAYANT MENON

Introduction

Integrating South and East Asia—Economics of Regional Cooperation and Development

Background and Rationale for the Study

Since the early 1990s, there has been a marked increase in regional cooperation and integration (RCI) amongst the economies in South and East Asia. Economic reforms in the People's Republic of China (PRC) since the 1980s, greater trade and investment openness in India and the rest of South Asia since the 1990s, and the emergence of regional production networks provided the initial push for greater RCI both within and between the two subregions. Domestic policy reforms and global market forces have played the biggest role in driving RCI; but more recently, bilateral and regional-level initiatives are also helping to boost South and East Asian integration. Bilateral free trade agreements (FTAs) between South and East Asian economies have increased, from none in 2000 to 12 in 2016. Plurilateral arrangements are in place, such as the Bay of Bengal Initiative for Multi-Sectoral Technical and Economic Cooperation (BIMSTEC) and the Association of Southeast Asian Nations (ASEAN)–India Comprehensive Economic Cooperation Agreement (CECA). More are in the offing, with the Regional Comprehensive Economic Partnership (RCEP), an FTA which will link the economies of ASEAN, Australia, India, Japan, Republic of Korea, the PRC, and New Zealand; the Bangladesh–China–India–Myanmar (BCIM) Economic Corridor Initiative, which will connect India, Bangladesh, Myanmar, and Yunnan, PRC through a network of roads, railways, and waterways; and the PRC's 'One Belt and One Road' initiative, which will strengthen land and maritime connectivity between the PRC and economies in South and Southeast Asia. These and other initiatives are likely to pick up pace given the continued economic fragility in developed economies. If these initiatives succeed, they will revive economic ties between the two subregions that hark back to the ancient Silk Road, and both subregions could once again grow to dominate global trade.

These developments have ignited research interest in the prospects for linking South and East Asia. The Asian Development Bank (ADB) has been one of the institutions at the forefront of this inquiry. In 2009, ADB published two volumes on RCI between South and East Asia. The first, titled *Pan-Asian Integration: Linking East and South Asia*, analysed the determinants, benefits, and obstacles to closer economic cooperation and integration. The volume examined patterns of merchandise and services trade, investment, trade and monetary cooperation, infrastructure, logistics and trade facilitation, and developments in ASEAN and South Asian Association for Regional Cooperation (SAARC), and analysed the effects of alternative integration schemes using a Computable General Equilibrium (CGE) model. The second volume, titled *National Strategies for Regional Integration: South and East Asian Case Studies,* used a common framework to examine the relationship between regional economic performance and country-level strategies for regional integration. In 2015, ADB and the ADB Institute (ADBI) jointly published another volume titled *Connecting South Asia and Southeast Asia,* which focused on the role of 'hard' infrastructure and associated 'soft' infrastructure in promoting trade and investment between the two regions.

These knowledge products notwithstanding, comprehensive and quality research on this timely subject remains scarce. Filling this gap is critical for policymakers to fully grasp the policy implications—both domestic and regional—of growing cooperation between the two subregions.

In 2012, ADB contracted the Indian Council for Research in International Economic Relations (ICRIER) and the Korea Institute for

International Economic Policy (KIEP) to conduct another study, this time focusing on (i) domestic and regional policy options for increasing trade and investment between the two subregions; and (ii) challenges facing South Asian countries and small economies in particular, in order to help them catch up with their bigger, more developed, and more liberal East Asian counterparts. Apart from ICRIER and KIEP, ADB also drew upon the expertise of renowned academics and economists in Asia, including ADB's own experts on trade.

This volume begins with three chapters which provide an overview of the general trends in interregional trade and investment between South Asia and East Asia, and examine the potential role of FTAs in advancing further integration. Moving from this general exploration of trade and investment integration, the next three chapters examine the potential role of integration in spurring economic development and making trade more inclusive for small economies. The last four chapters, prepared by ICRIER, deal primarily with India and its integration with East Asia. This focus on India is warranted, given the size of India's economy relative to its neighbours, and its role as the biggest driver of integration in the subregion.

The second to fourth sections of this introduction provide a summary of the chapters, their major policy recommendations, and caveats which must be borne in mind when interpreting the findings. The final section concludes.

Integration between South and East Asia: General Trends and the Potential Role of Free Trade Agreements

The first chapter by Ganeshan Wignaraja presents evidence of increasing integration between South Asia and East Asia since the 1990s, with the value of total interregional trade increasing from \$12.7 billion in 1990 to around \$235.2 billion in 2013. Wignaraja notes that foreign direct investment (FDI) flows and FTAs between the two regions have also increased, albeit at a much slower pace. In South Asia, India and Pakistan are identified as leading this process of integration with East Asia.

Wignaraja emphasizes the role of FTAs as a tool for promoting greater regional cooperation. Using a CGE model, he presents empirical estimates of welfare effects from various FTA scenarios involving

South Asian and East Asian economies. As is well known, putting together and implementing CGE model involves assembling an appropriate database and making many analytical assumptions and calibration (rather than econometric estimation) of many of its parameters. Appropriate checks have to be employed to test the robustness of the findings with respect to changes in assumptions and calibration. Since only a limited number of checks for robustness are feasible, the findings have to be used with caution.

In the present case, Wignaraja finds that deeper economic integration efforts will greatly benefit South Asia, with a potential increase in gross domestic product (GDP) by 2.2 per cent on the low end and 8.9 per cent on the high end. However, these potential gains are premised on greater integration within South Asia itself.

Wignaraja highlights the proposed RCEP as a potential Pan-Asian FTA that could be useful for facilitating greater integration between South and East Asia. He views an expansion of the RCEP as one way of significantly enhancing integration.

Consistent with Wignaraja's findings, Choongjae Cho's chapter on the causal relationship between trade and FDI reports an increase in trade and FDI flows between India and four East Asian countries—Japan, the Republic of Korea, Singapore, and the PRC—since the late 2000s. Cho cites cumulative FDI statistics from April 2000 to March 2013 which reveal that Singapore and Japan were the first and third largest FDI investors in India. Cho also reports that FDI between the four East Asian countries to India has been accompanied by a considerable expansion in trade volume. India's trade and FDI linkages with the four major East Asian countries appear to be growing, relative to India's more traditional western trade and FDI partners, such as the United States (US), the United Kingdom (UK), Germany, and the Netherlands.

Cho's chapter adds to Wignaraja's analysis by digging a bit further to determine whether there is a causal relationship between bilateral trade and FDI. That is, to what extent does trade drive investment flows, and vice versa? Cho argues that examining causality between trade and FDI is crucial to evaluate the medium- and long-term dynamic effects of FTAs between countries in the two regions.

To investigate this relationship between trade and FDI, Cho uses bilateral trade and FDI volume data from the third quarter of 2004 to the fourth quarter of 2012 to examine whether trade and FDI between India and a number of East Asian countries, Germany, the UK, and the US are causally related in the temporal priority sense of Granger. His analysis reveals that while the correlation coefficients between trade and FDI in the case of India–East Asian countries were much higher than for India–Western countries, a causal relationship between bilateral trade- and FDI for India and the East Asian countries could not be established. In contrast, the test revealed a two-way causality in terms of UK–India, and a one-way causality in the case of the US–India (FDI causes trade), and Germany–India (trade causes FDI). This is despite the relatively poor performance of bilateral trade and FDI involving these countries in the late 2000s. Cho ascribes this result to the relatively longer history of economic relations between India and its Western partners, which he sees as more critical to establishing causality than a short-term increase in the volume of trade and investment flows. This is a plausible inference, although it does not follow from his econometrics of Vector Auto Regression that is non-structural.

Based on these results, what does Cho make of India's FTAs with East Asian countries, and their role in promoting trade and investment flows? Despite the lack of evidence to suggest causality, Cho remains an optimist, arguing that the FTAs may still 'contribute to enhanced inter-relationship between trade and FDI'. He writes: 'From this perspective, more measures for investment as well as trade have to be deployed in future FTA upgrade negotiations between India and East Asia. Furthermore, the two governments should further strengthen bilateral efforts to create a production division in the global supply chain through trade and FDI. These efforts will make it possible to compensate for the relatively low trade–FDI relationship and the short history of economic exchange between India and East Asian countries.'

From Wignaraja's and Cho's more general discussion of trends in trade and investment and the role of FTAs in integration, Jayant Menon's chapter delves into whether FTAs can play a role in supporting the growth or spread of production networks in Asia. Menon's chapter takes off from the premise that the spread of production networks confers major potential benefits to developing countries. He examines the different trade policy options for increasing South Asia's participation in these networks. More specifically, he asks whether FTAs between East and South Asian countries can increase participation, or whether other modalities should be pursued. Noting that empirical studies on FTAs and production networks have produced mixed results, Menon adopts a qualitative approach to his analysis.

Menon notes that the growth in product-fragmentation trade predated the proliferation of FTAs in Asia, which did not take off until the early 2000s. As such, it is clear that FTAs are not necessary for production networks; the question, therefore, lies in whether FTAs can support its further growth or its spread. Unlike many of the authors in this volume who hold a more favourable view of FTAs' role in trade policy, Menon cites a number of reasons why FTAs may not be the best instrument for promoting product fragmentation trade.

First, most component trade already travels duty-free or at low tariffs, either because of the International Technology Agreement (ITA, which means taxes on electronics components are generally zero), various duty-drawback or bonded warehouse schemes providing duty or tax rebates for re-exports, or because most multinationals locate themselves in duty-exempt export processing zones. Moreover, these schemes operate against a backdrop of low and falling tariffs on parts and components, which have more to do with unilateral actions than preferential ones. For these and other reasons, almost all studies point to very low utilization rates of FTAs, directly contradicting the assertion that they directly promote this or any other type of trade.

Second, because product fragmentation trade by definition involves limited processing or value added at each destination, they may not meet rules of origin (ROO) requirements. The FTAs are basically designed to promote trade in goods that are produced from beginning to end in a given country, and not trade involving parts and components and final assembly within production networks.

Third, countries involved in production networks gain most from trade facilitation and related trade and behind-the-border reforms. But almost all FTAs involving Asian countries are relatively shallow. Even if they deepen over time, FTAs are not likely to be the right trade policy instrument to promote the growth and spread of productions networks because unlike tariff liberalization, it is costly to try and remove non-tariff barriers (NTBs) or non-tariff measures (NTMs) in a preferential manner. Also, unlike export subsidies, it is impossible to remove production subsidies in a selective manner. Further, given the global nature of supply chains, regional FTAs are bound to be of limited value and can also choke off the natural spread of production networks.

For all of these reasons, Menon eschews regional FTAs in favour of a more multilateralist approach. He argues that the World Trade Organization (WTO) can still play a role through the multilateral agreement on trade facilitation signed at the Ministerial Summit in Bali in December 2013. But most of all, he argues that the best way to support the growth of production networks is through national liberalization and regulatory reforms in services and investment that address market access issues and barriers to entry, irrespective of nationality.

Harnessing Regional Integration for Development: The Case of Small Economies

The chapter by DiCaprio and Suvannaphakdy zero in on a group of countries that need to benefit the most from regional integration—least developed countries (LDCs). Based on United Nations (UN) data, there were 48 LDCs in 2014, including seven from South and East Asia—Afghanistan, Bangladesh, Bhutan, Nepal, Cambodia, Lao PDR, and Myanmar. Since 1971, several plans have been proposed by the UN Conference on Least Developed Countries to enable LDCs to graduate from their least developed status. The most recent is the Istanbul Programme of Action (2011) for the decade 2011–20, with the objective of graduating all LDCs by 2020. Thus far, the record of graduation is abysmal. Only four (Botswana in 1997, Cape Verde in 2009, the Maldives in 2011, and Samoa in 2014) have graduated and only two more, Equatorial Guinea and Vanuatu, are scheduled to graduate by December 2017.

The LDCs have only limited participation in regional value chain trade, but there is a common perception that plugging into global value chains (GVCs) will promote development in LDCs. Moreover, since LDCs' involvement in production fragmentation has been limited to low-technology sectors, such as garments and agrifood, very little attention has been given to electronics and automobile value chains, despite the latter having the densest networks and offering greater opportunities for diversification and upgrading.

DiCaprio and Suvannaphakdy examine how LDCs might slot into regional high-technology GVCs, particularly electronics and automobiles. Due to data constraints, DiCaprio and Suvannaphakdy employ a Grubel-Lloyd Index (GLI) to proxy for the usual indicators of GVC participation. Their analysis reveals two groups of countries that have very different outcomes. Track 1 countries have plugged into high-technology GVCs and have traded at least a quarter of these exports within GVCs. These countries have exports that are more globally focused, have moderate intra-industry trade, and have had fairly stable exports over time (that is, goods exported for 3 or more years over the 10-year period). In contrast, Track 2 countries also export network-eligible goods, but remain outside global supply chains. They have a more regional focus for exports, very limited intra-industry trade, and have a high proportion of 'exploratory' exports (goods exported for only 1 or 2 years over the 10-year period). The analysis also reveals that LDCs' participation in GVCs has not been driven by revealed comparative advantage. As such, the authors argue that 'any evidence of GVC participation is likely to be a feature of development aid, or production diversification by firms, or large intra-industry transfers of machinery or other parts falling into these categories of goods [none of which] are likely to be sustainable diversification strategies'.

Going forward, different sets of policy recommendations may be considered for these two groups of LDCs. For the more vulnerable countries in Track 2, horizontal policy support for manufacturing remains critical, particularly since the lack of revealed comparative advantage (RCA) across all exports suggests that promotion of trade capacity, infrastructure, and trade finance is needed. Track 2 countries also need to promote FDI and quality inputs, and focus on supportive legal frameworks, regulations, and trade policies. For the countries in Track 1, vertical policy support will be critical, but the bigger challenge lies in engaging the private sector to identify opportunities and bottlenecks; public–private dialogues will be important, especially when looking for partnerships.

DiCaprio and Suvannaphakdy also make some brief comments on the potential role of FTAs, particularly the Trans-Pacific Partnership (TPP) and the RCEP, in making GVC trade more inclusive. The authors opine that the RCEP has a better potential to offer opportunities for LDCs, given its more diverse membership which includes some LDCs (Cambodia, Lao PDR, and Myanmar), and the provisions in the RCEP's Guiding Principles which allow for 'appropriate forms of flexibility' and 'technical assistance and capacity building'. The TPP's outcomes are more uncertain; on the one hand, preferences can further reduce trade costs in favour of exports from Viet Nam, but on the other hand, the overall increase in trade could also result in greater demand from inputs elsewhere, including LDCs that are not part of the agreement. In any case, the authors emphasize that 'unless future FTAs directly address issues associated with the incorporation of LDCs, there is a very real possibility that they will increase rather than smooth spatial inequalities in Asia'.

The chapter that follows, by Paudel and Wagle, takes a closer look at the case of one LDC in South Asia—Nepal. More specifically, the authors assess the potential for increased bilateral trade between Nepal and its regional partners. Paudel and Waglé begin with an overview of the country's export performance and sophistication, and the distinct policy and logistical challenges it faces as a landlocked country.

Their analysis reveals that India's traditional role as Nepal's major trading partner has increased further over the past decade: India's share of Nepal's merchandise exports grew by about 28 percentage points between the periods 1999–2001 and 2009–11. Exports to Asian countries that are closer geographically have also increased, as have exports to Gulf states and Sub-Saharan Africa. In contrast, exports to the European Union (EU), North America, the member states of the European Free Trade Association (EFTA), and Northeast Asia have declined substantially. Paudel and Waglé attribute this increased 'regionalization' of Nepal's exports to the collapse of its apparel industry after the Multi-Fibre Agreement (MFA) was abolished, which also saw apparel exports halve in value over the past decade.[1]

[1] As is well-known, MFA was an egregious violation of the articles of General Agreement on Tariffs and Trade (General Agreement on Tariffs and Trade [GATT] 1947, 1994) and the WTO, namely, non-discrimination, national treatment, and prohibition of quantitative restriction (quotas). The MFA continued to exist as long as it did because the developed countries bought off possible opposition from developing countries with the rents that accrued to them from the country-specific, product-specific, non-transferable, and guaranteed quotas of MFA. The anticipated abolition of MFA and its replacement by global competition created uncertainty and adjustment problems, particularly for countries that were not competitive suppliers but relied on quotas to be able to sell in specific developed country markets.

Paudel and Waglé's analysis offers some good news: their examination of Nepal's export sophistication (EXPY)[2] reveals a relatively high EXPY, indicating that Nepal 'does have a foothold in manufacturing of goods that appear to present plenty of scope for technological upgrading, for such goods are also exported by higher-income countries', and 'its exports are not dominated by natural resources (fuel, minerals, or unprocessed commodities), whose abundance in poorly governed low-income countries is often associated with the chronic challenges of export diversification towards industrialization'.

The authors then present the results of an econometric analysis of the determinants of Nepal's bilateral export performance, using an updated gravity modelling framework. This technique enables incorporation of zero trade flows (one way and both ways), as well as the possibility of differing number of exporting firms across destinations and decomposition of trade flows into intensive and extensive margins. The model uses data on bilateral exports with at least 134 partners averaged over a 3-year period between 2009 and 2011, with the standard determinants of bilateral trade as exploratory variables.[3]

The results find that the largest share (over 60 per cent during 2009–11) of Nepal's exports went to India because of Nepal's religious, linguistic, cultural ties and proximity to India as well as its FTAs with India and its membership in South Asia Free Trade Agreement (SAFTA). The results also identify countries where Nepal 'over-exports', such as India, Bangladesh, and Sri Lanka, and countries where it 'under-exports', such as Japan, the Republic of Korea, and Indonesia. In light of these findings, exports can be deepened and diversified in the case of the first group, and greater market penetration be encouraged in case of the second group. The model predicts Nepal's exports to India (and for the same reason exports to the PRC) well. The prediction errors for

[2] The EXPY assesses the export baskets of countries by the incomes of countries that produce similar products, weighted by the share of those exports in the national total.

[3] Distance, contiguity, common language, common colonial power, log of GDP, log of GDP per capita, average weighted tariff, and the log of the remoteness index (computed by summing each country's distance with every other country, weighted by the latter's share in world GDP).

exports to other countries are generally 20 per cent or more. On the whole, the estimation of the gravity model is a useful illustration.

The results also emphasize that, in the case of Nepal, 'structural' factors such as geographical and cultural proximity and supply-side and logistical bottlenecks present a much more binding constraint than domestic and foreign trade policy–related distortions. Paudel and Waglé further note that 'trade cost disadvantages arising from landlockedness are compounded by Nepal's own macro-institutional failures (such as instability and civic disturbances) and micro-regulatory constraints'.

More worryingly, however, the results reveal that overall, Nepal appears to be 'under-exporting' compared to countries at similar levels of per capita income. Indeed, the authors point out that, were it not for Nepal's export of labour over the past 15 years, Nepal would almost certainly have faced a balance of payments crisis. Nepal's export performance is clearly suboptimal and should be made a development priority.

Nepal's dismal export performance in recent decades has been partly attributed to its inability to maintain competitiveness after the MFA was abolished. Sri Lanka's experience has been the exact opposite of Nepal's. Not only has Sri Lanka avoided being pushed out of the global apparel trade by larger, low-cost rivals, it has actually managed to maintain its world market share and remain embedded within the global apparel value chain. Athukorala and Ekanayake's case study of Sri Lanka's export-oriented apparel industry focuses on the structural adjustment and industrial upgrading which allowed the industry to thrive, despite the disappearance of preferential access and significant increases in manufacturing wages.

Athukorala and Ekanayake's analytical narrative makes use of secondary data sources as well as the results of interviews with senior officials of Joint Apparel Association Forum (JAAF), Export Development Board, and the Ministry of Industries and Trade, and the senior managers of 12 exporting firms that accounted for over 70 per cent of the total apparel exports in 2010–11. The authors adapt the global value chain approach pioneered by Gereffi (1994, 1999) and his co-authors, which sees industrial upgrading in 'demand responsive' industries as being driven by the global buyers of the final product, that is, 'lead firms'. The authors argue that the role played by the 'lead firm' in the process of industrial upgrading varies depending on whether the firm is a mass retailer, a speciality retailer, a brand marketer, or a brand manufacturer.

The authors identify four phases in the process of industrial upgrading in apparel manufacturing—cut, make, and trim (CMT) (simple assembly); original equipment manufacturing (OEM) (package contracting); original design manufacturing (ODM) (full packaging); and original brand manufacturing (OBM). A movement up from CMT to ODM is considered the major upgrading challenge faced by a firm in the apparel value chain.

Athukorala and Ekanayake's analysis reveals how the abolition of the MFA led to a major restructuring of sourcing strategies and networks, enabling buyers to streamline the number of countries/suppliers they deal with and focus on developing long-term strategic partnerships with the most important/efficient suppliers. This worked favourably for Sri Lanka.

Initially, Sri Lankan firms were involved in CMT, with international buyers (purchasing agents) providing market channels. But relationships built with lead firms allowed the role of pure indigenous firms to increase over time, with joint-venture operations playing a vital role. Meanwhile, the importance of the intermediary role of buying agents diminished as Sri Lankan firms forged direct links with speciality apparel retailers (for example, GAP, Marks & Spencer, and Abercrombie and Fitch) and brand marketers (for example, Victoria's Secret, Ralph Lauren, and Tommy Hilfiger).

There has been a notable increase in the local human capital base of the industry, with the dependence on foreign textile technicians virtually disappearing by the early 2000s. Sri Lanka has now become a supplier of textile technicians to the other apparel-producing countries in the region and beyond.

The industry has successfully faced increased competition in the post-MFA era through product diversification and improved marketing capabilities. There has been a significant shift away from the basic products to fashion-basic products: the authors report a notable increase in the share of knitted apparel in total apparel exports from 10.5 per cent in 2003–04 to 24 per cent in 2012–13, and increased concentration of exports in lingerie. Sri Lankan firms are now producing for speciality stores and/or brand marketers, and as a result, CMT firms have virtually disappeared. Roughly 60 per cent of exports are now by OEM firms and the rest by ODM firms. Some large firms have also ventured into production of fabrics, elastics, and imputes (for example, buttons, hangers, and packing material) required for apparel production.

The shift in export composition has been accompanied and/or aided by a greater emphasis on ethical employment practices. Sri Lankan apparel firms have an impressive track record of meeting corporate social responsibility, with the JAAF playing a key role through its Garments without Guilt programme. Sri Lanka is the only country in Asia to become a signatory to the 39th International Labour Organization (ILO) Convention prohibiting child labour. A number of large firms produce 'fair trade' clothing and have built environment-friendly factories. Wages in most firms are well above the minimum wage set by the government.

There has also been a notable shift in the direction of exports from the US to the EU, mainly because 'European demand patterns and the nature or marketing channels are much more compatible with the production and specialization patterns of the Sri Lankan apparel industry evolved over the past two decades'. That is, order sizes are generally smaller compared to the US's, and speciality stores and brand marketers play a relatively much more important role. This has further helped Sri Lanka carve out a niche in fashion-basic products.

As Athukorala and Ekanayake correctly point out, the experience of Sri Lanka suggests a broadening of our understanding of comparative advantage beyond the conventional, Ricardian sense of relative cost advantage, to include other non-price factors such as the human capital base, foreign trade and investment regimes, and other related aspects of the overall business environment.

Integrating South and East Asia: The Importance of India

India's efforts at integration with ASEAN began with India's Look East Policy initiated in the 1990s. The systemic economic reforms of 1991 (and the earlier hesitant and piecemeal economic reform in the 1980s), which eliminated or reduced many of the barriers to foreign trade and investment that had insulated India's economy from the world economy, likewise played a role. But two decades after the 1991 reforms, a number of significant barriers remain. Some crucial reforms, such as those relating to labour laws and infrastructure, have either not been undertaken or are yet to be completed.

Amongst the four studies done by ICRIER, two are of particular interest. The first by Kathuria, Kedia, and Balakrishnan focuses on high value manufacturing (HVM) and uses the product space framework popularized by Ricardo Haussman and Klinger (2007). A country's product space maps its export status at a point in time. In general, it is made up of a dense core and a periphery, where the products at the periphery are less sophisticated and have a lower income elasticity of demand than those at the core. The size of each product node represents the share of that product in the country's total exports.

The authors define HVM products in two alternative ways. The first is based on a product's outcomes in terms of its economic value (proxied by value added), social value (proxied by wages and salaries), and strategic value (proxied by number of employees). An HVM index based on each of these values is constructed and simply averaged to yield an aggregate HVM index for each product. The second is based on its enabling dimension in terms of the skill composition of its employees, its technological and capital intensities, and finally the flexibility in being able to respond to changing needs in a cost-effective manner.

The results based on the first definition show that although the HVM index for India stood at 7 compared to the PRC's 68, the top 10 industries by HVM show a substantial overlap both between PRC and other East Asian countries with India. This suggests that the HVM index has relatively low discriminatory power.

On the other hand, as is to be expected, there is no overlap in the top five industries using the second definition that emphasizes skills between India and the PRC in particular and also between India and East Asian countries. At one level this non-overlap implies that the potential of India's economic integration with East Asia to enhance the potential benefits from trade and technological flows that exploit the complementarities implicit in the non-overlap between the two, in the medium and long run, are significant. On the other hand, it could also be a barrier at least in the short run.

The analysis based on the product space framework is hard to interpret since it is largely, if not entirely, an empirical framework with no clear foundation in international trade theory. Of course, it is plausible to argue that in a forward-looking approach to exports, it would be more appropriate to build competitive capacity in products that are 'close' to those that India already exports, but have greater sophistication and are exported by countries with high per capita income. Beyond conceptualizing closeness from an empirical perspective and the density of product space, it is unclear whether there is any analytical foundation for the inferences drawn for future exports strategy based on the product space framework.

Be that as it may, the cross-country analysis of HVM exports at a 4-digit harmonized standard (HS) level of India, the PRC, Japan, and the Republic of Korea suggests that all countries have revealed comparative advantage in chemical and plastic products and in optical measuring instruments and parts and accessories thereof. The PRC, Japan, and the Republic of Korea have revealed comparative advantage in machinery and mechanical appliances, electrical equipment and parts thereof, and electronic products such as sound recorders and reproducers, amongst others.

The density of each of the nearly 200 HVM products that India is exporting but in which it has not revealed comparative advantage is defined as a suitably scaled sum of its proximity (that is, probability of exporting it) to each product with revealed comparative advantage that is being exported. The range of densities across products is small and the levels of densities are so low that all products with a potential to develop comparative advantage lie within a narrow range of densities. Two products from the chemical cluster exhibit both high densities and levels of sophistication. Whether an old-fashioned industrial policy of choosing the two as products to be promoted is appropriate is arguable. Despite some new supporters of such an industrial policy, it continues to be a risky policy with no rigorous and convincing empirical evidence as to its success.

The authors recognize that promoting HVM in India is a serious challenge and propose a two-pronged strategy. The first is to address the poor condition of infrastructure and undertake labour-market reforms that focus on flexibility. Regardless of its impact on HVM, such a policy is needed for many other reasons. The second is to promote selected HVM industries in clusters. This prong is yet another version of old-fashioned industrial policy. It is not persuasive, its recent revival amongst analysts notwithstanding. However, the authors recognize that moving up the value chain and upgrading within the value chain is a long drawn-out process and requires a combination of policy measures.

They neither mention explicitly India's integration with East Asia or other regions amongst the combination of policy measures nor do they rule it out.

The chapter by Tewari, Veeramani, and Singh reviews the relevant theoretical and empirical literature on regional integration as well as an analysis of trends and patterns of trade between India and East Asia. Its contribution is in documenting industry perspectives based on 20 'semi-structured and open ended' interviews of relevant firms and industry associations that are important for India's vertically integrated trade with ASEAN. Particularly interesting is the interview with Sundaram Motors which has been a long-term supplier of Auto Components to General Motors (GM). The adjustment of the relationship without rupture when GM found a cheaper supplier of components in Austria is instructive.

The authors find that several of the determinants of vertical specialization and production sharing in GVCs as identified in the literature are missing in Indian manufacturing. Levels of export-oriented FDI are low in India, and so are levels of local value addition. Credit availability is inadequate and interest rates are high; infrastructure including logistics support is poor. Uncertainty about land acquisition and its cost and about being able to get needed permits at the central and state levels is another deterrent.

The interviews with firms document how these deterrents affect their decisions and how they respond to them. They also present a hopeful picture of a manufacturing sector that is trying to upgrade its technology and is making headway in this regard. On the other hand, they suggest that the FTAs that India has concluded with advanced countries do not result in FDI inflows that enhance India's capacity to supply domestic and export markets, but only to export to India's large market from their home bases. This is no surprise since given India's long history of hot-house industrialization under heavy tariff protection, an FTA with India enables the advanced country to export to India at little or no tariff without having to engage in costlier tariff-jumping FDI.

Although none of the chapters from ICRIER note it, the PRC deliberately courted investment by Chinese firms experienced in producing and exporting to world markets, particularly labour-intensive goods; this helped PRC succeed as an export platform. Even before the PRC's accession to WTO in 2001, it had acquired a dominant share in labour-intensive manufacturing while India's declined. Unfortunately India does not have a diaspora experienced in manufacturing and exporting labour-intensive goods.

Anwarul Hoda and Durgesh Kumar Rai's chapter seeks to investigate the main factors responsible for India's poor performance in the global economic arena, and its low participation in international production-sharing agreements. The authors examine India's circumstances vis-à-vis three East Asian comparators—Malaysia, Thailand, and the PRC. The study is based almost entirely on secondary data from national and multinational official and non-official sources. The analysis covers external barriers (for example, most favoured nation [MFN] tariffs) and domestic barriers such as transport infrastructure and logistics, availability of land and electric power, labour laws, internal taxation, and the role of special economic zones (SEZs). The finding that the pertinent barriers are all domestic is important, since the barriers have been identified time and again and not much progress has been made in addressing them. This, in effect, implicitly shifts the onus for failure squarely on domestic political economy.

Hoda and Rai also list a large number of domestic barriers to trade and investment in India. It is unclear whether their restrictive effect is greater for trade in parts and components that characterize participation in GVCs compared to trade in other goods and services.

The last chapter by Arpita Mukherjee and Tanu M. Goyal is primarily a descriptive study using both primary data from a survey of a purposive sample of stakeholders in India and Thailand and secondary data from various official domestic and international sources on various trade and regional cooperation agreements. The authors note that the services sector contributes significantly to the GDP and employment in East and South East Asian countries as it does in India. The main objective of the study is to understand how services can be traded within the region and how it can lead to improved efficiency, market integration, and creation of value chains. Its primary focus is bilateral trade between India and Thailand in the context of their Comprehensive Economic Cooperation Agreement (CECA). The study finds commonalities as well as differences between the two countries in their approach to services trade. Both have restrictive FDI regimes and are selective about the movement of people (natural persons) under Mode 4 of the General Agreement on Trade in Services (GATS) of WTO. The differences arise in large part from the fact that India is a major exporter mostly to developed countries of information technology (IT) and information technology enabled services (ITeS) while Thailand's interest is in tourism, alternative healthcare, and logistics. Indian companies have a global market focus while Thai companies restrict theirs to their domestic and East Asian markets. Not surprisingly, the survey conducted by the authors reveals that the major barriers to physical connectivity and seamless supply chains are FDI restrictions, regulatory barriers, and procedural delays. The authors conclude that these barriers can be removed by domestic reforms in the two countries. They make the general point that in bilateral (such as the India–Thailand CECA) and regional agreements on services, the negotiators do no go beyond their unilateral liberalizations and seek only to firm up (that is, bind) the commitments to those positions. The authors point out that binding commitments to levels achieved under unilateral liberalization is nonetheless beneficial.

★ ★ ★

The chapters in this volume evince growing trade and investment linkages between South and East Asia over the last two decades. These linkages can only grow stronger in the years ahead, as trade and investment policy reforms deepen, regional production networks widen, and new regional cooperation agreements come into effect.

Econometric analyses presented here and in other studies suggest that the gains from further integration could be substantial, opening up opportunities for higher growth and employment. While both subregions stand to benefit from stronger linkages, the potential gains for South Asia could be considerably greater. East Asia has already been reaping the benefits of greater openness; East Asian countries have plugged into regional and global production networks and moved up the value chain. In contrast, South Asia has been a laggard and will need to catch up. South Asian countries are still mostly involved in low value manufacturing (employment-intensive sectors such as textiles, leather and footwear, and food processing), and are present at the low end of the global and regional production networks for most industries. The need to focus on HVM is clear. As the biggest economy in South

Asia, there has been a steady growth in India's integration with global production networks, but compared to East Asian firms, Indian firms are relatively less integrated. Indian firms are more focused on the large domestic market rather than exports, and in general, India imports products of higher value or stage of processing than it exports.

While the challenges may be more pressing for South Asia, both subregions will have to overcome a number of hurdles to increase integration and fully reap the benefits of greater openness. Some of these hurdles are physical constraints such as a country's size and geography. Other hurdles have to do with policy distortions, including high MFN tariffs, substantial non-tariff barriers, poor trade facilitation, a restrictive business environment, and weak property rights. There is also the wider phenomenon of insufficient investments in human capital.

Overcoming these hurdles will require a slew of interventions. Greater investments and improvements in the quality of cross-border infrastructure will be necessary to overcome size and geography. This will be particularly important for small countries, whose size restricts domestic demand and supply capacity and limits the number of market participants, and landlocked countries, whose geography make it difficult to connect with external markets. Further reductions in trade and investment protection are necessary, as are improvements in trade facilitation. There are some differences in opinion as to how these objectives can be best achieved. Some have more favourable views of FTAs as a means for lowering tariff and non-tariff barriers; others argue that multilateralization remains the most efficient and effective option. This volume has presented the pros and cons of both options, but ultimately policymakers will choose what is more feasible based on national priorities, capacities, and geopolitical interests.

What is clear across the board is that regional interventions will not amount to much without the implementation of a wider programme of domestic structural reforms and greater investment in human capital. East Asia's success has been founded on unilateral reforms rather than regional agreements. Despite the proliferation of FTAs, it is unilateral reforms that will continue to have the biggest impact, not just for domestic economies but for regional economies and the global economy as a whole. While this may sound like old news to most policymakers, it nonetheless bears repeating.

References

Gereffi, Gary. 1994. 'The Organization of Buyer-driven Global Commodity Chains: How US Retailers Shape Overseas Production Networks', in Gary Gereffi and M. Korzeniewicz (eds), *Commodity Chains and Global Capitalism*. Westport, Connecticut: Preager, pp. 95–122.

———. 1999. 'International Trade and Industrial Upgrading in the Apparel Commodity Chain', *Journal of International Economics*, 48(1): 37–70.

Hausmann, R. and B. Klinger. 2007. 'The Structure of the Product Space and the Evolution of Comparative Advantage', CID Working Paper No. 146, Harvard University, Cambridge, Massachusetts.

1

GANESHAN WIGNARAJA

Assessing the Experience of South Asia–East Asia Integration*

In 2014, the new Modi government adopted the Act East policy signaling a more proactive approach towards East Asia than in the past.[1] The details of the new approach are being developed at the time of writing but involve inviting East Asian economies to participate in India's ongoing economic transformation and joint projects. In May 2015, India and the People's Republic of China (PRC) signed deals worth $22 billion during Modi's visit to PRC (*Financial Times*, 17 May 2015). India's original Look East Policy was introduced in 1992 after the end of the Cold War and the start of economic reforms to strengthen relations with economically important Association of Southeast Asian Nations (ASEAN) and other East Asian economies. In time, India became a founding member of the East Asia Summit in 2005 as a forum for dialogue amongst 18 leaders and the ASEAN–India Free Trade Area (AIFTA) came into effect in 2010. Furthermore, in 2012, India and East Asian economies began

* The views expressed in this chapter are solely the author's and are not to be attributed to the Asian Development Bank (ADB). I am most grateful to T.N. Srinivasan, Jayant Menon, and two reviewers for comments. I am also grateful to Menaka Arudchelvan for efficient research assistance.

[1] Parameswaran (2014) notes that Modi unveiled India's Act East policy in Myanmar at the ASEAN Summit on 12 November 2014 and reiterated it at the East Asia Summit on 13 November 2014.

negotiations for the Regional Comprehensive Economic Partnership (RCEP). The rest of South Asia lacks a formal look or act east policy but some economies have sought closer economic ties with East Asia. For instance, the Pakistan–PRC Free Trade Agreement (FTA) took effect in 2007 and FTA negotiations between the PRC and Sri Lanka began in 2014.

The Modi government's Act East policy has reignited a debate on the impact of closer Pan-Asian economic integration involving South and East Asian economies.[2] A particular concern is whether smaller South Asian economies will gain from Pan-Asian integration schemes with East Asian economies and India. This chapter assesses the experience of Pan-Asian integration since the 1990s and focuses on three questions in this debate: (i) How much has Pan-Asian trade and foreign direct investment (FDI) grown?; (ii) What impedes further Pan-Asian integration?; and (iii) Who gains from closer Pan-Asian integration? This chapter seeks to improve our understanding of the impact of Pan-Asian integration on South Asian economies, and contribute to the sparse academic literature on the topic.[3]

The second section of the chapter analyses flows of traditional trade, global production network trade, and FDI. The third section explores impediments to Pan-Asian integration relating to trade barriers and regulations, services trade, FTAs, and infrastructure. The fourth section discusses the results of a quantitative assessment of various Pan-Asian policy scenarios. The last section concludes.

Regional Trade and Foreign Direct Investment Flows

A Shift in Regional Integration Priorities

In ancient times, there were ties between India and East Asia. For instance, between about 200 BC and until around the 15th century,

[2] South Asia includes the eight South Asian Association for Regional Co-operation (SAARC) members (Afghanistan, Bangladesh, Bhutan, India, the Maldives, Nepal, Pakistan, and Sri Lanka). East Asia includes the 10 ASEAN members, the PRC, Japan, and the Republic of Korea.

[3] For a recent selection, see Kumar, Sen, and Asher (2006); Kumar, Kesavapany, and Chaocheng (2008); Francois, Rana, and Wignaraja (2009b, 2009c); and ADB and ADBI (Asian Development Bank Institute; 2015).

India and various Southeast Asian kingdoms were linked by cultural, political, and trade relations. But these relations diminished over time.

Two distinct periods in South Asia–East Asia economic integration can be identified in the modern era: (i) a period of limited regional integration from about 1945 until the late 1980s; and (ii) a period of intensifying efforts at regional integration from 1990 until the present.

Before 1990, South and East Asian economies were relatively isolated from one another in terms of economic relations (Rana and Dowling 2009). There was limited bilateral trade and investment flows in goods or services. There was also little talk in policy circles of Pan-Asian integration using active regional integration policies. The only FTA that covered the two subregions was the Asia-Pacific Trade Agreement (APTA). The relative isolation between the two subregions before 1990 stems from a lack of political signals to foster South Asia–East Asia integration, barriers to regional trade and investment, poor regional connectivity, and cultural and linguistic barriers.

After the Second World War, South and East Asia viewed the benefits of globalization differently and followed different development strategies. Following independence from British rule in 1947, India and Pakistan adopted import-substituting industrialization strategies with high import tariffs, licensing to control entry into industries, and other forms of state intervention. The private sector and exports in India and Pakistan were shackled by an anti-export bias in the trade regime. Influenced by the prevailing anti-globalization economic philosophy, the smaller South Asian economies, to varying degrees, also adopted a similar development strategy. Growth and trade in inward-oriented South Asia thus largely stagnated.

Meanwhile, after an initial import substitution period, East Asian economies (initially the Republic of Korea and Taipei,China, and then ASEAN) switched to outward-oriented development strategies in the 1960s and 1970s. New emphasis was given to liberalizing trade, attracting export-oriented FDI via export-processing zones, and using the market mechanism for resource allocation (World Bank 1993). By embracing globalization, East Asia rapidly industrialized and emerged as one of the world's most prosperous regions with a notable middle class as a source of final demand.

The period after 1990 to the present has been marked by intensifying efforts at regional integration between South and East Asia. Several factors explain the shift in regional integration priorities (Dasgupta, Pitigala, and Gourdon 2012; Francois, Rana, and Wignaraja 2009a).

First, South Asian economies have adopted more market-friendly trade and investment regimes through a gradual implementation of economic reforms. Sri Lanka was the earliest South Asian economy to start a reform process in 1977. India initiated partial reforms in the 1980s and major reforms in the post-1991 period. The other South Asian economies initiated reforms only in the 1980s and 1990s.

Second, financial crises have encouraged industrial and economic restructuring in Asia. In the decade since the Asian financial crisis of 1997/98, East Asia reemerged into the global economy with high growth, impressive flows of export-oriented FDI, and localization of production networks geared towards regional markets. Following the global financial crisis of 2008, East and South Asian economies have increasingly rebalanced trade and FDI towards growth in faster recovering regional economies and away from slower recovering industrial economies. The giant dynamic economies of the PRC and India have increased their economic relations with each other and acted as growth poles in their respective subregions.

Third, transport, communications, and logistics costs in Asia have fallen significantly amid technological progress and productivity gains. These factors have helped spur the fragmentation of manufacturing throughout Asia through global production networks and supply chains.

Fourth, as discussed in this chapter, FTAs involving the two subregions have spread to liberalize intra-Asian trade and investment. These FTAs are partly a result of increasing recognition of the business opportunities from a large and growing Asian market, India's Look East Policy, and slow progress in the World Trade Organization (WTO) Doha Round talks.

Traditional Trade Flows

Table 1.1 shows that South Asian exports to East Asia (in US dollar terms) grew rapidly at 13.2 per cent per year between 1990 and 2013, while imports from East Asia grew at 13.7 per cent. The value of total trade between South and East Asia amounted to $235.2 billion in 2013 (up from $12.7 billion in 1990). India (which makes up 75.3 per cent of

South Asia's trade with East Asia) saw double-digit growth in trade with East Asia. Bangladesh, Pakistan, and Sri Lanka have also experienced growth in imports with East Asia but exports have lagged. The region's least developed countries (Afghanistan, the Maldives, and Nepal) are at the early stages of trade with East Asia.

The share of South Asia's exports to East Asia increased from 14.5 per cent to 17.9 per cent between 1990 and 2013 and the share of imports

TABLE 1.1 Growth in South Asia's Trade with East Asia, 1990–2013

	Value in 2013	Annual Average Growth (%)	East Asia Share of Total (%)	
	$ million	1990–2013	1990	2013
Exports				
South Asia	67,914	13.2	14.5	17.9
India	60,477	14.7	14.6	19.4
Pakistan	4,665	7.0	17.6	17.6
Bangladesh	1,783	11.2	9.3	6.5
Sri Lanka	843	6.8	9.9	8.0
Nepal	60	6.6	6.6	7.6
Maldives	75	7.0	30.1	32.3
Afghanistan	12	6.7	2.0	2.0
Imports				
South Asia	167,327	13.7	22.8	27.9
India	116,697	16.1	15.8	25.0
Pakistan	20,411	10.5	27.6	37.9
Bangladesh	17,578	12.0	35.5	44.5
Sri Lanka	8,514	10.1	35.2	39.8
Nepal	2,720	10.0	51.5	39.1
Maldives	567	8.0	70.1	40.2
Afghanistan	839	4.7	60.4	10.1

Notes: No data for Bhutan; East Asia refers to the 10 Association of Southeast Asian Nations member states, the People's Republic of China, Japan, and the Republic of Korea.

Source: Computed from International Monetary Fund Direction of Trade Statistics Database. Available at http://data.imf.org/?sk=9D6028D4-F14A-464C-A2F2-59B2CD424B85&ss= 1390030341854 (accessed in July 2014).

from 22.5 per cent to 27.9 per cent (see Table 1.1). Underlying this shift towards East Asia is a realignment of India towards East Asia, which accounts for one-fifth of India's exports and a quarter of its imports in 2013. Similarly, Pakistan has also had a shift in its trade with East Asia. However, the rest of South Asia shows varying degrees of trade orientation towards East Asia. India's experience suggests that trade with East Asia offers South Asia a potentially dramatic enlargement of its economic horizons, making available a far greater regional market with which it can integrate.

A shift is also visible within the destination of South Asia's trade with East Asia. Reflecting global trends, Japan has declined in importance while the PRC, the Republic of Korea, and ASEAN economies have become more important. The share of South Asia's exports to Japan fell from 57.8 per cent to 12.0 per cent between 1990 and 2013. Meanwhile, the share of the PRC rose from 3.0 per cent to 26.6 per cent, Singapore from 13.4 per cent to 20.4 per cent, Indonesia from 3.8 per cent to 8.1 per cent, and Viet Nam from 0.5 per cent to 8.2 per cent.

The commodity composition of trade between South and East Asian economies tends to reflect inter-country differences in comparative advantages[4] (natural resources, capital, labour, and technology) and levels of economic development. With an abundance of natural resources and labour, South Asia's exports to East Asia are weighted towards such products. Meanwhile, South Asia's imports from East Asia mainly consist of finished and high-technology goods reflecting an abundance of capital and technology. To illustrate this pattern of trade, Table 1.2 provides the leading items in India's trade with East Asia since 1991. India's main exports to East Asia include natural resource–intensive products (mineral fuels, pearls, stones, and iron ore), cotton, fish, non-ferrous metals and ores, granite, leather, oil cake, as well as some skill- and technology-intensive goods (chemicals, plastics, ships, and machinery). In contrast, East Asia's leading exports to South Asia feature products such as computers and integrated circuits; television,

[4] Analyses of revealed comparative advantages at the product level in South and East Asian trade are contained in Scollay and Pelkmans-Balaoing (2009) and Dasgupta, Pitigala, and Gourdon (2012). These studies conclude that South Asian countries exhibit a relatively narrow range of comparative advantages compared to East Asia.

TABLE 1.2 India's Top 10 Traded Commodities with East Asia (% share of total exports and total imports)

Commodity Code	Commodity Description	2000	2012
Share of total exports			
27	Mineral fuels, mineral oils, and products of their distillation	0.0	8.1
71	Natural or cultured pearls, precious or semi-precious stones, precious metals	17.5	6.8
52	Cotton	4.6	2.5
29	Organic chemicals	1.0	2.1
26	Ores, slag, and ash	8.0	1.7
89	Ships, boats, and floating structures	0.0	1.3
74	Copper and articles thereof	0.1	1.2
84	Nuclear reactors, boilers, machinery and mechanical appliances; parts thereof	0.1	1.2
72	Iron and steel	0.1	1.0
10	Cereals	0.1	1.0
Share of total imports			
85	Electrical machinery and equipment, and parts thereof	10.6	15.8
84	Nuclear reactors, boilers, machinery, and mechanical appliances	13.4	15.0
27	Mineral fuels, mineral oils, and products of their distillation	5.7	9.5
71	Natural or cultured pearls, precious or semi-precious stones, precious metals	0.5	6.8
29	Organic chemicals	3.9	6.3
15	Animal or vegetable fats and oils	4.5	6.2
72	Iron and steel	6.8	4.1
39	Plastics and articles thereof	3.7	3.1
89	Ships, boats, and floating structures	2.7	3.0
87	Vehicles other than railway or tramway rolling-stock	2.2	6.4

Source: UN Comtrade database. Available at http://comtrade.un.org/data/ (accessed in July 2014).

radio, and telecommunications equipment; motor vehicles and motor vehicle parts; and chemicals and fuels. Where there is two-way trade in the same industry, East Asian exports tend to be at a higher level of processing. For the steel industry, India's leading exports to East Asia include ferro-alloys, pig iron, and rolled steel; East Asia's leading exports to South Asia include rolled steel of a heavier grade.

Global Production Network Trade

The rapid expansion of trade and FDI over decades has become the engine of economic growth in East Asia and is increasingly important in South Asia. Traditional trade and FDI flows in East Asia have been progressively replaced by a new form of industrial organization centered on sophisticated global production networks and supply chains (Baldwin 2013). In this type of industrial organization, production processes are fragmented into several slices and located in different countries in East Asia to reduce production costs of multinational corporations (MNCs). Production fragmentation has spurred growing intra-regional trade in intermediate goods (mostly parts and components) in East Asia. The spread of production networks has spurred East Asia's global rise to the converted 'Factory Asia' league with rapid growth over a long period. The PRC has strikingly emerged as the factory of the world and the largest trader in Asia. Production networks have made East Asia more prosperous than ever before and are transforming the world economy. However, there is little sign of the spread of production networks beyond East Asia to South Asia. The evidence suggests that South Asian economies play a relatively small role in global production networks compared to the pivotal role of East Asian economies.

Table 1.3 presents average shares of global production network exports for South Asian economies and others for three sub-periods during 2001–13.[5] Production network exports are defined as trade in parts and components using the gross trade approach of Athukorala (2011). More specifically, it includes total exports of SITC 75–79 and SITC 87–88 and parts and components exports (that is, SITC 58, 62, 65, 66, 69, 71, 72, 73, 74, 81, 82, 84, and 89). The data shows that South

[5] Unfortunately, data was not available on inter-regional network trade between South Asia and East Asia.

Asia's share of world production network exports increased from 0.95 per cent of global production network exports to 1.58 per cent between 2001–04 and 2009–13. This trend has been fuelled by an increase in the world shares of India from 0.45 per cent to 0.84 per cent and Bangladesh from 0.26 per cent to 0.49 per cent. Meanwhile, the world shares of Pakistan and Sri Lanka have stagnated during this period. The data also underlines the important role of East Asia in global production networks. Thus, the PRC makes up as much as 24.99 per cent of world production network exports. The ASEAN economies as a group account for 9.34 per cent, Japan for 7.90 per cent, and the Republic of Korea for 4.85 per cent.

TABLE 1.3 Average Shares of World Production Network Exports,[a] 2001–13 (%)

	2001–04	2005–08	2009–13
South Asia	0.95	1.23	1.58
India	0.45	0.68	0.84
Pakistan	0.11	0.11	0.12
Bangladesh	0.26	0.33	0.49
Sri Lanka	0.12	0.11	0.12
Nepal	0.01	0.00	0.00
Maldives	0.01	0.00	0.00
Afghanistan	0.00	0.00	0.00
Bhutan	0.00	0.00	0.00
Memo Items			
Southeast Asia[b]	9.61	9.29	9.34
PRC	12.54	19.20	24.99
Japan	11.12	9.61	7.90
Korea, Republic of	4.16	4.89	4.85

Notes: PRC = People's Republic of China. [a] Production network exports are defined as trade in parts and components and computed using the gross trade approach of Athukorala (2011). More specifically, it includes total exports of SITC 75–79 and SITC 87–88 and parts and components exports (that is, SITC 58, 62, 65, 66, 69, 71, 72, 73, 74, 81, 82, 84, and 89).

[b] The total for the 10 Association of Southeast Asian Nations (ASEAN) members.

Source: UN Comtrade database. Available at http://comtrade.un.org/data/ (accessed in July 2014).

Regional Foreign Direct Investment Flows

Data on regional FDI flows is more limited than trade statistics. Data on greenfield investments[6] suggests that FDI flows between South and East Asia have nearly doubled from $5.0 billion in 2003 to $8.2 billion in 2013 but from a low base. The FDI flows from less developed South Asia to more developed East Asia are lower than the flow the other way. As Table 1.4 shows, annual flows of FDI from South Asia to East Asia were only about $4 billion in 2003–13. Meanwhile, FDI flows from East Asia to South Asia were more than double at over $10 billion.

TABLE 1.4 Foreign Direct Investment Flows of South Asia, 2003–13 ($ million)

	East Asia to South Asia			South Asia to East Asia		
	Annualized Average 2003–13	Cum-ulative 2003–13	Share (%)	Annualized Average 2003–13	Cum-ulative 2003–13	Share (%)
South Asia	10,248	112,731	100.0	4,047	44,522	100
India	8,602	94,621	83.9	4,014	44,157	99.2
Pakistan	796	8,760	7.8	15	165	0.4
Bangladesh	123	1,352	1.2	9	94	0.2
Sri Lanka	233	2,568	2.3	6	70	0.2
Maldives	132	1,452	1.3	NA	NA	NA
Nepal	23	258	0.2	3.3	36.5	0.1
Afghanistan	311	3,421	3.0	NA	NA	NA

Note: Figures cover only greenfield investments. NA = not available.
Source: Estimated from fDi Markets. Available at https://www.fdimarkets.com/ (accessed on 2 November 2016).

[6] fDi Markets defines greenfield investments as cross-border investment in a new physical project or expansion of an existing investment that creates new jobs and capital investment. Joint ventures are included where they lead to a new physical operation. However, mergers and acquisitions as well as other equity investments—generally the largest element of FDI inflows—are not tracked by fDi Markets. Hence, the data in Table 1.4 understate the magnitude of regional FDI flows.

Cumulative FDI flows from East Asia to South Asia in 2003–13 were \$112.7 billion. In contrast to trade flows, Japan (with 36.9 per cent of cumulative FDI inflows in 2003–13) is the leading foreign investor in South Asia. The Republic of Korea (19.7 per cent) and the PRC (18.5 per cent) come next. Singapore (11.6 per cent) and Malaysia (10.3 per cent) follow someway behind. Nataraja (2010) argues that Japanese inward investment to India is below potential, reflecting a hesitation amongst Japanese MNCs with regard to India.[7] The explanation is said to lie in constraints in India's investment climate, such as poor infrastructure, strict labour laws, and cumbersome business procedures. These issues will be explored further in the next section.

Like trade, India dominates regional FDI flows accounting for 99.2 per cent of cumulative FDI flows from South Asia to East Asia in 2003–13 and 83.9 per cent of cumulative FDI flows from East Asia to South Asia in 2003–13. Other South Asian economies have invested little in East Asia but have received some East Asian FDI. Pakistan notably accounts for 7.8 per cent of cumulative FDI flows from East Asia to South Asia.

Cumulative FDI inflows from East Asia to India during 2003–13 are diversified. The largest FDI activity is automotives and parts (22.2 per cent). This is followed by metals (18.2 per cent); real estate (6.2 per cent); communications (4.0 per cent); consumer electronics (4.0 per cent); engines and turbines (4.0 per cent); industrial machinery, equipment, and tools (3.9 per cent); and semiconductors (3.9 per cent). Meanwhile, India's outflows of FDI to East Asia are concentrated in resource activities (34.0 per cent in metals and 14.1 per cent in coal, oil, and gas) and service activities (10.3 per cent in financial services, 8.5 per cent in software and information technology [IT] services, 2.2 per cent in transportation, and 2.2 per cent in hotels and tourism).

[7] Case studies of Japanese subsidiaries or joint ventures in India by Roy Choudhury (2009) suggest that in the telecommunications and pharmaceuticals sectors, India has become a potential destination for research and development activity because of its relatively cheap but highly qualified technical human resources. Furthermore, Japanese firms value trust in their partner and each of the firms that has a joint venture in India spent a long time deciding on the partnership.

The leading East Asian investor is Japan (with 35 per cent of cumulative FDI into India during 2003–13) and nearly half of this went into automotive and parts. Japanese FDI also went into machinery and tools, electronics, chemicals, and rubber. The Republic of Korea (19 per cent of cumulative FDI into India) comes next and one-third of Korean FDI went into metals and another one-fifth into automotives and parts. The PRC is third (13 per cent of cumulative FDI) and just under half of this is in metals and another one-fifth is in engines and turbines. Singapore is fourth (with 11 per cent of cumulative FDI) and one-third of this is in real estate and another quarter is in semiconductors.

Impediments to Pan-Asian Integration

While the pace of South Asia–East Asia economic integration has picked up since 1990, many impediments at national and regional levels remain, which can hamper the process. Four key impediments are (i) trade barriers and cumbersome business procedures, (ii) barriers to services trade, (iii) risk of insufficient depth and business use of FTAs, and (iv) gaps in infrastructure.

Trade Barriers and Cumbersome Business Procedures

Open, market-friendly policy regimes are critical for promoting international trade and investment as well as South Asia–East Asia integration. Lower trade barriers and streamlined business procedures lower trade costs and facilitate the spread of production networks. Although tariff protection has been falling in South Asia, overall levels are typically higher than in East Asia. Table 1.5 shows import tariffs for agriculture and manufactures for 1990 and 2013 along with information on non-tariff measures (NTMs) implemented during the period 2009–13 and the World Bank's Ease of Doing Business Rank. The average agricultural tariff in India is 33.5 per cent (2013), while for the PRC (reflecting a decade of accession to the WTO) it is 15.6 per cent. Interestingly, average manufacturing tariffs for the PRC and India are similar at 9.0 per cent and 10.2 per cent respectively (2013), with India showing a large reduction between 1990 and 2013. Furthermore, while tariffs seem low in many East Asian countries, NTMs can be reduced. During the post-global financial crisis era, the number of NTMs implemented

TABLE 1.5 Ease of Trading across Borders and Doing Business

	Simple Average MFN Tariffs for Agriculture (%)		Simple Average MFN Tariffs for Manufactures (%)		NTMs Imple-mented	Ease of Doing Business Rank (out of 189 economies)
	1990	2013	1990	2013	2009–13	2013
India	77.0	33.5	84.1	10.2	206	134
Pakistan	45.5	15.4	NA	13.2	16	110
Bangladesh	99.5	16.8	123.1	13.4	1	130
Sri Lanka	38.1	25.7	27.0	7.5	10	85
Maldives	18.2	18.3	NA	20.8	1	95
Nepal	9.4	13.8	18.9	12.0	2	105
Afghanistan	NA	7.1	NA	5.7	1	164
Bhutan	14.3	41.4	15.5	18.9	0	141
Memo Items						
PRC	42.5	15.6	43.9	9.0	98	96
Indonesia	20.1	7.5	19.3	6.7	68	120
Korea, Republic of	11.4	52.7	7.8	6.8	19	7
Malaysia	12.7	8.9	9.4	5.5	9	6
Thailand	40.5	29.9	41.7	8.3	11	18
Philippines	23.1	9.9	20.9	5.7	5	108
Viet Nam	17.7	16.2	14.3	8.3	21	99

Note: Where data is not available, the most recent year is used. MFN = most favoured nation, NTM = non-tariff measure, PRC = People's Republic of China.

The NTMs are policy measures, other than customs tariffs, that can potentially have an effect on trade costs by changing prices, quantity traded, or a combination of both. The aforementioned data covers 22 types of NTMs including bail-out/state-aid measure; trade defense measures (anti-dumping [AD], countervailing duties [CVD], safeguard); non-tariff barrier (not otherwise specified); export taxes or restriction; investment measure; migration measure; export subsidy; public procurement; import ban; trade finance; import subsidy; quota (including tariff rate quotas); state-controlled company; competitive devaluation; state trading enterprise; subnational government measure; sanitary and phytosantiary measure; intellectual property protection; consumption subsidy; local content requirement; other service sector measure; and technical barrier to trade).

Source: World Bank. World Integrated Trade Solutions, available at http://wits.worldbank.org/ (accessed on 2 November 2016) for MFN tariffs; Global Trade Alert Database. Available at http://www.globaltradealert.org/site-statistics (accessed on 2 November 2016) for non-tariff measures; and World Bank (2013).

were 98 for the PRC, 68 for Indonesia, and 19 for the Republic of Korea. These figures compare with 206 for India, 16 for Pakistan, and 10 for Sri Lanka.

According to the World Bank Ease of Doing Business indicators, East Asia is typically a more open destination than South Asia. As the earliest adopter of economic reforms, in South Asia, Sri Lanka has the highest rank (85th) within the subregion. The Maldives (95th) comes next. However, the large South Asian economies (Bangladesh, India, and Pakistan) achieve rankings well in excess of 100. Meanwhile, Malaysia is ranked 6th, the Republic of Korea 7th, and Thailand 18th. Hence, East Asia serves as a more preferred destination for FDI than South Asia. East Asia also benefits more from the potential for regional integration of industries through a dense network of global production networks and supply chains, as well as large domestic markets.

Efforts at trade liberalization and streamlining business procedures in South Asia need to be embedded in a wider programme of the so-called second-generation economic reforms to support inclusive growth.[8] Important measures would include fiscal consolidation, reform of state-owned enterprises, improvement of domestic competition policy, reforms to the civil service and delivery of public goods, and reforms to institutions that create human capital (such as health and education).

Potential for Services Trade and Barriers

Studies suggest that services have been on the rise in output in Asia. From 45 per cent of the average share in 1990, the services sector made up 48.5 per cent of gross domestic product (GDP) in 2010 (Noland, Park, and Estrada 2013). In newly industrializing economies of East Asia such as the Republic of Korea; Hong Kong, China; and Taipei,China, the services sector has GDP shares of 60–90 per cent. In the ASEAN economies (with the exception of Singapore and the Philippines), the sector makes up less than 50 per cent of GDP. South Asian economies have uniformly rapidly growing services sectors, particularly India, Sri Lanka, and Nepal where shares have risen by 15–20 percentage points respectively.

[8] For assessments of reform and the case for second-generation reforms in South Asia, see Dee (2012) and Wignaraja (2011, 2012).

The services sector is also an important contributor to trade in South and East Asia. The average share of services trade in GDP in South Asian economies was 13 per cent in 2013 compared with 25 per cent in East Asia.[9] India and Sri Lanka are outliers in South Asia, with shares of 15 per cent and 11 per cent respectively. Pakistan (6 per cent), Bangladesh (6 per cent), and Nepal (11 per cent) have quite low shares. East Asia has an even greater diversity in services trade between high and low shares: Singapore (92 per cent), Thailand (27 per cent), Malaysia (26 per cent), Indonesia (6 per cent), and the PRC (6 per cent).

Overall estimates of the magnitude of trade in services between South and East Asia are not available, but there is evidence of modest growth in selected sectors between Japan and India. According to the Organisation for Economic Co-operation and Development (OECD) services trade data, between 2008 and 2012, Japan's services exports to India increased from $1.6 billion to $2.1 billion while Japan's services imports from India remained static at $758 million and $751 million (OECD 2016).[10] Other commercial services (up from $1.2 billion to $1.5 billion) were the main sector in Japan's exports to India, followed by transportation (up from $373 million to $467 million) and travel (up from $81 to $137 million). Other commercial services (up from $515 million to $535 million) were Japan's main service import from India, followed by travel ($92 million to $167 million) and transportation (down from $149 million to $47 million).

More generally, there is significant potential for services trade between South Asia and East Asia. India's IT services exports grew at 14.5 per cent over the 2011–12 period and was valued at $51.8 billion (Reserve Bank of India 2013). There is considerable potential for further expansion as top Indian IT firms are currently attempting to diversify

[9] The figures in this paragraph were estimated from the World Bank's *World Development Indicators Database*, available at http://databank.worldbank.org/data/reports.aspx?source=world-development-indicators (accessed in March 2016).

[10] Unfortunately, OECD data is only available for Japan–India services trade and not for other East Asia–South Asia trade such as PRC–India services trade. OECD data taken from 'OECD Statistics on International Trade in Services Detailed Tables by Partner Country', available at https://stats.oecd.org/Index.aspx?DataSetCode=TISP (accessed in March 2016).

their markets using various strategies, such as setting up offices in the PRC to serve the local market and to attract Japanese outsourcing business by employing workers from the PRC and Japan to overcome the language barriers.

Contractual construction and labour services are the PRC's major service sectors, especially in Asia (Findlay, Ochiai, and Dee 2009). In South Asia, Pakistan is one of the most important markets for contractual construction service exports from the PRC. The PRC also has some history of construction and labour exports to Sri Lanka and Bangladesh. Meanwhile, South Asian and ASEAN countries export labour services, and remittances from these economies are also increasing. Japan and the Republic of Korea may provide selective opportunities for migration as their respective workforces age.

However, there is evidence of important impediments to trade and investment inhibiting trade in services between the regions. Table 1.6 provides a services trade restrictiveness index from the World Bank. The data for the developing countries was collected through surveys in 2012, while the OECD countries covered were taken from various publicly available sources such as General Agreement on Trade in Services (GATS) commitments and offers, WTO reports, and Economic Intelligence Unit reports, amongst others. This attempts to capture the policies and regulations that discriminate against foreign services or foreign-service providers as well as certain key aspects of the overall regulatory environment that have a notable impact on trade in services. A high score suggests greater restrictiveness. Measuring services trade restrictiveness is a difficult undertaking beset by data gaps and subjective judgments. Bearing this qualification in mind, the data suggests that India[11] has greater restrictions on trade in services than large East Asian economies such as the PRC, Japan, and the Republic of Korea. Trade in services restrictions in Bangladesh, Nepal, and Sri Lanka are slightly lower (or comparable) with levels in the Philippines, Indonesia, Thailand, and Malaysia. There are concerns particularly in South Asia

[11] According to WTO (2011), ownership limits were a particular impediment to the development of financial services in India. An FDI up to 100 per cent was permitted in other major services sectors in India. But, 'specific market access conditions or permits were applicable, which in some cases may be more restrictive than an explicit cap on foreign ownership' (WTO 2011: xiii).

about the large costs of adjustment to liberalization of services trade on unemployment, poverty, and loss of universal access to basic services (Kelegama 2009). Some South Asian countries have thus adopted a cautious approach to services trade liberalization.

TABLE 1.6 Services Trade Restrictiveness Index

South Asia	
India	65.7
Bangladesh	44.2
Nepal	42.9
Sri Lanka	38.2
Pakistan	28.3
East Asia	
Philippines	53.5
Indonesia	50.0
Thailand	48.0
Malaysia	46.1
Viet Nam	41.5
PRC	36.6
Cambodia	23.7
Japan	23.4
Korea, Republic of	23.1
Others	
US	17.7
UK	14.3

Note: PRC = People's Republic of China, US = United States, UK = United Kingdom.

The World Bank's Services Trade Restrictions Database collects information on services trade policy across 103 countries, 5 sectors (telecommunications, finance, transportation, retail, and professional services), and the key modes of service supply. A high score suggests greater restrictiveness.

Source: World Bank Services Trade Restrictions Database. Available at http://iresearch.worldbank.org/servicetrade/ (accessed in March 2016).

Enhancing services trade between South and East Asia will be a challenging process. First, a major cooperative effort at national and regional levels is needed, especially in South Asia, to improve the data on the services sector and services trade (Kelegama 2009). Second, it will involves creating competitive services markets through a combination of policy reforms, productivity improvements, and investments in infrastructure and human capital (Noland, Park, and Estrada 2013).

A Risk of Insufficient Depth and Business Use of Foreign Trade Agreements

Preferential liberalization is a relatively recent phenomena in South Asia–East Asia economic relations (Asher and Sen 2008; Scollay and Pelkmans-Balaoing 2009). By December 2013, nine FTAs were in effect between South and East Asian countries, with eight taking effect since 2004. More FTAs are being negotiated. Furthermore, these FTAs have only involved South Asia's two largest economies, India and Pakistan. While it is early days in South Asia–East Asia FTAs, two concerns arise.

First, the agreements in effect vary in their provisions to reduce trade barriers. Table 1.7 summarizes our assessment of liberalization in major South Asia–East Asia FTAs in the areas of goods, services, and regulatory barriers.[12] Our results suggest that South Asia–East Asia FTAs fall into two types: (i) limited agreements that deal mainly with barriers to goods trade, and (ii) agreements that extend liberalization beyond goods trade to tackle services and regulatory barriers. The APTA, the PRC–Pakistan FTA, and the Pakistan–Malaysia FTA are mainly goods agreements. The remaining FTAs listed in Table 1.7 are somewhat more comprehensive. The ASEAN–India FTA initially covered goods liberalization but has recently expanded to cover services and investment. The India–Singapore FTA excludes agriculture and transit but has reasonable coverage of services and cooperation enhancement

[12] Goods liberalization evaluates the speed and coverage of tariff liberalization based on the criteria for FTAs in the WTO General Agreement on Tariffs and Trade. Services liberalization evaluates the number of services sectors covered based on the WTO General Agreement on Trade in Services. Coverage and liberalization in intellectual property, investment, government procurement, trade facilitation, and competition were based using criteria for individual issues such as adherence to international agreements such as the WTO Agreement on Trade-Related Aspects of Intellectual Property Rights and the Government Procurement Agreement.

TABLE 1.7 Scope and Depth of South Asia–East Asia Free Trade Agreements

	Goods Liberalization	Services Coverage	Deep Integration
India–Japan FTA (2011)	Relatively fast	Some	Deep
India–Malaysia FTA (2011)	Relatively fast	Some	Moderate
ASEAN–India FTA (2010)	Gradual	Excluded	Shallow
India–Republic of Korea FTA (2010)	Gradual	Comprehensive	Moderate
India–Singapore FTA (2005)	Relatively Fast	Comprehensive	Limited
Pakistan–Malaysia FTA (2008)	Limited	Some	Limited
Pakistan–PRC FTA (2007)	Gradual	Some	Limited
APTA (1976)	Limited	Excluded	Shallow

Note: ASEAN = Association of Southeast Asian Nations, FTA = free trade agreement, PRC = People's Republic of China, APTA = Asia-Pacific Trade Agreement.
Source: Author's assessment based on the methodology outlined in Wignaraja, Ramizo, and Burmeister (2013).

provisions. The India–Republic of Korea FTA also has reasonable coverage of services and moderate coverage of regulatory barriers while the India–Japan FTA covers some services and has wider coverage of regulatory barriers. In general, there seems room for improvement in the coverage of services and regulatory issues in South Asia–East Asia FTAs.

Second, use of tariff preferences in South Asia–East Asia FTAs differs between agreements. We were able to obtain some information on export value using FTA preferences from national sources in Thailand, Malaysia, and Viet Nam for a few FTAs (Thailand–India FTA, ASEAN–India FTA, and Pakistan–Malaysia FTA). The Thai data obtained from the Ministry of Commerce of Thailand show an increase in the combined utilization rate of the Thailand–India FTA and the ASEAN–India FTA from 17.6 per cent to 36.6 per cent between 2005 and 2011. The Viet Nam data obtained from the Ministry of Industry and Trade of Viet Nam also indicate an increase in utilization of the ASEAN–India FTA between 2010 and 2011, but its 2011 figure (7.4 per cent) is lower than that of Thailand. However, the Malaysian data gathered from the

Ministry of International Trade and Industry of Malaysia indicates a significant increase in utilization of the Pakistan–Malaysia FTA from 1.4 per cent to 74.3 per cent between 2006 and 2010.

Thus, the evolving trend towards South Asia–East Asia FTAs carries two risks: a tendency towards insufficient liberalization and depth of agreements as well as suboptimal preference use. Asia should pursue a geographically broad scheme, instead of an expanding web of bilateral and subregional agreements. Against slow progress in the WTO Doha Round trade talks, a Pan-Asian FTA can promote continuing liberalization, induce structural reforms, and widen market access across the region. With a view to making the proliferation of FTAs between South and East Asia 'stepping stones' rather than stumbling blocks to multilateralism and to reduce inefficiencies due to overlapping rules of origin and others, policymakers may wish to adopt the concept of 'open regionalism' and broaden FTAs by creating as large and as wide a market as possible.

In this vein, one major pan-Asian FTA under negotiation is noteworthy. In November 2012, ASEAN members and their FTA partners (including India, Japan, the PRC, the Republic of Korea, Australia, and New Zealand) agreed to negotiate an RCEP that would result in the world's largest trading bloc covering 40 per cent of world trade. The first round of RCEP negotiations took place in the middle of 2013 with the ambitious goal of finishing in 2015.[13] But that initial deadline has passed and the RCEP talks are likely to continue in 2017. India is the only South Asian economy to join the negotiations thus far. This will give Indian business a greater opportunity to access markets in East Asia, to integrate into regional production networks, and to invest in information technology services sectors in East Asia. It will also expose Indian business to competition on the domestic market and facilitate upgrading of skills and technology. None of the other South Asian economies has expressed a desire to join the RCEP, but this may change if they become concerned about being left out of the large regional integration group.

[13] See Chia (2015) for a comprehensive assessment of mega-FTAs including RCEP. Wignaraja (2014) examines the implications of RCEP membership for India.

Gaps in Infrastructure

Asia's trade performance and its ability to attract FDI depend fundamentally on efficient, reliable, and seamless infrastructure (Asian Development Bank [ADB] and Asian Development Bank Institute [ADBI] 2009). The spread of global supply chains in East Asia means that manufacturing activities have been dispersed over geographical space connected by trade in parts, components, and services. India has gradually been incorporated into supply chains through FDI from Japan, the Republic of Korea, and ASEAN economies. Investment in cross-border infrastructure, multimodal transport systems, and logistics are critical to facilitate South Asia–East Asia supply chain integration.

Detailed technical studies of infrastructure connectivity assess different transport options to efficiently and seamlessly integrate South and East Asia trade (Arnold 2009; ADB and ADBI 2015). These studies have also identified several missing links and bottlenecks—particularly in sea and land transport—in connectivity between South and East Asia. They find that the dominant mode for freight transport between South and East Asia remains ocean transport and this situation is expected to continue for the foreseeable future. International shipping lines serving the South Asia–East Asia region operate on the equatorial route connecting East Asia and the Persian Gulf and the Mediterranean. The introduction of larger container ships and expansion of feeder services have supported trade growth. However, problems have been identified in the facilities and operational efficiency of public ports (such as Chittagong Port in Bangladesh, Kolkata Port in India, and Yangon Port in Myanmar) and links between ports and road networks.[14]

Furthermore, it is suggested that the recent opening up of Myanmar through political and economic reforms means that land transport (both road and rail) will have an increasing role in bilateral trade within

[14] In Chittagong Port, the size of vessels that are able to call is limited by the width and curvature of the Karnaphuli River. Rail and road traffic between Chittagong Port and Dhaka also created severe bottlenecks. Yangon Port also has several problems, including limited accessibility to large vessels, poor road conditions between the Thilawa port area and the bridge leading to Yangon, high container charges, obsolete facilities in Yangon Port, frequent blackouts and insufficient generators, and lack of cargo equipment (see ADB and ADBI 2015).

Asia, but major improvements are needed (ADB and ADBI 2015). New land corridors between India and the PRC through Bhutan and Nepal are required, necessitating large investments. For instance, a minimum investment of $18 billion is needed for road creation and improvement totalling 26,000 kilometres of roads to complete the Asian Highway project. Land access to ports is also important for landlocked countries. With respect to the intra-regional rail network, the Trans-Asian Railway (TAR) network includes about 10,500 kilometres of missing links that need to be constructed to provide for an unbroken TAR network. Moreover, the incompatibility of gauges (track widths) in India, Bangladesh, Thailand, and Myanmar means that trans-shipment will be required even after rail links are developed. Air transport is growing in importance as the value of commodities traded between the two regions increases; however, the growth in air freight has lagged behind that of ocean transport and is likely to continue to do so.

Inter-country comparisons of the quality of infrastructure are difficult due to measurement problems, statistical gaps, and the inherently subjective nature of such evaluations (ADB and ADBI 2009). Table 1.8 provides one such evaluation based on a survey of global business leaders' perceptions and available hard data indicators on ports, roads, railways, and air transport. A value of 7 in the scoring system used shows the best possible situation and 1 the worst. The data suggests that the quality of infrastructure in South Asian economies typically lags behind East Asian economies. In terms of the quality of overall infrastructure, South Asia's largest economies fare poorly: India has a value of 3.9, Pakistan 3.3, and Bangladesh 2.8. Sri Lanka (4.8) and Bhutan (4.9) are exceptions in South Asia. By comparison, the Republic of Korea has a value of 5.6, Malaysia 5.5, and the PRC 4.3. Interestingly, the Philippines and Viet Nam underperform in East Asia.

Thus, while improvements have occurred in regional infrastructure, South Asia in particular has a large unfinished agenda to improve the quantity and quality of its infrastructure.

Quantifying the Gains from Pan-Asian Integration

Model-based studies are a useful tool to quantitatively assess the impact of various policy scenarios for Pan-Asian integration between South and East Asian economies. Multi-country computable general

Table 1.8 Quality of Infrastructure, 2013

	Quality of Overall Infrastructure	Road	Railroad	Port	Air Transport	Electricity Supply
India	3.9	3.6	4.8	4.2	4.8	3.2
Pakistan	3.3	4.0	2.5	4.5	3.2	2.0
Bangladesh	2.8	2.8	2.4	3.5	3.2	2.2
Sri Lanka	4.8	4.7	3.6	4.2	4.8	5.0
Nepal	2.9	2.7	1.1	2.7	3.0	1.6
Bhutan	4.9	4.3	NA	2.2	3.5	5.9
Memo Items						
PRC	4.3	4.5	4.7	4.5	4.5	5.7
Korea, Republic of	5.6	5.8	5.7	5.5	5.8	4.3
Indonesia	4.0	3.7	3.5	3.9	4.5	5.2
Thailand	4.5	4.9	2.6	4.5	5.5	5.2
Malaysia	5.5	5.4	4.8	5.4	5.8	5.8
Philippines	3.7	3.6	2.1	3.4	3.5	4.0
Viet Nam	3.4	3.1	3.0	3.7	4.0	4.0

Note: NA = not available, PRC = People's Republic of China.

1 = worst possible situation, 7 = best situation.

Quality of infrastructure is one of the indicators used to measure global competitiveness in an annual survey conducted by the World Economic Forum. The scores are based on opinions of business leaders in a survey conducted in 148 economies.

Source: World Economic Forum (2013).

equilibrium (CGE) models more comprehensively evaluate gains to South Asian economies from alternative Pan-Asian policy scenarios than partial equilibrium models like gravity models. A CGE modelling approach incorporates the complex relations between prices, markets, and income. A multi-country CGE model permits taking account of the effects of a changing world economic environment as well as feedback linked to bilateral trade liberalization and reductions in trade costs resulting from better physical connectivity.

There are a few CGE studies on South and East Asian economies due to the recent origin of South Asia–East Asia integration schemes and limited CGE modelling capacity in South Asia. These studies vary in their modelling assumptions made, unit of analysis used, and policy scenarios considered. An early study by Bandara and Yu (2003) used a global CGE model to evaluate the effects of tariff elimination under a South Asia–ASEAN FTA. They pessimistically report that all South Asian countries, including India, would incur welfare losses from such an FTA, while ASEAN as a whole would see modest gains. However, more recent and comprehensive simulation studies report different results.

As part of the work related to the Comprehensive Asia Development Plan (CADP) prepared by the Economic Research Institute for ASEAN and East Asia (ERIA) for the East Asian Summit, Kumagai et al. (2013) used the Institute of Developing Economies (IDE)/ERIA Geographical Simulation Model—a detailed regional model—to estimate the impacts on the cumulative increase of GDP of countries in the two regions from 2010 to 2030 relative to the base case for a number of connectivity projects, including the Mekong–India Economic Corridor (MIEC), the Dawei and Kyaukphyu deep-sea ports in Myanmar, and the India–Myanmar–Thailand Trilateral Highway. For the MIEC alone, they found cumulative impacts of over 5 per cent for Cambodia, Myanmar, Thailand, and Viet Nam, and over 2.5 per cent for India.

Regarding trade integration, a CGE study by Mohanty and Pohit (2008) shows welfare gains for members of the ASEAN+3–India FTA ranging from $52 billion for a simple FTA (involving only liberalization of tariffs) to $114 billion for a more comprehensive FTA (involving liberalization of tariffs as well as reduction in barriers to investment and services).

Using a slightly different regional unit of analysis (ASEAN+3 economies and South Asia), Francois and Wignaraja (2008 and 2009) estimate large gains of about $260 billion, or 2 per cent of GDP, from an East and South Asian FTA, under conservative assumptions. Countries obtaining relatively large positive income impacts (over 2 per cent) include the Republic of Korea, Indonesia, Malaysia, the Philippines, Singapore, Thailand, Viet Nam, India, and Sri Lanka. In addition, India sees somewhat larger gains from an ASEAN+3 and South Asia policy scenario than an ASEAN+3 and India policy scenario. This result indicates that India has an incentive to include the rest of South Asia in a regional integration scheme with East Asia than doing it alone with East Asia.

While a broad ASEAN+3 and South Asia policy scenario is desirable from an economic welfare point of view, current political events in Asia may rule it out for some time. At the time of writing, Japan–PRC tensions persist over disputed islands, which make it difficult for early conclusion of regional integration arrangements involving Asia's two largest economies. Uncertainties also exist over the state of India–PRC political relations given growing competition between these rising powers in Asia. Accordingly, political considerations suggest that it be useful to explore policy scenarios with a narrower geographical coverage (for example, between South Asian and Southeast Asian economies) which act as a building bloc for eventual Pan-Asian integration. It is also useful to consider policy scenarios with varying degrees of deep integration efforts.

The results of a CGE exercise by Wignaraja et al. (2015) involving South and Southeast Asian economies are reported here. The study uses an advanced CGE model featuring recent innovations in heterogeneous-firms trade theory into the CGE framework. Policy scenarios are included featuring full liberalization of tariff barriers, a 50 per cent reduction in non-tariff barriers (NTBs), and improvements in infrastructure (both physical infrastructure and software like trade and transport facilitation) manifest in reductions in trade costs. A long-run time framework for ambitious deepening liberalization is assumed. Liberalization of these barriers is assumed over the period 2016–25 and is compared relative to the baseline forecasts, with projections finishing in 2030.

Table 1.9 reports the broad welfare effects for the three policy scenarios from the study:

1. South Asia–Southeast Asia Policy Scenario 1: Removal of all tariffs associated with South Asia–Southeast Asia trade but no changes in NTBs and other trade costs.

TABLE 1.9 Effects of South Asia/Southeast Asia Trade Initiatives in 2030, Income (equivalent variation as % of GDP), on South Asia and Southeast Asia, Relative to Baseline

Country	SA/SEA1	SA/SEA2	SA/SEA3
Total South Asia	2.2	3.2	8.9
India	2.3	3.3	8.7
Pakistan	0.8	1.8	7.0
Bangladesh	0.4	1.2	6.9
Sri Lanka	1.3	2.9	14.1
Nepal	5.4	9.0	30.0
Other South Asia	5.2	8.3	31.7
Total Southeast Asia	1.9	2.5	6.4
Indonesia	2.3	2.4	5.0
Malaysia	2.8	3.6	9.7
Philippines	0.2	0.6	1.9
Singapore	3.1	4.8	14.4
Thailand	1.7	2.3	6.1
Viet Nam	0.6	2.0	7.0
Cambodia	–0.3	–0.1	0.6
Lao PDR	–0.1	–0.1	–0.1
Other ASEAN	0.1	0.5	2.3

Note:

- EV = equivalent variation, GDP = gross domestic product, SA = South Asia, SEA = Southeast Asia, Lao PDR = Lao People's Democratic Republic, ASEAN = Association of Southeast Asian Nations.
- SA/SEAFTA1 = removal of all tariffs across SA and SEA over 2016–25; SA/SEAFTA2 = SA/SEA1 + 50% cut in NTBs; SA/SEAFTA3 = SA/SEAFTA2 + 15% reduction in trade costs relevant to South Asian–Southeast Asian trade.
- Other South Asia includes: Afghanistan, Bhutan and Maldives.
- Other ASEAN includes: Brunei Darussalam and Myanmar

Source: Wignaraja et al. (2015).

2. South Asia–Southeast Asia Policy Scenario 2: Scenario 1 plus a 50 per cent cut in NTBs.
3. South Asia–Southeast Asia Policy Scenario 3: Scenario 2 plus a 15 per cent cut in trade costs pertaining to South Asia–Southeast Asia trade. This ambitious scenario represents the deepest integration efforts amongst the three scenarios.

Strikingly, deeper South Asia–Southeast Asian economic integration efforts result in large and notable gains for the two subregions in all scenarios. Under Scenario 1, South Asia's GDP increases by 2.2 per cent and Southeast Asia's GDP by 1.9 per cent relative to the baseline, indicating that tariffs continue to hamper gains from trade between the subregions. All South Asian economies gain. The smallest South Asia economies—Nepal and other South Asian economies—exhibit the largest gains (over 5 per cent of GDP). India comes next (over 2 per cent of GDP). Sri Lanka, Pakistan, and Bangladesh experience smaller gains than others.

Even bigger gains, however, occur when NTBs and trade costs related to improvements in infrastructure fall. Scenario 3 shows a four-fold increase in GDP for South Asia (8.9 per cent) relative to the baseline and a three-fold increase in GDP for Southeast Asia (6.4 per cent). All economies within South Asia gain with Nepal and other South Asian economies witnessing the largest gains. Notable gains are also visible for India (8.7 per cent), Sri Lanka (14.1 per cent), Pakistan (7.0 per cent), and Bangladesh (6.9 per cent).

The outcome of these policy scenarios implicitly assumes that South Asia is internally quite well integrated. However, earlier studies argue that the South Asia Free Trade Agreement (SAFTA) process involving the eight South Asian Association for Regional Cooperation (SAARC) members has lost momentum and that South Asia remains one of the least integrated regions globally (Khan 2012; Weerakoon 2010). Fears of domestic industries in smaller South Asian economies being swamped by cheap Indian imports, restrictions on India–Pakistan trade, bureaucratic inertia, and security concerns explain the limited progress in South Asian integration.

Nonetheless, to illustrate potential benefits of South Asian integration, Wignaraja et al. (2015) also report the outcome of a deep integration South Asian policy scenario. This scenario seems useful as SAFTA has had a goods agreement in effect for some years and a services agreement took effect in 2012 as an expansion of SAFTA. Efforts are also being made to improve cross-border roads to link India's Northeast with neighbouring economies. A deep-integration South Asian policy scenario (with removal of all tariffs, a 50 per cent cut in NTBs and a 15 per cent reduction in trade costs) increases South Asia's GDP by 2.1 per cent relative to the baseline.[15] This figure compares with a 0.4 per cent rise in South Asia's GDP for a policy scenario of only tariff removal.

* * *

Against the backdrop of the Modi government's Act East policy, this chapter assessed the experience of Pan-Asian economic integration, particularly for South Asia, by examining the growth of regional trade and FDI, impediments to further integration and the welfare gains from integration policy scenarios.

Three important points emerge from the research.

First, there is evidence of increased economic integration between South and East Asia, but the process is uneven.[16] Traditional bilateral trade flows have grown rapidly from a small base since 1990, led by India and, to a lesser extent, Pakistan. South Asia, including India, is largely absent from production network trade which has characterized East Asia's rise as the global factory. The FDI flows, particularly from East Asia to South Asia, have increased but levels are smaller than regional trade flows reflecting higher costs and risks of setting up overseas plants rather than trading from home. Additionally, the bulk of East Asian FDI goes to India. Little regional policy integration has occurred with only a few recent South Asia–East Asia FTAs focusing on India and Pakistan. India's smaller South Asian neighbours are in the early stages of integration with East Asia—imports from East Asia have grown, but exports, network trade, FDI, and FTAs have lagged.

Second, a myriad of problems come in the way of further economic integration between South and East Asia. These include trade barriers and cumbersome procedural bottlenecks affecting business, barriers to services trade, a risk of insufficient depth and business use of FTAs, and gaps in infrastructure. The data suggests that these problems are

[15] Earlier studies, which look mostly at goods trade liberalization, not surprisingly suggest smaller gains for South Asia from a South Asian FTA. Accordingly, Bandara and Yu (2003) suggest gains for South Asia of $771.4 million, ADB and UNCTAD (United Nations Conference on Trade and Development; 2008) of $858.3 million, and Siriwardana (2003) of $4 billion.

[16] With the benefit of a few additional years of data, our conclusion about the pace of South Asia–East Asia economic integration is more nuanced and qualified than earlier studies (for example, Asher and Sen 2008).

particularly challenging in South Asian economies and in poorer Southeast Asian economies. Coherent remedies include continuing the lowering of trade protection and implementing a wider programme of domestic structural reforms, reducing barriers to services trade, developing a deep Pan-Asian FTA, and investing more and improving the quality of cross-border infrastructure.

Third, deep regional integration efforts generate notable welfare gains for all participants in South Asia–East Asia policy scenarios. The results of a quantitative CGE exercise indicate that South Asia–Southeast Asia integration can be a useful building block for wider Pan-Asian integration. Tariff removal produces reasonable gains for both South and Southeast Asian economies. However, the welfare gains are multiplied manifold when deeper integration efforts (involving reducing non-tariff barriers and reducing trade costs through infrastructure improvements) are factored in. Interestingly, India's smaller South Asian neighbours gain significantly from tariff reduction and even more so from deeper integration efforts. Furthermore, integration within South Asia is a necessary condition for realizing the benefits of South Asia–Southeast Asia integration.

Thus, South Asia–East Asia economic integration represents a work in progress but will benefit all participating economies in the long run. It is likely to entail a multi-track, multi-speed process with different participating rates by different economies. A big and coordinated effort is needed at national and regional levels, particularly in South Asia, to ensure future success. India may be well positioned to play such a coordinating role under the Modi government's Act East policy.

References

ADB and ADBI. 2009. *Infrastructure for a Seamless Asia*. Manila and Tokyo: ADB and ADBI.

———. 2015. *Connecting South Asia and Southeast Asia*. Manila and Tokyo: ADB and ADBI. Available at https://www.adb.org/sites/default/files/publication/159083/adbi-connecting-south-asia-southeast-asia.pdf (accessed on 29 September 2016).

ADB and UNCTAD. 2008. *Quantification of Benefits from Economic Cooperation in South Asia*. New Delhi: Macmillan India.

Arnold, J. 2009. 'The Role of Transport Infrastructure, Logistics, and Trade Facilitation in Asian Trade', in J. Francois, P.B. Rana, and G. Wignaraja (eds), *Pan-Asian Integration: Linking East and South Asia*, pp. 351–438. Basingstoke, UK: Palgrave Macmillan.

Asher, M. and R. Sen. 2008. 'India and Asian Economic Integration', in N. Kumar, K. Kesavapany, and Y. Chaocheng (eds), *Asia's New Regionalism and Global Role: Agenda for the East Asia Summit*, pp. 105–40. New Delhi and Singapore: Research and Information System for Developing Countries and Institute of Southeast Asian Studies.

Athukorala, P. 2011. 'Production Networks and Trade Patterns in East Asia: Regionalization or Globalization?', *Asian Economic Papers*, 10(1): 65–95.

Baldwin, R. 2013. 'Global Supply Chains: Why They Emerged, Why They Matter and Where They Are Going', in D.K. Elms and P. Low (eds), *Global Value Chains in a Changing World*. Geneva: World Trade Organization.

Bandara, J. and W. Yu. 2003. 'How Desirable Is the South Asian Free Trade Area?', *World Economy*, 26(9): 1293–323.

Chia, S.Y. 2015. 'Emerging Mega-FTAs: Rationale, Challenges and Implications', *Asian Economic Papers*, 14(1): 1–27.

Dasgupta, D., N. Pitigala, and J. Gourdon. 2012. 'South Asia's Economic Prospects from Global Rebalancing and Integration', in P. Dee (ed.), *Economic Reform Processes in South Asia: Toward Policy Efficiency*, pp. 23–42. Abingdon, UK: Routledge.

Dee, P. (ed.). 2012. *Economic Reform Processes in South Asia: Toward Policy Efficiency*. Abingdon, UK: Routledge.

Financial Times. 17 May 2015. Available at https://www.ft.com/content/88de2eea-fc60-11e4-ae31-00144feabdc0 (accessed on 29 September 2016).

Findlay, C., R. Ochiai, and P. Dee. 2009. 'Integrating Services Market', in J. Francois, P.B. Rana, and G. Wignaraja (eds), *Pan-Asian Integration: Linking East and South Asia*, pp. 245–350. Basingstoke, UK: Palgrave Macmillan.

Francois, J.F. and G. Wignaraja. 2008. 'Economic Implications of Asian Integration', *Global Economy Journal*, 8(3): 1–46.

———. 2009. 'Pan-Asian Integration: Economic Implications of Integration Scenarios', in J. Francois, P.B. Rana, and G. Wignaraja (eds), *Pan-Asian Integration: Linking East and South Asia*, pp. 487–536. Basingstoke, UK: Palgrave Macmillan.

Francois, J., P.B. Rana, and G. Wignaraja. 2009a. 'Introduction and Overview', in J. Francois, P.B. Rana, and G. Wignaraja (eds), *Pan-Asian Integration: Linking East and South Asia*, pp. 1–62. Basingstoke, UK: Palgrave Macmillan.

———. (eds). 2009b. *National Strategies for Regional: South and East Asian Case Studies*. London: Anthem Press.

Francois, J., P.B. Rana, and G. Wignaraja. (eds). 2009c. *Pan-Asian Integration: Linking East and South Asia*. Basingstoke, UK: Palgrave Macmillan.

Kelegama, S. 2009. 'Introduction: Opportunities and Risks of Liberalizing Trade in Services', in S. Kelegama (ed.), *Trade in Services in South Asia: Opportunities and Risks of Liberalization*, pp. 1–22. New Delhi: Sage Publications.

Khan, M. 2012. 'India–Pakistan Trade: A Roadmap for Enhancing Economic Relations', in P. Dee (ed.), *Economic Reform Processes in South Asia: Toward Policy Efficiency*, pp. 191–206. Abingdon, UK: Routledge.

Kumagai, S., K. Hayakawa, I. Isono, S. Keola, and K. Tsubota. 2013. 'Geographical Simulation Analysis for Logistics Enhancement in Asia', *Economic Modelling*, 34(C): 145–53.

Kumar, N., R. Sen, and M. Asher. (eds). 2006. *India–ASEAN Economic Relations: Meeting the Challenges of Globalization*, pp. 165–81. New Delhi and Singapore: Research and Information System for Developing Countries and Institute of Southeast Asian Studies.

Kumar, N., K. Kesavapany, and Y. Chaocheng. (eds). 2008. *Asia's New Regionalism and Global Role: Agenda for the East Asia Summit*. New Delhi and Singapore: Research and Information System for Developing Countries and Institute of Southeast Asian Studies.

Mohanty, S.K. and S. Pohit. 2008. 'Welfare Gains from Regional Economic Integration in Asia: ASEAN+3 or EAS', in N. Kumar, K. Kesavapany, and Y. Chaocheng (eds), *Asia's New Regionalism and Global Role: Agenda for the East Asia Summit*. New Delhi and Singapore: Research and Information System for Developing Countries and Institute of Southeast Asian Studies.

Nataraja, G. 2010. 'India–Japan Investment Relations: Trends and Prospects', ICRIER Working Paper No. 245, Indian Council for Research on International Economic Relations, Delhi.

Noland, M., D. Park, and G.B. Estrada. 2013. 'Developing the Services Sector as an Engine of Growth for Asia: An Overview', in D. Park and M. Noland (eds), *Developing the Services Sector as an Engine of Growth for Asia*, pp. 2–50. Manila: Asian Development Bank.

Rana, P.B., and M. Dowling. 2009. *South Asia: Rising to the Challenge of Globalization*. Singapore: World Scientific Press.

Reserve Bank of India (RBI). 2013. 'India's Exports of Computer Services 75.2% of Total Software Services Exports in 2011–12: RBI Survey', press release. Available at http://rbidocs.rbi.org.in/rdocs/PressRelease/PDFs/IEPR42SUR0713.pdf (accessed on 5 September 2016).

Roy Choudhury, S. 2009. 'Japan's Foreign Direct Investment Experiences in India: Lessons Learnt from Firm Surveys', ICRIER Working Paper No. 243, Indian Council for Research on International Economic Relations, Delhi.

Parmeswaran, P. 2014. 'Modi Unveils India's Act East Policy to ASEAN in Myanmar', *The Diplomat,* 17 November. Available at http://thediplomat.com/2014/11/modi-unveils-indias-act-east-policy-to-asean-in-myanmar/ (accessed on 29 September 2016).

Scollay, R. and A. Pelkmans-Balaoing. 2009. 'Current Patterns of Trade and Investment', in J. Francois, P.B. Rana, and G. Wignaraja (eds), *Pan-Asian Integration: Linking East and South Asia*, pp. 63–162. Basingstoke, UK: Palgrave Macmillan.

Siriwardana, M. 2003. 'Trade Liberalization in South Asia: Free Trade Area or Customs Union', *Journal of South Asian Studies*, XXVI(3): 309–29.

Weerakoon, D. 2010. 'SAFTA: Current Status and Prospects', in S. Ahmed, S. Kelegama, and E. Ghani (eds), *Promoting Economic Cooperation in South Asia Beyond SAFTA*, pp. 71–88. New Delhi: Sage.

Wignaraja, G. 2011. *Economic Reforms, Regionalism, and Exports: Comparing China and India* (Policy Studies No. 60). Honolulu, Hawaii: East–West Center.

———. 2012. 'Commercial Policy and Experience in the Giants: China and India', in M. Kreinin and M. Plummer (eds), *The Oxford Handbook of International Commercial Policy*, pp. 252–88. Oxford: Oxford University Press.

———. 2014. 'The Regional Comprehensive Economic Partnership: An Initial Assessment', in T. Guoqiang and P. Petri (eds), *New Directions in Asia-Pacific Economic Integration*, pp. 93–105. Honolulu: East West Center.

Wignaraja, G., D. Ramizo, and L. Burmeister. 2013. 'Assessing Liberalization and Deep Integration in FTAs: A Study of Asia–Latin America FTAs', *Journal of East Asian Economic Integration*, 17(4): 385–416.

Wignaraja, G., P. Morgan, M. Plummer, and F. Zhai. 2015. 'Economic Implications of Deeper South Asian-Southeast Asian Integration: A CGE Approach', *Asian Economic Papers*, 14(3, August): 63–81.

World Bank. 1993. 'East Asian Miracle Economic Growth and Public Policy', A World Bank Policy Research Report, Oxford University Press, New York. Available at http://documents.worldbank.org/curated/en/975081468244550798/Main-report

———. 2013. *Doing Business 2014: Understanding Regulations for Small and Medium-Size Enterprises*. Washington, D.C.: World Bank Group. Available at http://www.doingbusiness.org/rankings (accessed on 29 September 2016).

World Economic Forum. 2013. *Global Competitiveness Report*. Geneva. Available at https://www.weforum.org/ (accessed on 29 September 2016).

WTO. 2011. *Trade Policy Review: India*. Geneva: World Trade Organization.

2

CHOONGJAE CHO

The Causal Relationship between Trade and Foreign Direct Investment

Implication for India and East Asian Countries*

Since the 1980s, full-fledged economic liberalization and deregulation have increased the volume of trade and foreign direct investment (FDI). These have also led to increased economic interdependence—in other words, the economic integration amongst countries. Volume of trade and FDI amongst various countries increased approximately by 9 and

* The study was presented at the Asian Development Bank (ADB)-Korea Institute for International Economic Policy (KIEP)-Indian Council for Research on International Economic Relations (ICRIER) Workshop, held in October 2012 in Seoul, the Republic of Korea. In the workshop, the relationship between the Republic of Korea and India was analysed. I would like to thank Rajat Kathuria from ICRIER, Ramesh Subramaniam and Jayant Menon from ADB and Junkyu Lee, International Economic Advisor for the Ministry of Strategy and Finance, the Republic of Korea who made valid comments. The analysis included more countries and the analytical methods were also reinforced.

30 times between 1980 and 2011 respectively, which in turn led to an increase in world GDP by about six-fold (United Nations Conference on Trade and Development [UNCTAD] 2012). Therefore, it is argued that FDI and trade are main drivers of economic growth and economic integration.

Economic integration between South and East Asia has shown significant progress since the 1980s. In particular, India, the largest country in South Asia, and East Asian countries such as the Republic of Korea, the People's Republic of China (PRC), Japan, and Singapore have made great efforts towards economic integration. India is attractive to these four countries in that it has immense market potential. In addition, as the Indian government emphasized in its Look East Policy,[1] East Asia is strategically very important for India's economic growth and diplomacy. The Indian government has been trying to establish a strong economic relationship with East Asian countries. Currently, India has free trade agreements (FTAs) with Singapore, the Republic of Korea, the Association of Southeast Asian Nations (ASEAN), and Japan. These FTAs (Republic of Korea–India, ASEAN–India, Japan–India) came into force in 2006, 2010 and 2011, respectively.

The FDI from the four East Asian countries to India has led to a considerable increase in trade volume. Based on cumulative FDI statistics from April 2000 to March 2013, Singapore and Japan were the first and third largest FDI investors in India.[2] From 2002 to 2010, East Asia's share in India's total trade increased from 10.9 per cent to 16.2 per cent, while the share of the European Union (EU) and the United States (US) decreased to 15.2 per cent and 7.8 per cent from 21.7 per cent and 14 per cent, respectively.[3]

In this context, East Asian countries and India are making efforts to accelerate economic integration between them. This chapter is designed to explore the policy implications of accelerating economic integration between India and East Asian countries. Although various studies on this subject have been attempted in the past, this chapter

[1] India's Look East policy represents its efforts to cultivate extensive economic and strategic relations with the nations of East Asia.

[2] If Mauritius, a tax-haven country, is included, they would be ranked second and fourth.

[3] The figures were estimated using data issued from the Ministry of Commerce and Industry, Government of India.

focuses on the causal relationship between trade and FDI between India and East Asian countries since the 2000s. In other words, the purpose of this chapter is to examine the causal links (unidirectional, bidirectional, or independent) between trade and FDI and its policy implications.

Study of the causal relationship between trade and FDI will help us determine the focus and direction of policy sets and policy choices. It will help us to predict the effects of FTAs launched from the late 2000s. Lee and Song (2007) argue that identifying causality between trade and FDI is an important issue in order to evaluate the dynamic effect of FTAs in the medium and long run (Lee and Song 2007, pp. 28–29). The dataset employed in this chapter includes countries such as the US, United Kingdom (UK), Germany, and the Netherlands, which have traditionally been major trade and FDI partners of India before the emergence of East Asian countries.

This chapter consists of five sections. The first section introduces the background and purpose of this study. The second section presents trends in trade and FDI between India and East Asian countries, vis-à-vis other external partners. A brief review of the literature on the relationship between trade and FDI is included in the third section. Empirical data, model, and analysis are elaborated in the fourth section. The last section concludes with policy implications.

Trend of Trade and Foreign Direct Investment between India and East Asia

Trade

Trade volume between India and East Asian countries has significantly increased since 2000. The PRC's performance in particular has been outstanding: trade volume between India and the PRC increased sharply by about 30 times, from $2.3 billion in 2000 to $67.8 billion in 2011. In the case of Singapore, the amount of trade with India in 2000 was almost the same as the PRC; but India–Singapore trade also increased by about 10 times and reached $21.3 billion by 2011. During the same period, the trade volume between the Republic of Korea and India increased by 13 times, from $1.3 billion to $17.7 billion. On the other hand, while trade between Japan and India appeared very prosperous in 2000 (with the highest volume amongst four countries), Japan–India trade increased only by about five times since, from $3.6 billion in 2000 to $18.6 billion in 2011, which represents the lowest figure amongst the four countries.

In terms of each country's share in India's total trade, the PRC's share has more than doubled from 4.1 per cent in 2002 to 8.9 per cent in 2011. While Singapore's share has increased to 3.7 per cent in 2011 from 2.5 per cent in 2002, the Republic of Korea's share rose only slightly from 1.9 per cent to 2.1 per cent during the same period. Japan's share decreased by 1 percentage point from 3.3 per cent to 2.3 per cent during the same period.[4]

Looking into India's trade volume vis-à-vis partner economies, Japan, Singapore, the PRC, and the Republic of Korea ranked 5th, 9th, 10th, and 17th in 2000, respectively (Table 2.1). However the ranks of Singapore, the PRC, and the Republic of Korea increased to 8th, 2nd, and 12th, respectively, in 2011 (Table 2.2). Japan actually experienced a drop in its rank, from 5th to 11th over the same period. Meanwhile, the ranks of India's traditional trade partners, the US, UK, and Germany, are falling sharply. The US, the immovable number 1 in 2000, dropped to 3rd in 2011. Germany also dropped to 6th from 4th. The UK, a firm number 2 till 2000, plunged to 17th in 2011.

Foreign Direct Investment

Cumulative FDI flow into India from April 2000 to March 2013 was about $193.4 billion. Singapore and Japan were the first and third largest FDI investors in India during the same period, with cumulative FDI of about $19.5 billion and $14.6 billion, respectively. The share of Singapore's FDI was about 10 per cent, while that of Japan was 7.5 per cent (Table 2.3). Singapore's annual FDI in India rose dramatically between 2006 and 2007. In 2005, the Singapore–India Comprehensive Economic Cooperation Agreement (CECA) and Double Taxation Avoidance Act became effective. Since then, FDI inflows from Singapore to India have soared from $321 million in 2005 to $4.2 billion in 2011. In 2006, Japan and India upgraded their relationship from a Global Partnership to a Global Strategic Partnership, and mutually agreed to establish a Comprehensive Economic Partnership. Since then, as in the

[4] Most figures were estimated from the CEIC 'India Premium Database'.

TABLE 2.1 India's Top-20 Trade Partners in 2000/01[a] ($ million)

Rank	Economy	Export	Import	Total Trade	Trade Balance
1	US	9,305.12	3,015.00	12,320.12	6,290.12
2	UK	2,298.71	3,167.92	5,466.63	–869.21
3	Belgium	1,470.56	2,870.05	4,340.60	–1,399.49
4	Germany	1,907.57	1,759.59	3,667.15	147.98
5	Japan	1,794.48	1,842.19	3,636.67	–47.7
6	Switzerland	437.7	3,160.14	3,597.85	–2,722.44
7	Hong Kong, China	2,640.86	852.11	3,492.97	1,788.75
8	UAE	2,597.52	658.98	3,256.51	1,938.54
9	Singapore	877.11	1,463.91	2,341.03	–586.8
10	PRC	831.3	1,502.20	2,333.50	–670.89
11	Italy	1,308.75	723.58	2,032.33	585.17
12	Malaysia	608.15	1,176.80	1,784.95	–568.65
13	France	1,020.01	640.81	1,660.82	379.2
14	Australia	405.87	1,062.76	1,468.63	–656.89
15	Saudi Arabia	822.94	621.12	1,444.06	201.82
16	Russia	889.01	517.66	1,406.67	371.35
17	Republic of Korea	450.78	893.76	1,344.54	–442.98
18	South Africa	310.67	1,021.91	1,332.58	–711.24
19	Netherlands	880.09	437.53	1,317.63	442.56
20	Indonesia	399.75	910.24	1,310.00	–510.49
Total of top 20 economies		***31,256.95***	***28,298.26***	***59,555.24***	***2,958.71***
India's total		**44,560.28**	**50,536.44**	**95,016.43**	**–5,976.17**

Note: US = United States, UK: United Kingdom, UAE = United Arab Emirates, PRC = People's Republic of China.

[a] Indian fiscal year criteria (from April 2000 to March 2001)

Source: Ministry of Commerce and Industry, Government of India, 'Directorate General of Commercial Intelligence and Statistics Online Data'. Available at www.dgciskol.nic.in (accessed on 27 September 2016).

case of Singapore, Japanese FDI in India has jumped from $116 million in 2006 to $3.1 billion in 2011.[5]

[5] The figures are from the CEIC 'India Premium Database'.

TABLE 2.2 India's Top-20 Trade Partners in 2011/12[a] ($ million)

Rank	Economy	Export	Import	Total Trade	Trade Balance
1	UAE	36,265.15	38,436.47	74,701.61	–2,171.32
2	PRC	13,503.00	54,324.04	67,827.04	–40,821.04
3	US	36,152.30	24,343.73	60,496.03	11,808.57
4	Saudi Arabia	9,783.81	34,130.50	43,914.31	–24,346.69
5	Switzerland	1,116.98	29,915.78	31,032.76	–28,798.79
6	Germany	7,244.63	14,373.91	21,618.54	–7,129.28
7	Iraq	1,278.13	20,155.94	21,434.07	–18,877.81
8	Singapore	13,608.65	7,754.38	21,363.03	5,854.27
9	Hong Kong, China	12,278.31	8,078.58	20,356.89	4,199.74
10	Indonesia	5,331.47	14,774.27	20,105.75	–9,442.80
11	Japan	6,099.06	12,514.07	18,613.14	–6,415.01
12	Republic of Korea	4,201.49	13,461.25	17,662.73	–9,259.76
13	Kuwait	1,060.80	16,569.63	17,630.43	–15,508.83
14	Nigeria	2,739.41	13,826.02	16,565.43	–11,086.60
15	Qatar	687.05	15,616.58	16,303.63	–14,929.53
16	Belgium	5,506.63	10,087.16	15,593.80	–4,580.53
17	UK	8,611.72	6,553.74	15,165.47	2,057.98
18	Iran	3,351.07	11,603.79	14,954.86	–8,252.72
19	Malaysia	4,442.67	10,435.00	14,877.66	–5,992.33
20	Australia	2,348.23	12,026.25	14,374.48	–9,678.02
Total of top 20 economies		***175,610.56***	***368,981.09***	***544,591.66***	***–193,370.5***
India's total		**300,274.11**	**491,945.04**	**792,215.62**	**–191,670.93**

Note: UAE = United Arab Emirates, PRC = People's Republic of China, US = United States, UK = United Kingdom.

[a] Indian fiscal year criteria (from April 2011 to March 2012)

Source: Ministry of Commerce and Industry, Government of India, 'Directorate General of Commercial Intelligence and Statistics Online Data'. Available at www.dgciskol.nic.in (accessed on 27 September 2016).

In contrast, the total share of the Republic of Korea's FDI in India was about 0.6 per cent over the same period, with cumulative FDI of about $1.2 billion. But during the 1990s, the Republic of Korea was one

TABLE 2.3 Cumulative Economy-wise Foreign Direct Investment Inflows from April 2000 to March 2013

Rank	Economy	FDI Inflows (Rs crore)[a]	FDI Inflows ($ million)	Share in Total FDI Inflows
1	Mauritius	341,124	73,666	38.1
2	Singapore	90,182	19,460	10.1
3	UK	80,458	17,548	9.1
4	Japan	70,094	14,550	7.5
5	US	50,922	11,121	5.8
6	Netherlands	42,378	8,965	4.6
7	Cyprus	32,328	6,889	3.6
8	Germany	25,512	5,480	2.8
9	France	16,864	3,572	1.9
10	UAE	11,307	2,422	1.3
13	Republic of Korea	5,821	1,231	0.6
15	Hong Kong, China	4,769	1,028	0.5
19	Indonesia	2,825	610	0.3
21	Malaysia	2,730	549	0.3
30	PRC	1,428	278	0.1
Subtotal		778,742	167,369	86.6
Grand Total		896,912	193,403	100.0

Note: FDI = Foreign Direct Investment, UK = United Kingdom, US = United States, UAE = United Arab Emirates, PRC = People's Republic of China.

[a] 10 million rupees

Source: Ministry of Commerce and Industry, Government of India, 'Department of Industrial Policy and Promotion FDI Statistics'. Available at www.dipp.nic.in/English/Publications/FDI_Statistics/FDI_Statistics.aspx (accessed on 27 September 2016).

of the largest FDI investors in India from East Asia, along with Japan (Table 2.4). Thus, from 1991 to 2001, the Republic of Korea's share in total FDI was 3.5 per cent. Three big conglomerates—Samsung, LG, and Hyundai—began to invest in India in the mid-1990s. However, during the 2000s, FDI of the Republic of Korea in India was relatively

TABLE 2.4 Cumulative Country-wise Foreign Direct Investment Inflows from 1991 to 2001

Rank	Country	FDI Inflows (Rs crore)[a]	FDI Inflows ($ million)	Share in Total FDI Inflows
1	Mauritius	22,908	5,733	36.8
2	US	11,250	2,969	18.1
3	Japan	4,601	1,187	7.4
4	Germany	3,166	846	5.1
5	UK	2,755	777	4.4
6	Netherlands	2,847	761	4.6
7	Republic of Korea	2,189	594	3.5
8	France	1,828	466	2.9
9	Italy	1,630	402	2.6
10	Singapore	1,485	399	2.4

Note: FDI = Foreign Direct Investment, US = United States, UK = United Kingdom.

[a] 10 million rupees

Source: Ministry of Commerce and Industry, Government of India, 'Department of Industrial Policy and Promotion FDI Statistics'. Available at www.dipp.nic.in/English/Publications/FDI_Statistics/FDI_Statistics.aspx (accessed on 27 September 2016).

smaller than Singapore's and Japan's. From 1991 to 2005, the cumulative share of FDI from the Republic of Korea decreased to 2.3 per cent (Table 2.5).

Chinese FDI in India is much smaller compared to other countries. The PRC's total share of FDI in India was just 0.1 per cent from April 2000 to March 2013, amounting to about $52 million during the entire 2000s. Recently, FDI from the PRC into India increased to about $50 million in 2011 and $138 million in 2012, respectively.

Meanwhile, the US, Germany, and the Netherlands have also continued to invest in India, but their status has been decreasing. From 1991, the year of the reform, to 2001, they were the first, third, and fifth largest FDI contributors to India, respectively. But from 2000 to 2012, the US and Germany dropped to fourth and seventh, respectively. The Netherlands has stayed at number 5. Only the UK increased in rank from the fourth to the second in the same period.

TABLE 2.5 Cumulative Country-wise Foreign Direct Investment Inflows from 1991 to November 2005

Rank	Country	FDI Inflows (Rs crore)[a]	FDI Inflows ($ million)	Share in Total FDI Inflows
1	Mauritius	46,794	10,976	37.2
2	US	20,023	4,892	15.9
3	Netherlands	8,457	1,985	6.7
4	Japan	8,436	2,014	6.7
5	UK	7,962	1,910	6.3
6	Germany	5,408	1,331	4.3
7	Singapore	3,895	940	3.1
8	France	3,230	768	2.6
9	Republic of Korea	2,899	749	2.3
10	Switzerland	2,482	605	2.0
Subtotal		109,586	26,170	87.1
Grand Total		151,605	36,704	100.0

Note: FDI = Foreign Direct Investment, US = United States, UK = United Kingdom.

[a] 10 million rupees

Source: Ministry of Commerce and Industry, Government of India. 'Department of Industrial Policy and Promotion FDI Statistics'. Available at www.dipp.nic.in/English/Publications/FDI_Statistics/FDI_Statistics.aspx (accessed on 27 September 2016).

Literature Review and Distinction

The interaction between FDI and trade has become complicated with economic integration, while the importance of the relationship between trade and FDI has increased over the years. Although researchers have theoretically and empirically studied the relationship between trade and FDI, it is still under debate.[6]

[6] There have been many studies on the relationship between trade and investment and the relationship between intra-industry trade and investment with industry- or company-level data, but those introduced here are mainly studies on the relationship between trade and investment with macroeconomic-level data.

According to the traditional Hecksher-Ohlin assumption, trade and FDI have a substitute relationship (Mundell 1957). Moreover, some studies (Caves 1957) assume that exports and FDI can be mutual alternatives with respect to entering foreign markets, implying that there is a substitutive relationship between export and FDI. Gray (1998) argued that market-seeking FDI and trade are substitutes, while efficiency-seeking FDI and trade are complementary. In other studies the motives for FDI were divided into three categories: the horizontal motivations (Markusen 1984; Markusen and Venables 1998), the vertical motivations (Helpman 1984; Helpman and Krugman 1985), and the knowledge-capital model (Markusen and Maskus 2001), which combines both the horizontal and vertical motivations (Jang 2011, p. 1629). Theoretically, horizontal FDI is designed to place production close to foreign consumers and thereby avoid trade costs (Jang 2011, p. 1629); it is a substitute to trade as in the relationship between market-seeking FDI and trade. On the other hand, vertical FDI and trade are complementary, since vertical FDI is driven by the distance of production costs rather than trade costs.

When these existing theories and hypotheses are applied to FDI inflows from East Asian countries to India, it is evident that the horizontal and vertical FDI motivations are working simultaneously. High trade costs such as overall high tariffs, the import ban on durable goods with very high tariffs, and lower labour cost were especially active in inducing FDI to India. Therefore, finding the relationship between trade and FDI in India–East Asia countries will require a deeper analysis of the approach relying on the nature of FDI. But India's FDI statistics as well as the country-specific statistics by FDI motivations are very limited, which is why we try to find the causality between trade and FDI in this chapter. This chapter includes the western countries—traditional economic partners of India—in the dataset to bring greater clarity in understanding the relationship between trade and FDI between India and the East Asian countries. Further, this would help us decipher the effect of the quantitative expansion of India–East Asia trade and FDI since the late 2000s and find the policy implications of accelerating economic integration between both.

The literature on the causal relationship between trade and FDI includes Hsiao and Hsiao (2006), who argued that FDI caused exports, in turn leading to economic growth in the eight East and Southeast Asian economies (the PRC, the Republic of Korea, Taipei,China, Hong Kong, China, Singapore, Malaysia, the Philippines, and Thailand) from 1986 to 2004. Likewise, Min (2003) also supported that FDI inflows stimulated exports in Malaysia.

However, Liu, Wang, and Wei (2001) found different results in the case of the PRC's trade and FDI with 19 countries from 1984 to 1998. They found that the growth rate of PRC's imports caused the growth in inward FDI from home countries, which in turn, caused the growth of exports from PRC to the home country.

In the case of Mexico, Pacheco-Lopez (2005) found bi-directional Granger causality between exports and FDI, and between imports and FDI. She interpreted the result as liberalization of FDI easing access of multinational corporations to the country and promoting exports. In addition, an increase in exports led to an increase in imports in the case of Mexico.

There are a few studies on the causal relationship between trade and FDI in the case of India. Jayachandran and Seilan (2010) performed a causality test amongst trade, FDI, and economic growth in India from 1970 to 2007 but did not find a significant connection between trade and FDI.

In the case of the Republic of Korea, the results by Lee and Song (2008) were almost unique; applying the Granger causality test method and employing annual data from 1970 to 2004, they found that trade led to FDI between the Republic of Korea and the US, and the Republic of Korea and the PRC, while FDI caused trade between the Republic of Korea and Japan.

Data, Methodology, and Estimation

Analysed Countries and Data

The eight countries employed for analysis include the Republic of Korea, Japan, Singapore, the PRC, and four other countries—the US, UK, Germany, and the Netherlands. All of these are the top countries in terms of trade and FDI with India.

Amongst top trade partners to India, oil-importing countries like the United Arab Emirates (UAE), Saudi Arabia, Iraq, and a gold-importing country, Switzerland, were excluded. Amongst the top FDI partners to India, tax-haven countries such as Mauritius and Cyprus, with cumulative FDI inflows of less than $1 billion by March 2013, were also excluded.

In this chapter, bilateral trade and FDI volume data is used. Quarterly data from the third quarter of 2004 to the fourth quarter of 2012 was utilized. All of the data came from the Ministry of Commerce and Industry in India and was obtained from the CEIC database (CEIC n.d.). The reason that this study could not cover the data before 2004 is that there is no continuous FDI data by countries before 2004 because the Government of India changed the FDI estimation criteria two or three times since. As a result, there was discontinuity with respect to data before 2004.

In this study, trade data included bilateral exports and imports, while FDI data included inflow to India from each country. The FDI inflow from India to each country was too small and sporadic to be included.

Table 2.6(a) is the basic description of the data used in this study. Both trade and FDI data have a positive value. Skewness and kurtosis values for every data show that they are not normally distributed. Most of the data distribution has a skewed right and more or less-peck rather than a normal distribution. As a result, the values of Jarque-Bera are not significant.

Looking at the trade and FDI graph (Figure 2.1), the trade data shows a generally increasing trend. That means trade of all individual countries with India increased over time. In contrast, while FDI has generally trended upward, the level is lower and more irregular than trade. Therefore, the primary integral data or the first difference integral data is used in this study.

The PRC–India FDI has been excluded from the analysis due to problems with the PRC's FDI inflow data. In the 34 quarters covered by the analysis, the volume of FDI was zero in four quarters, and seven quarters had FDI less than $100,000.[7]

Both trade and FDI show positive correlation coefficients. In particular, coefficients for the Netherlands, Singapore, and Japan are very high, at more than 68 per cent. The coefficient for the Republic of Korea is over 46 per cent. Germany, and the UK's coefficients are about 37 per cent and 36 per cent, respectively. The US is unique, with very little correlation between trade and investment.

[7] See the graph CI in Figure 2.1.

TABLE 2.6(a) The Basic Descriptions of the Data

	KT	JT	CT	ST	UST	UKT	GET	NET
Mean	2,912.89	2,903.26	11,067.57	3,911.29	10,003.1	2,986.73	4,055.48	1,976.70
Median	2,982.12	2,646.62	10,569.26	3,744.31	9,253.985	2,859.57	4,114.25	1,951.99
Maximum	5,188.63	5,340.46	21,084.5	8,426.34	15,399.26	4,465.81	6,438.37	3,972.12
Minimum	1,170.47	1,358.57	3,226.41	1,711.55	5,067.01	1,699.94	1,732.26	634.85
Standard Deviation	1,148.74	1,178.876	5,231.77	1,506.386	3,295.585	698.0934	1,305.82	931.2171
Skewness	0.110011	0.528781	0.249807	0.774205	0.39918	0.352515	–0.02001	0.257637
Kurtosis	1.77407	2.162149	1.952326	3.519314	1.883065	2.111449	1.902606	2.125693
Jarque-Bera	2.197695	2.578946	1.908582	3.778621	2.67031	1.822668	1.708324	1.459054
Probability	0.333255	0.275416	0.385085	0.151176	0.263117	0.401988	0.42564	0.482137
Sum	99,038.56	98,711.08	376,297.5	132,984.1	340,105.5	101,549.1	137,886.6	67,208.12
Sum of Squared Deviation	43,547,528	45,861,707	9.03E+08	74,883,534	3.58E+08	16,082,035	56,270,510	28,616,457
Observations	34	34	34	34	34	34	34	34

(*Contd.*)

Table 2.6(a) (*Contd.*)

	KI	JI	CI	SI	USI	UKI	GEI	NEI
Mean	33.86	280.00	8.17	563.76	271.74	279.45	145.16	227.78
Median	22.8	160.28	0.585	424.655	233.655	125.365	66.365	197.59
Maximum	135.96	1,234.19	105.85	2,671.44	867.29	2,476.89	1,255.18	543.05
Minimum	0.64	12.82	0	4.9	57.12	6.56	17.73	6.5
Standard Deviation	32.84653	301.3317	20.15392	559.4996	184.8313	488.415	219.6597	170.3706
Skewness	1.471411	1.483816	3.691328	1.81869	1.70787	3.38118	3.951758	0.275566
Kurtosis	4.750801	4.760423	17.58002	7.186454	5.994206	14.41875	20.43918	1.751398
Jarque-Bera	16.61112	16.86674	3.78E+02	43.57233	2.92E+01	2.49E+02	519.3366	2.638903
Probability	0.000247	0.000217	0	0	0	0	0	0.267282
Sum	1,151.39	9,520.33	278	19,168.16	9,239.48	9,501.36	4,935.47	7,744.59
Sum of Squared Deviation	35,603.52	2,996,426	13,403.96	10,330,312	1,127,367	7,872,123	1,592,262	957,862.3
Observations	34	34	34	34	34	34	34	34

Note: KT and KI represent the Republic of Korea–India trade volume and FDI inflow to India from the Republic of Korea, respectively
KT, JT, CT, ST, UST, UKT, GET, NET represent trade between India and the Republic of Korea, Japan, People's Republic of China, Singapore, the US, UK, Germany, and the Netherlands, respectively. KI, JI, CI, SI, USI, UKI, GEI, and NEI represent FDI inflows to India from the Republic of Korea, Japan, People's Republic of China, Singapore, the US, UK, Germany, and the Netherlands, respectively.

Source: Prepared by author using EView.

Correlation and causation are conceptually and theoretically different. High correlation does not equal causation. Although the correlation is high, causal relationship could be low or missing. This is why this study tests for Granger causality between bilateral trade and FDI by countries (Table 2.6(b)).

Methodology

To figure out the causal relationship between FDI and trade, a bivariate vector autoregression (VAR) format was employed. The VAR Granger causality test, designed and developed by Granger (1969), Engel and Granger (1987), and Johansen (1991), amongst others, suggests researchers to follow a three-stage procedure for the estimation.

TABLE **2.6(b)** The Correlation Coefficient between Trade and Foreign Direct Investment by Countries

Countries	Coefficient
Republic of Korea–India	0.461145
Japan–India	0.682405
Singapore–India	0.695252
US–India	0.008990
UK–India	0.366477
Germany–India	0.389577
Netherlands–India	0.717258

Note: US = United States, UK = United Kingdom.

Source: Prepared by author using EView.

The first-step is to determine whether each time series data is stationary. The natural logarithm conversion data and the first-difference natural logarithm conversion data are tested through Augmented Dickey and Fuller (ADF) statistics.

The second step is to investigate the bivariate cointegration between each trade and FDI data converted to the natural logarithm and the first-difference natural logarithm data using Johansen's cointegration test.

The two aforementioned steps provide the proper data and analysis method. Engel and Granger (1987) and Johansen (1991) recommended

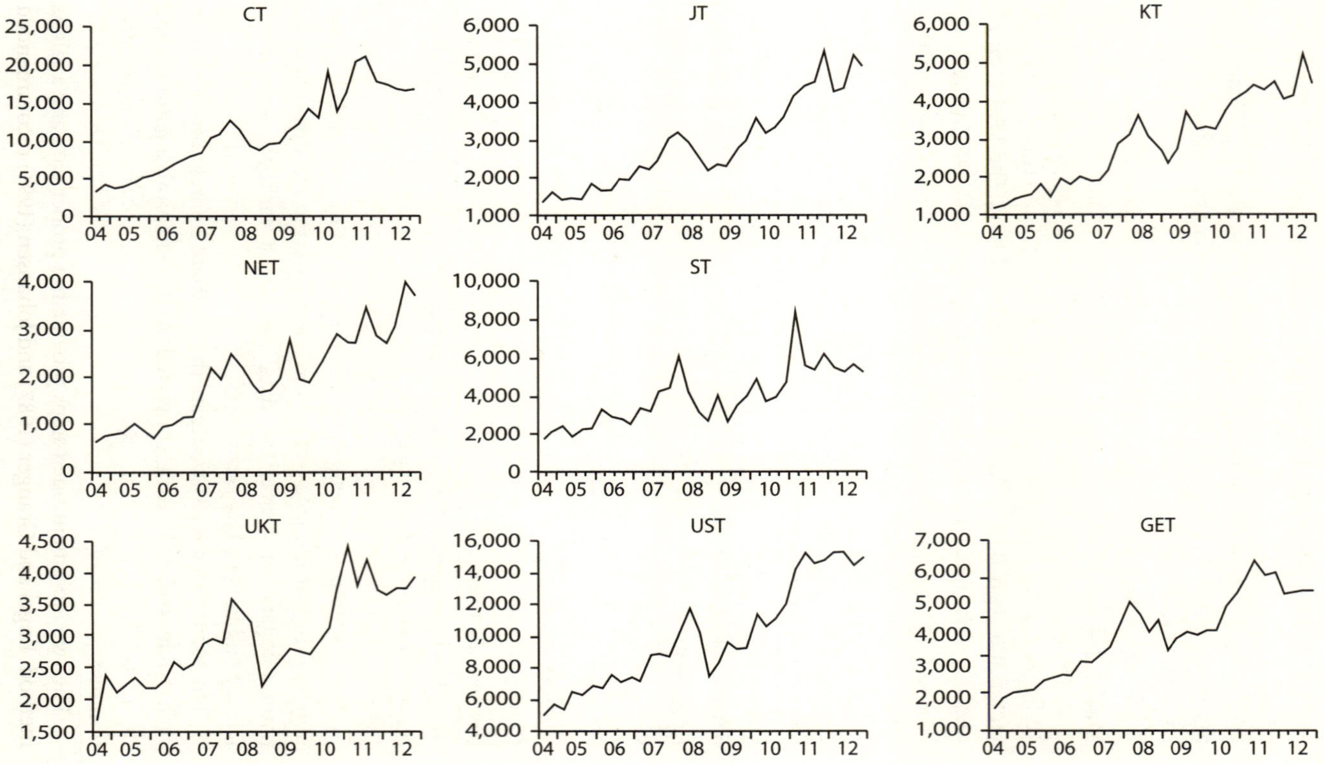

CT
JT
KT
NET
ST
UKT
UST
GET
04 05 06 07 08 09 10 11 12

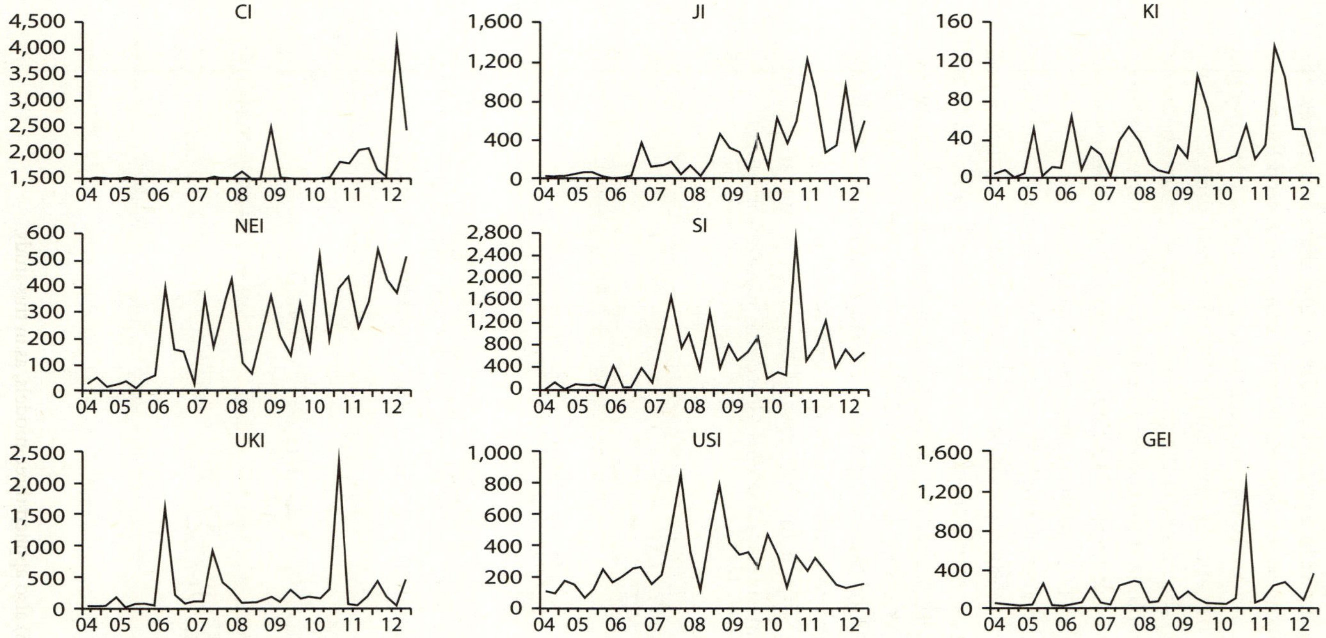

FIGURE 2.1 Trade and Foreign Direct Investment Variables by Countries

Note: KT and KI represent the Republic of Korea–India trade volume and FDI inflow to India from the Republic of Korea, respectively. KT, JT, CT, ST, UST, UKT, GET, NET represent trade between India and the Republic of Korea, Japan, People's Republic of China, Singapore, the US, UK, Germany, and the Netherlands, respectively. KI, JI, CI, SI, USI, UKI, GEI, and NEI represent FDI inflows to India from the Republic of Korea, Japan, People's Republic of China, Singapore, the US, UK, Germany, and the Netherlands, respectively.

Source: Prepared by author using EView.

that when each time series data is stationary and there is the presence of cointegration between the two sets of data, the natural logarithm conversion data as a level data is better for the unrestricted VAR Granger causality test. They also recommended that, when each time series data is not stationary, but there is the presence of cointegration between both, the natural logarithm conversion data (level data) could be used with vector error correction VAR Granger causality test. The reason is that the possibility of spurious regression is low in that case.

Relying on the aforementioned method, the three estimation equations could be established as follows. Let X_t, Y_t be a stationary time series with zero means respectively (u_t=0, v_t=0). The simple causal equation is (1). The definition Granger causality is as follows: If Y_t is causing X_t provided some γ_j is not zero. Similarly X_t is causing Y_t if some c_j is not zero. If both of these events occur, there is said to be a feedback relationship between X_t and Y_t (Granger 1969, p. 431).

In this study,[8] first, if the level data of X_t and Y_t is stationary and has cointegration, an unrestricted VAR Granger Equation 1 is applied.

$$X_t = \sum_{i=1}^{m} \beta_i X_{t-i} + \sum_{j=1}^{n} \gamma_j Y_{t-j} + u_t$$

(Equation 1)

$$Y_t = \sum_{i=1}^{a} b_i Y_{t-i} + \sum_{j=1}^{r} c_j X_{t-j} + v_t$$

Second, if the level data of X_t and Y_t is not stationary but has cointegration, an error correction VAR Granger Equation 2 is applied.

$$X_t = \alpha + \sum_{i=1}^{m} \beta_i X_{t-i} + \sum_{j=1}^{n} \gamma_j Y_{t-j} + \delta ECM_{t-1} + u_t$$

(Equation 2)

$$Y_t = \alpha + \sum_{i=1}^{a} b_i Y_{t-i} + \sum_{j=1}^{r} c_j X_{t-j} + dECM_{t-1} + v_t$$

[8] Ghosh (2006) also applied three models, as in this study.

Third, if the level data of X_t and Y_t is stationary but has no cointegration, instead of level data, the first-difference data with an unrestricted VAR Granger Equation 3 is applied.

$$\Delta X_t = \sum_{i=1}^{m} \beta_i \Delta X_{t-i} + \sum_{j=1}^{n} \gamma_j \Delta Y_{t-j} + u_t$$
$$\Delta Y_t = \sum_{i=1}^{a} b_i \Delta Y_{t-i} + \sum_{j=1}^{r} c_j \Delta X_{t-j} + v_t \qquad \text{(Equation 3)}$$

Through Equation 1, 2, or 3, if the null hypothesis could be rejected unilaterally, Y_t or X_t Granger causes X_t or Y_t, respectively. If the null hypothesis could be rejected simultaneously, Y_t and X_t Granger cause each other.

Estimation

Unit Root and Cointegration Test

To examine whether the data is stationary, the ADF unit root test was conducted. Table 2.6(c) presents the results of the ADF test on the natural logarithms conversion data and the first-difference of the natural logarithms conversion data. As a level data, the Republic of Korea–India, Singapore–India, and the Netherlands–India data was stationary at the 10 per cent significance level at least. The data of Japan–India, UK–India, and Germany–India had one side stationary—in trade or FDI. In the case of the US–India, the trade- and FDI-level data is not stationary at any significant level. But every first-difference data was stationary at 1 per cent significance except for one data series—Singapore–India trade (Table 2.6(c)).

Next, Johansen cointegration tests were conducted to determine unrestricted VAR Granger causality or error correction Granger causality with level data. This is to check the existence of cointegration between trade- and FDI-level data. To find each optimal lag interval, Akaikie Information Criterion (AIC) was performed before the Johansen cointegration tests. In the Johansen cointegration test, constant and trend option was applied.

TABLE 2.6(c) The Results of Augmented Dickey and Fuller Unit Root Tests

		Log (level)	Log First–Difference
Republic of Korea–India	Trade	−3.397*	−7.202***
	FDI	−5.565***	−8.347***
Japan–India	Trade	−2.977	−6.515***
	FDI	−4.610***	−5.041***
Singapore–India	Trade	−3.963**	−2.198
	FDI	−5.646***	−12.615***
UAE–India	Trade	−3.706**	−5.981***
	FDI	−4.149**	−5.829***
US–India	Trade	−2.701	−5.595***
	FDI	−1.579	−5.462***
UK–India	Trade	−2.927	−6.593***
	FDI	−5.840***	−6.376***
Germany–India	Trade	−2.217	−5.832***
	FDI	−6.340***	−6.825***
Netherlands–India	Trade	−3.770**	−6.534***
	FDI	−6.836***	−5.985***

Note: FDI = Foreign Direct Investment, UAE = United Arab Emirates, US = United States, UK = United Kingdom.

*, **, *** mean statistically significant at 10%, 5%, and 1%, respectively.

Source: Prepared by author using EView.

Table 2.6(d) shows the results of both the trace test and the maximum eigen value test. The level data of the Republic of Korea–India and the Netherlands–India had one more cointegration at 0.1 per cent significance level. Further, Japan–India, the US–India, UK–India, and Germany–India had a cointegration between each of their trade- and FDI-level data. But only the level data of Singapore–India was unclear in regard to the existence of cointegration.

Granger Causality Test

According to the results of the ADF and Johansen cointegration tests (Table 2.6(e)), the appropriate Granger causality equations and data are as follows. In the cases of the Republic of Korea–India and

TABLE 2.6(d) The Results of Johansen Cointegration Tests

	Hypothesized Number of CE(s)	Eigen Values	Trace Statistic	Max-Eigen Statistic
Republic of Korea–India	None	0.56	31.78(23.34)*	20.63(17.23)*
	At most 1	0.35	11.14(10.66)*	11.14(10.66)*
Japan–India	None	0.84	51.20(23.34)*	46.04(17.23)*
	At most 1	0.18	5.15(10.66)	5.15(10.66)
Singapore–India	None	0.30	17.07(23.34)	11.42(17.23)
	At most 1	0.16	5.65(10.66)	5.65(10.66)
US–India	None	0.67	35.54(23.34)*	27.80(17.23)*
	At most 1	0.26	7.73(10.66)	7.73(10.66)
UK–India	None	0.54	32.53(23.34)*	25.14(17.23)*
	At most 1	0.20	7.39(10.66)	7.39(10.66)
Germany–India	None	0.81	46.70(23.34)*	42.10(17.23)*
	At most 1	0.16	4.60(10.66)	4.60(10.66)
Netherlands–India	None	0.57	39.10(23.34)*	27.09(17.23)*
	At most 1	0.31	12.01(10.66)*	12.01(10.66)*

Note: US = United States, UK = United Kingdom, ( ) is 0.1 critical value, * denotes rejection of hypothesis at the 0.1 level.
Republic of Korea–India, Japan–India, US–India, and Germany–India were applied 8 lag, Singapore–India, UK–India, and Netherlands–India were applied 1 lag.
Source: Prepared by author using EView.

the Netherlands–India, the level data with unrestricted VAR Granger Causality test (Equation 1) could be applied because their level data are stationary and cointegrated. Moreover, in the cases of Japan–India, the US–India, UK–India, and Germany–India, the level data with a vector error correction VAR Granger test (Equation 2) could be applied because their level data is not stationary but has cointegration. Only the Singapore–India case, in which the level data is stationary but has no cointegration, could be applied by the unrestricted VAR model with log first difference data in this analysis (Equation 3).

In general, 1 or 2 years' lag was utilized in many Granger causality analyses between trade and FDI. In this study 2 years' (8 quarters) lag interval was also applied. The results of the estimation are presented

TABLE 2.6(e) The Applied Data and Model by Countries

Data/Model	Destination Countries
Level data with Unrestricted VAR Granger Model (Equation 1)	Republic of Korea–India, Netherlands–India
Level data with Vector Error Correction VAR Granger Model (Equation 2)	Japan–India, US–India, UK–India, Germany–India
The first-difference data with Unrestricted VAR Model (Equation 3)	Singapore–India

Note: VAR = vector auto regression, US = United States, UK = United Kingdom.
Source: Prepared by author using EView.

in Table 2.6(f). The estimation results show that India and East Asian countries such as the Republic of Korea, Japan, and Singapore had no causality between trade and FDI. However India and non-East Asian countries such as the US, UK, and Germany had causal relations between trade and FDI. UK–India had a bi-directional relation between trade and FDI. In the case of the US–India and Germany–India, trade and FDI were uni-directional, with causality running from FDI to trade and trade to FDI, respectively.

Policy Implication

Since the late 2000s economic exchange between India and East Asia has become increasingly active. The trade and FDI linkages between India and East Asian countries such as the Republic of Korea, the PRC, Japan, and Singapore appear to be more active than India's linkages with the Western countries such as the US, UK, Germany, and the Netherlands, who were major trade and FDI partners for India previously. The correlation coefficients between trade and FDI in cases of India–East Asian countries were much higher than for India–Western countries.

However, the causal relationship between bilateral trade and FDI for India and the East Asian countries elicited results contrary to our expectations. In the Republic of Korea–India, Japan–India, and Singapore–India bilateral relationships, the causality between trade and FDI could

TABLE 2.6(f) The Granger Causality Estimation Results

	Null Hypothesis	Chi-Square	Probability	Results
Republic of Korea–India	FDI does not cause trade	10.535	0.229	Not Rejected
	Trade does not cause FDI	8.924	0.348	Not Rejected
Japan–India	FDI does not cause trade	12.649	0.124	Not Rejected
	Trade does not cause FDI	4.111	0.846	Not Rejected
Singapore–India	FDI does not cause trade	6.310	0.612	Not rejected
	Trade does not cause FDI	5.805	0.669	Not rejected
US–India	FDI does not cause trade	26.427	0.000	Rejected***
	Trade does not cause FDI	2.211	0.973	Not Rejected
UK–India	FDI does not cause trade	21.773	0.005	Rejected**
	Trade does not cause FDI	28.148	0.000	Rejected***
Germany–India	FDI does not cause trade	4.871	0.771	Not Rejected
	Trade does not cause FDI	22.044	0.004	Rejected**
Netherlands–India	FDI does not cause trade	6.886	0.548	Not Rejected
	Trade does not cause FDI	6.994	0.537	Not Rejected

Note: FDI = Foreign Direct Investment, US = United States, UK = United Kingdom. All were given 8 lag.

*, **, *** mean statistically significant at 10%, 5% and 1% respectively.

Source: Prepared by author using EView.

not be found. In contrast, in the case of the US–India, UK–India and Germany–India, while their bilateral trade and FDI was relatively poor in the late 2000s, the relationship showed the two-way or one-way causality, respectively.

The estimation results raise new research questions such as the effect of the exchange term or scale and the motives for FDI on the relationship between trade and FDI. But those questions could not be answered clearly in this study because of limitations in data and the analytical model.

In spite of the limitations, the estimation results could provide us with policy implications. The results suggest that bilateral trade and FDI causal relationship is determined more by long-term economic exchange than a short-term increase in the volume of trade or FDI. In other words, the UK, the US, and Germany are old and established economic partners for India just as the US, Japan, and the PRC are the major (and established) economic partners for the Republic of Korea. East Asian countries, namely, the Republic of Korea, Japan, and Singapore, have a relatively short history of economic exchange with India in comparison to Western countries such as the UK, US, and Germany. The context of this study is similar to Lee and Song (2008) which showed that the causal relationship between bilateral trade and FDI in the US, Japan, and the PRC with the Republic of Korea appeared to be unidirectional.

In fact, before the 1991 reform in India, these Western countries engaged in extensive economic exchanges with India. According to the Indian Investment Center, from 1981 to 1990, the total FDI inflow from the West was about $9.5 billion. Amongst them, the US (25 per cent), Germany (16 per cent), and the UK (7 per cent) accounted for 48 per cent, while they mainly invested in chemicals (34 per cent), electronics (19 per cent) and machinery (4 per cent) sectors (Akhtar 2013). In terms of the number of joint ventures in 1984, amongst the total of 412 companies, 189 companies belonged to the United Kingdom (46 per cent), 90 were from the US (22 per cent), and 47 companies from Germany (11 per cent) (Dhar 1998).

In this situation, the question of the effectiveness of bilateral FTAs which are now in force between India and the Republic of Korea, Japan, and Singapore may be raised. Paradoxically, despite what this chapter's findings may suggest, these FTAs may still contribute to enhanced interrelationship between trade and FDI although the causal relationship has not been found yet.

Even with the uncertainty of the causal relationship between bilateral trade and FDI, India and East Asian countries will eventually have to promote trade and FDI simultaneously rather than to focus on one or the other. From this perspective, more measures for investment as well as trade have to be deployed in future FTA upgrade negotiations between India and East Asia. Furthermore, the two governments should further strengthen bilateral efforts to create a production division in the global supply chain through trade and FDI. These efforts will make it possible to compensate for the relatively low trade–FDI relationship and the short history of economic exchange between India and East Asian countries.

* * *

While this study focuses on the analysis of the causal relationship between bilateral trade and FDI, it had its limitations especially in terms of data employment and operation. The limitations of statistical data on Indian FDI inflow prevented us from making a more detailed analysis. For example, the study could not reflect on the fact that each country differs in its history and pattern regarding its trade and FDI with India. If those facts had been taken into account and then analysed, the policy implications would be much clearer. In addition, inclusion of variables, such as industry or business level, may have increased the validity of the model.

References

Akhtar, G. 2013. 'Inflows of FDI in India: Pre and Post Reform Period', *International Journal of Humanities and Social Science Invention*, 2(2): 1–11.

Caves, R.E. 1957. 'International Trade and Industrial Organization: Problems, Solved and Unsolved', *European Economic Review*, 28(3): 377–95.

CEIC. n.d. 'India Premium Database'. Available at www.ceicdata.com (accessed on 27 September 2016).

Dhar, B. 1998. 'Foreign Controlled Companies in India: An Attempt and Identification', *Institute for Studies in Industrial Development Working Paper* 1988/03.

Ghosh, S. 2006. 'Steel Consumption and Economic Growth: Evidence from India', *Resource Policy*, 31: 7–11.

Granger, C. 1969. 'Investigating Causal Relations by Econometric Models and Cross-Spectral Methods', *Econometrica*, 37: 24–36.

Gray, H.P. 1998. 'International Trade and Foreign Direct Investment: The Interface', in J.H. Dunning (ed.), *Globalization, Trade and Foreign Direct Investment*, pp. 19–28. Oxford: Elsevier.

Helpman, E. 1984. 'A Simple Properties of Generalized Method of Moments Estimator', *Journal of Political Economy*, 92(3): 457–71.

Helpman, E. and P. Krugman. 1985. *Market Structure and International Trade*. Cambridge, Massachusetts: MIT Press.

Hsiao, F.S.T. and M.C.W. Hsiao. 2006. 'FDI, Export and Growth in East and Southeast Asia: Evidence from Time-Series and Panel Data Causality Analyses', *Journal of Asian Economics*, 17(6): 1082–106.

Jayachandran, G. and A. Seilan. 2010. 'A Causal Relationship between Trade, Foreign Direct Investment and Economic Growth for India', *International Research Journal of Finance and Economics*, 42: 74–88.

Jang, Y.J. 2011. 'The Impact of Bilateral Free Trade Agreements on Bilateral Foreign Direct Investment amongst Developed Countries', *World Economy*, 34(9): 1628–51.

Johansen, S. 1991. 'Estimation and Hypothesis Testing of Cointegration Vectors in Gaussian Vector Autoregressive Models, *Econometrica*, 59(6): 1551–80.

Lee, J.H. and J.S. Song. 2007. 'Is There a Two-Way Linkage Between Trade and FDI?: Evidence from Korea's Major Trading Partners', *International Area Studies*, 3(25–41), 28–29.

———. 2008. 'Is There a Two-Way Linkage between Trade and FDI?: Evidence from Korea's Major Trading Partners', *International Area Studies*, 3: 25–41.

Liu, X., C. Wang, and Y. Wei. 2001. 'Causal Links between Foreign Direct Investment and Trade in China', *China Economic Review*, 12: 190–202.

Markusen, J. 1984. 'Multinationals, Multi-Plant Economies, and the Gains from Trade', *Journal of International Economics*, 16(3–4): 205–26.

Markusen, J. and A. Venables. 1998. 'Multinational Firms and the New Trade Theory', *Journal of International Economics*, 46(2): 183–203.

Markusen, J. and K. Maskus. 2001. 'General Equilibrium Approaches to the Multinational Firm: A Review of Theory and Evidence', NBER Working Paper 8334.

Min, B.S. 2003. 'FDI and Trade: Links in the Case of Malaysia', *Journal of the Asia Pacific Economy*, 8(2): 229–50.

Mundell, R.A. 1957. 'International Trade and Factor Mobility', *American Economic Review*, 47(June): 321–25.

Pacheco-Lopez, P. 2005. 'Foreign Direct Investment, Exports and Imports in Mexico', *World Economy*, 28(8): 1157–72.

3

JAYANT MENON

Can Free Trade Agreements Support the Growth or Spread of International Production Networks in Asia?*

One of the defining characteristics of trade patterns in East Asia is the high share of manufacturing trade taking place with global production networks ('fragmentation trade') in regional trade, so much so that the description 'Factory Asia' is now commonplace. This share is much higher in East Asia than in more integrated regions of the world, such as the European Union (EU) and in North America under the North

* I am particularly grateful to Prema-chandra Athukorala for extensive comments provided on an earlier draft. I also thank Chris Milner, Innwon Park, and participants at the Asian Development Bank (ADB)–Korea Institute for International Economic Policy (KIEP) workshop on Integrating South and East Asia in Seoul, 22–23 October 2012, and those at the Globalisation and Economic Policy (GEP) conference at the University of Nottingham, Malaysia Campus, 19–20 February 2013, for useful comments and discussions. Anna Cassandra Melendez and Luca Burmeister provided excellent research assistance. The views expressed in this chapter are those of the author and do not necessarily reflect the views and policies of the ADB, or its Board of Governors or the governments they represent.

American Free Trade Agreement (NAFTA). If fragmentation trade characterizes trade flows, then trade policy in the region has come to be dominated by the proliferation of free trade agreements (FTAs), particularly since 2000. The growth in the number of FTAs has been so rapid that it is now known as the 'noodle bowl' of criss-crossing, and often overlapping, FTAs. Are the two related and, if so, how? Asian countries' engagement in global production sharing began well before the new-found penchant for forming FTAs. Thus, clearly, the real issue here is not whether FTAs are necessary for this form of international exchange but if FTAs can promote further growth of production network trade. This chapter attempts to answer these questions.

Empirical testing of the FTA–network trade nexus is complicated by an endogeneity problem—the possibility that the causation can run either way (Baier and Bergstrand 2007). These countries' engagement in global production networks predates the formation of FTAs; trade expansion through global production sharing could well have facilitated the formation of FTAs (Grunwald and Flamm 1985). Since about 2000, the proliferation of FTAs and rapid expansion of network trade have gone hand in hand; coexistence (determined by various common 'third' factors) does not mean causation. In addition to this, there are difficulties in isolating the impact of intra- versus inter-regional FTAs, since they have not only spread concurrently, but are likely jointly determined (Menon 2009). Indeed, these factors may account for the mixed findings of previous empirical studies,[1] leaving no clear conclusion on the existence, nature, or direction of the relationship. Therefore, this chapter employs a qualitative approach that carefully examines the characteristics of both product fragmentation trade and FTAs in Asia to ascertain possible linkages.

In doing this, it seeks to address questions such as the following. Given differences in the characteristics of product fragmentation trade and trade in final goods, are FTAs the right instrument to promote the former? Can rules of origin (ROOs) be designed in a way that can accommodate product fragmentation trade? Does the existence of other agreements, such as the International Technology Agreement (ITA) and various duty drawback schemes, affect the efficacy of FTAs in

[1] See, for instance, Hayakawa and Yamashita (2011), Orefice and Rocha (2011), Brooks and Ferrarini (2012), and literature cited therein.

promoting product fragmentation trade? Are Asian FTAs deep enough to affect this type of trade, and if not, is deepening these agreements the answer? What other trade policy instruments need to be considered in promoting the growth and spread of production networks? These are key questions that need to be addressed in a comprehensive manner in order to understand the relationship between FTAs and production networks. The existing literature has failed to do this in a systematic way, and we hope to fill this gap.

We begin in the second section by reviewing the rapid rise in the number of FTAs in Asia. In the third section, we examine the growth in product fragmentation trade in Asia and the pattern of such trade, including its geographic and commodity composition, and assess the quality of FTAs in Asia in order to judge how they may affect product fragmentation trade. Since product fragmentation trade can be affected by either changes in tariffs or other trade costs such as trade facilitation, we examine each separately. The fourth section focuses on tariffs, while the fifth deals with trade facilitation. The final section concludes.

The Proliferation of Free Trade Agreements in Asia

The Doha Round of the World Trade Organization (WTO) has stalled, indefinitely. Partly as a reflection of this, bilateral FTAs have proliferated. Every country in the world today, with the exception of Timor-Leste, is a member of at least one plurilateral free trade agreement (PTA) and/or bilateral trade agreement (BTA), and most are members of multiple BTAs.

While Asia[2] was a relative latecomer to preferential liberalization through participation in FTAs, the region has been catching up rapidly of late. Asia has been at the center of a massive surge in the number of FTAs in a little less than a decade. Figure 3.1 tracks the growth of FTAs that involve at least one economy from the region, together with their status of implementation. Between 1983 and 1999, the number of FTAs in the region grew at a slow but steady pace. From 2000, however, this growth started to accelerate. Between 2000 and 2005, the number of FTAs that were signed or under negotiation more than doubled from

[2] Defined here to include countries in the Pacific, including Australia and New Zealand.

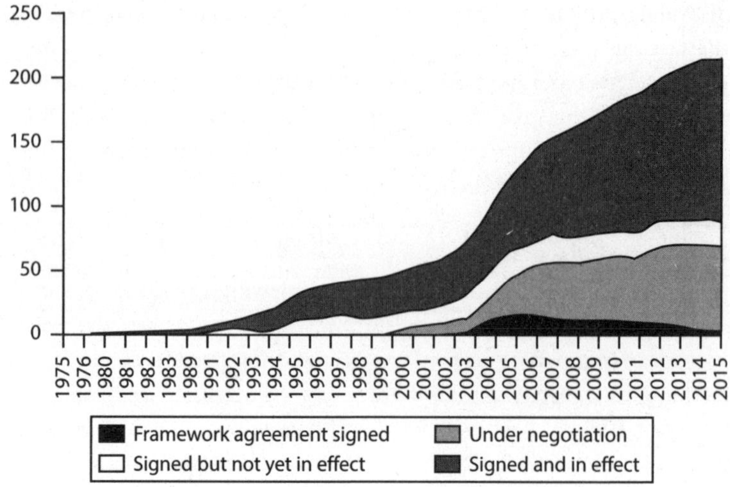

FIGURE 3.1 Free Trade Agreements by Status: Asia (cumulative, selected years)

Note: Framework agreement signed = The parties initially negotiate the contents of a framework agreement, which serves as a framework for future negotiations. Negotiations launched = The parties, through the relevant ministries, declare the official launch of negotiations or set the date for such, or start the first round of negotiations. Signed but not yet in effect = Parties sign the agreement after negotiations have been completed. However, the agreement has yet to be implemented. Signed and in effect = Provisions of Free Trade Agreements come into force, after legislative or executive ratification.

Source: Data generated by the Asia Regional Integration Center, Asian Development Bank (data as March 2015).

51 to 123; since 2005, this number has nearly doubled again to reach 215 by March 2015. Of these 215 FTAs, 145 have been signed, out of which 126 are already in effect. Another 70 FTAs are currently under negotiation.

The continuing popularity of FTAs is evinced by the even more significant rise in the number of proposed agreements, which has multiplied twenty-fold from 3 proposals in 2000 to the proposal of 60 potential agreements by March 2015 (Figure 3.2). The rapid growth in FTAs has been largely driven by the proliferation of BTAs. The number of BTAs that are signed or under negotiation has grown at an incredible pace in Asia, increasing by almost four-fold from 46 in

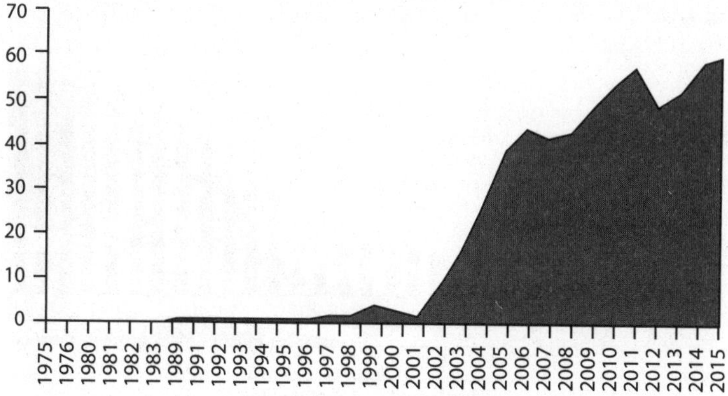

FIGURE 3.2 Proposed Free Trade Agreements: Asia (cumulative, selected years)
Note: Proposed = The parties consider a Free Trade Agreement; governments or relevant ministries issue a joint statement on its desirability or establish a joint study group/joint task force to conduct feasibility studies.
Source: Data generated by the Asia Regional Integration Center, Asian Development Bank (data as March 2015).

2000 to 155 by March 2015. This accounts for close to three-quarters of all FTAs in the region to date (Figure 3.3). Table 3.1 presents the geographic distribution of BTAs. The numbers clearly show that the vast majority of BTAs involve one Asian country and one country outside of the region. This same trend can be seen in the geographic distribution of plurilateral FTAs (Table 3.2).

Countries in East and Southeast Asia have been the most active in establishing linkages outside of the region. In South Asia, India and Pakistan have been actively pursuing FTAs with countries outside the subregion, particularly in East and Southeast Asia (Table 3.3). However, the smaller South Asian countries have been keener to establish links within the subregion. Countries in Central Asia have been as equally interested in signing FTAs with outside countries as with each other, presumably to restore favourable trading conditions that existed prior to the collapse of the Soviet Union.

A breakdown of the FTAs by economy reveals that the Association of Southeast Asian Nations (ASEAN)+6 countries—the 10 ASEAN members plus Australia, the People's Republic of China (PRC), India, Japan, the Republic of Korea, and New Zealand—sit at the top of the table. As of March 2015, Singapore leads the group with a total of 33 FTAs, of

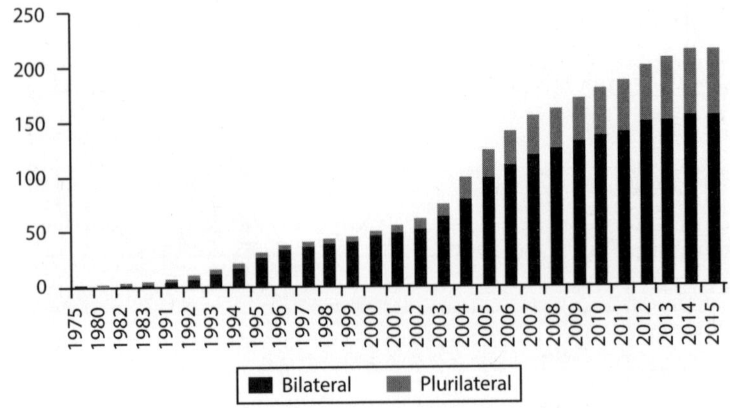

FIGURE 3.3 Free Trade Agreements by Scope: Asia (cumulative, selected years)
Note: Bilateral refers to a preferential trading arrangement involving only two parties. Plurilateral refers to a preferential trading arrangement involving more than two parties.
Source: Data generated by the Asia Regional Integration Center, Asian Development Bank (data as March 2015).

which 21 are currently in effect. India comes in second with a total of 28 FTAs, 13 of which are in effect. Japan has 24 FTAs, while the Republic of Korea and the PRC each have a total of 22 FTAs. Within ASEAN, Thailand, Malaysia, and Indonesia are not far behind with 22, 21, and 17 FTAs, respectively (Figure 3.4).

The FTAs involving ASEAN+6 countries have increased at an even faster rate than Asia's FTAs as a whole, growing more than ten-fold from 14 in 2000 to 148 by March 2015. To date, ASEAN+6 countries account for almost 70 per cent of the total FTAs in Asia (Figure 3.5). Not surprisingly, of the 148 FTAs involving ASEAN+6 countries, most are BTAs involving an ASEAN+6 country and a trading partner outside Asia (Table 3.4).

The outcome of this proliferation of often overlapping BTAs and PTAs has been described as the 'spaghetti bowl' effect, or in the Asian region, the 'noodle bowl' effect. The effect of the rise of the mega-regionals, on the other hand, has been described as fragmenting the world trade system to make it appear more like a jigsaw puzzle (Menon 2014b). Both refer to the increased cost of doing business, and welfare losses associated with trade diversion, due to inconsistencies between

TABLE 3.1 Bilateral Free Trade Agreements by Geographic Area: Asia, 2015

Bilateral FTAs	2015
Within subregion	
Central and West Asia	17
East Asia	5
Oceania	1
South Asia	6
Southeast Asia	1
Across subregions	
East Asia + Oceania	7
East Asia + South Asia	4
East Asia + Southeast Asia	13
South Asia + Oceania	2
Southeast Asia + Oceania	7
Southeast Asia + South Asia	7
The Pacific + Oceania	1
With Non-Asian Countries	
Central and West Asia + Non-Asia	21
East Asia + Non-Asia	27
Non-Asia + Oceania	3
South Asia + Non-Asia	10
Southeast Asia + Non-Asia	20
The Pacific + Non-Asia	3
Total	**155**

Note: Central and West Asia = Armenia, Azerbaijan, Georgia, Kazakhstan, Kyrgyz Republic, Tajikistan, Turkmenistan, Uzbekistan
East Asia = People's Republic of China, Hong Kong, China, Japan, Republic of Korea, Mongolia, Taipei,China
South Asia = Afghanistan, Bangladesh, Bhutan, India, Maldives, Nepal, Pakistan, Sri Lanka
Southeast Asia = Brunei Darussalam, Cambodia, Indonesia, Lao People's Democratic Republic, Malaysia, Myanmar, Philippines, Singapore, Thailand, Viet Nam
Source: Data generated by the Asia Regional Integration Center, Asian Development Bank (data as March 2015).

TABLE 3.2 Plurilateral Free Trade Agreements by Geographic Area: Asia, 2015

Plurilateral FTAs	2015
Asian Plurilateral	11
Asian Plurilateral + Asian Country	6
Non-Asian Plurilateral + Asian Country	29
Cross-regional Plurilateral	8
Non-Asian Plurilateral + Asian Plurilateral	2
Cross-regional Plurilateral + Asian Country	3
Cross-regional Plurilateral + Non-Asian Plurilateral	1
Total	**60**

Note: Asian Plurilateral refers to groupings of more than two countries where all the members are Asian countries.
Cross-regional refers to groupings of more than two countries where the members are a combination of Asian and non-Asian countries.
Source: Data generated by the Asia Regional Integration Center, Asian Development Bank (data as March 2015).

various elements of the agreements.[3] But there are those who contend that FTAs have played and will continue to play a key role in stimulating product fragmentation trade. Is this in fact the case?

The Growth in Product Fragmentation Trade

The share of trade emanating from production networks worldwide is much higher in East and Southeast Asia than in any other region in the world (Table 3.5). In 2009/10, product fragmentation exports accounted for 62.5 per cent of total manufacturing exports in the region, compared with the world average of 52.8 per cent. Parts and components accounted for more than half of total product fragmentation exports in the region during the same period. This share is much larger than the share of parts and components amongst world exports and intra-regional exports in the EU and NAFTA.

[3] These include, for instance, different schedules for phasing-out tariffs, different ROOs and exclusions, conflicting standards, and differences in rules dealing with anti-dumping and other regulations and policies (Pangestu and Scollay 2001).

TABLE 3.3 Free Trade Agreements between South and East Asian Countries

In Effect
1. Asia Pacific Trade Agreement (1976)
2. India–Singapore CECA (2005)
3. Pakistan–PRC FTA (2007)
4. Pakistan–Malaysia CEPA (2008)
5. India–Republic of Korea CEPA (2010)
6. India–ASEAN CECA (2010)
7. India–Malaysia CECA (2011)
8. India–Japan CEPA (2011)
9. Preferential Tariff Arrangement-Group of Eight Developing Countries (2011)
Signed (Not in Effect)
10. Pakistan–Indonesia FTA
11. Trade Preferential System of the Organization of the Islamic Conference
Under Negotiation
12. BIMSTEC
13. India–Indonesia CECA
14. India–Thailand FTA
15. Pakistan–Singapore FTA
16. Regional Comprehensive Economic Partnership
17. Sri Lanka–PRC FTA

Note: CECA = Comprehensive Economic Cooperation Agreement, PRC = People's Republic of China, FTA = Free Trade Agreement, CEPA = Comprehensive Economic Partnership Agreement, ASEAN = Association of Southeast Asian Nations, BIMSTEC = Bay of Bengal Initiative for Multi-Sectoral Technical and Economic Cooperation.
Source: Data generated by the Asia Regional Integration Center, Asian Development Bank (data as March 2015).

While a high and rising share of intra-regional exports consists of fragmentation trade, the bulk of final goods are exported to countries outside the region (Athukorala 2011). As noted in the previous section, despite recent increases in South–South trade, much of developing Asia's trade prospects is still dependent on markets outside the region.

One option under consideration in Asian policy circles for supporting regional trade growth in the face of slow growth in world demand is

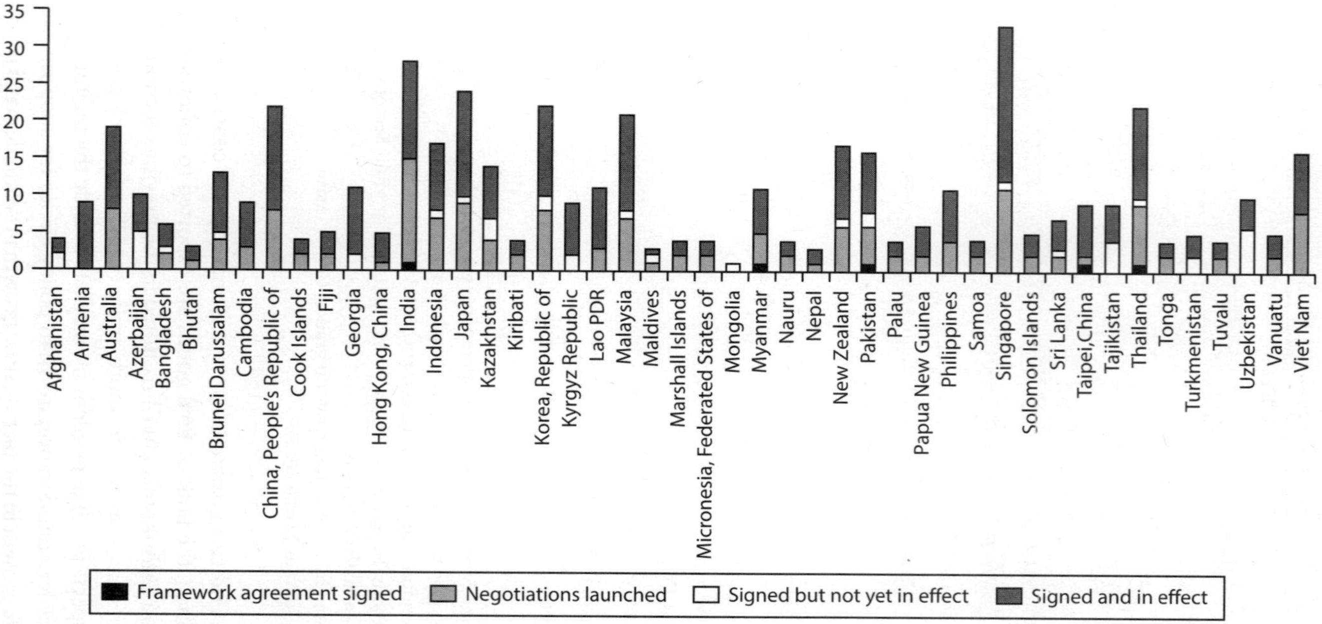

FIGURE 3.4 Free Trade Agreements by Economy: Asia, 2015

Notes: Framework agreement signed = The parties initially negotiate the contents of a framework agreement, which serves as a framework for future negotiations. Negotiations launched = The parties, through the relevant ministries, declare the official launch of negotiations or set the date for such, or start the first round of negotiations. Signed but not yet in effect = Parties sign the agreement after negotiations have been completed. However, the agreement has yet to be implemented. Signed and in effect = Provisions of free trade agreement come into force, after legislative or executive ratification.

Source: Data generated by the Asia Regional Integration Center, Asian Development Bank (data as March 2015).

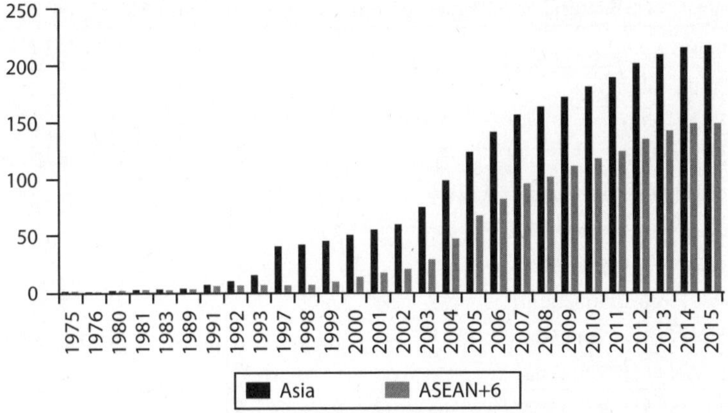

FIGURE 3.5 Free Trade Agreements: Asia and ASEAN+6 (cumulative, selected years)
Note: ASEAN+6 = ASEAN plus Australia, the People's Republic of China, India, Japan, Republic of Korea, and New Zealand.
Source: Data generated by the Asia Regional Integration Center, Asian Development Bank (data as March 2015).

to form a region-wide FTA. The ASEAN-led Regional Comprehensive Economic Partnership (RCEP), formally endorsed at the 19th ASEAN Summit held in November 2011, is one such example. The RCEP will initially include all ASEAN+6 countries in forming the largest FTA in Asia. Apart from potentially harmonizing the various intra-regional BTAs, the formation of such blocs is often touted as carrying the potential to support the growth and spread of production networks. The argument put forward is as follows: trade within global production networks is expected to be more sensitive to tariff changes than trade in final goods because of multiple border crossings. Consequently, a 1 percentage point reduction in tariff rates within the consolidated bloc leads to a decline in the cost of production of a vertically integrated good by a multiple equal to the number of borders crossed within the bloc, rather than a 1 per cent decline in the cost of a final good. Tariff reductions may also make it more profitable for goods that were previously produced entirely in one country to become vertically specialized. Consequently, in theory, the trade-stimulating effects of FTAs would be higher for product fragmentation trade than for trade in final goods, other things remaining unchanged.

Table 3.4 Bilateral Free Trade Agreements: ASEAN+3 and ASEAN+6, 2015

Region	2015
Within subregion	
ASEAN+3	15
ASEAN+6	36
Across subregion (within Asia)	
ASEAN+3 + Non-ASEAN+3	9
ASEAN+6 + Non-ASEAN+6	14
With Non-Asian Countries	
ASEAN+3 + Non-Asia	39
ASEAN+6 + Non-Asia	45

Note: ASEAN+3 = ASEAN plus the People's Republic of China, Japan, and the Republic of Korea.
ASEAN+6 = ASEAN plus Australia, the People's Republic of China, India, Japan, the Republic of Korea, and New Zealand
Within subregion means both countries are ASEAN+3 (ASEAN+6) members.
Across subregion means one is an ASEAN+3 (ASEAN+6) member with its partner an Asian country but not an ASEAN+3 (ASEAN+6) member.
Source: Data generated by the Asia Regional Integration Center, Asian Development Bank (data as March 2015).

Preferential Tariff Reductions and Product Fragmentation Trade

It is sometimes argued that the proliferation of FTAs has supported intra-regional trade through the spread of production networks, and that their continued growth will be enhanced by expanding or increasing the number of FTAs. The logic behind this assertion rests on the fact that unlike trade in final goods, product fragmentation trade generally involves multiple border crossings. With this difference between the two, it is argued that trade within global production networks is generally more sensitive to tariff changes than is trade in final goods (Yi 2003). Since a tariff can be levied each time a good-in-process crosses a border, the reduction or elimination of tariffs within the free trade area can lead to a multiplier effect whereby the cost savings is a multiple determined by the number of border crossings within the FTA. Furthermore, tariff reductions of this type may make it more profitable for goods that were previously produced entirely in one country to become vertically

TABLE 3.5 Share of Network Products in Manufacturing Trade, 2009/10 (%)

	Parts and components	Final assembly	Total network trade
(a) **Exports**			
Developing East Asia	**35.2**	**27.3**	**62.5**
PRC	25.7	32.5	58.2
Taipei,China	44.2	25.6	69.8
Republic of Korea	43.2	28.4	71.6
ASEAN	44.7	24.8	69.5
Indonesia	21.54	17.7	39.1
Malaysia	54.6	22.2	78.8
Philippines	73.3	14.5	87.8
Singapore	49.5	17.2	66.7
Thailand	30.1	34.3	64.4
Viet Nam	11.2	7.6	18.8
India	12.3	4.2	16.5
Developed economies	**25.2**	**23.6**	**48.8**
Developing economies	**47.3**	**44.5**	**55.6**
World	**29.2**	**23.6**	**52.8**
(b) **Imports**			
Developing East Asia	**42.2**	**17.1**	**61.3**
PRC	44	19.8	63.7
Hong Kong, China	48.5	13.5	62.1
Taipei,China	38.9	16.8	55.7
Republic of Korea	31.9	17.4	49.3
ASEAN	47.9	16.2	64.1
Indonesia	21.8	15.8	37.7
Malaysia	50	22	72
Philippines	61.3	17.4	78.6
Singapore	60.4	17.3	77.7
Thailand	36.1	12.4	48.5
Viet Nam	19.1	9.7	28.5
India	22.9	17	39.9
Developed economies	**23.4**	**25.5**	**48.9**
Developing economies	**33.6**	**19.9**	**53.5**
World	**27.3**	**23.3**	**50.7**

Note: ASEAN = Association of Southeast Asian Nations.

Source: Athukorala (2011).

specialized, exploiting differences in cost competitiveness across members of the FTA. Consequently, in theory, the trade-stimulating effects of FTAs could be higher for product fragmentation trade than for trade in final goods, other things being equal. This theoretical possibility alone has led some to conclude, somewhat prematurely it would seem, that FTAs, or their expansion, can support production networks (for example, Kawai and Wignaraja 2013).

How does this pan out in practice in Asia? Should policymakers pursue more FTAs to capture the multiplier effect from tariff reductions on product fragmentation trade? There are a number of reasons for policymakers to be wary in considering this option for Asia. The compelling reason for avoiding the FTA option is that it is simply unnecessary. First and foremost, for a number of reasons most, if not all, product fragmentation trade already travels duty-free or at very low tariffs across the region. Most important is the Information Technology Agreement (ITA), a multilateral agreement of the WTO. As noted earlier, most product fragmentation trade in Asia involves products classified as electronics parts and components. Products covered under the ITA include computer hardware and peripherals, telecommunications equipment, computer software, semiconductor manufacturing equipment, analytical instruments, and semiconductors and other electronic components (Table 3.6). This covers almost all constituent products involved in fragmentation trade classified to this category.

As shown in Table 3.7, all of the key players in production networks in Asia are signatories of the ITA, including the PRC; Japan; the Republic of Korea; the five original ASEAN members (ASEAN5); Hong Kong, China; and Taipei,China. Asian economies had the largest volumes of trade upon joining the ITA in the period spanning from 1997 to 2008. They continue to be the biggest users of the agreement (Tables 3.8, 3.9). In 2010, Asian members accounted for around two-thirds of global ITA exports and nearly half of global ITA imports (Tables 3.10, 3.11). The three largest users of the ITA were the PRC; Singapore; and Taipei,China. When combined with the Republic of Korea and Japan, these five economies accounted for over half of total ITA exports. As Anderson and Mohs (2010, p. 13) point out, '[a] prominent feature of expanding ITA trade is the broadening participation of Asian countries, particularly [the PRC], and an increasingly important role for other developing countries.' Furthermore, since ITA participants must eliminate their tariffs on a most favoured nation (MFN) basis, even non-ITA signatories that are members of the WTO will enjoy duty-free access to these products. The initiative to update the agreement to create ITA II will further enhance its use, by expanding membership and product coverage, as well as dealing with technological changes that affect product classification.

How about fragmentation trade outside the electronics parts and components sector? Here again it appears that FTAs have little to offer since most of the firms involved in production networks (mostly multinational enterprises) are located in export processing or free trade zones (EPZs or FTZs). Those operating outside FTZs normally enjoy import duty exemptions under duty–drawback and bonded warehouse schemes.

These factors operate against a backdrop of low and falling tariffs on parts and components, which have more to do with unilateral actions than preferential ones. In this respect, Vezina (2010) suggests that a highly liberalizing race-to-the-bottom unilateralism occurred in emerging Asia in the 1980s and 1990s (see also Baldwin 2010 and 2011). Vezina (2010) argues that unilateral tariff-cutting in Asia's emerging economies has been driven by competition to attract foreign direct investment (FDI) from Japan. As a result, the trade-weighted preference margin for intra-ASEAN trade in 2008 was a mere 2.3 per cent, while 72.9 per cent of trade travelled at a 0 MFN rate (WTO 2011).

Using spatial econometrics, he shows that tariffs on parts and components, a crucial locational determinant for Japanese firms, converged across countries following a contagion pattern, driving them to lower and lower levels. In a study on autos, auto parts, and hard disk drives in ASEAN, Cheewatrakoolpong, Sabhasri, and Bunditwattanawong (2013) conclude that investment promotion policies contributed more to the emergence of international production networks than FTAs. The many country-sector studies by the United Nations Economic and Social Commission for Asia and the Pacific (UNESCAP 2011a) also came to the general conclusion that FTAs, in their current form, have had little or no impact on production networks in the region.

The findings of Vezina (2010), Cheewatrakoolpong, Sabhasri, and Bunditwattanawong (2013), and UNESCAP (2011a) apply to emerging Asia, and mainly the original ASEAN economies of Malaysia, Thailand, Singapore, Indonesia, and the Philippines. How about other Asian

Table 3.6 Representative Information Technology Agreement Products and Number of HS Codes, by Attachment

	Number of HS Codes	Sample Products
Attachment A1	112	*Computers and computer peripherals*: Personal computers, laptops, workstations, monitors, keyboards, hard drives, CD-ROM drives, smart cards, printers, scanners, and other input/output units
		Telecommunications equipment: Telephone sets, cordless phones, mobile handsets, pagers, answering machines, switches, routers, hubs, modems, fibre optic cables
		Semiconductors: Microprocessors, integrated circuits, printed circuits, diodes, resistors
		Software: Magnetic tapes, unrecorded media
		Office equipment: Certain photocopy machines, fax machines, cash registers, adding machines, calculators, automatic teller machines (ATM)
		Scientific and measuring devices: Spectrometers,chromatographs, flow meters, gauges, optical radiation devices
		Other: Loudspeakers, still digital cameras, parts
Attachment A2	78	*Semiconductor manufacturing equipment (SME)*: Etching and stripping apparatus, vapour deposition devices, sawing and dicing machines for wafers, spinners, ion implanters, wafer transport, handling and storage machines, injection molds, optical instruments, parts and accessories
Attachment B	131	Computers, electric amplifiers, flat-panel displays, network equipment, monitors, pagers, CD and DVD drives, plotters, printed circuit assemblies, removable storage devices, set-top boxes

Note: Attachment B products are covered regardless of where they are classified in the HS system. ITA Committee members have made attempts to narrow divergences in the customs classification of some Attachment B products (WTO G/IT/W6/Rev.3), though there is no agreed-upon list. The authors use such codes as a proxy.

Source: Anderson and Mohs (2010).

TABLE 3.7 Information Technology Agreement Membership Asian Countries (ITA trade upon joining the agreement)

Country	Year joined ITA	Total ITA trade ($ million) upon joining agreement	Share of ITA trade (%)	
			Total Asia	Total ITA
Malaysia	1997	58,416	16.18	13.13
China, People's Republic of	2003	250,202	69.32	56.23
Thailand	1997	22,368	6.2	5.03
Philippines	1997	21,460	5.95	4.82
India	1997	3,077	0.85	0.69
Georgia	1999	38	0.01	0.01
Viet Nam	2007	5,375	1.49	1.21
Kyrgyz Republic	1999	26	0.01	0.01
Total Asia		360,962	100	81.13
Total ITA member countries[a]		444,937		

Note: ITA = Information Technology Agreement.
[a] Only includes members which joined the ITA between 1997–2008.
Source: Anderson and Mohs (2010).

economies in South Asia and Central and West Asia? Tariffs and other barriers to trade remain relatively high in many parts of South Asia, and many Central Asian countries are not yet members of the WTO. As noted in the second section, a number of these countries are also actively pursuing FTAs. If FTAs have not played much of a role in promoting the growth or spread of production networks in Southeast Asia, can they help countries in these other regions participate in production networks? The short answer is that it is highly unlikely, for a number of reasons. A key factor relates to a defining characteristic of FTAs, which is their preferential nature.

Even if we put aside the ITA, FTZs, and duty-drawback schemes, it appears that FTAs are still unlikely to play an effective role in promoting this type of trade due to their need to protect the provision of preferences by excluding non-members. The impact that preferential tariff reductions can have on product fragmentation trade relates to the need to implement ROOs in order to exclude trade that does not comply

TABLE 3.8 Information Technology Agreement Exports as a Share of Each Economy's Exports

Rank	Main Exporters	Value ($ billion)			Share of Total Exports (%)			Share of Manufactured Goods Exports (%)			Share of SITC 7 Exports (%)			Share of SITC 75-77 Exports (%)		
		1996	2005	2010	1996	2005	2010	1996	2005	2010	1996	2005	2010	1996	2005	2010
1	PRC	11.3	186.8	386.5	7.5	24.5	24.5	8.9	26.7	26.2	32.0	53.0	49.5	44.7	66.5	67.1
4	Singapore[a]	38.1	103.9	122.5	30.5	45.2	34.8	36.7	56.6	48.3	46.2	77.0	68.2	53.1	91.1	85.9
5	Taipei,China	33.4	66	100.6	28.9	34.8	36.8	31.0	38.4	41.1	57.4	70.0	74.7	78.1	90.1	93.4
6	Korea, Republic of	25.6	78.3	97.9	19.7	27.5	21.0	22.3	30.3	23.8	37.9	45.1	37.1	63.9	79.5	79.3
7	Japan	81.9	98.7	84.5	19.9	16.6	11.0	21.0	18.1	12.4	28.7	25.9	18.4	65.6	70.4	58.1
8	Malaysia	21.7	56.2	60.5	27.7	39.7	30.4	36.7	53.2	45.4	50.1	73.5	69.3	56.4	80.2	77.9
10	Thailand	8.9	21.9	31.3	16.0	19.9	16.0	23.2	26.3	22.4	42.2	44.5	38.0	54.0	68.4	65.6
11	Philippines	8.6	26.1	29.2	41.9	63.3	56.7	50.6	71.1	66.6	74.0	85.0	80.9	78.3	93.3	88.8
15	Viet Nam	0	1.2	5	0.0	3.7	6.9	0.0	7.4	10.8	0.0	38.3	43.6	0.0	53.3	58.6
16	India	0.5	1	4.3	1.5	1.0	2.0	2.5	1.7	3.7	18.2	9.5	13.5	52.6	36.3	50.3
17	Indonesia	1.6	4.7	3.9		5.5	2.5		11.7	6.7		34.6	19.9		47.0	30.8
21	Hong Kong, China	4.9	3.9	1.9	2.7	1.3	0.5	3.0	1.4	0.5	8.4	2.6	0.8	10.5	2.8	0.9

Note: PRC = People's Republic of China.

[a] Includes significant re-exports

Source: UNCTAD (United Nations Conference on Trade and Development; 2012) and WTO (2012).

TABLE 3.9 Information Technology Agreement Imports as a Share of Each Economy's Imports

Rank	Main Importers	Value ($ billion)			Share of Total Imports (%)			Share of Manufactured Goods Imports (%)			Share of SITC 7 Imports (%)			Share of SITC 75-77 Imports (%)		
		1996	2005	2010	1996	2005	2010	1996	2005	2010	1996	2005	2010	1996	2005	2010
2	PRC	12.9	169.3	291.7	9.3	25.7	20.9	11.8	34.5	32.8	23.6	58.3	53.1	62.8	83.5	81.1
4	Singapore[a]	25.4	75.6	86.7	19.3	37.8	27.9	23.5	50.3	43.1	33.4	67.7	60.2	47.5	88.0	85.1
5	Japan	40.6	64.3	69.1	11.6	12.5	10.0	21.7	23.4	20.0	47.7	48.6	42.8	75.2	73.4	63.0
6	Taipei,China	14.3	46.3	56.5	14.0	25.5	22.5	19.4	35.4	34.6	35.3	62.1	62.2	60.7	95.7	99.1
8	Korea, Republic of	19.7	45.1	54.5	13.1	17.3	12.8	20.3	28.5	22.7	36.0	54.6	44.2	81.8	85.3	79.8
9	Malaysia	14.2	44.3	50.2	18.2	38.8	30.5	22.1	49.1	41.7	30.4	67.4	61.6	47.5	86.7	85.4
10	Thailand	6.6	20.2	26.9	9.1	17.1	14.7	11.9	25.1	22.2	19.3	44.9	41.8	42.9	76.6	73.0
12	Philippines	7.7	22.9	18.8	22.2	46.3	32.2	28.6	60.6	48.1	42.8	80.0	68.3	69.2	93.6	91.2
13	India	1	10.5	16.7	2.6	7.5	4.8	4.9	13.9	11.7	9.7	27.3	23.5	35.6	60.8	52.0
17	Hong Kong, China	10.7	10.9	14.1	5.3	3.6	3.2	6.2	4.1	3.8	14.5	7.0	5.7	19.8	7.9	6.3
19	Indonesia	2.1	1.8	11.5		2.4	8.5		3.8	13.3		7.2	24.4		18.6	64.5
24	Viet Nam	0.3	2.1	6.3	2.7	5.7	7.4	3.5	8.2	10.3	9.5	22.8	25.4	25.4	57.8	55.7

Note: PRC = People's Republic of China.

[a] Includes significant re-exports

Source: WTO (2012) and UNCTAD (2012).

Table 3.10 Asian Information Technology Agreement Members' ITA Exports (volume, share of world trade, and average annual growth)

Rank	Main Exporters	Value ($ billion)			Share of World ITA Trade (%)			Average Annual Change (%)	
		1996	2005	2010	1996	2005	2010	1996–2010	2005–2010
1	PRC	11.3	186.8	386.5	2.1	15.8	27.5	29	16
4	Singapore[a]	38.1	103.9	122.5	6.9	8.8	8.7	9	3
5	Taipei,China	33.4	66.0	100.6	6.1	5.6	7.2	8	9
6	Korea, Republic of	25.6	78.3	97.9	4.7	6.6	7.0	10	5
7	Japan	81.9	98.7	84.5	14.9	8.4	6.0	0	-3
8	Malaysia	21.7	56.2	60.5	4.0	4.8	4.3	8	1
10	Thailand	8.9	21.9	31.3	1.6	1.9	2.2	9	7
11	Philippines	8.6	26.1	29.2	1.6	2.2	2.1	9	2
15	Viet Nam	0.0	1.2	5.0	0.0	0.1	0.4	45	32
16	India	0.5	1.0	4.3	0.1	0.1	0.3	17	35
17	Indonesia	1.6	4.7	3.9	0.3	0.4	0.3	7	-4
21	Hong Kong, China	4.9	3.9	1.9	0.9	0.3	0.1	-7	-14

Note: ITA = Information Technology Agreement, PRC = People's Republic of China.

[a] Includes significant re-exports

Source: WTO (2012).

TABLE 3.11 Asian Information Technology Agreement Members' ITA Imports (volume, share of world trade, and average annual growth)

Rank	Main Importers	Value ($ billion)			Share of World ITA Trade (%)			Average Annual Change (%)	
		1996	2005	2010	1996	2005	2010	1996–2010	2005–2010
2	PRC	12.9	169.3	291.7	2.3	13.6	18.8	25	11
4	Singapore[a]	25.4	75.6	86.7	4.6	6.0	5.6	9	3
5	Japan	40.6	64.3	69.1	7.4	5.1	4.5	4	1
6	Taipei,China	14.3	46.3	56.5	2.6	3.7	3.6	10	4
8	Korea, Republic of	19.7	45.1	54.5	3.6	3.6	3.5	8	4
9	Malaysia	14.2	44.3	50.2	2.6	3.5	3.2	9	3
10	Thailand	6.6	20.2	26.9	1.2	1.6	1.7	11	6
12	Philippines	7.7	22.9	18.8	1.4	1.8	1.2	7	–4
13	India	1.0	10.5	16.7	0.2	0.8	1.1	22	10
17	Hong Kong, China	10.7	10.9	14.1	1.9	0.9	0.9	2	5
19	Indonesia	2.1	1.8	11.5	0.4	0.1	0.7	13	44
24	Viet Nam	0.3	2.1	6.3	0.1	0.2	0.4	25	24

Note: [a] Includes significant re-exports.

Source: WTO (2012).

with or meet minimum requirements. First, unlike trade in final goods, formulating and implementing ROOs for production network trade is far more complicated. If the conventional value-added criterion is employed, it is highly unlikely that intermediate inputs emanating from outside the region will qualify. This is because the activities involved are low value-added by their very nature. If, on the other hand, the change in tariff-line-based ROOs is applied, then this may disqualify inputs from both outside and inside the region once they travel across the next border. This is because trade in parts and components generally belong to the same tariff codes at the HS-6 digit level, which is the normal base for designing this type of ROO. The following illustrative example, provided by Athukorala and Kohpaiboon (2011), is compelling: electrical appliance assembly plants in Thailand, which use imported bare printed circuit board (BPCB) together with other locally procured electronic components (for example diode, integrated circuits, semi-conductors) to printed circuit board assembly (PCBA) for export are not eligible for FTA concessions because BPCBs and PCBAs belong to the same HS code (853690).

Second, the process of international product fragmentation is characterized by the continuous emergence of new products. Given the obvious administrative problems involved in revising ROOs in tandem, these product inventions and innovations naturally open up room for unnecessary administrative delays and/or the tweaking of rules as a means of disguised protection (Elek 2008).

Therefore, countries in South and Central Asia are unlikely to be able to use FTAs as a trade policy instrument to promote their engagement in production networks in an effective way. This is not to suggest that FTAs cannot have an impact in these countries. Highly preferential concessions provided on a bilateral basis in an otherwise highly trade-restrictive environment is bound to have an impact. Indeed, these conditions provide an almost perfect setting for trade diversion to thrive. In this environment, utilization of FTA concessions could become firm or industry specific, presenting economy-wide distortions that reduce national welfare as ramifications of the well-known theory of the second-best. Furthermore, they are likely to mainly affect intensive margins—the amount of a good traded, rather than extensive margins—the range of goods that are traded, further limiting potential benefits of participating in production networks. They are also self-limiting by nature. The preferential nature of FTAs stands in the way of what we have observed to be the natural expansion of production networks in countries and regions actively involved in the process. By limiting the scope to members only, or specific firms of industries, growth is likely to be choked-off over time. Production networks survive by growing and spreading across countries and sectors, in response to relative factor price adjustments and related developments, and FTAs are not designed to accommodate either of these features of their expansion.

A living example of successful spread, or of a new entrant successfully joining production networks, is provided by the experience of Viet Nam. In recent years, regional production networks have begun to spread beyond their original Southeast Asian bases to Viet Nam in particular (Athukorala and Tien 2012). This appears to have little to do with FTAs but instead the market-oriented policy reforms which started in the late 1980s and that gathered momentum in the 1990s. Most, if not all, of these reforms were national actions undertaken unilaterally, as part of the *doi moi* reform programme, as well as related factors such as satisfying requirements of WTO accession. To date, Viet Nam remains one of the least active in pursuing FTAs in this region. From about the late 1990s, part and component assembly began to emerge, mostly with the involvement of small- and medium-scale investors from Taipei,China and the Republic of Korea and only one major global player, Hitachi from Japan. When Intel arrived in February 2006 to set up a $300 million testing and assembly plant (subsequently increased to $1 billion) in Ho Chi Minh City however, a whole host of other manufacturers soon followed suit (see Athukorala and Kohpaiboon 2013).

In sum, when it comes to tariff liberalization, it appears that FTAs have been largely irrelevant. The factors described here combine to account for the embarrassingly low utilization rates of FTAs in Asia reported in almost all studies, directly contradicting the assertion that FTAs matter in promoting this or any other type of trade. Indeed, the estimated impacts of these FTAs in studies assuming full utilization may greatly exaggerate their benefits (Menon 2014a, 2014b). Rather than promoting production networks, it is more likely that product fragmentation trade has prospered despite the noodle bowl of overlapping FTAs in the region.

The preferential nature of FTAs can also thwart the natural expansion of production networks by limiting their growth to members of the bloc. This applies particularly to countries trying to participate in production networks for the first time, using FTAs to substitute for generally high tariffs and other barriers. The process of product fragmentation, which involves not only part and components but also final assembly, is a global rather than a regional phenomenon. Not only are parts and components production and final assembly usually conducted in different countries, and usually quite a number of them with the former, final demands for the finished products are generally found in countries outside the region (Athukorala and Kohpaiboon 2012).

Even proposals for mega-FTAs, such as the recently proposed RCEP, would exclude about two-thirds of the countries in the region, depending on how Asia is defined. Experience also suggests that creating such mega-FTAs tends to be possible only through resorting to the lowest—rather than highest common denominator, thereby making their concessions weak or even redundant (Menon 2009).[4] This is often necessary in order to secure consensus. Putting aside the difficulties in creating such consolidated mega-blocs, every South Asian country (except India) and all Central Asian countries would fall outside RCEP. This would not only disadvantage the excluded countries, but it would also hurt RCEP's members by limiting the switching and spreading of tasks that serves to sustain production networks. Therefore, to support the natural growth of production networks, it would be more useful if these preferences were multilateralized, and offered to all on an MFN basis, rather than consolidated within discriminatory FTAs, however large. Apart from supporting the growth of production networks, it would also remove trade diversion and the costs associated with implementing ROOs, while increasing the benefits that flow from non-discriminatory trade. Baldwin (2013) raises considerable concern over the recent trend

[4] In South Asia, for instance, the establishment of a region-wide FTA had little effect on intra-regional trade and no effect in neutralizing existing BTAs. To the contrary, the FTA has been largely rendered redundant while the BTAs have thrived. For instance, 93 per cent of Sri Lanka's exports to India currently enter duty-free under the relevant BTA. The Bangladeshi minister of commerce, Amir Chowdury, explains why: 'When it comes to (our) regional FTA, big economies like India and Pakistan may not offer handsome duty cuts due to distinct interests with an individual country. But they may offer large duty cuts in bilateral FTAs with Bangladesh.' This is why Bangladesh and other South Asian countries continue to pursue BTAs with each other (and outsiders) even after the formation of the consolidated FTA. See also Hill and Menon (2008).

to group regional blocs around the world together to create mega ones, pointing to how they can only lead to further 'fragmentation and exclusion', and goes further to call for a new institution—a second WTO—to govern the process of liberalizing global supply chain trade. Although the likelihood of a new institution emerging is low, the WTO Trade Facilitation Agreement adopted at the Bali Ministerial Conference in 2013, may serve to deliver the kind of reforms required to support production networks (see the fifth section).

Although the creation of consolidated regional blocs, or the expansion of FTAs to include other members of the region, appears unlikely to be able to support the growth or spread of production networks, what about cross-regional FTAs? If an FTA is concluded with a country or bloc that represents a major destination for final goods, then the prospects for the FTA to affect production networks could be different. Take, for example, the case of a potential Japan–US FTA. If the concessions within the FTA are sufficient to promote a significant increase in exports of final goods from Japan to the US, then the FTA could potentially support the growth—although not necessarily the spread—of production networks within the region. Similarly, the recent trend to pursue tie-ups between plurilateral FTAs (*The Economist* 2012) could indirectly spur product fragmentation trade if the linkages result in increased demand for final goods. That is, an increase in demand for final goods produced within production networks would drive an increase in product fragmentation trade in the region. Although this may support the growth in product fragmentation trade involving existing participants within production networks, it may not affect the spread to new members.

Trade Facilitation

Product fragmentation trade is the output of complex production systems characterized by the establishment of global value chains. These networks are dependent on efficient logistics and the reduction of 'services link cost' (Jones and Kierzkowski 1990; Hesse and Rodrigue 2004). As Memedovic et al. (2008) point out, the benefits arising from production networks cannot be realized without co-developments in modern logistics services underpinned by innovations in containerization, intermodal transport, and the application of information technology in physical distribution and materials management. Logistics is a wide-ranging concept, but from the point of view of cross-border movements of product fragmentation trade, the relevant aspect is trade facilitation.[5] Countries involved in production networks and the trade that they generate stand to gain the most from facilitating trade. The question then is how effective are FTAs in moving forward the trade facilitation agenda. Even though production networks preceded the proliferation of FTAs, has the growth in product fragmentation trade led to a deepening of existing FTAs, or the advent of new, deeper ones, particularly in relation to trade facilitation?

If FTAs are largely redundant when it comes to reducing tariffs on product fragmentation trade, then they have proven largely incapable of addressing trade facilitation aspects that matter when it comes to promoting this type of trade in Asia.

A number of studies also confirm the failure of many of the FTAs involving an Asian partner to deepen their coverage, and to deal adequately with trade facilitation issues. In a major study assessing the quality of FTAs, WTO (2011) finds that most of the FTAs show relatively limited WTO-plus or General Agreement on Trade in Services (GATS)-plus commitments in their design. In particular, ASEAN countries other than Singapore have shown relatively limited WTO-plus or GATS-plus commitments. Sally (2007) argues that Asian FTAs are by-and-large preferential tariff agreements on a limited range of goods. Even the better ones are trade-light and barely WTO-plus in that they do not seriously tackle non-tariff and regulatory barriers. In short, almost all FTAs involving Asian countries are relatively shallow, focusing on tariff reductions. Even when new WTO-plus issues are

[5] Although there is no universally accepted definition of trade facilitation, it is usually taken to refer to reforms aimed at making complicated and time-consuming cross-border trade procedures less inefficient. In other words, the idea is to cut the often excessive amount of red tape at the border. More formally, the Doha Ministerial Declaration (WTO 2001) refers to trade facilitation as 'expediting the movement, release, and clearance of goods, including goods in transit'. Persson (2008) suggests that another popular way to define the issue is to refer to the simplification and harmonization of international trade procedures, where such procedures are the activities, practices, and formalities involved in collecting, presenting, communicating, and processing data required for the movement of goods in international trade. This is the broad definition that we employ here. See also WTO (2015).

covered by FTAs, the areas embodying legally enforceable—and therefore substantive—commitments are relatively few; generally avoid trade facilitation; and tend to address investment, competition policy, intellectual property rights, and the movement of capital. Table 3.12 illustrates this for a selection of FTAs between countries in South and East Asia.

In sum, Asian FTAs generally tend to focus on tariff liberalization rather than trade facilitation or other WTO-plus or GATS-plus issues. In this way, Asian FTAs appear unlikely to be able to support the growth or spread of production networks by facilitating the trade in parts and components.

Since product fragmentation trade continues to grow within certain subregions of Asia, a related question is whether higher levels of trade in parts and components increase the likelihood of signing deeper agreements. In other words, does the causation run in the reverse direction, from increased product fragmentation trade leading to deeper FTAs over time, rather than vice versa? There is some evidence to support the reverse causality argument, but the relevant studies are not confined to Asia. For instance, Orefice and Rocha (2011) examine 96 FTAs reported to the WTO between 1958 and 2010. After taking into account other FTA determinants, they find that a 10 per cent increase in the share of product fragmentation trade over total trade increases the depth of an agreement by approximately 6 percentage points. Hayakawa and Yamashita (2011) consider over 250 FTAs with trade flows distinguished into parts and components and final goods for 1979–2008. Their gravity equation estimates suggest that the concurrent year effects of FTA formation on trade in parts and components are unseen, whereas FTAs have positive and pervasive effects on both types of trade flows 6 years and 9 years after FTA formation.

Although it is likely that these results are heavily influenced by the deeper FTAs signed between developed countries, could it be that Asian FTAs will evolve to be the same over time, and eventually contribute to the growth and spread of production networks? To the contrary, there is an emerging sentiment of resistance towards the upgrading of FTAs into deeper Comprehensive Economic Partnership Agreements (CEPAs) in the region. To cite just a few recent examples, the Indonesian Chamber of Commerce has voiced concern over such progression in a general way, while Sri Lanka has also rejected calls for a CEPA with India. The deepest of the proposed mega-blocs, the Trans-Pacific

TABLE 3.12 Depth of South and East Asian Free Trade Agreements

FTA	Government Procurement Chapter	Investment Chapter	Trade Facilitation Chapter	Competition Policy	Intellectual Property Rights	New Issues (overall)
APTA (1976)	No provision	No provision	No provision	No provision	No provision	Shallow
India–Singapore CECA (2005)	No provision	Standard	Standard	No provision	Standard	Limited
Pakistan–PRC FTA (2007)	No provision	NA	No provision	No provision	No provision	Shallow
Pakistan–Malaysia CEPA (2008)	No provision	Standard	Above standard	No provision	Standard	Limited
India–Republic of Korea CEPA (2010)	No provision	Above standard	Above standard	No provision	Standard	Moderate
India–ASEAN CECA (2010)	No provision	No provision	Standard	No provision	No provision	Shallow
India–Malaysia CECA (2011)	No provision	Above standard	Above standard	No provision	No provision	Limited
India–Japan CEPA (2011)	Standard	Standard	Above standard	Standard	Above standard	Moderate

Note: FTA = Free Trade Agreement, APTA = Asia-Pacific Trade Agreement, CECA = Comprehensive Economic Cooperation Agreement, CEPA = Comprehensive Economic Partnership Agreement, ASEAN = Association of Southeast Asian Nations.

Source: Author's own elaboration.

Partnership (TPP), was concluded in 2015, but its prospects for coming into force continue to remain uncertain. The next step for the TPP is for it to be ratified by the respective legislatures. This is expected to happen within about 2 years, although some countries may face challenges in getting the agreement passed by their legislatures. For now, there is still continuing uncertainty over the fate of the ratification process with the US Congress; if either the US and/or Japan fail to ratify the agreement, it cannot survive irrespective of what other countries do. Even if this is a temporal issue, however, there is a fundamental reason for avoiding FTAs as a trade policy instrument in promoting trade facilitation or other forms of liberalization in support of production networks.

That fundamental reason, as with tariff liberalization, relates to the need to be preferential or discriminatory in the provision of the concession or reform. But unlike tariff liberalization, it is often difficult or costly to remove non-tariff barriers or measures (NTBs, NTMs) in a preferential manner. It is usually impractical for these types of concessions to be exchanged in a discriminatory fashion—once an NTB or NTM is removed, the cost of excluding non-members is likely to be high, if not prohibitive, like with most public goods. This difficulty and associated cost vary by type of measure. While export subsidies or export licensing, for example, could be offered or applied preferentially, production subsidies cannot be reduced in the same way. With reducing production subsidies arguably the biggest barrier to reforming agricultural trade, the problem is real.

Even if it were possible to exclude third parties, this could seriously derail the reform programme. A recent study by UNESCAP (2011b) notes that preferential treatment negotiated with selected trading partners typically involves additional documentary requirements. The study presents evidence of significant delays associated with such requirements since FTAs have adopted different approaches to the rules on substantive measures relating to trade facilitation. Moreover, differences in their scope, depth, and level of detail have often translated into varying degrees of administrative inefficiency, through a maze of different procedures applied to respective trading partners under different FTAs.

If the costs associated with complying with FTA-based trade facilitation provisions are high, then the benefits that flow are also generally quite low, when compared with other modalities of liberalization. The results reported in Dee (2006) show that if deep economic integration initiatives were limited to reform of regulations that explicitly discriminated against foreigners, and that the reforms were undertaken on a preferential basis, they would add only trivially to the gains from preferential liberalization of tariffs on merchandise trade. Dee (2006) therefore concludes that 'there may be a few limited areas where FTAs can usefully supplement a domestic regulatory reform program... [but] because they tend to be preferential—even in their "new age" provisions—they tend to focus reform efforts away from where the big gains are to be made'. These big gains can only be realized through unilateral regulatory reform in the East Asian region. Due to more comprehensive coverage that targets the non-discriminatory restrictions which add to real resource costs, comprehensive unilateral reform would yield gains of more than five times that of an FTA.

Although such unilateral actions that also deal with incumbency, whether domestic or foreign, are optimal, is there a role that the WTO can play in coordinating the reform effort in a non-preferential manner? The difficulty of reaching agreement on Doha's ambitious all-or-nothing single-undertaking programme—aimed at addressing a wide variety of issues—is becoming increasingly clear. Attention has therefore shifted towards a compromise involving sectoral deals, including one that addresses trade facilitation. The WTO Trade Facilitation Agreement adopted at the Bali Ministerial Conference in 2013 could go some way towards delivering the kind of reforms required to support production networks.

On an average, trade-weighted tariffs account for about 5 per cent of trade costs, while logistical and other trade facilitation costs are about double that at 10 per cent. Originally, it was expected that a comprehensive and wide-ranging WTO-based trade facilitation agreement would bring these logistical costs down by half, or to an average of 5 per cent, which is the equivalent of removing all tariffs. In order to conclude the agreement, however, the final version adopted was less ambitious than originally planned. Furthermore, a lot will depend on how the agreement is implemented, and it is still too early to be able to judge the extent to which it will significantly affect the growth or spread of production networks. Therefore, unilateral actions should continue to be pursued wherever possible.

* * *

It is sometimes argued that the proliferation of FTAs in Asia has supported intra-regional trade through the spread of production networks, and that their continued growth will be enhanced by expanding or increasing the number of FTAs. However, empirical studies have produced mixed results, possibly resulting from dual causality and difficulties in isolating the impact of intra- versus inter-regional FTAs, which have increased concurrently. Therefore, this chapter employs a qualitative approach that carefully examines the characteristics of both product fragmentation trade and FTAs in Asia to ascertain possible linkages. Although it is clear that FTAs are not necessary for the growth or spread of production networks, since product fragmentation trade preceded the advent of FTAs, can their promotion support the further growth or spread of these networks? In this chapter, we argue that there are a number of reasons for policymakers to be wary of pursuing this option. First is the fact that almost all studies point to low utilization rates of FTAs, directly contradicting the assertion that they matter in promoting this or any other type of trade. Indeed, the estimated impacts of these FTAs in studies assuming full utilization may greatly exaggerate their benefits. Second, and this may explain the reason behind the first reason, most if not all product fragmentation trade already travels at duty-free or at very low tariffs across the region, either because of the ITA, which covers trade in electronics parts and components; various duty-drawback schemes; or the fact that most multinationals operate out of EPZs, where they are duty-exempt.

Rather than promoting production networks, it is more likely that product fragmentation trade has prospered despite the noodle bowl of overlapping FTAs in the region. Intra-regional FTAs appear to have had little effect on either the growth or spread of production networks. Inter-regional FTAs, on the other hand, may have been able to indirectly support the growth of production networks amongst existing members but not the spread to new ones. The FTAs are designed to promote trade in final goods, or goods which are produced from beginning to end in a given country, and not the type of fragmentation trade involving parts and components and final assembly within production networks. Also, almost all FTAs involving Asian countries are relatively shallow, focusing on tariff reductions rather than addressing trade facilitation and other NTBs that could have a greater impact on promoting production networks. Even if they were to deepen over time, it is difficult or costly to remove NTBs in a preferential manner. For these reasons, it would be more useful if FTA preferences were multilateralized and other accords offered to all on an MFN basis. This would remove trade diversion and the need to implement ROOs, along with the associated cost and confusion, as well as increase the benefits that flow from non-discriminatory trade. Combined with national liberalization actions that deal with incumbency issues, irrespective of nationality, this would be the best way to support the growth of production networks in current participants and their spread to new ones.

References

Anderson, M. and J. Mohs. 2010. 'The Information Technology Agreement: An Assessment of World Trade in Information Technology Products', *Journal of International Commerce and Economics* (web version), January. Available at https://www.usitc.gov/publications/332/journals/05_andersonmohs_itagreement.pdf (accessed on 28 September 2016).

Athukorala, P.C. 2011. 'Production Networks and Trade Patterns in East Asia: Regionalization or Globalization?', *Asian Economic Papers*, 10(1): 65–95.

Athukorala, P.C. and A. Kohpaiboon. 2011. 'Australian–Thai Trade: Has the Free Trade Agreement Made a Difference?', *Australian Economic Review*, 44(4): 457–67.

———. 2012. 'Intra-regional Trade in East Asia: The Decoupling Fallacy, Crisis and Policy Challenges', in M. Kawai, M. Lamberte, and Y.C. Park (eds), *The Global Financial Crisis and Asia: Implications and Challenges*, pp. 262–91 New York: Oxford University Press.

———. 2013. 'Global Production Sharing, Trade Patterns and Industrialization in Southeast Asia', in I. Coxhead (ed.), *Handbook of Southeast Asian Economies*, pp. 139–161. London: Routledge.

Athukorala, P.C. and T.Q. Tien. 2012. 'Foreign Direct Investment in Industrial Transition in Vietnam', *Journal of the Asia-Pacific Economy*, 17(3): 446–63.

Baier, S. and J. Bergstrand. 2007. 'Do Free Trade Agreements Actually Increase Members' International Trade?', *Journal of International Economics*, 71(1): 72–90.

Baldwin, R. 2010. 'Unilateral Tariff Liberalisation', *The International Economy: Journal of The Japan Society of International Economics*, 14: 10–43.

———. 2011. '21st Century Regionalism: Filling the Gap between 21st Century Trade and 20th Century Trade Rules', *CEPR Policy Insight*, 56(May).

———. 2013. 'The WTO and Global Supply Chains', *East Asia Forum*. Available at http://www.eastasiaforum.org/2013/02/24/the-wto-and-global-supply-chains/ (accessed on 6 September 2016.

Brooks, D.H. and B. Ferrarini. 2012. 'Vertical Gravity', ADB Economics Working Paper Series. No. 303, ADB, Manila.

Business Standard. 2012. 'Sri Lanka Not Keen on CEPA with India', 24 August. Available at http://www.business-standard.com/india/news/sri-lanka-not-keencepaindia/484201/ (accessed on 1 October 2016).

Cheewatrakoolpong, K., C. Sabhasri, and N. Bunditwattanawong. 2013. 'Impact of the ASEAN Economic Community on ASEAN Production Networks', ADBI Working Paper No. 409, Asian Development Bank Institute, Tokyo. Available at https://www.adb.org/sites/default/files/publication/156264/adbi-wp409.pdf (accessed on 28 September 2016).

Dee, P. 2006. 'East Asian Economic Integration and its Impact on Future Growth', *World Economy*, 30(3): 405–23.

Elek, A. 2008. 'Immunizing Future Protectionist: Preventing the Emergence of More Sensitive Sectors', Asia Pacific Economic Papers No. 372, Australia–Japan Research Centre, Australian National University, Canberra, Australia.

The Economist. 2012. 'Regional Deals Are the Only Game in Town for Supporters of Free Trade. Are They Any Good?', 22 December.

Grunwald, J. and K. Flamm. 1985. *The Global Factory: Foreign Assembly in International Trade*. Washington, D.C.: Brookings Institution Press.

Hayakawa, K. and N. Yamashita. 2011. 'The Role of Preferential Trade Agreements in Facilitating Global Production Networks', *Journal of World Trade*, 45(6): 1181–207.

Hesse, M. and J.P. Rodrigue. 2004. 'The Transport Geography of Logistics and Freight Distribution' *Journal of Transport Geography*, 12(3): 171–84.

Hill, H. and J. Menon. 2008. 'Back to Basics on Trade', *Far Eastern Economic Review*, 171(5 June): 44–47.

Jakarta Globe. 2012. 'Nation Must Review Its Trade Pacts, Kadin Says', 2 September. Available at http://bilaterals.org/spip.php?page=print&id_article=22005 (accessed on 28 September 2016).

Jones, R.W. and H. Kierzkowski. 1990. 'The Role of Services in Production and International Trade: A Theoretical Framework', in R.W. Jones and A.O. Krueger (eds), *The Political Economy of International Trade: Essays in Honor of Robert Baldwin*, pp. 31–48. Oxford: Basil Blackwell.

Kawai, M. and G. Wignaraja. 2013. 'Patterns of Free Trade Areas in Asia', Policy Studies No. 65. East West Center, Honolulu.

Memedovic, O., L. Ojala, J.P Rodrigue, and T. Naula. 2008. 'Fuelling the Global Value Chains: What Role for Logistics Capabilities?', *International Journal of Technological Learning, Innovation and Development*, 1(3): 353–74.

Menon, J. 2009. 'Dealing with the Proliferation of Bilateral Free Trade Agreements', *World Economy*, 32(10): 1381–407.

———. 2014a. 'Multilateralization of Preferences versus Reciprocity when FTAs are Underutilized', *World Economy*, 37: 1348–66.

Menon, J. 2014b. 'From Spaghetti Bowl to Jigsaw Puzzle? Fixing the Mess in Regional and Global Trade', *Asia and the Pacific Policy Studies*, 1(3): 470–83.

Orefice, G. and N. Rocha. 2011. 'Deep Integration and Production Networks: An Empirical Analysis', Staff Working Paper ERSD-2011-11, Economic Research and Statistics Division, World Trade Organization, Geneva.

Pangestu, M. and R. Scollay. 2001. 'Regional Trading Arrangements: Stock Take and Next Steps', paper presented at the PECC Trade Policy Forum sponsored by the Thai Ministry of Commerce, Bangkok, 12–13 June.

Persson, M. 2008. *Trade Facilitation and the Extensive and Intensive Margins of Trade*. Nottingham: University of Nottingham.

Sally, R. 2007. 'Looking East: The European Union's New FTA Negotiations in Asia', Jan Tumlir Policy Essays 03/2007, ECIPE, Belgium.

UNCTAD, 2012. UNCTADstat Database [Online]. Merchandise trade matrix - product groups, exports and imports in thousands of dollars, annual, 1995-2011. Retrieved from: http://unctadstat.unctad.org/wds/ReportFolders/reportFolders.aspx

UNESCAP. 2011a. *Fighting Irrelevance: The Role of Regional Trade Agreements in International Production Networks in Asia: A Study by the Asia-Pacific Research and Training Network on Trade*. New York: UN.

———. 2011b. *Trade Facilitation in Regional Trade Agreements*. Bangkok: UNESCAP.

Vézina, P.L. 2010. 'Race-To-The-Bottom Tariff Cutting', IHEID Working Paper December, The Graduate Institute of International Studies (IHEID), Geneva.

WTO. 2001. 'Ministerial Conference, Fourth Session—Ministerial Declaration', Doha, 9–14 November 2001, WT/MIN(01)/DEC/1.

———. 2011. *World Trade Report 2011*. Geneva: WTO.

———. 2012. 15 Years of the Information Technology Agreement. Trade, innovation and global production networks. Geneva: World Trade Organization. https://www.wto.org/english/res_e/publications_e/ita15years_2012full_e.pdf

———. 2015. 'Trade Facilitation'. Available at https://www.wto.org/english/tratop_e/tradfa_e/tradfa_e.htm (accessed on 6 September 2016).

Yi, K.M. 2003. 'Can Vertical Specialization Explain the Growth of World Trade?', *Journal of Political Economy*, 111(1): 52–102.

4

ALISA DICAPRIO
SITHANONXAY SUVANNAPHAKDY

Are Asia's Least Developed Countries Gaining from Regional Integration?

An Initial Look at Participation in Advanced Manufacturing Value Chains

From the beginnings of the postcolonial period, regional integration has been billed as a tool for economic development. Many of the United Nations (UN) regional commissions promoted regional ties to facilitate integration of newly independent nations into the international economy (see, for example, Greenaway and Milner 1990; Neuman 1979). Still today, this is firmly embedded in the policy goals of nations.

However, subsequent research has shown that the benefits of integration are unevenly distributed (for example, Feenstra 1996; Hur and Park 2012). The poorest countries in the block are those which are least likely to capture the full benefits of integration. The reasons for asymmetry of benefits range the spectrum from lack of productive capacity in the lower income partner to the asymmetric bargaining context.

The UN and other donors have recognized the need to address the challenges of the poorest countries. The Istanbul Programme of Action

(IPoA)[1] which was signed in 2011 includes the objective of graduating half of the UN's list of least developed countries (LDCs) by 2020 (United Nations Conference on Trade and Development [UNCTAD] 2012; IPoA 2011, section III, para 28). History illustrates the difficulties of this goal. In the 50 years since LDCs have been recognized as a category, only four countries have succeeded in meeting the graduation requirements.[2]

Structural transformation is central to the UN's graduation plan and has been important to the success of today's advanced economies. Yet LDCs continue to struggle with this endeavour. The UN has decided to focus on commodities and agricultural activity in their efforts to promote graduation (UNCTAD 2012). In this chapter, we will show that while this is a good strategy for some LDCs, it may not be appropriate for those who have made some headway into global high technology manufacturing global value chains (GVCs).

Recent trends in manufacturing have altered the context in which countries pursue economic development. In 1800, Great Britain industrialized by pushing the production possibilities frontier forward through invention. In 1970, the Republic of Korea industrialized by moving to the frontier via innovation. Today, the reduction of average tariff rates and the fragmentation of production networks is offering a very different global environment for industrializing countries. This has led some authors to suggest that development will happen very differently in the future (Baldwin 2011).

The fragmentation of the production process has opened up new possibilities for export diversification across the globe. While production network trade is anchored by three core areas—the European Union (EU), Japan, and the US (Baldwin 2011; Ferrarini 2011), cross-border production chains encompass numerous proximate countries (Johnson and Noguera 2012; Baldwin and Lopez-Gonzalez 2013). For Asia's LDCs, their position within a regional hub puts them at a very good position to link into high-technology networks.

The rise of production network trade has been particularly dynamic in Southeast Asia. The fact that trade in production networks has grown

[1] Available at http://www.unohrlls.org/UserFiles/File/IPoA.pdf (accessed on 1 October 2016).

[2] Botswana in 1994, Cape Verde in 2007, Maldives in 2011, and Samoa in 2014. The next review will happen in 2018.

faster than manufacturing trade overall underscores its importance in the region (Athukorala 2011). The ASEAN's share in total production network trade has risen from about 5 per cent in 1991 to almost 9 per cent in 2011 (Wignaraja, Krueger, and Tuazon 2013). Malaysia and Thailand dominate this trade with more than 40 per cent of a combined share of regional production network trade.

There is evidence that LDCs have successfully taken advantage of production fragmentation. Though LDCs remain marginal players in international trade, imports of intermediates have increased five-fold between 2000 and 2011—compared to a little over two-and-a-half-fold increase for the world in general (Mahanta 2013). Most of this manufactured trade growth has been in low-technology sectors such as textiles and apparel and agrifood. As a result of this reality, research on GVCs and LDCs almost completely ignores LDCs' experiences in advanced technology sectors.

Yet advanced technology value chains are those which have the greatest development potential. Within manufacturing, automobile and electronics value chains are amongst the densest and with the greatest potential for diversification. Hidalgo et al. (2007) suggest that lack of connectedness to advanced sector GVCs contributes to the difficulty poor countries face in converging to the income levels of rich countries.

Product space analysis identifies where LDCs might slot into value chains given their existing set of endowments and exports, while it begins with the reality that LDCs do not tend to produce within the 'dense core' of production networks (Hidalgo et al. 2007). They also point out that countries tend to move into new goods which are related to those in which they already specialize, which suggests a path. Furthermore, in their discussion of complexity and development, Hausmann and Hidalgo (2009) suggest that countries then tend to converge to the income level associated with their capability set. Thus for LDCs, there is benefit in diversifying the activities that use that set.

In the next two sections, we detail the experience of countries in two tracks of manufacturing experiences that we have identified from the data. The first track includes those LDCs which not only export into value chains, but are competitive in some categories. We will suggest that these countries are best positioned to implement vertical policies to support further development of these sectors. The second track includes countries which also export into these sectors, but which are considerably further behind in implementing the support structures that are needed to promote competitiveness. For these countries, we suggest that horizontal policies to improve economic productivity more generally would be the most efficient use of both domestic and international resources.

Asia's Position in Global Value Chains

The fragmentation of global production processes began most aggressively in low-technology sectors such as textiles and apparel but quickly spread to advanced technology sectors as production was modularized. Asia occupies a central role in both low and high technology GVCs as a result of the region's combination of high-skilled labour and cheap resources in relatively close proximity. The past decade has seen the People's Republic of China (PRC) entering a central role in the trajectory of both GVC types.

In order to assess the potential opportunities advanced GVC trade holds for LDCs, we need to first understand the space Asia occupies in global GVC trade. Since proximity is a good predictor of whether a country will join a GVC, the setup of networks within Asia will have implications for LDCs regardless of their current position within GVCs. Low-technology sectors, described here by the example of textiles and apparel trade, have knit together many of the low-cost producers in Asia for supply to the United States and the EU. High-technology sectors, such as electronics, also have an important global hub in Asia. But their production sites are not as widely spread and have experienced consolidation away from many of the more peripheral suppliers in recent years. We present the setup of both low- and high-technology GVCs to illustrate that the more prominent role LDCs play in low-technology GVCs is not a function of market forces alone.

Low-Technology Global Value Chains: Textiles and Apparel

Low-technology GVCs have extensive engagement with countries in Asia at all levels of development. Sectors such as agrifood and textiles and apparel often seen as 'starter' industries in the development process require limited technology at the lowest levels. These are also the sectors which moved most aggressively abroad once fragmentation began.

Of the GVCs, textiles and apparel has received the most extensive empirical attention since it was one of the first industries to disperse geographically (see, for example, Gereffi 1999; ITC [International Trade Classification] 2013a). It is a buyer-driven GVC where networks are largely determined by branded retailers, such as Nike, which outsource production. The process of fragmentation has resulted in a significant decline in production in developed countries to the point where most processing and manufacture now occurs in developing countries. There are three key importing markets including the US, the EU, and Japan (Gereffi and Frederick 2010). The economic fortunes of these markets determine the expansion and consolidation of this GVC.

Fragmentation in textiles and apparel was driven by a highly distortionary international quota regime. When high-output economies such as the PRC and Hong Kong, China reached their quota ceilings, production was subcontracted to countries which had available quota left. This led to early expansion into lower income countries located near major exporters. The importance of this is underscored by Fernandez-Stark, Bamber, and Gereffi (2011) finding that the majority of their sample countries entered the global apparel value chain as a result of preferential regimes. While the quota system has been phased out and protectionist measures have declined over time, bilateral and regional tariff preferences continue to influence trade flows in this sector.

While most countries in Asia are involved in the textile and apparel trade, there has also been a great deal of consolidation following the phase out of the Multi-Fiber Arrangement which ended the global system of quotas in 2005 and more recently the end of special safeguards on PRC in 2008. By 2008, the top five developing countries—the PRC, Bangladesh, India, Turkey, and Viet Nam—accounted for 45.5 per cent of total apparel trade (Fernandez-Stark, Bamber, and Gereffi 2011). The PRC's position in particular has ramped up rapidly. In a period of only 4 years, it became the major supplier of all three major import markets (Bair and Peters 2006). The future organization of the sector hinges on the extent to which the PRC continues to dominate textiles and apparel trade (Morris and Barnes 2009).

The LDCs play a prominent and important role in production for low-technology GVCs. Low income countries account for three-quarters of global apparel exports (Fernandez-Stark, Bamber, and Gereffi 2011). The literature has emphasized that this is because low-technology GVCs are more appropriate for the production capacity and institutional quality that LDCs have to offer. At the lowest stages of the value chain, formal skills requirements are low and skills gaps are addressed through on-the-job training. However, as we have seen here, the initial organization of the textile and apparel GVC was driven by tariff preferences which impacted trade costs.

High-Technology Global Value Chains

Asia functions as a key global hub for GVCs in advanced-technology sectors such as electronics and automobiles. For developing countries which have been successful in plugging into these GVCs, electronics and automotive production have served as propulsive features of their development process as a result of the wide opportunities they present for diversification and value added improvements.

In contrast to the textile and apparel example given before, the advanced technology sectors are producer-driven (Figure 4.1). This organizational style is used where technology is proprietary and strict quality standards exist at various levels of production. Major manufacturers, such as Samsung, are engaged in both design and production and as a result have stronger ties to their network of producers and assemblers (Organisation for Economic Co-operation and Development [OECD] 2013).

The fragmentation process in these sectors was driven largely by trade liberalization. Rapid expansion occurred through the 1990s in Asia, plateauing only with the Asian Financial Crisis in 1998 (Humphrey and Memedovic 2003). Expansion continued upon recovery and today encompasses even low-income countries in the region.

High-technology GVCs favour proximity to assembly hubs in their geographic expansion. As a result, and in contrast to low-technology GVCs, regional hubs are considerably tighter and tend to produce largely for supply to the region. These GVCs include LDCs but the links are more tenuous. We see, for example, a substantial contraction in the geographic spread of both electronic and automotive production sites following the 2008 global financial crisis.

What Does Least Developed Countries' Participation in Advanced Global Value Chains Look Like?

Asia's substantial engagement in both high- and low-technology GVCs have positioned trade as the driver of growth for countries in the

FIGURE 4.1 Global Concentration of Automobile and Electronics Networks (three hubs)

(a) Automobile Sector

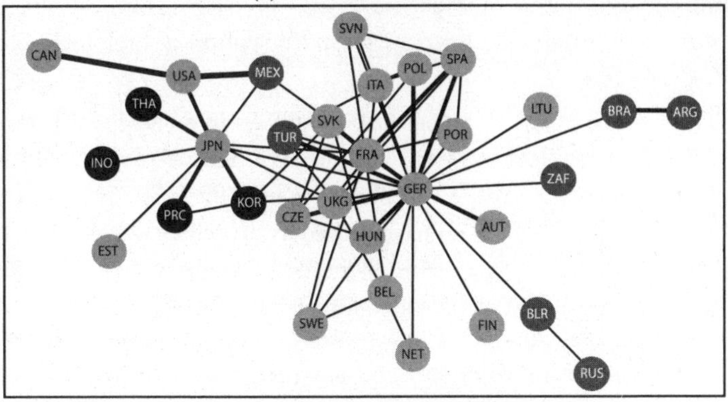

(b) Electronics Sector

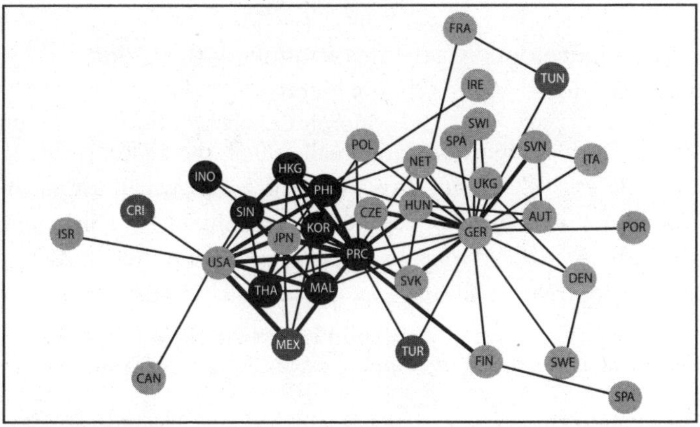

Note: ARG = Argentina, AUT = Austria, BEL = Belgium, BLR = Belarus, BRA = Brazil, CAN = Canada, CRI = Costa Rica, CZE = Czech Republic, DEN = Denmark, EST = Estonia, FIN = Finland, FRA = France, GER = Germany, HKG = Hong Kong, China, HUN = Hungary, INO = Indonesia, IRE = Ireland, ISR = Israel, ITA = Italy, JPN = Japan, KOR = Republic of Korea, LTU = Lithuania, MAL = Malaysia, MEX = Mexico, NET = Netherlands, PHI = Philippines, POL = Poland, POR = Portugal, PRC = People's Republic of China, RUS = Russia, SIN = Singapore, SPA = Spain, SVK = Slovak Republic, SVN = Slovenia, SWE = Sweden, SWI = Switzerland, THA = Thailand, TUN = Tunisia, TUR = Turkey, UKG = United Kingdom, USA = United States, ZAF = South Africa.

Source: Ferrarini (2011).

region. However, the extent to which this trade has been extended to include LDCs varies considerably. There has been extensive exploration in the literature of the role of LDCs in low-technology GVCs (see, for example, Gereffi and Memedovic 2003; ITC 2013a; ITC 2013b). But we have very little idea of what their participation in high-technology GVCs looks like.

This section seeks to address this issue directly. In particular, we examine three features of LDC export activity that may be connected to advanced GVCs. We begin by asking if LDCs export the types of goods used in advanced sector GVCs. Then, is there evidence that any of these exports are involved in value chain trade? Finally, are these exports comparative-advantage goods or are they being exported despite a comparative disadvantage? The answers to these questions will enable us to then determine whether LDC activities in these sectors are likely to contribute to growth given the current regional environment.

Are Least Developed Countries Producing the Goods Advanced Global Value Chains Need?

While the total proportions are small, all of the LDCs included in our sample export non-negative values of goods which are included in electronics and automobile GVCs (see Table 4.1). This supports the hypothesis that the fragmentation of production will enable low-capacity countries to produce non-traditional exports. Since these products are exported, we can assume that they meet at least minimal quality standards needed to compete on the international market.

TABLE 4.1 Exports of Goods Used in Automotive and Electronics Global Value Chain Trade, 2011 ($ million)

	Total Exports	Electronics Exports	Automotive Exports
Cambodia	13,500	294	295
Bangladesh	26,666	121	123
Lao PDR	2,900	3	11
Myanmar	8,210	7	2
Nepal	817	7	6

Note: Lao PDR = Lao People's Democratic Republic.

Source: United Nations Comtrade.

In Table 4.1, we can see the beginnings of a dichotomy between sample LDCs from their volume of exports. Bangladesh and Cambodia both export more than $100 million, while the other LDCs top out at $11 million. The only substantial differences we know between these countries at this point is that Bangladesh and Cambodia have both been highly successful in the textiles and apparel GVC. While this indicates a familiarity with international trade rules, it does not necessarily reflect any ties to regional trade since their apparel exports are largely destined for the US and EU.

We can put the high export LDCs in perspective by comparing their advanced GVC trade to that of regional leaders (Figure 4.2). This shows us that LDC trade in these sectors is dwarfed by the volume of exports of the core value chain players in Asia.

In Asia, advanced sector GVC trade is largely concentrated in middle income countries. While both Cambodia and Bangladesh have seen growth in trade in advanced GVC sectors over the decade examined, this does not compare to the gains made by regional leaders such as Thailand and Malaysia. India's growth in 2011 offers a relatively clear split between middle income and low income countries in the region.

But the experience of Viet Nam offers some insight into the potential growth path for LDC participation in advanced sector GVCs. Within a decade, Viet Nam went from a position as a low income country with

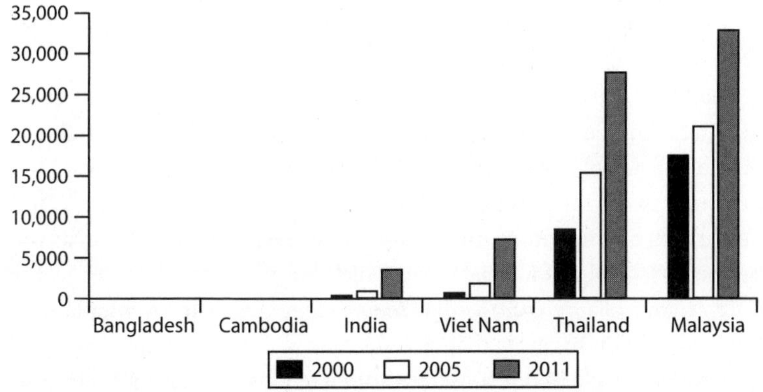

FIGURE 4.2 Total Exports of Automotive Global Value Chain Goods ($ million)
Note: Bangladesh data is from ITC based on HS 1996 data. Converted to SITC 3.
Source: Authors' calculation based on UN Comtrade and ITC data.

an export mix not very different from LDC to a middle income country which has become a more significant player in the region's value chain trade. This came from a clear government vision which involved using policy instruments and close state-business relations to leverage the country's cheap labor with supportive foreign direct investment (FDI) policies (Thomsen 2007).

Are Least Developed Countries Plugged into Advanced Sector Global Value Chains?

We now turn to take a more precise look at LDC exports of GVC-eligible goods to gauge the extent to which these exports are a part of value chain trade. The divergence we saw amongst LDCs in terms of their export volumes is again present in their GVC participation indicators. We will show that there are two distinct groups of LDCs—those which have successfully plugged in and those which are export eligible goods, but do not yet show evidence that they are involved in GVCs.

Due to severe data constraints, the usual indicators of GVC participation are not available for most LDCs. To address this issue, we employ a Grubel-Lloyd Index (GLI) to proxy for value chain participation. The GLI is more traditionally used as a measure of intra-industry trade since it simply indicates whether the country is also importing components of this good. However because of the absence of input-output tables for these countries, it is the most reasonable alternative measure for the presence of value chain trade.

Table 4.2 illustrates that Bangladesh and Cambodia, the two countries with the largest volume of GVC-eligible exports, have traded at least a quarter of these exports within GVCs. From here, we will identify these two countries as Track 1. In Bangladesh, GVC trade was particularly strong in automotive components, but was affected negatively by the 2008 global financial crisis which led to a consolidation in this GVC. Cambodia by contrast has seen the greatest improvements since the crisis, which suggests that its links may be more sustainable.

Though Track 1 countries are more likely to be sending their automotive and electronics exports through the channel of GVCs, the extent of participation fluctuates year to year. Table 4.3 illustrates the inconsistency of intra-industry trade for an electronics intermediate product

TABLE 4.2 Grubel-Lloyd Index for T1 and T2 (sample goods) Grubel-Lloyd Index>0.65, 2005–11 (%)

	Bangladesh		Cambodia		Lao PDR		Myanmar		Nepal	
	Electronics	Automotive	Electronics	Automotive	Electronics	Automotive	Electronics	Automotive	Electronics	Automotive
2005		25			5	8	5			17
2006		25			9	8	5	8		8
2007		13				8	5		5	
2008			7			8	5	8	5	8
2009			7	25						
2010			7	13						
2011				38						

Source: Authors' calculations based on UN Comtrade data.

TABLE 4.3 Cambodia's Exports of SITC 763 (2007–11)

Commodity	Year	Grubel-Lloyd Index
S3 763	2007	0.0705
S3 763	2008	0.5353
S3 763	2009	0.6897
S3 763	2010	0.3367
S3 763	2011	0.6066

Source: Authors' calculations based on UN Comtrade data.

in Cambodia. This product is exported every year and the volumes are increasing consistently. Yet it does not always show evidence of being a part of GVC trade based on the GLI threshold of 0.65.

The second group of LDCs, which we call Track 2, also export electronics and automotive products, but show only limited evidence that they are a part of regional supply chains. Intra-industry trade indicators for Track 2 countries are consistently below 0.65 and often well below. This suggests that most trade is inter-industry which does not leave much room for production network trade. Figure 4.3 illustrates the degree of intra-industry trade for four selected goods from Lao PDR. There is only one good (SITC 77313) that exhibits the presence of intra-industry trade and this is inconsistent over the period.

This split between Track 1 and Track 2 countries reflects some of the warnings the literature issues for poor countries. Hidalgo et al.

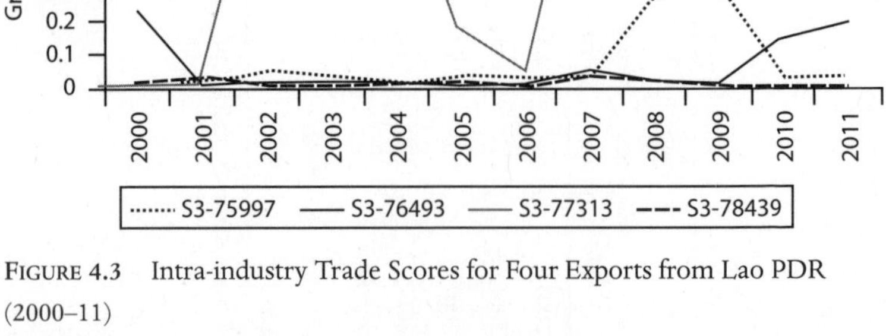

FIGURE 4.3 Intra-industry Trade Scores for Four Exports from Lao PDR (2000–11)
Source: Authors' calculations based on UN Comtrade data.

(2007) mention that studies of product space show that only some poor countries are benefitting from GVC trade. Baldwin (2011) also suggests that network exports have limited spillovers in the overall economy. The inconsistent exports shown by Track 2 countries slot them both into this latter category.

Are Least Developed Countries' Global Value Chain Exports Competitive?

While exports illustrate the capacity of LDCs to produce GVC-eligible goods at trade-level quality, and GLI score provide evidence that at least some of these exports are within GVCs, neither gives us any indication about the competitiveness of exports. At least some of the country case study literature has noted that these exports are not competitive in the usual sense because they are either a function of a development project or they are shipments of machinery for repair (for example, for the case of Lao PDR, see Stirbat, Record, and Nghardsaysone 2011).

The ambiguity in whether LDC GVC exports are competitive stems from the questionable relevance of the indicator used to measure this outcome. Revealed comparative advantage (RCA) is used to indicate if a sector is sustainable given the available factors of production. This traditional measure of competitiveness would conclude that most LDCs are exporting advanced sector products at a comparative disadvantage. Only Cambodia shows improving RCA scores in its automotive exports since 2008. Bangladesh also offers some trending years of increasing RCA, but this disappears before 2008. All Track 2 countries show only some inconsistent evidence of comparative advantage in some years.

Rather than assert that this means exports are unsustainable, we instead discount low RCA scores as unsuitable for GVC analysis. Others have pointed out that RCA does not have the same explanatory power when trade is fragmented (Baldone, Sdogati, and Tajoli 2007; Dai 2013). Baldwin and Venables (2010) point out that, for example, parts may move against their comparative costs as a result of proximity benefits. Others have noted that using value added data can change revealed comparative advantage results in important ways (Koopman et al. 2011).

Since traditional measures may not be suitable for GVC analysis, and the lack of LDC data restricts us from employing proposed alternatives, we instead focus on the question of whether there is evidence that activities associated with pursuing GVC participation might contribute to longer term development outcomes. By taking a broader focus on activities rather than specific indicators, we can evaluate the set of experiences of both Track 1 and Track 2 countries.

Could Global Value Chain Activities Reduce Economic Vulnerability?

Given the dichotomy in LDC experiences, we now approach the question of whether either group's participation or attempted participation in GVCs might contribute to broader development outcomes. Since graduation from LDC status is widely seen as a positive indicator of development, we ask if LDC's pursuit of GVC trade might impact the LDC indicators.

In particular, we focus on the economic vulnerability indicator (EVI) used by the UN. There are three measures that all together identify whether a country is categorized as an LDC (see Table 4.4). These include the EVI, a human assets index (HAI), and a low-income criterion. Trade in the automobile and electronics GVCs does not directly impact the HAI and given the limited proportion of advanced sector exports in total exports, it is unlikely to impact the low-income criterion.

There are two indicators within the EVI that are most likely to be impacted by GVC trade—merchandise export concentration and the instability of exports of goods and services. In short, to the extent that GVC trade results in stable export diversification, it can improve the EVI. The product space literature predicts that diversification should occur into products that are 'near' existing exports. But others warn that new exports are unlikely to become established exports. Thus we explore whether there has been diversification at the five-digit Standard International Trade Classification (SITC) level with a particular eye on survival rates.

Both Track 1 and Track 2 countries exhibit changes in the extensive margin of exports from year to year. This suggests that there are at least attempts to explore whether production of new items can be competitive. But though countries change the exact products that they are exporting every year, many have very low survival rates (Figure 4.4).

TABLE 4.4 Least Developed Country Indicators

Low-Income Criterion	Human Assets Index	Economic Vulnerability Indicator
Gross national income per capita < $992	Nutrition	Population size
	Health	Remoteness
	Education	Merchandise export concentration
	Adult literacy	Share of agriculture, forestry, and fisheries in gross domestic product
		Share of population living in low elevated coastal zones
		Instability of exports of goods and services
		Victims of natural disasters
		Instability of agricultural production

Source: UN-OHRLLS. Available at http://www.unohrlls.org/UserFiles/File/IPoA.pdf (accessed on 1 October 2016).

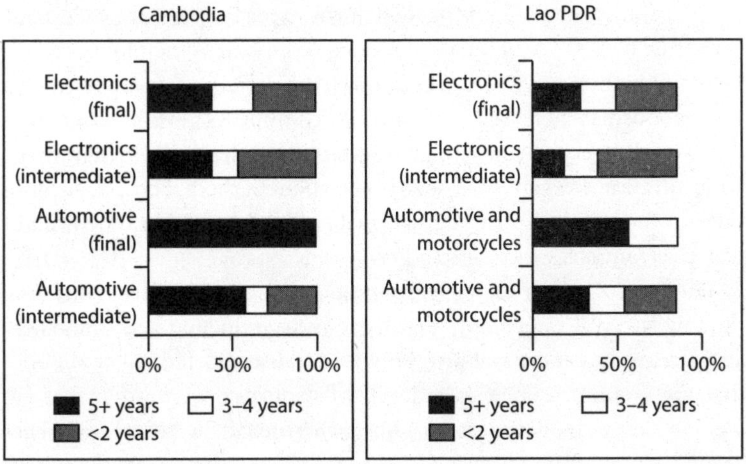

FIGURE 4.4 Sustainability of Exports Index (Cambodia and Lao PDR 2000–11)
Note: Lao PDR = Lao People's Democratic Republic.
Source: Authors' calculations based on UN Comtrade data.

Figure 4.4 offers two illustrative examples of the difference between Track 1 and Track 2 countries' export survival rates. We define an 'established' export as one which has been exported for 5 years or more. A 'potential' export is one that has been exported 3 to 4 years during the sample period, not necessarily consecutively. This suggests that there is some continued production of the good and that the cost structure has been revealed. Finally 'exploratory' exports are those which have been exported 2 years or less during the sample period. We consider these to be exporters exploring their ability to produce these goods, but there is no indication that they are competitive.

For Cambodia, at least 50 per cent of all of its exports of automotive and electronics GVCs goods are exported for more than 3 years. This suggests that new exports are more likely to stick. By contrast, Lao PDR's exports are most likely to be exported less than 3 years. This implies that these exports are of the exploratory type where the cost structure of the economy is still being examined. The lack of consistent exports over time suggests that Track 2 countries are not building on specific sector capacity for these exports. If this were the case, we would expect to see export values and volumes increasing steadily over time, or at least maintaining similar levels.

In terms of the EVI, it is likely that the export experience of Track 1 countries such as Cambodia can reduce economic vulnerability. This is the combination of two activities. First, the variety of advanced sector GVC goods has increased over time which improves export diversification overall, especially given that these countries have very high rates of concentration so even small changes can benefit them. Second, survival rates of these new exports are reasonable and suggest that they will not negatively impact export instability.

For Track 2 countries, while exploration does increase diversification, the low survival rates imply that there is no reduction and potentially an increase in export stability. However it is important to remember that these countries also have levels of export concentration that are well above the global average. Thus by virtue of the information that briefly exported goods provide about the capacity to produce near goods with the countries' given factors of production their activities around GVC trade should be seen as positive for the development process.

Does the Trajectory of Regional Integration Increase the Potential of Least Developed Countries to Participate in Advanced Global Value Chains?

The LDCs as a class have struggled to sustain links to GVC trade in advanced technology manufacturing. The existing literature recognizes this and drops LDCs out of most studies of these sectors. Yet, even the most capital-intensive final products have slices in the value chain that are labour-intensive and which offer room for LDC participation. If we have a better idea of what these spaces look like, we can make more effective recommendations about how LDCs can use them.

Our findings confirmed that LDCs operate at the periphery of advanced technology sectors such as automobiles and electronics. We also showed that participation is not driven by efficiency as measured by revealed comparative advantage. These two facts alone suggest that any evidence of GVC participation is likely to be a feature of development aid, or production diversification by firms, or large intra-industry transfers of machinery or other parts falling into these categories of goods. None of these are likely to be sustainable diversification strategies.

However, we also showed that LDCs fall into two distinct groups in terms of their GVC experience over the past decade. This leads us to make two different sets of policy recommendations. For countries in Track 1, which have seen the most success in plugging into advanced sector GVCs, cooperation with and support for the specific needs of the private sector in these sectors is critical for expansion. The success of efforts to capture more GVC share will depend on the ability to identify and support the skills shortages and institutional needs of these sectors. The identification of these needs can help countries more efficiently target aid for trade and other resource flows.

For countries in Track 2, which have largely produced only experimental exports in these sectors, the investment base is not sufficiently stable to target policies in the same way. Governments here should consider filtering the cost of production information generated by experimental exports into a form that can be used by firms as they continue to explore. Horizontal policies are most appropriate in this case. These can be guided by needs identified by World Trade Organization's (WTO's) survey of exporters in LDCs (see WTO 2013).

Of course, country-specific policies are only one way that GVC participation is impacted. Due to the regional environment in which GVC are seated, LDCs should also consider the implications of changes in the regional operating structure. This is particularly important for Asian LDCs given the negotiations towards two region-wide FTAs that will seek to reduce barriers to trade. Up till now, regional integration in Asia has features that promote the spatial reach of GVCs, but it has not ensured that all countries benefit equally. Could the two new FTAs impacting Asia make GVC trade more inclusive?

The Trans-Pacific Partnership (TPP) is an upgrading of an existing set of trade preferences amongst countries both inside and outside of Asia. No LDCs are involved in negotiations, which are expected to conclude in 2015. However, some of the most dynamic economies in terms of their engagement with advanced sector GVCs, such as Malaysia, Singapore, and Viet Nam, are involved in negotiations. While the negotiating texts are not yet public, it is expected that there will be significant elevation of standards and a reduction of non-tariff barriers. This will make trade much smoother between member countries.

For LDCs, this could have two opposing effects. First, the conclusion of TPP will reduce the barriers facing Viet Nam which has performed extremely well over the last decade. Viet Nam produces many of the same goods as the LDCs and with this added reduction of trade costs, core economies may favour Viet Nam's inputs. But a second effect will come from the likely expansion of trade between core economies in Asia and the US market. Increased trade will result in greater regional demand for inputs which may spillover to cost competitive LDCs (for example, Track 1), particularly as Viet Nam moves into higher value segments of advanced sector GVCs.

Another major regional initiative is the Regional Comprehensive Economic Partnership (RCEP). This covers all of ASEAN plus Australia, the PRC, India, New Zealand, the Republic of Korea, and Japan. In contrast to TPP, RCEP will include some of the region's LDCs. Cambodia, Lao PDR, and Myanmar are all negotiating partners. Negotiations are still at an early stage, but we can already identify two elements that have the potential to open greater opportunities to LDCs seeking to advance in higher technology GVC trade.

As a result of the developmental distance between negotiating countries, the Guiding Principles released in 2011 acknowledge that the final text should include 'appropriate forms of flexibility' and 'provisions for technical assistance and capacity building may be made available'. This can be used to assist Track 2 countries to implement horizontal policies that will lower business risk which could attract more diverse FDI to explore potentially sustainable GVC products. By assisting LDCs to reach regional levels of standards and regulations, this will also improve productive capacity more generally.

A second feature that is likely to widen the geographic spread of GVCs in Asia in a way favourable to LDCs comes from the inclusion of developed economies. When both developed and developing countries are included in an FTA, the WTO requires that it follows the rules set out in Article XXIV of the General Agreement on Tariff s and Trade (GATT). This means that tariffs must eventually reach zero amongst the group within the medium term, and substantially all traded goods must be covered. In practice, many of Asia's larger countries have favoured partial and staged liberalization in their existing agreements. This is reflected by their relatively high average tariff rates—India's average most favoured nation (MFN) rate is 12.6 per cent, the Republic of Korea's is 12.1 per cent and the People's Republic of China (PRC) is 9.6 per cent. If the RCEP follows the WTO guidelines and if sensitive goods are not excluded, WTO-mandated reduction in barriers to trade could reduce trade costs from LDC exports and improve trade flows with core GVC economies in the region.

These conclusions underscore both the importance and the challenges of transforming the potential of regional integration into actual outcomes. Integration amongst economies in Asia drives the GVC trade that has become a key growth activity. Amongst LDCs, while the Track 1 economies may have reached a stage where they can pull themselves into advanced sector GVCs, Track 2 LDCs still need assistance. But unless future FTAs directly address issues associated with the incorporation of LDCs, there is a very real possibility that they will increase rather than smooth spatial inequalities in Asia.

References

Athukorala, P. 2011. 'Production Networks and Trade Patterns in East Asia: Regionalization or Globalization?', *Asian Economic Papers*, 10(1): 65–95.

Bair, J. and E. Peters. 2006. 'Global Commodity Chains and Endogenous Growth: Export Dynamism and Development in Mexico and Honduras', *World Development*, 34(2): 203–21.

Baldone, S., F. Sdogati, and L. Tajoli. 2007. 'On Some Effects of International Fragmentation of Production on Comparative Advantages, Trade Flows and the Income of Countries', *World Economy*, 30(11): 1726–69.

Baldwin, R. 2011. 'Trade and Industrialization after Globalization's 2nd Unbundling: How Building and Joining a Supply Chain are Different and Why It Matters', Working Paper No. 17716, NBER, Cambridge, Massachusetts.

Baldwin, R. and A. Venables. 2010. 'Spiders and snakes: Offshoring and agglomeration in the global economy', *Journal of International Economics*, 90(2): 245–54.

Baldwin, Richard and Javier Lopez-Gonalez. 2013. 'Supply-Chain Trade: A Portrait of Global Patterns and Several Testable Hypotheses', NBER Working Paper No. 18957.

Collier, P. 2007. *The Bottom Billion: Why the Poorest Countries Are Failing and What Can Be Done About It*. Oxford: Oxford University Press.

Dai, L. 2013. 'The Comparative Advantage of Nations: How Global Supply Chains Change Our Understanding of Comparative Advantage', M-RCBG Associate Working Paper Series No. 15, University Kennedy School, Harvard.

Feenstra, R. 1996. 'Trade and Uneven Growth', *Journal of Development Economics*, 49(1): 229–56.

Fernandez-Stark, Katrina, Penny Bamber, and Gary Gereffi. 2011. *The Offshore Services Global Value Chain: Workforce Development and Global Value Chains in Developing Countries*. USA: Duke University.

Ferrarini, Benno. 2011. 'Mapping Vertical Trade', ADB Economics Working Paper No. 263.

Gereffi, G. 1999. 'International Trade and Industrial Upgrading in the Apparel Commodity Chain', *Journal of International Economics*, 48(1): 37–70.

Gereffi, G. and S. Frederick. 2010. 'The Global Apparel Value Chain, Trade and the Crisis: Challenges and Opportunities for Developing Countries', World Bank Policy Research Working Paper No. 5281.

Gereffi, G. and O. Memodovic. 2003. 'The Global Apparel Value Chain: What Prospects for Upgrading by Developing Countries?', Sectoral Studies Series, United Nations Industrial Development Organization (UNIDO).

Greenaway, D. and C. Milner. 1990. 'South-South trade: Theory, Evidence and Policy', *The World Bank Research Observer*, 5(1): 47–68.

Hausmann, R. and C. Hidalgo. 2009. 'The Building Blocks of Economic Complexity', CID Working Paper No. 186.

Hidalgo, C., B. Klinger, A-L. Barabasi, and R. Hausmann. 2007. 'The Product Space Conditions the Development of Nations', *Science*, 317(5837): 482–87.

Humphrey, John and Olga Memedovic. 2003. 'The Global Automotive Industry What Prospects for Upgrading by Developing Countries', UNIDO Sectoral Studies Series.

Hur, J. and C. Park. 2012. 'Do Free trade Agreements Increase Economic Growth of Member Countries?', *World Development*, 40(7): 1283–94.

ITC. 2013a. *LDCs and Global Value Chains: Using Aid for Trade to Seize New Opportunities*. Geneva: ITC.

———. 2013b. *Identifying Asian LDC's High Potential Export Sectors*. Geneva: ITC.

Johnson, Robert and Guillermo Noguera. 2012. 'Proximity and Production Fragmentation', *American Economic Review*, 102(3): 407–11.

Koopman, R., W. Powers, Z. Wang, and S-J. Wei. 2011. 'Give Credit where Credit is Due: Tracking Value Added in Global Production Chains', Working Paper No. 16426, NBER, Cambridge, Massachusetts.

Mahanta, Ankur. 2013. *Connecting Least-developed Countries to Value Chains*. Geneva: WTO.

Morris, M. and J. Barnes. 2009. 'Globalization, the Changed Global Dynamics of the Clothing and Textile Value Chains and the Impact on Sub-Saharan Africa', UNIDO Working Paper No. 10/2008.

Neuman, P. 1979. 'Regionalism in Developing Areas: UN Regional Economic Commissions and their Relations with Regional Organizations', in B. Andemicael (ed.), *Regionalism and the United Nations*, pp. 339–96. New York: Oceana Publications .

OECD. 2013. *Interconnected Economies: Benefitting from Global Value Chains*. Paris: OECD.

Stirbat, L., R. Record, and K. Nghardsaysone. 2011. 'Exporting from a Small Landlocked Economy: An Assessment of Firm-Product-Destination Survival Rates in the Lao PDR', Working Paper No. 5695, World Bank, Washington, D.C.

Thomsen, L. 2007. 'Accessing Global Value Chains? The Role of Business-State Relations in the Private Clothing Industry in Vietnam', *Journal of Economic Geography*, 7(6): 753–76.

UNCTAD. 2012. *Enabling the Graduation of LDCs: Enhancing the Role of Commodities and Improving Agricultural Activity*. Geneva: UNCTAD.

Wignaraja, G., J. Krueger, and A. Tuazon. 2013. 'Production Networks, Profits and Innovative Activity: Evidence from Malaysia and Thailand', ADBI Working Paper No. 406.

WTO. 2013. 'Connecting the Least Developed Countries to Value Chains', WTO Working Paper. Available at https://www.wto.org/english/res_e/booksp_e/ldc_oecd_e.pdf (accessed on 28 September 2016).

5

RAMESH PAUDEL
SWARNIM WAGLÉ

Nepal's Trade Performance and Potential with Regional Partners

The 48 least developed countries (LDCs), by definition, have low income, poor human assets, and vulnerable economies. A significant subset, 16 of these LDCs, including Nepal, is also landlocked, which re-enforces their low-income status by constraining their full utilization of world markets for international exchange of goods, services, capital, and ideas. The LDCs account for about 2 per cent of global output and 12 per cent of world population. By sheer headcount of poor people, they matter. Indeed, if LDCs of Asia alone were a single country, they would be the third largest in the region, if not the world. The LDCs, however, lag behind substantially in trade. While they contribute to less than 1 per cent of world commerce, 75 per cent of their exports are accounted for by seven countries and a handful of products like oil, minerals, and garments.

This chapter takes Nepal as a representative LDC[1] to understand better the challenges faced by LDCs to integrate further with the regional and world economy. We analyse Nepal's merchandise trade performance, relate it to the policy framework in place, and conduct an

[1] Nepal has chaired the Global Coordination Council of the Group of LDCs in recent years.

empirical estimation of the potential for trade expansion in the region using a gravity model. Further, we present the export scenario of Nepal analysing estimates of over- and under-reliance on regional export markets, including East Asian countries. The study is structured as follows. In the second section, we present an overview of Nepal's recent performance in trade (mainly exports). The third section elaborates on Nepal's trade policies, trade costs, and the logistic environment. The fourth section describes the econometric model, methodology, and results of Nepal's state of bilateral trade with countries in the geographical vicinity, spanning the Gulf countries in the west (where Nepal sends hundreds of thousands of migrant workers) to Australia and New Zealand in the east. The final section concludes.

An Overview of Trade Performance

Export Patterns and Trends

Nepal adopted import substitution rather than export promotion strategies until the early 1990s. The economic reforms initiated two decades ago opened up the economy, and the steady rise of imports until 1997 was perhaps as expected. What stands out is the rapid rise in imports in the 2000s—fuelled by rising inflow of remittances and official aid—at the same time exports have been stagnant, never crossing the $1 billion mark in nominal terms. The upper panel of Figure 5.1 captures goods trade, which indicates negative trade balance throughout the period. The lower panel presents services trade which stands in contrast to performance in goods because the country's services exports exceeded imports until about 2005, after which there was a reversal.

The story of stagnant exports is stark not just in terms of absolute numbers, but also when expressed relative to the size of the economy. While the overall trade-to-gross domestic product (GDP) ratio peaked in 1997 and has declined since, the increasing share of imports in total trade has kept the overall trade ratio at around 40 per cent; however, when imports are stripped off total trade, the secular decline in exports relative to GDP is unmistakable (Figure 5.2).

Figure 5.3 presents a picture of 'adjusted openness', which is the trade-to-GDP ratio adjusted for per capita income, relative to other countries that are also landlocked or in the region. Countries tend to trade more as they become richer, but at a decreasing rate. In this figure,

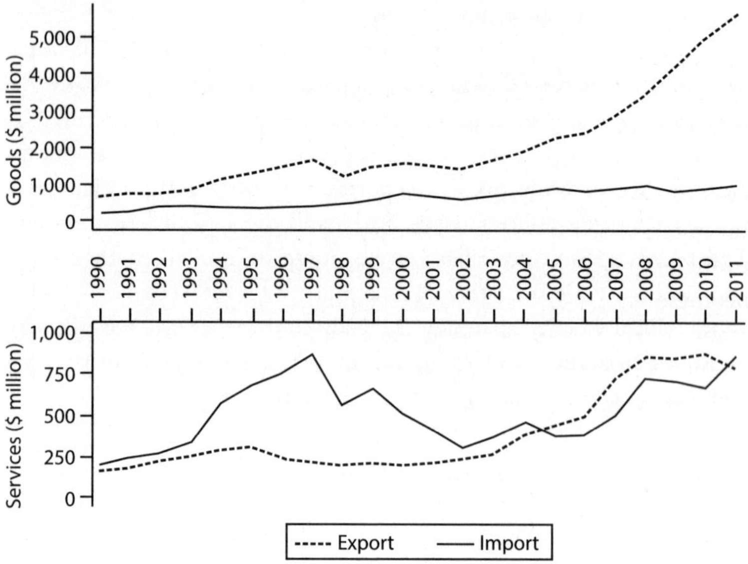

FIGURE 5.1 Nepal's Trade Balance
Source: World Bank (2013b).

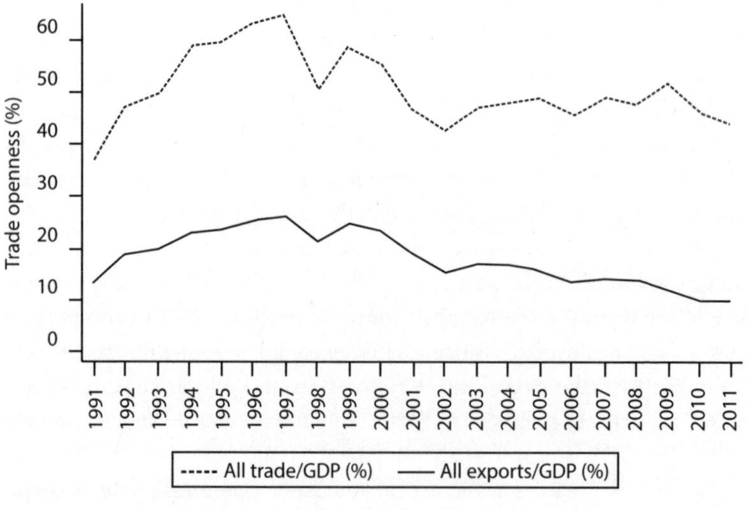

FIGURE 5.2 Trade Trend
Note: GDP = gross domestic product.
Source: World Bank (2013b).

the actual level of export orientation of countries is compared with the level one would expect to reach for their economic affluence measured by GDP per capita. The latter is estimated by regressing trade or export-to-GDP ratio on the log of GDP per capita as well as its squared value for a balanced panel of 155 economies. Relative to countries at similar levels of per capita income, Nepal remains an under-trader (left panel). But in terms of exports to GDP, Nepal's performance is not only the lowest amongst a group of countries with comparable per capita incomes, but almost in the entire world, irrespective of income. This relative picture confirms that the absolute stagnation discussed earlier is a matter of grave policy challenge. It is ironical that without Nepal's 'successful' export of labour over the past 15 years, in lieu of labour embodied in merchandise exports, the country would almost certainly have faced a balance of payments crisis.

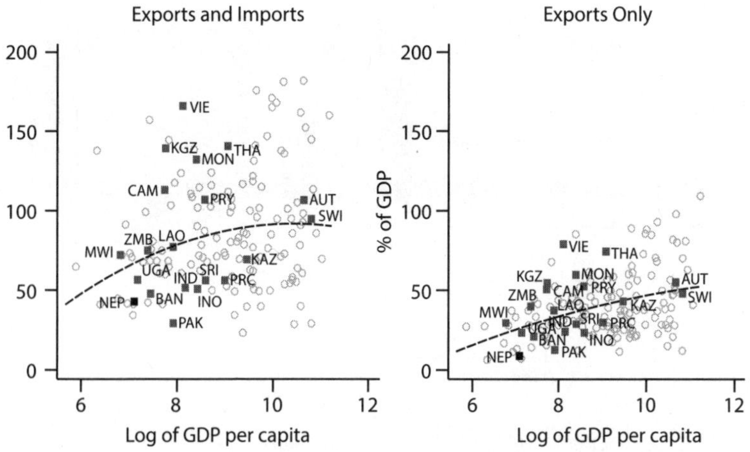

FIGURE 5.3 Relative Trade Openness

Notes: GDP = Gross Domestic Product, AUT = Austria, BAN = Bangladesh, CAM = Cambodia, IND = India, INO = Indonesia, KAZ = Kazakhstan, KGZ = the Kyrgyz Republic, LAO = Lao People's Democratic Republic, MON = Mongolia, MWI = Malawi, NEP = Nepal, PAK = Pakistan, PRC = People's Republic of China, PRY = Paraguay, SRI = Sri Lanka, SWI = Switzerland, THA = Thailand, UGA = Uganda, VIE = Viet Nam, ZMB = Zambia.

(a) Curve is a quadratic fit of trade/GDP regressed on the log of GDP per capita and its squared value.

(b) A balanced panel of 155 economies.

Source: World Development Indicators.

Geographical Orientation

In terms of the reach of exports, India has always been a major market, easily explained by lower trade costs attributable to geographical and cultural proximity. The relatively 'open' border, abetted by Nepal's peg of its currency with the Indian rupee, has further facilitated bilateral trade. What is striking, however, is that over the past decade, there has been a substantial reorientation of Nepal's trade towards India. Figure 5.4 presents the market reach of exports in two different time periods: 1999–2001 and 2009–11. About 64 per cent of merchandise exports in 2009–11 went to India, an increase of about 28 percentage points from a decade earlier.

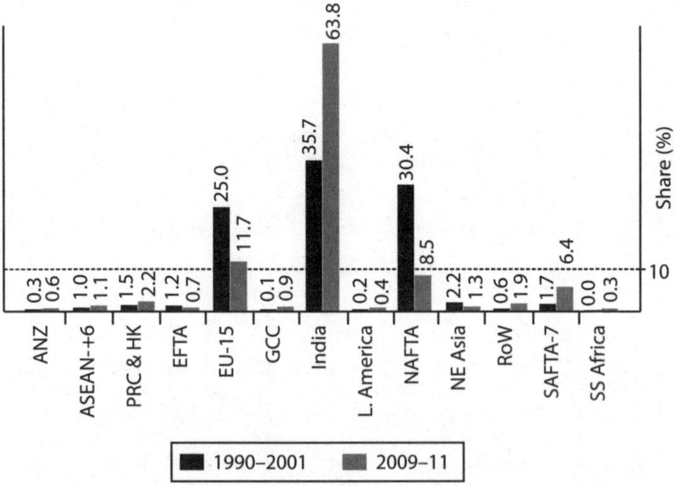

FIGURE 5.4 Nepal's Export Destinations

Note: ANZ = Australia and New Zealand, ASEAN+6 = ASEAN plus Australia, the People's Republic of China, India, Japan, Republic of Korea, and New Zealand, PRC = People's Republic of China, HK = Hong Kong, China, EFTA = European Free Trade Association, EU-15 = Austria, Belgium, Denmark, Finland, France, Germany, Greece, Ireland, Italy, Luxembourg, Netherlands, Portugal, Spain, Sweden, United Kingdom, GCC = Gulf Cooperation Council consists of Saudi Arabia, Kuwait, the United Arab Emirates, Qatar, Bahrain, and Oman, L. America = Latin America, NAFTA = North American Free Trade Agreement, NE Asia = Northeast Asia, RoW = Rest of the World, SAFTA-7 = South Asian Free Trade Agreement, SS Africa = Sub-Saharan Africa.

Source: UN Comtrade (2014).

During this period, exports to the European Union (EU) declined significantly to about 12 per cent from 25 per cent earlier. The decline in exports to North America was even more dramatic, from 30 per cent to 8 per cent. Exports to other regions, such as the member states of the European Free Trade Association (EFTA) and Northeast Asia have also declined substantially. Exports to economies that are closer geographically, in the Asia-Pacific rim, such as Australia and New Zealand, Association of Southeast Asian Nations (ASEAN), the People's Republic of China (PRC) and Hong Kong, China and South Asia have increased. Exports to Gulf states and Sub-Saharan Africa have also increased, albeit from a low base. This increased 'regionalization' of Nepal's exports can be directly attributed to the collapse of its apparel industry, following the termination of the World Trade Organization (WTO) Agreement on Textiles and Clothing.

Export Composition and Sophistication

The composition of products exported from Nepal in 2001 and 2011 are reported in Figure 5.5. Nepal has a comparative advantage in

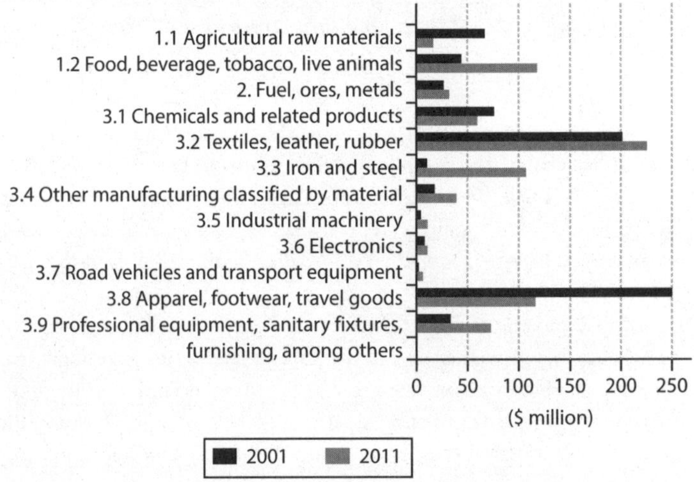

FIGURE 5.5 Export Composition
Note: 1. Mirrored export figures.
Source: UN Comtrade (2014).

labour-intensive manufactures and primary products. But as already mentioned, the most significant of manufactured exports—apparel—more than halved in value during the past decade. There were some gains in material-based manufactures, as well as processed food, beverages, tobacco, and live animals, which crossed the $100 million mark. Textile (fabric)- and leather-related products were the largest in 2011. There was some gain in the export of ores and metals, and also of industrial machinery, electronics and road vehicles and transport equipment.

Amidst the gloomy export statistics, it may come as a surprise that Nepal's export basket is 'richer' than what its average per capita income suggests. This is shown in Figure 5.6 where Nepal lies above the regression line in a scatter plot of about 100 developing countries that the World Bank has classified as either low or middle income. This is based on one of the measures of export sophistication (EXPY) which assesses the export baskets of countries by the incomes of countries that produce similar products, weighted by the share of those exports in the national total.[2] By observing the movement of EXPY indices over time, we cannot definitively say if rising export sophistication pulled up per capita incomes, or countries moved into production of more sophisticated exports after average incomes rose. However, Hausmann and Klinger (2007) have shown for a large pool of countries that export

[2] EXPY is preceded by the calculation of the 'income content' of products (PRODY). It is calculated by combining the methods of Hausmann, Rodrik, and Hwang (2006) and Lall, Weiss, and Zhang (2006). The premise is that products largely exported by rich countries are 'revealed' as sophisticated. We divide 148 countries into 10 income groups, sorted by their level of real GDP per capita in 2007–08. The income content of each product is the sum of the average GDP per capita income of these ten groups weighted by the ratio of the share of the product in a group's basket to the sum of shares of the product in the overall export basket of all income groups. The weights sum to unity, and are a variant of the revealed comparative advantage (RCA) index. Treating these ten groups as hypothetical countries, we attach the weighted mean per capita income of each group proportionately to the products they export. This assigns implicit productivity numbers to products based on the income character of their exporters.

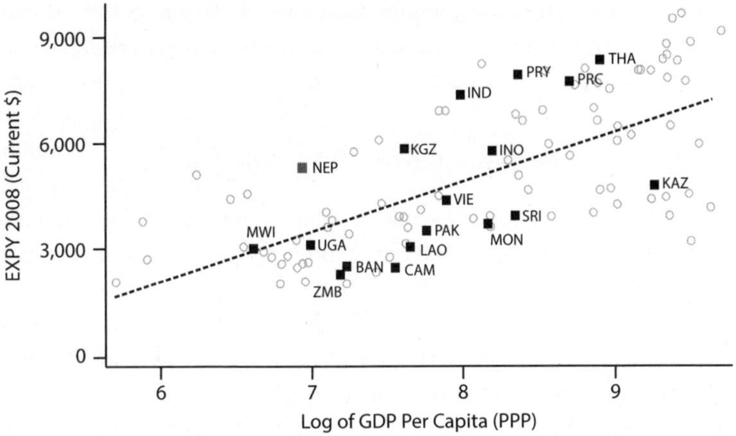

FIGURE 5.6 Export Sophistication

Note: EXPY = Export sophistication, GDP = Gross Domestic Product, PPP = Purchasing Power Parity, BAN = Bangladesh, CAM = Cambodia, IND = India, INO = Indonesia, KAZ = Kazakhstan, KGZ = the Kyrgyz Republic, LAO = Lao People's Democratic Republic, MON = Mongolia, MWI = Malawi, NEP = Nepal, PAK = Pakistan, PRC = People's Republic of China, PRY = Paraguay, SRI = Sri Lanka, THA = Thailand, UGA = Uganda, VIE = Viet Nam, ZMB = Zambia.

(a) Only low- and middle-income countries used in the regression

Source: World Bank (2013b).

sophistication at present is a good predictor of economic growth in the future.[3]

The caveat is that if sophistication is measured based on the final value of assembled good, it is likely to overestimate the ability of countries to produce complex, high-value (intermediate) products. Nonetheless, compared to landlocked countries at similar levels of per capita income (such as Uganda and Zambia), Nepal's relatively high EXPY indicates two facts: first, it does have a foothold in manufacturing of goods that appear to present plenty of scope for technological upgrading, for such goods are also exported by higher-income countries; and, second, its exports are not dominated by natural resources (fuel, minerals, or

[3] Felipe, Kumar, and Abdon (2010) also estimate that a 10 per cent increase in EXPY at the beginning of period raises growth by about 0.5 percentage point.

unprocessed commodities) whose abundance in poorly governed low-income countries is often associated with the chronic challenges of export diversification towards industrialization.

Trade Policy Regime, Costs and Logistics

Nepal has gone through three distinct phases of trade policy—(almost) free trade between 1923 and 1956, protectionism (1956–86), and a relatively open regime from 1986. Nepal embarked on market-oriented policy reforms in the mid-1980s replacing the inward-oriented policy that failed to fulfil growth and development objectives (Karmacharya 2001; Sharma 2001). However, a major policy reform occurred in the early 1990s (Acharya, Khatiwada, and Aryal 2003). One of the major indicators of policy direction in international economics is openness, which is measured mainly in three ways: the Sachs-Warner criteria, tariff rates, and trade as percentage of GDP. All of these indicators have their shortcomings but together they provide a useful indication of trade orientation,[4] which is that Nepal has maintained a relatively open trade regime since 1991.

Since about 2001, the trend towards greater liberalization was slightly reversed with the imposition of select import taxes in addition to customs duties and this situation remain unchanged until 2010 (Pursell 2011). However, Nepal was also the first LDC to join the WTO through a negotiated process in April 2004, which locked in its commitments to reform laws and gradually liberalize goods and services. Table 5.1 presents the weighted average applied tariff rates for all products in Nepal and India. The data are averages over 5-year periods, which show that during 1990–95, Nepal's tariff rates were lower, at 22 per cent on average compared to almost 60 per cent in India. During 1995–2000, Nepal's rates remained unchanged, while India reduced tariff rates to 26 per cent. Nepal's tariff rates were lower than those of India from 2000 to 2005. The average rate declined in Nepal from 2005 to 2010, falling to 15.5 per cent, but India reduced much faster in this period, to an average of just 7 per cent. This suggests that Nepal has the space to

[4] The five criteria consist of thresholds on average tariff rates, coverage of non-tariff barriers on imports, black market premium exceeding 20 per cent, presence of export marketing board, and a socialist political regime.

TABLE 5.1 Weighted Average Applied Tariff Rate: Comparison with India (%)

Period Average	Nepal	India
1990–95	22.1	59.6
1995–2000	22.1	26.0
2000–05	17.2	22.0
2005–10	15.5	7.2

Source: World Bank (2013b).

further reform its trade policies, aligning them closely with those of its main trading partner(s).

Like trade, the Government of Nepal started to promote foreign direct investment (FDI) with the enactment of the Foreign Investment and Technology Transfer Act in 1992 and the Industrial Enterprises Act, 1992. Since then, foreign investors and domestic investors have been treated alike, with favourable visa conditions for foreign investors (Rana and Pradhan 2005). Despite the de jure legal provisions, however, FDI inflows have not picked up because of constant political instability. Unlike countries in East Asia at comparable levels of per capita income, like Cambodia, Nepal has not quite managed to join global value chains where trade and FDI complement and reinforce each other.

Landlocked countries face inevitable barriers to trade because of their location, often remote and distant from navigable rivers or seas (Collier and Gunning 1999; Faye et al. 2004). A growing body of literature has highlighted the negative impact of trade costs on the volume of trade (Anderson and Wincoop 2004). Finger and Yeats (1976) found that transportation costs are comparatively higher for products exported from developing countries compared to products exported from developed countries. Amjadi and Yeats (1995) concluded that high transportation costs and trade policies were responsible for the weak trade performance in Sub-Saharan Africa during much of the second half of the past century.

Trade costs typically comprise of transportation, tariffs, and costs associated with unreliable supply chains due to the poor infrastructure and administrative burdens imposed by transit countries. Faye et al. (2004) argue that transportation and insurance costs are higher in landlocked countries by about 9 per cent because of the long distance to seaways, but also because of the costs associated with the unreliable supply chain caused by administrative burdens and other customs procedures (Arvis, Raballand, and Marteau 2007). The literature suggests that landlockedness imposes exogenous costs on exports, making them not only expensive, but also more vulnerable and uncompetitive.

While trade policies play a vital role in improving export performance (Alvarez 2011; Santos-Paulino 2002), other factors are also important in geographically handicapped countries like Nepal. On trade logistics, exporters from Nepal have to travel more than 1,000 kilometres to reach Kolkata seaport in India via road, the dominant mode of transport in and out of Nepal. The alternative seaport is Chittagong in Bangladesh, which is almost at a similar distance to Kolkata, but involves first a narrow crossing of the Indian territory (about 17 kilometres) which nonetheless has proven to be a logistically prohibitive route so far. Nepal's transportation costs could be substantially reduced if India extended transit facilities to reach the seaport in Bangladesh (Dubey 2010). In addition, as part of the infrastructure for trade, three Inland Clearance Depots (ICD) dry ports are operating in Bhairahawa, Birgunj, and Biratnagar (all along the border with India) but the quality and operation of these dry ports have not been efficient enough to reduce transportation costs to render traded goods competitive.

An alternative mode of transportation for international trade is air cargo, which is more cost effective generally for light products. In Nepal, only 17.6 million kilograms of cargo (imports and exports) were handled by air services in 2009 via 20 international airline networks in 35 countries. About 17 per cent of total exports used air transportation in the same year. Railway transport could be a more efficient way to connect to Kolkata seaport to export to third countries; it would also be an effective means of transport to connect to the wider Indian market which has one of the biggest railway networks in the world. Unfortunately, Nepal has an unreliable and highly limited (about 56 kilometres) railway facility to connect with the Indian rail network. Of the mere 56 kilometres of railway lines, only 29 kilometres are being used partly because of managerial inefficiency (Rajkarnikar 2010). Moreover, the railway network has never been a priority item on the agenda of the policymakers despite it having great potential in the flat Terai region, if not in the mountains.

Of course, none of the logistical difficulties are preordained. They can be improved together with macroeconomic management, political stability, and public investments. It currently fares quite poorly in both the World Bank's Trading Across Borders indicators (as part of Doing Business), as well as the logistics performance index (LPI). The latter is constructed based on the efficiency of customs clearance, quality of trade and transport infrastructure, condition of shipments, quality of logistic service, and consignment handling, using a number of qualitative and quantitative indicators. In 2012, Nepal ranked 151st out of the 155 countries surveyed (World Bank 2013a). On average, the time required to export a standard container full of goods from Nepal is substantially higher—41 days, compared to 5 days in the top ranking countries in the world.

Trade cost disadvantages arising from landlockedness are compounded by Nepal's own macro-institutional failures (such as instability and civic disturbances) and micro-regulatory constraints. For example, the documents needed to export reflect the lengthy procedures to engage in international trade. On average, Nepali exporters are required to fill out nine documents to get government approval for exporting, compared to five in other landlocked countries. Processing and inland costs associated with exporting a 20-foot container, as estimated by the World Bank, is about $2,000, which is almost double that in India or Bangladesh; it is also higher than in several other landlocked LDCs (Figure 5.7). The summary of the Ease of Doing Business and indicators of trade logistics for Nepal compared against global benchmarks are presented in Table 5.2.

Bilateral Exports: Model, Variables, and Data

We assess Nepal's bilateral export performance vis-à-vis all its active export destinations using the latest methodology in gravity modelling along the lines of Helpman, Melitz, and Rubinstein (2008), henceforth HMR. The HMR technique controls for country selection bias and firm heterogeneity bias even with aggregate country-level trade data (see Table 5.3 for results). We use data on bilateral exports with at least 134 partners averaged over a 3-year period between 2009 and 2011. The explanatory variables are the standard determinants of bilateral trade: distance, contiguity, common language, common colonial power, as

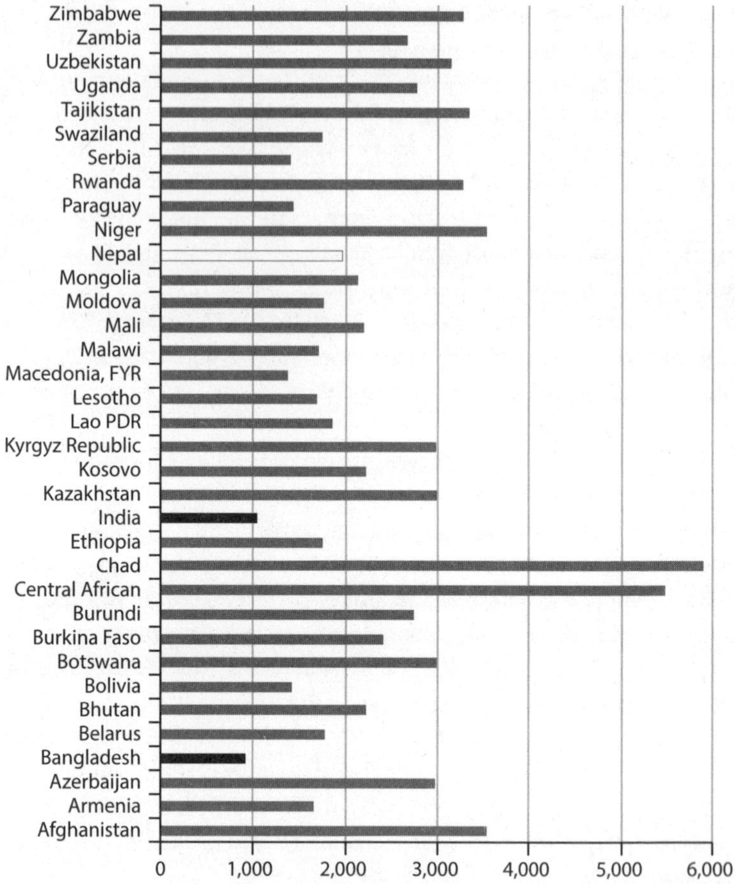

FIGURE 5.7 Cost of Processing Export Shipment in Landlocked Developing Countries and Nepal's Neighbours

Notes: Macedonia, FYR = former Yugoslav Republic, Lao PDR = Lao People's Democratic Republic.

Source: World Bank (2013a).

well as the log of GDP, log of GDP per capita, average weighted tariff, and the log of the Remoteness index (computed by summing each country's distance with every other country, weighted by the latter's share in world GDP). In the model specification given as follows, α is a constant term, subscripts i and j refer to Nepal and its trading partners, respectively. The last term, ε_{ij} is the stochastic error term and β_s are the coefficients of individual explanatory variables. The details of the

TABLE 5.2 Nepal's Logistic Indicators

	Ease of Doing Business Rank	Logistics Performance Index	Time Taken to Export	Documents Required for Export	Cost of Exporting
Nepal	108	2.2	41	11	1,975
Best in the World	1	5	5	2	450

Notes: Ease of doing business ranking of 183 countries (best is 1) in 2011. Logistics Performance Index: overall (1 = low and 5 = high), time to export-days (5–80 days); documents to export: number of documents to export (2–11 documents), and costs to export per container ($450–$5,902) in 2015.
Source: World Bank (2015).

variables, their description, sources, and expected sign are explained in Table 5.3.

The estimated model is as follows:

$$\log(Export)_{ij} = \alpha + \beta_1 \log(GDP)_j + \beta_2 \log(GDP\ percapita)_j + \beta_3 \log(Remoteness)_j + \beta_4 (Tariff)_i + \beta_5 \log(Distance)_j + \beta_6 (FTA)_{ij} + \sum_{ij} (Dummy)_{ij} * D_{ij} + \varepsilon_{ij}$$

Of the 161 export destination countries in the Comtrade dataset, 27 have either zero or extremely low values.[5] When data series is expressed in logarithm, zero values drop out of the sample even though they may contain important information about trade costs.[6] We control for such 'sample selection' bias by creating an inverse Mills ratio from the Probit estimation (column 1 in Table 5.4). This is the first stage. For identification, we use a valid exclusion restriction that affects the propensity of two countries engaging in bilateral trade, but not the volume of trade after the trading relationship is established. In other words, this exclusion restriction affects the fixed cost of exporting, but not the variable cost.

[5] Positive export values under $1,000 are treated as 'zero'. We do not discount the possibility that some zeros are just missing or unreported values.

[6] Ad-hoc adjustment in the extant literature of adding 1 to 0 and then retaining the full sample in the regressions is flawed.

TABLE 5.3 Description and Sources of Variables

Variables	Sources	Descriptions	Expected Sign
Export	Comtrade	Bilateral exports from Nepal to trading partners, (mirrored) value in US dollar, averaged between 2009 and 2011. Where mirror data is missing, actual values reported by Nepal are used, multiplied by an ad hoc cost, insurance and freight conversion factor of 1.1; when mirrored values are less than actual, the latter used.	NA
GDP	WDI	GDP in current US dollar, then expressed in logarithm.	(+)
GDP per capita	WDI	GDP per capita in current US dollar, then expressed in logarithm.	(+)
Distance	CEPII	Distance in kilometres between two countries using the great circle formula which uses latitudes and longitudes of each country's most populated cities or official capital.	(–)
Remoteness	Computed by authors based on CEPII data and WDI	Log of the sum of a country's bilateral distance with all other countries in the world, weighted by the share of the GDP of the partner country in total world GDP.	(–)
Tariff	WDI	Weighted mean applied tariff is the average of effectively applied rates weighted by the product import shares corresponding to each partner country. When the effectively applied rate is unavailable, the most favoured nation rate is used.	(–)
FTA		1 for a bilateral preferential trade agreement in existence between Nepal and importing countries during a year of observation; 0 otherwise.	(+)

Contiguity	CEPII gravity data set	Dummy variable, 1 if trading partner borders with Nepal, 0 otherwise.	(+)
Common ethnic language	CEPII gravity data set	Dummy variable; 1 if the partner has the common ethnic language, 0 otherwise.	(+)
Colony	CEPII gravity data set	Dummy variable, 1 if the partner was with same colonial with Nepal.	(+)
Fixed Trade Cost	Doing Business Indicators (World Bank)	The cost associated with all procedures required to export and import goods. Includes the costs for documents, administrative fees for customs clearance and technical control, customs broker fees, terminal handling charges, and inland transport.	(–)

Notes: GDP = gross domestic product, WDI = World Development Indicators, CEPII = The French Centre d'Etudes Prospectives et d'Informations Internationales, FTA = Free Trade Agreement.

Source: CEPII (2013), World Bank (2013a, b).

Table 5.4 Determinants of Nepal's Bilateral Exports

	(1) Probit	(2) OLS	(3) HMR	(4) Bias I	(5) Bias II
GDP	0.317***	0.607***	0.616***	0.787***	0.876***
	0.085	0.084	0.135	0.111	0.087
GDP per capita	–0.04	0.593***	0.503***	0.629***	0.598***
	0.123	0.13	0.131	0.113	0.098
Remoteness	–0.143	0.986	0.714	1.056*	1.004*
	0.795	0.597	0.508	0.571	0.518
Weighted Tariffs	–0.043	–0.033	–0.068	–0.055	–0.099***
	0.035	0.038	0.042	0.04	0.038
Distance	0.065	–0.555**	–0.518*	–0.540*	–0.516*
	0.265	0.279	0.262	0.286	0.278
Contiguity	–	2.708***	3.732***	2.942***	1.718**
	–	0.972	1.145	0.695	0.808
Common Language	–	3.435***	4.021***	4.367***	4.832***
	–	1.076	1.181	1.143	0.961
FTA	–	2.488***	4.687***	4.724***	3.822***
	–	0.898	0.521	1.346	0.881
Fixed Trade Cost	–0.688**	0.162			
	0.322	0.321	0	0	0
Inverse Mills Ratio			–1.229		3.398***
			2.937	0	0.854
Z1 (Control for heterogeneity)			–12.532*		
			6.587		
Z2 (Control for heterogeneity)			5.072**		
			2.206		
H1 (Control for heterogeneity)				–0.586*	
				0.313	
N	153	134	134	134	134
R-squared		0.7	0.76	0.71	0.74

Notes: GDP = gross domestic product, FTA = free trade agreement, OLS = ordinary least square.

* Robust standard errors reported in the second line corresponding to each variable.

** Statistical significance indicated as * for $p<0.1$, ** for $p<0.05$ and *** for $p<0.01$.

*** Sample selection bias is controlled by the Inverse Mills Ratio and firm selection is controlled by a polynomial whose coefficients include those on Z1 and Z2.

We consider an index from Doing Business 2008 created by combining the fixed export and import cost associated with processes, fees, and inland transportation as a valid exclusion restriction. From the inverse Mills ratio, we also create a control for unobserved heterogeneity.[7] Both terms are included in a non-linear and ordinary least squares regressions. Since the coefficients are similar, we prefer the bias-corrected ordinary least square (OLS) method.

Importantly, the coefficients of the bias-corrected model (column 3) are different from coefficients obtained from a simple OLS (column 2). The coefficient of GDP (of the partner country) is significant and higher in the bias-corrected model. The coefficients of variables measuring bilateral distance, sharing of a common border or ethnic language, and having a free trading agreement are all statistically significant, with coefficients for shared border and language much higher in the bias-corrected mode (3) than the simple OLS model (2). The coefficient of weighted tariffs is not a significant determinant of exports from Nepal.

In columns 4 and 5, we decompose the country and firm heterogeneity biases to assess which of the two biases is more prominent. Column 4 reports results controlling only for heterogeneity bias and not the selection bias. In column 5, only the sample selection bias is corrected. While coefficients on some variables in column 4 are close to those in column 3, and those in column 5 are closer to the magnitudes reported in the benchmark regression (column 2), it is difficult to infer which of the two biases dominate from the results in columns 4 and 5. A priori, however, because the problem of zero bilateral flows between the country pairs does not appear to be too serious, the control for unobserved heterogeneity would have been expected to produce most of the bias in this gravity-like model.

Conditional on the bilateral characteristics (and the corrections for the two biases), Figure 5.8 depicts economies to which Nepal 'under-exports' above the 45-degree line, and those to which it 'over-exports' below it. This figure shows that controlling for the aforementioned standard explanatory variables, Nepal's export values vary quite significantly even across countries that are geographically equidistant. Along the Pacific Rim, Nepal's exports are—as would be predicted—

[7] It is a polynomial of the sum of the inverse Mills ratio and the fitted values of the latent variable in the selection equation.

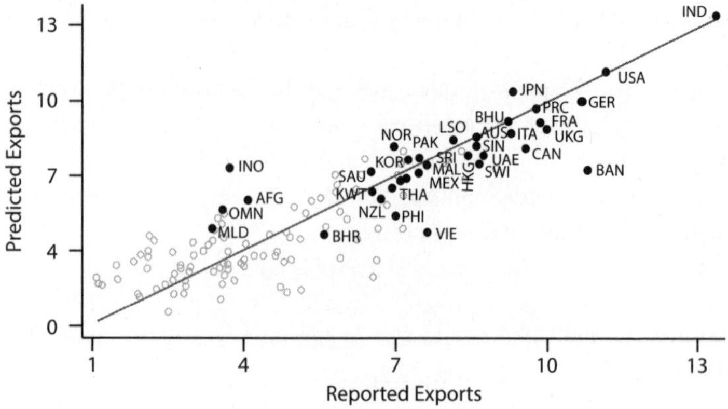

FIGURE 5.8 Gravity Estimates of Bilateral Exports

Notes: AFG = Afghanistan, AUS = Australia, BAN = Bangladesh, BHR = Bahrain, BHU = Bhutan, CAN = Canada, FRA = France, GER = Germany, HKG = Hong Kong, China, IND = India, INO = Indonesia, ITA = Italy, JPN = Japan, KOR = Republic of Korea, KWT = Kuwait, LSO = Lesotho, MAL = Malaysia, MEX = Mexico, MLD = Maldives, NOR = Norway, NZL = New Zealand, OMN = Oman, PAK = Pakistan, PHI = Philippines, PRC = People's Republic of China, SAU = Saudi Arabia, SIN = Singapore, SRI = Sri Lanka, SWI = Switzerland, THA = Thailand, UAE = United Arab Emirates, UKG = United Kingdom, USA = United States, VIE = Viet Nam.

(a) Mirrored export values in log of US$ (in thousands, averaged 2009–2011).

(b) Mirrored values replaced by actual export values for 2009–2011 when missing or less than actual.

Source: UN Comtrade (2014).

with Australia and New Zealand, but below potential with both Japan and the Republic of Korea as well as Indonesia. Nepal's exports to Thailand, Malaysia, Viet Nam, and the Philippines are not suboptimal.

In South Asia, Nepal's exports to India, Bangladesh, and Sri Lanka are above what would be predicted, but it under-exports to Pakistan, Afghanistan, and the Maldives. In countries belonging to the Gulf Cooperation Council (GCC), which are home to hundreds of thousands of temporary migrants from Nepal, export volumes are as expected or more with the United Arab Emirates (UAE) and Qatar, but below potential with Saudi Arabia and Oman. Focusing on these countries above the fitted line, Nepal can increase the export level to a higher level. For preliminary estimates of the magnitude of over- or under-exporting, see Table 5.5.

On the whole, the country pines for the levels of export achievement it reached after the reforms of the 1990s. There has since been a sharp deterioration in productivity and export competitiveness while imports have surged on the back of rising remittances, which as a share of national income is the highest in the world for a relatively populous

TABLE 5.5 Estimates of Over- and Under-Reliance on Regional Export Markets, 2009–11

Country	Actual	Predicted	Discrepancy (%)
Bangladesh	48,782.0	1,415.6	97.1
Viet Nam	2,108.1	110.2	94.8
Philippines	1,116.9	219.3	80.4
UAE	6,189.5	2,485.5	59.8
New Zealand	810.9	429.7	47.0
Thailand	1,028.1	688.7	33.0
Singapore	5,307.6	3,737.9	29.6
Qatar	1,183.7	839.8	29.1
Malaysia	1,747.6	1,275.3	27.0
Sri Lanka	2,037.7	1,639.1	19.6
Australia	5,422.0	4,748.5	12.4
PRC	17,557.8	16,583.0	5.6
India	631,842.5	668,985.7	–5.9
Pakistan	1,771.9	2,183.9	–23.3
Korea, Republic of	1,401.8	2,006.1	–43.1
Saudi Arabia	659.2	1,288.9	–95.5
Japan	11,062.4	33,051.2	–198.8
Maldives	28.5	132.8	–366.1
Afghanistan	58.7	413.8	–604.3
Oman	36.0	284.0	–688.1
Indonesia	41.4	1,538.6	–3,613.6

Note: Export values in $ thousand. UAE = United Arab Emirates; PRC = People's Republic of China.

Source: Authors' calculations.

country. The massive transfers have likely induced a 'Dutch Disease'. The non-tradable sector has expanded as a result of a 'resource movement' effect and a 'spending' effect,[8] leading to a contraction of manufacturing and a rise in the real exchange rate. Since the exchange rate of the Nepalese rupee is pegged to the Indian rupee, the pressure on the Nepalese rupee to appreciate against currencies, other than India's, has also aggravated export competitiveness.

* * *

In this short chapter, we have undertaken a broad-brush examination of Nepal's export performance in recent years and discussed some policy and supply-side challenges faced by a typical landlocked LDC. Following such an overview, we econometrically analysed the state of the value of Nepal's exports, averaged between 2009 and 2011, in several countries in the region. The aim was to see which of the explanatory variables stood in prominence in determining the magnitude of bilateral flows, and to identify some of the countries where Nepal may look to for greater regional integration.

The results demonstrate that partners' GDP and trade costs (as proxied by gravity variables like distance, contiguity, and common language) are two of the main determinants of Nepal's bilateral exports. While this result is partly accounted for by Nepal's growing trade with India, a generalizable policy inference is that it will be difficult for countries like Nepal to engage more actively in international trade without first addressing their supply-side and logistical bottlenecks. They present a much more binding constraint than policy-related distortions at home or in the import markets (for example, tariffs).

Over the past decades, the decline in Nepal's exports, relative to GDP, as well as its major reorientation towards regional markets like India happened in tandem with the intensification of civil conflict as

[8] The first effect is caused when mobile factors are sucked into the booming sector (overseas) and wages are bid up at home, causing other tradable sectors to contract. The second effect is a result of resources flowing into the economy that creates extra demand for labor in the non-tradable sector. Because demand for non-traded goods increases their prices go up. Prices of traded goods, however, are set internationally, so they do not rise. This is, by definition, an appreciation of the *real* exchange rate, that is, the rise of the *relative* price of non tradables to tradables.

well as the termination of global quotas end-2004 that governed trade of apparel for four decades. That Nepal was not able to maintain its competitiveness after the distortionary quotas were abolished reaffirms the salience of supply-side factors in trade.

The analysis also shows great variance in Nepal's exports to subsets of countries that may lie close to each other geographically. This suggests that exports could be deepened and diversified in countries where it is seen to over-export, and greater penetration could be encouraged in countries where it under-exports. Newer trade issues such as trade in services, regional trade and investment agreements, and attempts to latch on to regional and global value chains deserve greater policy priority. Experience of the past decade suggests that foremost, this would require a modicum of political stability and the removal of pressing bottlenecks in trade-related infrastructure.

References

Acharya, M., Y.R. Khatiwada, and S. Aryal. 2003. *Structural Adjustment Policies and Poverty Eradication*. Kathmandu, Nepal: Institute for Integrated Development Studies.

Alvarez, R. 2011. 'Export Transitions', *Journal of International Trade and Economic Development*, 20(2): 221–50.

Amjadi, A. and A.J. Yeats. 1995. 'Have Transport Costs Contributed to the Relative Decline of Sub-Saharan African Exports?', Policy Research Working Paper No. 1559, World Bank.

Anderson, James and Eric Van Wincoop. 2004. 'Trade Costs', *Journal of Economic Literature*, 42(3): 691–751.

Arvis, Jean-Francois, Gael Raballand, and Jean-Francois Marteau. 2007. 'The Cost of Being Landlocked: Logistics Costs and Supply Chain Reliability', World Bank Policy Research Working Paper No. 4258.

Collier, Paul and Jan Willem Gunning. 1999. 'Why Has Africa Grown Slowly?', *Journal of Economic Perspectives*, 13(3): 3–22.

Dubey, M. 2010. 'Regional Economic Integration in South Asia: The Development of Institutions and the Role of Politics', in Rafiq Dossani, Daniel C. Sneider, and Vikram Sood (eds), *Does South Asia Exist? Prospects for Regional Integration*, pp. 53–84. The Water H. Shorenstein Asia-Pacific Research Centre, New York.

Faye, M.L., J.W. Mcarthur, J.D. Sachs, and T. Snow. 2004. 'The Challenges Facing Landlocked Developing Countries', *Journal of Human Development*, 5(1): 31–68.

Felipe, J., U. Kumar, and A. Abdon. 2010. 'As You Sow Shall You Reap: From Capabilities to Opportunities', Working Paper No. 613, Asian Development Bank.

Finger, J.M. and A.J. Yeats. 1976. 'Effective Protection by Transportation Costs and Tariffs: A Comparison of Magnitudes', *Quarterly Journal of Economics*, 90(1): 169–76.

Hausmann, R. and B. Klinger. 2007. 'The Structure of the Product Space and the Evolution of Comparative Advantage', CID Working Paper No. 146, Harvard University.

Hausmann, R., D. Rodrik, and J. Hwang. 2006. 'What You Export Matters', NBER Working Paper No. 11905, Cambridge, Massachusetts.

Helpman, Elhanan, Marc Melitz, and Yona Rubinstein. 2008. 'Estimating Trade Flows: Trading Partners and Trading Volumes', *Quarterly Journal of Economics*, 123(2): 441–87.

Karmacharya, B. 2001. 'Economic Reforms in Nepal and Their Implications for Trade, Economic Growth, Inequality and Poverty', *South Asia Economic Journal*, 2(1): 87–103.

Lall, S., J. Weiss, and J. Zhang. 2006. 'The Sophistication of Exports: A New Trade Measure', *World Development*, 34(2): 222–37.

Pursell, G. 2011. *Routledge Handbook of South Asian Economies*. Routledge, London, UK.

Rajkarnikar, P.R. 2010. 'Adequacy and Effectiveness of Logistic Services in Nepal: Implication for Export Performance', Working Paper Series No. 79, Asia-Pacific Research and Training Network on Trade, Bangkok.

Rana, M.S. and S. Pradhan. 2005. 'Implementation Evaluation of Foreign Direct Investment Policy in Nepal', Policy Paper No. 11, Economic Policy Network, Kathmandu, Nepal.

Santos-Paulino, A.U. 2002. 'Trade Liberalisation and Export Performance in Selected Developing Countries,' *Journal of Development Studies*, 39(1): 140–64.

Sharma, Kishor. 2001. 'Liberalisation, Growth and Structural Change: Evidence from Nepalese Manufacturing', *Applied Economics*, 33(10): 1253–61.

World Bank. 2013a. 'Logistics Performance Index'. Available at http://data.worldbank.org (accessed on 16 April 2013).

———. 2013b. 'World Development Indicators'. Available at http://data.worldbank.org (accessed on 16 April 2013).

———. 2015. 'World Development Indicators'. Available at http://data.worldbank.org (accessed on 28 May 2015).

PREMA-CHANDRA ATHUKORALA
RAVEEN EKANAYAKE

Repositioning in the Global Apparel Value Chain in the Post Multi-fibre Arrangement Era

Strategic Issues and Evidence from Sri Lanka

The geography of global apparel production and trade has been in a state of flux following the termination, with effect from 1 January 2005, of the export quotas imposed under the Multi-fiber Arrangement (MFA). The widespread expectation in the lead-up to the MFA abolition was that in a quota-free global apparel market, the large low-cost countries (such as the People's Republic of China [PRC] and India) and countries in close proximity to the major markets (such as Mexico, Turkey, and some Eastern European countries) would gain market shares at the expense of other countries where the apparel sector had grown under quota protection.[1] The actual outcome over the past 4 years has, however, brought many surprises. As predicted, the PRC has become by far the biggest gainer, and many countries in Africa and

[1] For a comprehensive survey of the relevant literature, see Nordås (2009).

Latin America whose 'export competitiveness' relied heavily on the quota system have lost market shares. However, a number of countries such as Bangladesh, Cambodia, Sri Lanka, Viet Nam, Indonesia, Honduras, Nicaragua, and Peru have maintained or increased market shares. Interestingly, Bangladesh—a 'predicted' massive loser—has emerged as the third largest developing country exporter (after the PRC and Turkey), surpassing India. Contrary to expectations, sourcing of clothing by retailers in the United States (US) and European Union (EU) from regional suppliers has decreased in the face of rapid growth in procurement from low-cost Asian countries. There have also been contrasting patterns with regard to the geographic profile of export from individual countries, with market share losses in some importing countries compensated by increase in exports to other destinations (Gereffi and Frederick 2010; Staritz 2011).

Understanding these inter-country differences in export performance is vital for crafting national policies for facilitating adjustment and industrial upgrading in the clothing industry in the post-MFA era. This chapter aims to contribute towards this end through a comparative case study of the impact of the MFA on structural adjustment in the clothing industry in Sri Lanka. Much has been written about how the complexities of country- and product-specific system of MFA quotas has shaped global trade patterns and export performance of individual exporting countries. However, there is a dearth of empirical evidence on the experiences of individual countries in the post-MFA era. Sri Lanka provides an interesting subject for a case study of the subject at hand. For over three decades, Sri Lanka's apparel industry has remained deeply embedded within the global clothing supply chain. The industry has managed to maintain its world market share, in spite of the disappearance of assured market access provided by export quotas under the MFA and significant increases in manufacturing wages relative to the other low-wage countries in the regions. A number of large Sri Lankan firms have consolidated their position in world apparel trade as credible suppliers to leading brand name owners in the world apparel trade. Analysing the Sri Lanka experience would, therefore, help understand the importance of non-price factors in determining export success in the post-MFA era.

In order to understand how MFA abolition impacts the export performance of a given country, it is necessary to go beyond the standard trade data analysis and probe its experience in the context of changing governance patterns of the global apparel value chain. For this purpose we draw on the global value chain (GVC) framework developed by Gereffi and others, which has become the workhorse of multidisciplinary studies on developing countries' engagement in international division of labour within labour intensive consumer goods industries (Bair 2009; Gereffi 1994, 1999; Gereffi, Humphrey, and Sturgeon 2005).

The study is based on data pieced together from various secondary sources and information gathered from field research carried out in Sri Lanka in November 2012 and July–August 2013. The secondary sources include unpublished investment approval and monitoring records of the Sri Lanka Board of Investment; unpublished exporter-level customs data disaggregated by commodity, destination, and the mode of shipment; the United Nations (UN) Comtrade database; the news clipping collection at the Institute of Policy Studies, Colombo; and company websites. As part of field research, face-to-face interviews were conducted with top executives of 11 apparel exporting firms of varying sizes, and senior officials of the Joint Apparel Association Forum (JAAF), Ceylon Chamber of Commerce, Sri Lanka Export Development Board, and the Ministry of Industry and Commerce.

The chapter is structured as follows: The second section introduces the GVC framework. The third section provides an overview of the way MFA moulded the world apparel trade for over 30 years and the challenges faced by exporting countries during the post-MFA era. The fourth section surveys the initial conditions and policy reforms which underpinned the origin and expansion of the export-oriented apparel industry in Sri Lanka. The fifth section provides an analytical narrative of the beginnings and evolution of Sri Lanka's engagement in the apparel value chain, focusing specifically on the role of the international buyers and the specific socio-economic factors which shaped the relationship between international buyers and the domestic apparel producers. The sixth section probes Sri Lanka's performance in apparel exports, paying particular attention to the emerging trends and patterns following MFA abolition. The seventh and eighth sections draw on the available literature to place the Sri Lankan experience in a comparative perspective. The key findings and inferences are summarized in the final section.

Global Value Chain Framework

The GVC approach is an offshoot of world-system research. It ties the concept of the value chain developed by international business scholars directly to the global organization of 'demand-responsive' industries. The term 'value chain' encompasses the entire range of activities required to bring a particular product to the market. A demand-responsive industry is one that is economically organized 'backward' in direct response to the demand from global buyer of the final product (the 'lead firms'). Using information on final demand collected through point-of-sales information or other means such as focus group surveys, the lead firms locate manufacturers that can produce the goods at quality and quantity levels required by the consumers (Hamilton and Gereffi 2009). The standard labour-intensive consumer goods industries such as clothing, toys, sports goods, and footwear are the prime examples of demand-responsive industries.

The GVC framework is built around the role of the lead firms as the key drivers in the formation and shaping of the GVC in demand-responsive industries. It postulates that global sourcing policies of lead firms shape production and trade patterns. The success of a developing-country firm entering export markets and achieving industrial upgrading—movement from low-value to increasingly high-value activities in the GVC—depends crucially on the links they forge with lead firms.

In its application to the global apparel industry, the GVC framework specifies four sequential phases in the process of industrial upgrading: cut, make, and trim (CMT) (simple assembly); original equipment manufacturing (OEM) (package contracting); original design manufacturing (ODM) (full-packaging); and original brand manufacturing (OBM) (Table 6.1). Moving from CMT to OBM is considered the major upgrading challenge faced by a firm in the apparel value chain. This upgrading trajectory involves acquiring an expanding set of capabilities in filling orders placed by the lead firms, which includes making samples, procuring or manufacturing the needed inputs, meeting international standards in terms of price and quality, and delivery, packing and shipping the finished goods. The full-package role requires manufacturers to coordinate the entire manufacturing process, including the procurement of fabric and other inputs. In addition to experience gained and the strong links developed with the buyers though OEM, there are two strategies that would help firms sustain their ODM status. The first strategy is to integrate the production process vertically (creation of backward linkages) to gain a competitive edge of improved quality and timely delivery of fabric and other ancillary inputs. In particular, since fabric is the most important input in the clothing chain, virtually all countries that want to develop full package capabilities need to develop a strong textile industry. The second strategy is the creation of a cross-border triangular manufacturing arrangement by setting up production bases in other countries to gain competitive advantage from differences in cost of production (mainly labour cost) in order to reap relative cost advantages and preferential market access.

The OBM status, which entails the firm developing its own brands, is the most advanced stage of industrial upgrading. It requires design and marketing capabilities in addition to the preconditions required for achieving ODM status. Transition from ODM to OBM status is difficult

TABLE 6.1 Firm/Country Capabilities within Global Clothing Value Chain

Capability	Nature of Operation
Cut, make and trim (CMT) assembly	A system of subcontracting in which the manufacturer is engaged in assembly of cloths—cutting fabric, sewing, and final trimming. Designing, procurement, and supply of fabric and other inputs, and shipment of the final product is handled by the buyer or his agent.
Original equipment manufacturing (OEM) (package contracting)	The manufacturer engages in sourcing and financing of piece goods (fabric), producing according to customer specifications, and packing for delivery to the buyer. In many cases, the buyer specifies material procurement, and handles shipment.
Original design manufacturing (ODM) (full packing)	The manufacturer carries out all steps involved in the production of a given brand, including design, fabric and other input purchase, cutting, sewing and trimming, packaging and delivery.
Original brand manufacturing (OBM)	The manufacturer carries out all steps involved in the production under his own brand name.

Note: CMT = cut, make and trim, OEM = original equipment manufacturing, ODM = original design manufacturing, OBM = original brand manufacturing.
Source: Gereffi (1999), Gereffi and Frederick (2010), and Hamilton and Gereffi (2009).

because of complex barriers to entry into developed-country markets. For many firms in developing countries, the viable strategy for achieving OBM would be to begin with brand development for the domestic maker or markets in neighbouring developing countries (Neidik and Gereffi 2006).

The way the relationship between the manufacturing firm (the supplier) and lead firms shape industrial upgrading of apparel-producing firms in a given country depends on the nature of activities the latter performs within the GVC. To understand the nature of this relationship, the GVC framework comes up with a four-way typology of lead firms: mass retailers (for example, Walmart, K-mart, Sears, Dillards, C&A), speciality retailers (L Brands,[2] Gap, Marks & Spencer, Mango, Abercrombie), brand marketers (Nike, Polo, Hugo Boss, Gucci, Victoria's Secret, Ralph Lauren, Inditex [Zara], Hennes & Mauritz [H&M]), and brand manufacturers (Wrangler, Levi's, Van Heusen, VF). Mass retailers normally do not directly deal with the manufacturers (do not undertake direct sourcing); they predominantly source through value-chain intermediaries (alternatively known as sourcing agents, international buyers, sourcing companies, jobbers, and packagers). The other three types use a mixture of direct sourcing and relying on value-chain intermediaries, with brand marketers and brand manufacturers generally placing a greater weight on direct sourcing compared to speciality retailers. Compared to sourcing through intermediaries, direct sourcing generally involves greater transmission of capabilities from the lead firm to the manufacturer, facilitating industrial upgrading.

In the early literature on GVC, the main (if not sole) focus was on the buyer–producer interaction, the role of the lead firm in placing the producers on a potentially dynamic learning curve. Recent applications of GVC framework have increasingly emphasized the importance of analysing this key linkage within the broader international and national institutional and policy contexts. On the international front, trade policy changes and regional or global trade preference schemes are an integral part of the operational environment within which the buyers operate. On the domestic front, historical legacies such as colonial links, trade and foreign investment policy, labour market reforms, and the quality of trade-related infrastructure have direct implications for determining

[2] Formerly known as Limited Brands Inc and The Limited Inc.

firms' capabilities in the upgrading process (for example, Feenstra and Hamilton 2006; Neidik and Gereffi 2006; Pipkin 2011).

Global Context: The Multi-fibre Arrangement and After

Apparel is the quintessential 'starter' industry of export-oriented industrialization in developing countries.[3] Given the labour intensity of production and low-entry barriers (low fixed cost and simple / well-diffused technology), the apparel industry is often seen as the gateway for the typical developing country to transition from primary commodity dependence to manufactured export expansion (Jones 2006). However, for much of the post-war era, developing countries' ability to enter this industry purely based on their comparative advantage and domestic policy reforms remained severely constrained by a complex system of country- and product-specific export quotas imposed by importing (developed) countries under the MFA.

The MFA, which came into effect in 1974, restricted trade in textile and apparel through a complex maze of country- and product-specific quotas, imposed by the individual importing countries either unilaterally or bilaterally. It went through four successive extensions of 5-year periods in 1978, 1982, 1986, and 1990, with each round encompassing a wider range of products and countries and thus remained a much-debated anomaly in the pre-World Trade Organization (WTO) world trading system for over 25 years.[4]

[3] In common usage, textile and apparel are often lumped together as a single industry. However, for the purpose of a meaningful discussion of the role of these products in the process of economic development, it is important to clearly distinguish between the two. This is because, in contrast to clothing, textile (yarn and fabric) production is more capital and skill intensive, and thus production remains largely confined to high-income (developed) or upper-middle income countries. The focus of this chapter is on clothing, although textile receives attention in the discussion on industrial upgrading within the global apparel value chain.

[4] For comprehensive accounts of the post-war trade restrictions in world textile and clothing trade and the MFA, see Irwin 2009, Krishna and Tan 1998, and Srinivasan 1998.

The introduction and the subsequent tightening of MFA quotas on exports from the newly industrializing economies (NIEs) in East Asia played an important role in the global spread of clothing industry. In response to binding MFA quotas, entrepreneurs from these economies (especially those from Hong Kong, China) moved production to low-wage countries in Asia and subsequently to even high-cost locations in Latin America and Africa. Thus, many countries with relatively low labour cost and limited technical or business skills 'benefitted' from the guaranteed market access provided by the MFA. This was, however, only a qualified, short-run benefit for the latecomers. Eventually, export restraints were imposed on these countries too at levels well below those enjoyed by established suppliers, effectively short-circuiting the industrialization process at a very early stage.

The MFA severely distorted the global spread of clothing industry in two ways. First, there was a clear developing-country bias in the implementation of quota restrictions. For instance, by the mid-1980s, over two-thirds of textile and clothing from developing countries to the US and EU were under MFA quotas. By contrast only about 2 per cent of exports from developed countries (which consisted solely of Japanese exports to the US) were under quota restrictions (Srinivasan 1998). This resulted in a notable reallocation of world production from quota-constrained developing-country suppliers to relatively low-cost countries in the developed world such as Italy, Portugal and Spain, which were high-cost countries by the developing country standards. Second, there were vast inter-country differences in restraint levels, with a bias in favour of first-comers and the politically powerful, subverting the original intention of providing opportunities to the most competitive (Keesing and Wolf 1988). The three established exporting economies in East Asia—Hong Kong, China, Republic of Korea and Taipei,China—were able to maintain international competitiveness even after their comparative advantage had eroded because the 'quota rent' was an effective buffer against escalating domestic cost pressure on profit margins. By contrast, quotas were imposed on new exporting countries purely based on initial rapid growth regardless of the low starting base. For instance, countries like Bangladesh and Sri Lanka had to face stringent quota restrictions in the US at very early stages of export expansion, despite their very low shares in total clothing imports to the US and the EU.

As part of the Uruguay Round of world trade negotiations concluded in 1994, the MFA was replaced by the Agreement on Textiles and Clothing[5] (ACT), which was designed to incorporate textile and clothing trade into the General Agreement on Tariffs and Trade (GATT) of the World Trade Organisation (WTO) so that protection could only take the form of non-discriminatory tariffs. The ACT put in place a programme for the elimination of MFA quota in four stages (1995, 1998, 2002, and 2004) over a 10-year period, with the adjustment heavily loaded towards the end of the period that ended in January 2005. Most importing countries did not go beyond the minimum liberalization required at the first three stages, leaving almost half of the quota removal to the very end of the transition period (31 December 2004). This 'back-loading' of the liberalization process meant that the final removal of quotas represented a systemic trade policy change that entailed considerable adjustment for all stakeholders. Some quantitative restraints on Chinese apparel ('China safeguards') remained in place in the US, EU, and Turkey after this date, as permitted under the PRC WTO accession protocol.[6] These safeguard quotas were also eliminated by the end of 2008.

Following the phasing-out of MFA quotas and the ending of the PRC safeguard, international buyers are now free to source textiles and apparel from any country, subject only to the system of tariffs. In the absence of quota protection, cost competitiveness is of course much more important in export success in the post-MFA era because 'quota rent' no longer distorts market prices. However, since they are no longer constrained by country-specific quotas, buyers would demand many more attributes in addition to price, such as product variety, quality, and timely delivery. Also since there are no limits on the amount procured

[5] In this chapter, we use the terms 'clothing' and 'apparel' interchangeably.

[6] The protocol PRC signed on its accession to the WTO in 2001 included a special Textile and Clothing Safeguard Provision ('China safeguards'). Under these safeguards, if a WTO member country felt that textiles and apparel exports from PRC threatened to impede the ordinary development trade in these products, it could request that PRC hold its exports of the given product to a level not greater than 7.5 per cent (6 per cent for wool products) above the amount entered its markers during the first 12 months of the most recent 14 months preceding the quest was made. The European Union and the US and Turkey invoked this safeguard provision immediately after MFA phase-out.

from a given country (or a firm) scale economies (the volume factor) could counterbalance the export competitiveness based purely on cost competitiveness. Thus, global apparel production is likely to become more concentrated amongst the most capable firms in a handful of low-cost production sites.

The MFA quotas prompted lead firms to rely heavily on value-chain intermediaries (sourcing agents) to coordinate the flow of orders from buyers in the US and Europe to a large number of apparel factories around the world. Sourcing agents provided lead firms with 'one-stop shopping' for the sourcing of goods: once the retailer came up with an order the packager filled that order by drawing on networks of contractors located in many countries. Following the abolition of quotas, lead firms have started to aggressively restructure their sourcing patterns to procure from fewer efficient suppliers worldwide and to develop long-term strategic partnership with core suppliers. This has also resulted in setting up local sourcing offices by some major buyers, bypassing their erstwhile sourcing agents. Some lead firms have moved their sourcing offices (involving local sourcing staff and quality control inspectors) closer to their main apparel suppliers (mainly Asia) and some have moved the design process and material selection offices as well (Fung et al. 2007; United States International Trade Commission [USITC] 2011).

The importance of non-price factors in export success in the post-MFA era has been further elevated by the ongoing process of 'lean retailing', a business strategy which has become widespread in apparel trade in developed countries since the mid-1990s (Abernathy et al. 1999; Abernathy, Volpe, and Weil 2006; Evans and Harrigan 2005; Harrigan and Barrows 2009). Lean retailing involves replenishing the range of clothes on offer on the shop floor in very short cycles (rather than seasonally, as was traditionally done), while defraying the inventory risk by holding low stocks.[7]

Lean retailing calls for close cooperation between the supplier and the buyer in order to achieve the desired levels of quality and reliability and timeliness of delivery. The retailers exchange point-of-sales

[7] This business strategy is generally more prevalent in 'fashion-basic products'—basic apparel products with some fashion content (such as lingerie, panties, sportswear and casualwear).

information with their suppliers, requiring them to replenish orders, in order to minimize inventory cost while ensuring continuous supply on the shopfloor. In the process of lean retailing, 'suppliers' warehouses and distribution centres act in many ways as virtual warehouses and distribution centres for the retailer' (Abernathy et al. 1999, p. 16). In response to this shift in risk, manufacturers must reshape planning methods, cost models, inventory practices, and production operations to match the sourcing strategies of the buyers. The buyers also increasingly require suppliers to undertake tasks such as labelling, packaging, and bar-cording which were traditionally done in the buyer's warehouses or distribution centres (Abernathy et al. 2006, Fung et al. 2007). Suppliers therefore need to adhere to *flexible manufacturing*[8] in order to enable to respond swiftly to changing demand, while cutting batch size and reducing inventories. In the post-quota world, buyers are likely to raise the bar ever higher on the responsiveness and flexibility required of their suppliers because now they have a wider choice, without being constrained by a country-product-specific quota regime.

A key determinant of a firm's success in flexible manufacturing is the backward integration of the production process: domestic availability of high quality fabric at competitive prices. Without quota restriction on the amount of production in a particular country, it can become cheaper for a country which produces both textiles and clothing to compete on world markets, thus avoiding transport costs of inputs, time delays, and management time needed to coordinate the fragmented supply chain (Audet 2007). During the MFA era, the textile industry did not migrate to developing country locations as fast as the clothing industry. In the post-MFA period, there are no more artificial obstacles (quotas) to prevent the emergence of a high-quality textile capacity in developing countries and stronger clusters of expertise. While low wages can still give developing countries a competitive edge in world markets, a strong domestic textile base can now play an important role in determining international competitiveness in the fashion-oriented and time-sensitive apparel markets by ensuring a quick turnaround time.

[8] Flexible manufacturing refers to the ability to customize a product, to produce to order, or shift quickly from production of one model to another on the same line in order to serve relatively small, specialized niche segments.

Lean retailing has increased the demand by the buyers for 'timeliness', ensuring a short and reliable time lag between the order and delivery. For products subject to rapid replenishment, direct costs related to labour, textile inputs, shipping and tariffs are balanced against the cost associated with lead times, inventory, and their attended risks. In those categories of apparel where replenishment is a major factor, countries located in proximity to major markets will, therefore, be at a considerable competitive advantage (of course if the other preconditions such as political stability and the quality of trade-related infrastructure are met). A possible substitute for proximity in meeting timeliness is airfreight, but shipping by air is commercially viable only for high-value, light products (Evans and Harrigan 2005).[9]

Another recent development in world apparel trade, which has significant implications for lead firms' sourcing decisions in a quota-free apparel trade, is the non-governmental organization (NGO)-led campaign in developed countries for imposing corporate social responsibility (CSR) norms (internationally accepted labour standards, taking care of employee wellbeing and meeting environmental standards) on developing-country exporters. The apparel industry has been at the forefront of the implementation of these ethical trading initiatives and social auditing practices because of the labour intensity of production (and the overwhelming dependence on female labour, a key focus of the high-profile anti-sweatshop campaign) and the environmental sensitivity of the production process (energy usage and waste water generation). 'Social audits' at the factory level have therefore become an important factor taken into account by apparel buyers (in particular speciality stores) in placing orders; [10] buyers are now demanding not only better prices and timely delivery, but also better conditions for workers and environmental friendly production ('greening of the industry') (Hale and Wills 2008; McIntyre 2008).

[9] L Brand, the big up-market women's clothing retailer in the US, adhere to a limit of 30 days for any order, frequently requiring to use airfreight as the mode of delivery (Fung et al. 2007, p. 2).

[10] 'When the buyers from Victoria's Secret and the other big brands come, working conditions is one of the first things they ask about. They have to, because they have customers asking them about it', says Mahesh Amalean, Managing Director of MAS Holdings, Sri Lanka's biggest clothing exporting firms (Friedman 2000, p. 178).

Sri Lankan Context: Initial Condition and Policy Reforms

In Sri Lanka commercial production of clothing began in the early 1960s. However, expansion of the industry remained severely constrained during the ensuing decade by a highly interventionist trade and industrial policy regime.[11] Unlike the textile industry, which was dominated by state-owned enterprises, apparel production continued to remain entirely a private sector activity. But importation of yarn and fabric, and other ancillary inputs needed for apparel production remained under stringent licencing. The state-owned companies, which dominated domestic textile industry, had limited capability to meet the input requirements of the apparel industry.

From about the late 1960s there was policy emphasis on promoting manufacturing exports through selective incentives and encouraging export-oriented FDI through selective incentives. The plethora of incentives introduced included an import duty rebate scheme, export-performance-related import entitlements, multiple exchange rates, and tax breaks for export-oriented foreign investment. These attempts largely failed, because the overall business climate of the country continued to be characterised by a significant 'anti-export' bias. Moreover, during the period from 1970 to 1977, widespread nationalization measures and threats, coupled with various economic controls, effectively marginalized the private sector in the economy. The 'quota-hopping' apparel firms of Hong Kong, China, therefore, bypassed Sri Lanka, notwithstanding its intrinsic advantages such as the strategic location, availability of cheap and trainable labour, and trade links forged during the colonial era.[12]

[11] For detailed historical surveys of Sri Lanka's trade and industry policy, see Athukorala and Rajapatirana (2000) and Cuthbertson and Athukorala (1990).

[12] Sri Lanka's missed opportunities are vividly illustrated in a comparison with Mauritius, the remote India-ocean island state which had much lesser favourable initial conditions compared to Sri Lanka. A thriving export-oriented clothing industry had developed in Mauritius by the mid-1970s, with the involvement of investors from Hong Kong, China who came there following the colonial trade roots to circumvent MFA quotas (Subramanian and Ray 2003, Wells 1980s, Gereffi 1999). A free trade zone set up in 1969, which effectively insulated the export sector from trade restrictions and labour-market rigidities in the rest of the economy regime, provided the setting for the expansion of clothing exports from Mauritius.

Rapid growth of the export-oriented apparel industry in Sri Lanka began only after the liberalization reforms initiated in 1977. The first round of reforms carried out during 1977–79 included elimination of quantitative import restrictions and significant reduction of import tariffs, revamping the foreign investment approval and monitoring process, the setting up of the Greater Colombo Economic Commission (GCEC) in 1978 with wide-ranging powers to establish and operate Export Processing Zones (EPZs) with an internationally competitive incentive package.[13] As an important part of the FDI policy, steps were also taken to enter into Investment Protection Agreements and Double Taxation Relief Agreements with the major investing countries. A guarantee against nationalisation of foreign assets without compensation was provided under the Article 157 of the new Constitution of Sri Lanka adopted in 1978.[14] A wide range of export promotion schemes, including an all-encompassing duty rebate scheme with flexible operational procedures, a manufacturing-in-bond scheme, and provision of equity and working capital, was introduced for export-oriented firms located outside FTZs under a newly established Export Development Board (EDB).

As part of a 'second wave' liberalization reform package introduced in early 1990s, most of the restrictions on the ownership structures of joint-venture projects located outside EPZs were abolished, and free-trade-zone privileges were extended to export-oriented ventures in all parts of the country (in addition to the ones located in the area demarcated by the original GCEC Act). The GCEC was reconstituted in 1991 under the new name of Board of Investment (BOI), and further

[13] The first investment promotion zone, at Katunayake near the Colombo International Airport (henceforth KEPZ), an area of approximately 160 square miles north of Colombo, was opened in June 1978. The remarkable success of the KEPZ paved the way for setting up a second EPZ in Biyagama (BEPZ) in 1982, a third in Koggala (KGEPZ) in June 1991.

[14] Following the nationalization of the foreign-owned gas and petroleum outlets during 1962–64, Sri Lanka became the first country against which the US government invoked the Hickenlooper Amendment, requiring the suspension of US aid to countries expropriating US property without compensation (Olson 1977). This constitutional guarantee was therefore vital to restore investor confidence.

liberalization of foreign trade. In 1992, BOI introduced a new incentive scheme ('The 200 Garment Factory Program') to entice the apparel industry to move to rural areas. Under this scheme, firms which set up factories in rural area were offered attractive tax incentives and access to bank credit and were also given priority in allocating export quotas under the MFA.

Import duties on textiles and yarn were abolished in 1998 to relieve apparel producers of administrative costs involved in using the duty rebate and bonded warehouse schemes. This was followed by the introduction of a Temporary Import for Export Processing (TIEP) scheme (as an alternative to the existing duty rebate and bonded warehouse schemes) to facilitate duty free accesses to other imported intermediate goods. Under this scheme, exporting firms were able to import inputs against a bank guarantee without paying all fiscal levies (tariffs and various para-tariffs)[15] and without requiring customs inspection of warehouses.

During the immediate post-reform years Sri Lanka scored very well on various factors relevant to foreign investors' perception. At the time, the international news media dubbed Sri Lanka 'the new investment centre of Asia' (*Far Eastern Economic Review*, 23 October 1978). This image was tarnished by the escalation of the separatist war from 1983. The Northern Province and large parts of the Eastern Province (which together account for one-third of Sri Lanka's total land area and almost 12 per cent of the population) remained mostly cut off from the national economy. Even in the rest of the country, prospects for attracting foreign investment, particularly in long-term ventures, was seriously hampered by the lingering fear of sporadic attacks by the rebels. However, Sri Lanka continued to remain an attractive location for clothing and other labour intensive industries, which are typically characterised by short pay-back periods, because of the availability of cheap and trainable labour and the liberal trade and investment policy regimes. Notwithstanding the massive military expenditure and its consequences for macroeconomic instability, the government also managed to avert real exchange rate misalignment through periodic adjustment in the exchange rate under a managed floating exchange rate regime.

[15] The Customs Ordinance permits reimbursement of only customs duties (import tariffs) under the duty rebate scheme.

Sri Lanka has a long history of trade union activism and worker militancy. Also, the organized labour market has long been characterized by significant rigidities, in particular, minimum wage legislation, restrictions on labour retrenchment and severance payments. Proposals in the original reform package of 1977 for reforming labour legislation to achieve greater labour market flexibility were never implemented because of successful legal challenges by the trade unions.[16] Following these failed reform attempts, the government adopted 'informal' strategies to resolve the contradiction between the existing rigid labour law and the need to provide enterprises located in EPZs with greater flexibility in labour management. First, greater care was taken in the recruitment of employees into the enterprises within the export processing zones; employees were recruited from applicants who were registered with the GCEC after prior police screening for trade union involvement. Second, a tight inspection process was introduced for monitoring daily entry of workers to EPZs. These 'informal' strategies proved workable because the trade union movement was in disarray following the crushing defeat of the centre-left parties in at the 1977 elections.

The extra-judiciary approach to achieving labour market flexibility proved less effective following the change of political leadership in 1994. The clothing industry also had begun to expand beyond the areas covered by the FTZs. According to BOI records, a number of foreign firms left the country during this period because of prolonged labour market disputes. However, the available data suggest that production disruption caused by trade union action continued to remain far less in clothing industry compared to the other industries.[17] By this time the apparel industry had become well established and employment conditions, particularly in large firms, had improved significantly, leaving little room for trade union action (as can be seen in the following lines). Moreover, the dominance of female workers in the work force was an important

[16] The only significant change achieved was the abolition under the GCEC Act of the ban on night-work for women in FTZ enterprises.

[17] According to the data on number of strikes and lost man-days reported in various issues of the *Sri Lanka Labour Gazette*, Department of Labour, Colombo.

source of industrial peace in the clothing industry.[18] The 'masculinist orientation' of political trade unionism in Sri Lanka hindered women from participation in trade unions. In any case, they did not have a compelling reason for joining unions because of the short-term nature of their employment; they typically remain in the labour force or a period of about 5 years before returning to their villages to move onto other forms of employment and getting married (Gunawardana 2007).

There has been some backsliding from liberalization reforms from about 2005, in particular after the end of the separatist war in May 2009 (Athukorala 2012). The foreign investment regime has become increasingly opaque/interventionist and there has been a significant increase in trade protection and the degree of variability of protection across product categories. International competitiveness (measured by the real exchange rate) had deteriorated in recent years, underpinned by a massive budget deficit and 'leaning against the wind' exchange rate policy. There has also been some reversal in trade liberalization with a range of new import taxes introduced in order to defray the costs of specific government services and/or to promote import-substituting domestic production. However, export-oriented firms continued to remain insulated from the distortion in the overall trade regime because of the EPZ scheme and the TIEP scheme which provide exporters with access to imported inputs at international prices.[19]

Expansion of Apparel Industry

Quota-hopping apparel firms' response to the liberalization reforms initiated in 1977 was swift and remarkable. By 1982 there were 16 foreign invested enterprises (FIEs) operating in the country, of which 13 were from Hong Kong, China, the major developing-economy exporter of garments at the time (Table 6.2). While MFA quota restriction was

[18] Young women drawn from the rural poor make up approximately 85 per cent of all workers in the garment industry.

[19] The duty rebate scheme is still in operation, but now the popular scheme is TIEP under which exporters can import inputs without making payments of both import duties and para tariffs (various fiscal levies). The duty rebate scheme is now mainly used by manufacturers that are focused on the local market and export only a small share of their output.

the major push factor, British colonial trade and business ties seem to have given firms of Hong Kong, China an inside track on investing in Sri Lanka (as in Mauritius and Jamaica) (Gereffi 1999).

Apparel exports from Sri Lanka began to come under MFA quotas as early as 1983 and the product coverage and the quota limit on each category expanded during the subsequent years.[20] The BOI, therefore, began to use the ability to produce non-quota products as a key criterion in approving new investment projects in the apparel industry. Consequently, from about the early 1990s, a number of East Asian firms whose entry was driven primarily by the quota-jumping motive left the country, and there were no new arrivals from these economies in non-quota categories, primarily because of the PRC's growing attraction as an alternative production location. However, there was no decline in the number of FIEs because there was a notable increase in the arrival of new investors from developed countries, in particular from the UK, Italy and Germany.

There has been a clear pattern of 'localization' in the ownership of apparel firms over the years, particularly from the mid-1990s. There were 109 BOI approved fully locally owned firms in operation (47 per cent of all BOI firms) in 2009, up from 14 (18 per cent) in 1994. In addition to these there were a large number of local firms opening under the normal business law of the country (non-BOI firms).[21] Moreover, there has been a notable shift in the ownership structure of FIEs from full foreign ownership to joint ventures with local investors. According to BOI data (not reported here for brevity), in 2002, only 8 per cent of all BOI-approved firms in operation (10 out of 121) were fully foreign owned, compared to 80 per cent (12 out of 16) in 1982. According to the information gathered from interviews, in the bulk of these joint ventures overall management is undertaken by local managers, with inputs from their foreign counterparts for GVC management.

At the formative stage, the Sri Lanka apparel industry was very much an integral part of the East Asia centred 'triangular apparel

[20] The Textile Quota Board was established at the Ministry of Textile Industries in 1992 to streamline quota allocation.

[21] According to firm-level customs records the number of exporting firms is much higher than the number of firms in operation according to the BOI records (see the fourth section).

TABLE 6.2 Source Economy Composition of Clothing Manufacturing Firms in Sri Lanka: 1982, 1994, 2002, and 2009

	1982	1994			2002			2009		
	Number of Firms	Number of Firms	Approved Invest-ment (%)	Planned Employ-ment (%)	Number of Firms	Approved Invest-ment (%)	Planned Employ-ment (%)	Number of Firms	Approved Invest-ment (%)	Planned Employ-ment (%)
Foreign invested enterprise	16	66	90.1	88.6	122	70.8	63.0	121	55.6	54.7
Developing economies	14	36	42.3	57.5	**72**	38.6	39.3	73	43.5	38.9
Hong Kong, China	13	16	23.5	31.1	34	26.1	26.2	24	26.5	15.8
Korea, Republic of	0	8	7.2	9.8	14	5.6	5.5	9	3.1	3.6
Taipei,China	0	1	0.3	1.8	8	2.1	2.2	2	0.6	1.2
India	1	2	0.1	1.3	3	0.3	0.8	13	3.8	8.7
Other[1]		9	11.2	13.5	13	4.6	4.5	25	9.5	9.6
Developed economies	2	30	47.8	31.2	50	32.2	23.7	48	12.1	15.8
Germany	0	6	8.1	10.2	10	7.4	4.7	8	0.3	1.3
Italy	0				4	3.2	2.7	6	1.1	1.5
Japan	0	5	26.5	5.0	5	0.8	2.3	2	0.3	0.1
UK	1	5	3.7	2.7	15	16.1	5.3	20	8.1	9.1
US	1	4	3.7	8.3	8	2.1	6.6	8	0.8	1.3
Other	0	10	5.9	4.9	8	3.5	2.0	4	1.5	2.5
Sri Lankan firms	7	14	9.9	11.4	133	29.2	37.0	109	44.4	45.3
Total	22	80	100	100	255	100	100	230	100	100

Note: Includes unclassified firms and firms with multi-country ownership.

Source: Compiled from official records of investment approval made available by the Board of Investment, Sri Lanka.

network' (*a la* Gereffi 1994) in which the East Asian firms acted as the intermediaries between foreign buyers and the apparel producing firms in Sri Lanka. The foreign buyers placed orders with the East Asian firms and the latter shifted some of the orders to affiliated factories in Sri Lanka. The affiliates shipped finished products directly to the foreign buyer under the quota issued to Sri Lanka by the importing country. The Sri Lankan (local) firms were predominantly subcontractors to these foreign affiliated companies.

From about the mid-1980s, the importance of triangular trade began to diminish owing to three important developments. First, as the volume of exports expanded, many international buyers began to set up buying offices in Sri Lanka. These buying offices soon began to play a crucial role in linking local firms with highly international markets. Second, the developed-country (mostly European) firms which set up production plants in Sri Lanka came with already established direct market links with retailers in their countries of origin. Third, more recently, a number of large local firms have begun to deal directly with lead firms based on market links established with the help of joint-venture operations with foreign firms. Some of these firms have set up their own sales offices in major importing countries and in Hong Kong, China. Buying offices are still catering to the demand of non-brand producers and small- and medium-sized firms.

The type of international buyers who came to the country had a significant implication for the evolution and industrial upgrading. Mass retailers (Wal-Mart, K-mart, Target, among others) never came to Sri Lanka because the MFA quota allocation systems (which was largely based on the country size) did not allow enough quotas for a given product for achieving scale economies needed to be a competitive supplier.[22] So from the beginning Sri Lankan exports were to speciality

[22] For instance, Epic, a Hong Kong, China based large scale supplier of trousers to mass retailers came to Sri Lanka in early 1990s, but soon left for Bangladesh because under the 'the complex web of quotas that dominated international trade in garments [it] could not get enough quota allocation to make one product' [trousers] .... in the ninny country' (Jacob 2013). (However the failed Sri Lankan operation gave Epic access to the pool of excellent managers; many of the Epic's managers in its Bangladesh operations are from Sri Lanka)

retailers and brand marketers such Marks & Spencer, JC Penny, and The Limited. These buyers sought greater variety and smaller orders that suit small scale operation of Sri Lankan firms. Moreover, these buyers, unlike the buyers for mass retailers, often worked closely with local manufacturers, imparting technical and managerial and marketing knowhow required for product improvement. Close links with brand marketers was accompanied by a shift in product mix from mass-market products to niche products, particularly women's underwear and bras, knitted intimate apparel and active wear. (See more on the change in product mixes in the next section.)

Some buyers of brand marketers made an even greater impact on updating local firms by becoming joint-venture partners in manufacturing. The role of Mast Industries, the overseas buying arm of The Limited, deserves particular attention. In the mid-1980s Mast set up joint ventures with two small local companies in Sri Lanka to produce intimate apparel (panties and brassiere) and casualwear. With marketing and technical knowhow obtained from this vital initial link, these two apparel firms (later renamed MAS Holdings and Brandix) have grown to become not only the two largest apparel exports in the country but also important players in these product lines at the world stage. They have also become multinationals in their own right, with production operations in a number of other countries, and have been instrumental in making Sri Lanka the design hub in South Asia (see Appendix 6A.2).

By the late 1990s Sri Lankan apparel industry had a well-developed customer base including well-known brand names such as Victoria's Secret, Marks & Spencer, Sainsbury's, Tesco, Hunkemoller, Abercrombie and Fitch, GAP, Liz Claiborne, Nike, Pierre Cardin, Ralph Lauren, and Tommy Hilfiger. Large apparel firms (at least the top ten companies) have established their own design centres which work closely with design teams of brand owners. Most large companies (in particular the top ten) have invested in computer aided design (CAD) and computer aided manufacturing (CAM), and electronic fitting ('e-fitting') which enable design decisions by visualizing the garment digitally, skipping the standard fit-on session with a model. They have also invested in supply chain enabling technologies such as the enterprise resource planning (ERP) computer system that integrates all data and processes of an organization into a unified system (a unified database to store data for various functions throughout the organization).

Like in many other second-tier exporting countries, the apparel industry in Sri Lanka started with cut, make, and trim (CMT) operations. In the beginning, local apparel firms were 'contract manufacturers' who produced according to the requirements of their customers. These firms received all the inputs (fabrics and accessories from the buyers) and just performed cutting and sewing. The industry was also heavily dependent on textile technicians imported from Hong Kong, China. It was common practice for international buying offices in Colombo to combine placing orders with local firms with sending textile technicians to monitor the production process (Athukorala and Lakshman 1985). At the time, the industry was often referred to as a 'glorified tailor shop' (Wijesiri and Dissanayake 2008).

From about the late-1990s, an increasing number of firms embarked on package contracting (original equipment manufacturing, OEM), which involves sourcing of fabrics and other inputs, producing according to customer specifications, and packaging for delivery. A number of these firms have now become full package manufacturers (or ODM). They offer a full range of services to customers, product development, pattern making, finishing, sourcing, manufacturing, and delivery. So far there has been only one successful case of a Sri Lankan firm (MAS Holdings, the largest in Sri Lanka) launching its own brand (a sign of graduating to OBM status), but the new lingerie brand still accounts for only a tiny share of its total exports (see Appendix 6A.2). According to tentative estimates provided by JAAF, ODM firms now account for about 60 per cent of total exports (by value)[23], with the balance coming from package contractors. The CTM activity has virtually become a relic of the past.

Going Global

In the mid-1990s a number of Sri Lankan apparel companies set up production plants in countries like Maldives, Madagascar, Bangladesh,

[23] This figure is comparable to the share in total exports of the top ten apparel firms (as we see later in the chapter).

Mauritius, and Kenya in order to circumvent MFA quota restrictions on their operations in Sri Lanka. These ventures employed Sri Lankan technicians, managers, and in some cases, Sri Lankan machinists. Some of these production bases (including all those set up in Maldives) were shifted back to Sri Lanka after MFA abolition; only those located in countries which continue to assure profitability due to tariff preferences and/or relatively low wages compared to Sri Lanka continue to remain in operation.

Following the MFA abolition, the three largest firms have set up plants in Viet Nam, Bangladesh and India (see Appendix 6A.2). Recently, a medium-size Sri Lankan firm set up a manufacturing plant in Jordan as a direct response to its US buyers, whose sourcing calculations have changed because of a free trade agreement between Jordan and the US. These firms are co-ordinating production in these countries to meet orders from their strategic buyers, reminiscent of the triangular manufacturing practices of the East Asian firms during the MFA era.

Backward Linkages

In many countries, the expansion of the export-oriented apparel industry was aided by a well-established textile base developed during the period of import-substitution industrialisation phase (Doner and Ramsey 1984; Feenstra and Hamilton 2006; Bonacich, et al. 1994; Tokatli and Kizilgun 2010; Tewari 2008a). However, as previously discussed, the expansion of apparel exports from Sri Lanka began without any support from a domestic textile base. The government-owned textile factories were closed down following liberalization reforms as they failed to face the new competitive market conditions. At the early stage of expansion of apparel exports, 'triangular trade' presumably discouraged the early emergence of textile factories. The East Asian firms operating in Sri Lanka found it profitable to supply yarn and textile from their established procurement sources in their home countries rather than attempting to produce them domestically. For these reasons, the domestic content of apparel exports was basically equivalent to the labour content (about 20 per cent), and the low level of backward integration was a major concern for policy makers (Kelegama and Foley 1999).

From about the mid-1990s the three largest firms (MAS Holdings, Brandix and Hidramani) began to set up a number of subsidiary companies to produce textile and ancillary inputs (hangers, bra moulding, packaging material, labels and buttons) as part of their strategy to prepare themselves for the abolition of MFA quotas. By this time the volume of exports also had reached levels that provide scale economies for fabric (in particular knitted fabric) production. In most cases these factories are joint ventures with foreign firms which had been established suppliers for many years. The most prominent cases are Ocean Lanka, a joint venture of Brandix, Hidramani and Fountain Set of Hong Kong, China (the largest manufacturer of weft knitted fabric in the world);[24] Textured Jersey, a joint venture between MAS Holdings and Brandix, and Textured Jersey (UK) (automated dye dispensing system); MAS Fabric Plant, a high-quality joint venture of MAS, Dogi International Fabrics of Spain and Elastic Fabrics of America (a $30 million weft knitted fabric factory); Stretchline Lanka, a joint venture of MAS Holdings and Stretchline UK (elastics for the production of lingerie and panties). Amongst these firms Stretchline has become a multinational in its own right, with production plants in four economies (PRC, Indonesia, Mexico, Honduras); sales offices in UK, the US, Hong Kong, China; and a research lab in UK jointly run with its parent company. A number of independent fabric and embroidery manufacturing firms have also emerged to serve apparel producing firms. The largest is Hayleys MGT Knitting Mills (denim producer), a joint venture between a local conglomerate, Hayleys Group and MGT Knitting Mills of Australia.

Currently, about 60 per cent of fabric used in apparel production in Sri Lanka is produced domestically: about 80 per cent of fabrics used in knitted apparel and about 20 per cent of woven apparel.[25] The bulk of the ancillary inputs (embroidery, hangers, labels, buttons, among others) are also produced domestically. The difference in the local content of fabric used between knitted and woven apparel can be explained by different investment requirements for establishing production plants for the two fabric types. The investment requirement for establishing

[24] Warp-knitted fabric is a synthetic stretch fabric used to make lingerie, swimwear, and sportswear

[25] Tentative estimates provided by JAAF.

a similar sized woven textile mill is about ten times of the investment required for a knit mill (Abernathy et al. 1999, Staritz 2011).[26]

Corporate Social Responsibility

Sri Lanka's labour market regime, notwithstanding the rigidities it created in hiring and firing of workers, was instrumental in preparing the apparel industry to effectively face the ethical workplace norms recently imposed by international buyers. Work conditions in Sri Lankan factories were already at a relatively high standard well before international buyers began to incorporate 'ethical trade' as an important element of their procurement policy. Sri Lanka had already become a signatory to (and remains the only country in Asia to do so) the 39 International Labour Organization (ILO) Core Convention covering workplace practices, prohibition of forced labour, prohibition of child labour, and ensuring better working conditions well before the export-oriented apparel industry took off. Employment of child labour has been curbed in Sri Lanka, and the minimum statutory age for employment is 18, with some conditional exemptions for those over 16. Stringent ruling of social compliance was rigorously enforced and monitored by the labour department and other bodies, including the BOI. The trade unions played an important role in ensuring adherence to these requirements. These initial labour market conditions reduced the likelihood of 'CSR transgression' by the buyers in the form of adding an extra level of accountability on the apparel manufacturers (Perry 2012).

Against this background, the upward movement in the value ladder of Sri Lankan apparel producers has been aided by a greater emphasis on ethical employment practices than many of its Asian competitors (Fernando and Almeida 2012; Ruwanpura and Wrigley 2011). In this, MAS Holdings took the lead in the mid-1980s as part of its emerging

[26] A knit fabric mill including dyeing and finishing unit of a viable economic size requires an investment of at least $3.5 million whereas the investment requirement for a similar factory in woven fabric amounts to at least $35 million. For this reason, in Bangladesh, as in Sri Lanka, the domestic fabric content of knitted apparel is almost four times that of woven apparels (Staritz 2011, p. 146).

role as a major supplier to Victoria's Secret (Appendix 6A.2). Following MAS's lead, the other apparel manufacturing firms have also established their own CSR programmes such as women empowerment programmes, and professional, vocational and technical training programmes for employees. Most firms provide workers with transport facilities, free breakfast, subsidized meals and medical care. They also actively engage in community services in rural areas where the factories are located. The 'Garments Without Guilt 'campaign launched by the JAAF has played a pivotal role in strengthening CSR commitments amongst apparel exporting firms and promoting Sri Lanka's name as an ethical clothing manufacturer (See Appendix 6A.1).

Some apparel factories in Sri Lanka have started to produce 'fair trade' clothing. These factories import organic and fair-trade cotton grown in India and Africa and then convert them into fabric in Sri Lanka. The three largest firms already supply organic cotton clothing for brand names such as Marks & Spencer and Tesco.[27] A number of local fabric companies like Ocean Lanka and Brandix Textiles have obtained fair-trade and organic accreditation from international certification bodies such as FLO-Cert GmbH in Germany and Institute of Marketecology (IMO) is Switzerland. With increasing global concern regarding climate change, a number of apparel firms have started investing in environmentally friendly products and production processes. A number of large firms have embarked on building 'green factories', which meet the international environmental standards.

Labour Market Transition

The expansion of the apparel industry following liberalization reforms was aided by an ample supply of cheap, trainable labour. At the time of reforms nearly a fifth of a labour force of about 5 million was out of work, with the bulk of unemployed concentrated in the age bracket of 18–25. The average wage of a factory worker at the time of reforms was about $33, which amounted to about 12 per cent of that in Hong Kong, China and was significantly lower compared to the other favoured clothing producers in the region such as Malaysia, Indonesia, and Philippines

[27] Tesco sells clothing designed by Katherine Hammett, a designer known for her political t-shirts and her ethical business philosophy.

and Mauritius (Athukorala and Rajapatirana 2000). In addition to their preparedness to take up low wage jobs, workers joining the newly set up apparel factories[28] had a much higher level of formal education (on average 10.3 years of schooling) compared to those in most other apparel exporting countries (Savachenko and Acevedo 2010). In addition, most of the female workers also came with years of experience in using the standard household sewing machine, the basic technology of which was not very different from that of the industrial sewing machine.[29] Consequently, a female apparel worker who joined the labour force as a helper took only two to three months to pick-up the skills required to become a machine operator, compared to three-to-six months taken by her Bangladeshi counterpart.[30]

Sri Lanka's track record of technical and tertiary education is not as impressive as its long-standing success with primary and secondary education. But the country did have a human capital base capable of acquiring within a short period technical and managerial skills required for the apparel industry once the economy was exposed to foreign trade and investment through liberalisation reforms.

There has been a notable improvement in the managerial and technical capability of the apparel industry over the past four decades, with public-private partnership playing a pivotal role. Since 1984, the University of Moratuwa (the main technical university in the country) has been offering diploma-level design courses in textile technology in collaboration with the London School of Fashion Design. In 2004, the university started offering a 4-year degree course in fashion

[28] Women accounted for over 85 per cent of total employment in the apparel industry (Nordås 2003).

[29] In the late 19th century the Sri Lankan subsidiary of the Singer Sewing Machine company launched a hire-purchase scheme with affordable monthly instalment payments through an island-wide network. This scheme soon became so popular that the sewing machine became an ubiquitous household asset and part of the bridal dowry. The combination of higher levels of formal education and basic training in using a household sewing machine made Sri Lankan factory workers easily trainable compared to their counterparts in other countries in the region.

[30] Based on interview with a Sri Lankan firm with operations in Bangladesh, and Savachenko and Acevedo, 2010 (Bangladesh).

development jointly with North Carolina State University College of Textiles. The JAAF played an important role in initiating this programme. The JAAF has also taken the initiative to offer a post graduate diploma in Marketing in collaboration with the Chartered Institute of Marketing in UK. Brandix, the second largest apparel producer, has been running its own training institution, the Brandix Clothing Training Institution (BCTI), since 1998. Recently, BCTI started offering a master's programme in textile technology in collaboration with the RMIT University in Melbourne.

Thanks to these initiatives, the dependence of Sri Lanka's apparel industry on foreign textile technicians (mostly from Hong Kong, China) had virtually disappeared by the dawn of the new millennium. Sri Lanka has also become a supplier of textile technicians and managers to other apparel-producing countries in the region and beyond (Jacob 2013, Staritz 2011).

The apparel industry has begun to experience labour shortages and wage increases in recent years. Various news reports in the first half of 2013 placed the number of unfilled vacancies between 30,000 and 50,000. The average hourly wage is now much higher than in Bangladesh, Viet Nam, Cambodia (and also possibly India and Indonesia) and approaching the levels in the PRC and the other East Asian clothing-producing countries (Table 6.3). Wages in almost all apparel firms are now well above the minimum wage set by the government (Sri Lankan rupees 9500, about $70).

An interesting conundrum in Sri Lanka's contemporary labour market scene is the coexistence of massive labour outmigration and labour scarcity faced by the garment industry, even though local wages are now comparable or even higher than the average wage received by female migrant workers who are mostly engaged in household services (Arunatilake, Jayawardena, and Weerakook 2011). Between 2002 and 2012, an average of about a quarter of a million Sri Lankans left annually for overseas employment, with the number increasing every year. The total number that left during 2008–12 was about 1.31 million, up from roughly 1.08 million during the previous 5 years. A tentative estimate suggests that the total stock of Sri Lankan overseas contract migrant workers had reached 2 million by 2011, amounting to over 14 per cent of the total working-age population of the country.

TABLE 6.3 Apparel Manufacturing Labour Cost in Selected Asian Countries: 2008 ($ per hour)

Thailand	1.29–1.36
Malaysia	1.18
Philippines	1.07
People's Republic of China	0.51–1.08
Prime coastal provinces	1.08
Other coastal provinces	0.86–0.94
Remote provinces	0.55–0.94
India	0.51
Indonesia	0.44
Sri Lanka[a]	0.43
Viet Nam	0.38
Pakistan	0.37
Cambodia	0.33
Bangladesh	0.22

Note: [a] At the time of fieldwork undertaken for this study (the third quarter of 2012), the average hourly wage was about 0.55, with the large firms paying an average wage of over 0.65. If the rate of inflation (measured by the consumer price index) is used as a rough guide to potential wage increases in individual countries, the Sri Lankan average for apparel manufacturing could have well exceeded that in Indonesia and India by this time.
Source: Jassin-O'Rourke Group (2008).

There are two possible reasons for the preference for overseas employment. First, foreign employment provides an opportunity for accumulating more saving since the cost of living (which is increasing rapidly in Sri Lanka) is covered as part of the overseas employment contract. Second, and perhaps more importantly, in a country where white-collar employment is highly valued as a result of universal free education, there is a stigma attached to working in a garment factory. Female garment workers are stereotyped as 'Juki Girls'—a derogatory name that comes from a popular brand of sewing machine. The long working hours involved is another reason for aversion to apparel industry jobs (Amelean 2006; Kelegama 2009, p. 591)

Labour shortages would have become a binding constraint much earlier if it were not for the 200 Garment Factory Scheme introduced in 1992. In the beginning, the apparel producers were hesitant to move to rural areas because of their concerns about transport costs and the need to be closer to international buyers operating in Colombo, but they eventually realized the advantage of locating closer to unexploited pockets of labour in the rural hinterland.[31] There is still a sizable pool of under-employed or unemployed female labour in rural areas who are reluctant to move to the industrial centres in the Western Province because of socio-economic reasons and they are prepared to work for relatively low wages.[32] Because of these reasons, in recent years most apparel producers have implemented their factory expansion programmes with a distinct rural bias. Following the end of the ethnic conflict in 2009, some large firms have started setting up factories in the Northern and Eastern provinces which remained virtually cut-off from the rest of the economy.

Post Multi-fibre Arrangement Export Performance

By the time of policy reforms in 1977, the export structure of Sri Lanka remained concentrated in a limited range of primary commodities, with manufactures accounting for only 4 per cent of total merchandise exports. Since then, manufacturing exports have expanded rapidly, with apparel playing the dominant role. Between 1977 and 2004, apparel exports increased from a mere $15 million (2.1 per cent of total exports) to over 2.8 billion (50.6 per cent) (Table 6.4). From 1992, apparel has become the single largest foreign exchange earner of the country. Over the years the composition of manufactured exports has diversified into other labour intensive and resource-based products, but apparel still accounts for over 40 per cent of total merchandise exports and over 60 of manufacturing exports.

[31] By the late 1990s, about 154 factories were in operation under the this scheme (Kelegama, 2006, p. 213).

[32] In late 2012, the average monthly wage of sewing machine operators in apparel factories located in Colombo district was about $125 compared to about $90 in the rest of the country.

TABLE 6.4 Apparel[a] Exports from Sri Lanka, 1970–2013

	$ million	Share of Apparel in		Share in World Apparel Exports
		Merchandise Exports (%)	Manufacturing Exports[b] (%)	
1970	1.4	0.4	0.9	–
1975	3.4	0.6	13.9	–
1977	15.1	2.1	13.8	–
1985	278.6	20.9	39.5	0.12
1990	637.0	33.3	53.2	0.91
1995	1,465.7	38.5	75.4	1.02
2000	2,775.8	52.0	76.6	1.10
2005	2,870.6	46.6	73.1	1.11
2006	3,048.8	45.1	72.1	1.03
2007	3,271.2	42.7	68.7	0.98
2008	3,434.3	42.1	67.5	1.01
2009	3,120.3	45.9	65.4	1.01
2010	3,356.3	42.0	56.9	1.07
2011	3,986.4	39.9	56.2	1.09
2012	3,783.8	43.1	57.1	1.11
2013	4,508.0	43.4	60.7	1.13
2014	4,930.0	44.3	61.3	1.13

Note: [a] Products belonging to commodity code 84 of the Standard International Trade Classification (SITC).

[b] Manufacturing is defined as SITC 5 to 8–68.

'–' denotes negligible.

Source: Compiled from United Nations Comtrade database and Central Bank of Sri Lanka Annual Report (various years).

In the lead-up to the MFA-quota abolition, Sri Lanka was amongst the countries expected to experience a significant contraction in exports in the quota-free era (Nordas 2009). This gloomy prediction has not materialized: Sri Lanka's average annual exports of apparel during 2010–14 amounted to $4.22 billion, up from $3.1 billion during the preceding 5 years (2005–09), a 31 per cent increase. Sri Lanka's share in world apparel exports did decline from about 1.10 per cent during 2000–04 to 1.01 during 2005–07. It has increased since then, reaching 1.13 per cent in 2014 (Table 6.4).

During the first 6 years of the post-MFA era, a widely held view was that Chinese safeguards (the invoking of safeguard provision by the EU and the US against imports from the PRC) and preferential access to the EU markets under the generalized system of preferences (GSP)[33] helped Sri Lanka to withstand the competitive pressure.[34] But the data is not consistent with this view. First, there was no significant overlap between the categories of apparel subject to the safeguards and the items that figured prominently in Sri Lanka's exports to the US and EU markets (Kelegama 2009). Apparel exports from Sri Lanka have, therefore, continued to increase after the termination of these safeguards. Second, contrary to a highly publicized prediction that 'losing GSP Plus would lead to a 4 per cent cut' (*The Economist* 2008), Sri Lankan apparel exports to the EU recorded a 34 per cent increase (from $1,616 million to $2,166 million) between 2010 and 2014 (CBSL [Central Bank of Sri Lanka] 2014, Table 71).

As discussed in the previous section, Sri Lanka's apparel industry had experienced significant industrial upgrading and carved out niches in a number of dynamic product lines (fashion-basic product) during the MFA era. The industry had also built a strong image of CSR, in particular relating to compliance with internationally agreed employment practices, and improved social and environmental standards. The human capital base and design capabilities of the industry had improved significantly, enabling it to swiftly respond to buyers' quest for variety. These non-price factors seem to have played a pivotal role in securing export orders, even though Sri Lanka is no longer a low-cost production base compared to many other apparel producing countries in the region. It is not possible to quantify the relative importance of price and non-price factors from a single country study of this nature, but the following discussion on the commodity composition, size distribution

[33] Under the EU-GSP scheme, Sri Lanka is eligible for an average non-reciprocal preference margin of about 2.2 per cent on clothing exports (the average GSP rate of 9.0 per cent compared to an average MFA tariff rate of 11.2 per cent). On July 2005, Sri Lanka became eligible for additional tariff concessions under the newly introduced GSP-Plus scheme, which offered duty free access to 7,200 products (including almost all clothing items). On 15 February 2010, the EU suspended GSP+ concessions to Sri Lanka (with effect from 15 August 2010) due to concerns about the violation of human rights (Abayasekara 2013).

[34] See Adhikari and Weeratunge (2007) and the works cited therein.

of firms, and direction of trade is illustrative of the relevance of these factors in understanding Sri Lanka's repositioning in the global apparel markets in the post-MFA era.

Commodity Composition

In order to examine the changing patterns of commodity composition of apparel exports from Sri Lanka, we use the three-way classification proposed by Abernathy et al. (1999 and 2006): fashion products, basic products, and fashion-basic products. Fashion products are those at high-end of the apparel value chain, such as dresses from Paris and Italian suits, the demand for which is largely driven by social status and deep-rooted cultural values. These products are expensive to produce and are not typically imported from developing countries. Basic products are the ones that remain in a retailer's or a manufacturer's collection for many seasons, such as men's white shirts or underwear. Fashion-basic products are variants on basic products which containing some fashion element (such as stone-washed jeans, pants with pleats or trim, fashion lingerie and intimate wear). Basic products account for the bulk (over a half) of internationally traded apparel products, with the other two categories each accounting for a quarter. However, over the past two decades, the third category has been the most dynamic, mainly because of the rapid increase in lean retailing. In these products, unlike in basic products, exporting is more than a simple price-cost game; speed and flexibility are crucial capabilities for firms wrestling with product proliferation. In basic apparels, low-wage nations, especially those with access to inexpensive textiles, have the potential for major market gains following the abolition of MFA quotas.

The available trade data does not permit (even at the highest degree of disaggregation they are reported in customs records) precise disaggregation of total exports into three categories. But the data does point to a clear pattern of concentration of Sri Lankan apparel exports in the fashion-basic category following the post-MFA era. This pattern is also consistent with the analytical narrative of structural changes in the apparel industry in the previous section and the information collected for the firm-level interviews.

Table 6.5 summarizes data on the commodity composition of apparel exports at three time points, focusing on the share accounted for by

Table 6.5 Sri Lankan Clothing Exports: Top 20 Standard International Trade Classification 5 Digit Products: 2000–01, 2005–06, and 2012–13

2000–01			2005–06			2012–13		
SITC Code	Product	Export Share (%)	SITC Code	Product	Export Share (%)	SITC Code	Product	Export Share (%)
84260	Women/girls trousers woven	9.6	84260	Women/girls trousers woven	13.5	84551	Brassieres	9.9
84140	Men/boy trousers woven	8.9	84140	Men/boy trousers woven	8.2	84140	Men/boy trousers woven	9.7
84270	Women/girls blouse woven	7.3	84540	T-shirts/singlets knit	8.0	84260	Women/girls trousers woven	9.8
84540	T-shirts/singlets knit	5.6	84482	Women/girls panties knit/crochet	7.2	84540	T-shirts/singlets knit	9.4
84530	Jerseys/pullovers	5.4	84551	Brassieres	6.4	84482	Women/girls panties knit	9.2
84130	Men/boys jackets woven	5.2	84530	Jerseys/pullovers	4.8	84691	Gloves knitted	4.7
84551	Brassieres	4.8	84270	Women/girls blouse woven	4.6	84426	Women/girls trousers knit	4.6
84151	Men/boys trousers cotton woven	4.7	84151	Men/boys trousers cotton	3.9	84822	Women nightwear woven	4.4
84230	Women/girls jackets woven	3.4	84250	Women/girls skirts woven	3.2	84151	Men/boys trousers cotton	3.5

84371	Men/boys trousers cotton knit	3.2	84691	Glove impregnated/coat knitted	2.8	84530	Jerseys/pullovers	3.2
84250	Women/girls skirts woven	3.2	84371	Men/boys trousers cotton knit/crochet	2.7	84270	Women/girls blouse woven	3.2
84240	Women/girls dresses woven	3.0	84230	Women/girls jackets woven	2.7	84240	Women/girls dresses woven	3.0
84482	Women/girls panties knit	2.7	84130	Men/boys jackets woven	2.4	84381	Men/boys under-wear knit	2.8
84282	Women nightwear woven	2.6	84470	Women/girls blouses knit	2.1	84512	Baby clothes knit	2.3
84512	Baby clothes knit	2.4	84426	Women/girls trousers knit	2.0	84564	Women/girls swimwear knit	2.2
84470	Women/girls blouses knit	2.0	84240	Women/girls dresses woven	1.9	84424	Women/girls dress knit	2.3
84691	Glove impreg/coat knitted	1.9	84483	Women/girls nightwear knit	1.5	84250	Women/girls skirts woven	1.7
84511	Baby clothes woven	1.7	84512	Baby clothes knit	1.5	84483	Women/girls skirts woven	1.5
84423	Women/girls jackets knit	1.1	84423	Men/boys jackets knit	1.4	84371	Men/boys trousers cotton	1.5
84159	Men/boys trousers fibre woven	1.1	84511	Baby clothes woven	1.1	84423	Women/girls jackets knit	1.2
	Total	79.8		Total	82.0		Total	90.2

Source: Compiled from UN Comtrade database.

the top 20 products.[35] The degree of concentration of exports in the top 20 products has increased over time from 80 per cent in 2001–01 to 90.2 in 2012–13. Amongst the top 20 products, women's clothing, which generally contain a higher fashion content, account for a much larger share: the share increased from 44 per cent to nearly 63 per cent in 2012–13. Amongst women's apparel, the prominent items are intimate wear: brassieres (SITC [Standard International Trade Classification] 84551) and panties (84482). This category accounted for nearly a fifth of total apparel exports in 2012–13, up from 7.5 per cent in 2000–01. Products such as men's business shirt and normal trousers (for both men and women), which generally have no fashion content, have virtually disappeared from the export product mix. This shift in product composition away from basic products to fashion-basic products is consistent with the information gathered from interviews: in almost all these 20 products, Sri Lankan firms are producing solely for speciality stores and/or brand-marketers.

The growing importance of Sri Lanka as a global supplier of intimate apparel is clearly shown in Figure 6.1. In 2013, Sri Lanka accounted for 8.3 per cent of total world exports of women/girls panties, up from an average annual figure of 2.2 per cent in 2000. Sri Lanka's world market shares of brassiere increased from 3.2 per cent to 7.4 per cent between these 2 years. In both products the increase in world market share was faster during the post-MFA years. Even in the other three products, the market shares have remained above that of total apparel exports during the post MFA era. The patterns of exports to the US and EU of these products (data not reported here due to space constraints) are remarkably similar to this aggregate picture.

In order to provide a more encompassing look at the emerging commodity profile of Sri Lanka's apparel exports, we computed revealed comparative advantage (RCA) indices at the SITC 5-digit level of commodity disaggregation. The RCA index measures a country's relative export performance in individual categories of a given product (in this case apparel, defined to encompass all 5-digit categories belonging to SITC 84) compared to that category's overall performance in world

[35] Products are identified at the five-digit level of the Standard International Trade Classification (SITC), which is closely comparable to the six-digit level of the Harmonised System (HS).

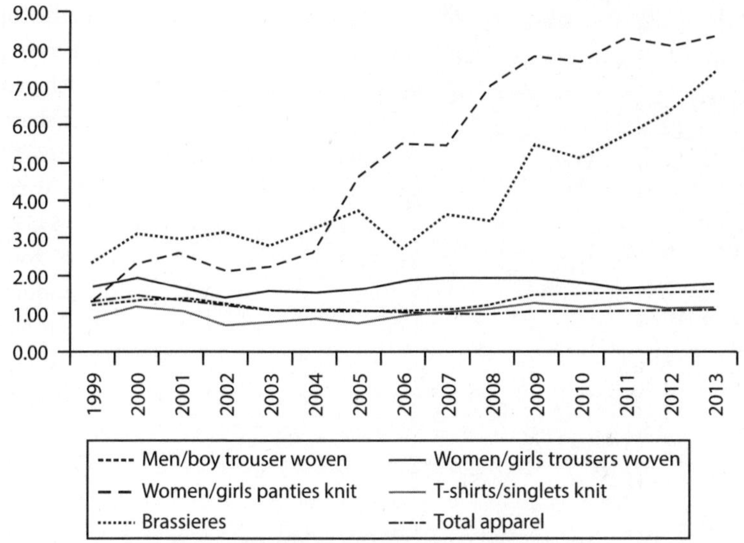

FIGURE 6.1 Sri Lanka's World Market Share in Total Apparel Exports and in the Top 5 Apparel Products (%)

Note: The top 5 apparel products were identified based on export value for 2011–2012.

Source: Based on data compiled from UN Comtrade database.

trade (Balassa 1965).[36] If the value of the RCA exceeds unity for a given product, the country is said to have 'revealed' comparative advantage in the production of that product. In contrast, an *RCA* index of below one implies that country is at a comparative disadvantage in the production of the related product.

The RCA indices are reported in Table 6.6 for all products for which RCA>1 (which we dub 'RCA products') in 2003–04 or 2012–13, in

[36] The RCA index:

$$RCA_{j,i,t} = \frac{X_{j,i,t} / \sum_i X_{j,i,t}}{\sum_j X_{j,i,t} / \sum_j \sum_i X_{j,i,t}}$$

where $X_{j,\,i,\,t}$ is the value of exports by country *j* of product *i* in year *t*. The numerator is the share of product *i* in total exports of country *j* in year *t* and the denominator is the share of product *i* in world (sum of all countries) exports in year *t*.

TABLE 6.6 Sri Lanka's Revealed Comparative Advantage in Apparel Exports and Export Composition: 2003–04 and 2011–12[a]

SITC Code[b]	Product	RCA[c]		Composition (%)	
		2003–04	2012–13	2003–04	2012–13
	(a) RCA-lost products[c]			11.75	3.75
84130	Men/boys jackets woven	2.95	0.43	4.80	0.59
84230	Women/girls jackets woven	1.56	0.4/58	3.66	0.82
84323	Men/boys jackets knit	1.29	0.57	0.69	0.62
84614	Gloves not knit	1.72	0.74	0.30	0.18
84423	Women/girls jackets knit	1.22	0.44	1.35	1.06
84829	Rubber clothing	2.98	0.06	0.22	0.00
84842	Headgear	2.51	0.35	0.12	0.03
84389	Men/boys underwear knit	1.13	0.33	0.06	0.02
84379	Men/boys trousers fibre	1.07	0.62	0.54	0.38
	(b) RCA-sustained products[d]			58.20	56.91
84140	Men/boys trousers woven	1.01	1.44	8.41	9.46
84151	Men/boys trousers cotton woven	1.49	1.328	4.37	3.40
84161	Men/boys underwear woven	1.06	1.34	0.40	0.21
84162	Men/boys pyjamas woven	1.00	2.32	0.17	0.19
84240	Women/girls dresses woven	2.15	1.02	2.80	2.95
84250	Women/girls skirts woven	2.09	1.75	4.20	1.72
84260	Women/girls trousers woven	1.39	1.56	11.51	9.33
84270	Women/girls blouses woven	2.22	1.21	6.96	2.96
84281	Women/girls petticoats woven	5.63	6.30	0.30	0.17
84282	Women/girls nightwear woven	3.78	2.93	1.60	0.63
84289	Women/girls underwear woven	1.86	1.09	0.84	0.32

84371	Men/boys trousers cotton knit	2.20	1.18	2.78	1.47
84481	Women/girls slips knit	2.05	5.85	0.11	0.27
84482	Women/girls panties knit	2.20	7.47	3.53	9.21
84483	Women/first nightwear knit	1.59	2.14	1.37	1.62
84511	Baby clothes woven	2.14	1.39	1.38	0.72
84512	Baby clothes knit	1.08	1.72	1.36	2.33
84551	Brassieres	2.70	5.53	5.43	9.95
84561	Men/boys swimwear not knit	6.65	1.28	0.68	0.08
	(c) RCA-gained products[e]			10.56	24.21
84381	Men/boys underwear knit	0.97	3.00	0.84	2.84
84382	Men/boys nightwear knit	0.51	1.44	0.14	0.36
84540	T-shirts/singlets knit	0.73	1.10	6.64	9.40
84426	Women/girls trousers knit	0.62	1.53	1.00	4.67
84562	Men/boys swim-wear knit	0.31	1.35	0.02	0.10
84564	Women/girls swim-wear knit	0.23	3.62	0.14	2.08
84691	Gloves knit	9.14	10.21	2.07	4.74
	Total [(a)+(b)+(c)]			80.52	84.72
	Other[f]			19.48	15.34

Notes: RCA = Revealed Comparative Advantage.

[a] 2-year average

[b] SITC = Standard International Trade Classification

[c] RCA>1 only in 2003–04

[d] RCA>1 in both 2003–04 and 2011–12

[e] RCA>1 only in 2011–12

[f] RCA<1 in both 2003–04 and 2011–12

Source: Compiled from UN Comtrade database.

order to help understand the change in RCA between pre- and post-MFA periods. The products are classified into three categories: 'RCA-lost': products that had RCA>1 in 2003–04 but RCA<1 in 2011–12; 'RCA-sustained' products: products with RCA>1 both in 2003–04 and 2012–13; and 'RCA-gained' products: products that had RCA<1 in 2003–04 but RCA>1 in 2012–13.

The change in RCA status of the products between 2003–04 and 2012–13 is indicative of the shift in Sri Lanka's revealed comparative advantage towards fashion-basic products during the post-MFA period. Most of the products which have lost RCA between the two time points (in particular, jackets of various types, rubber clothing, headgear, gloves, men's/boy's underwear), are generally classified as basic products. Both RCA-sustained and RCA gained groups are dominated by women's wear, which, as already mentioned, normally have high fashion content. In these groups, RCA indices are much larger for intimate apparel (women/girls slips, women/girls panties, brassieres, and swimwear) compared to the other products. Interestingly, all RCA-gained products are products using knitted fabrics; generally the fashion content is higher in knitted apparel compared to woven apparel. These products accounted for 24 per cent of total apparel exports in 2012–13, up from 10.5 per cent in 2003–04.

The time pattern of value, price (unit value), and volume indices of apparel export from Sri Lanka are also consistent with the structural shift in the commodity composition exports towards high-value products (Figure 6.2). The theory of trade protection predicts a general decline in export prices following abolition of quantitative export restrictions on a given product (Harrigan and Barrows 2009, Krishna and Tan 2001.[37] Consistent with this postulate, a number of recent studies have found a significant decline in prices of apparel imports in the US and other major markets, and also a decline in export prices in individual exporting country levels (Harrigan and Barrows 2009, Staritz 2011, USITC 2011). But in the Sri Lankan case, both volume and price

[37] There are two possible reasons for this. First, binding quotas push up process above the 'natural' market prices. Second, when the number of items that can be exported is limited, there can be a tendency on the part of the exporters to improve the quality and product to maximize export value within the quota limit).

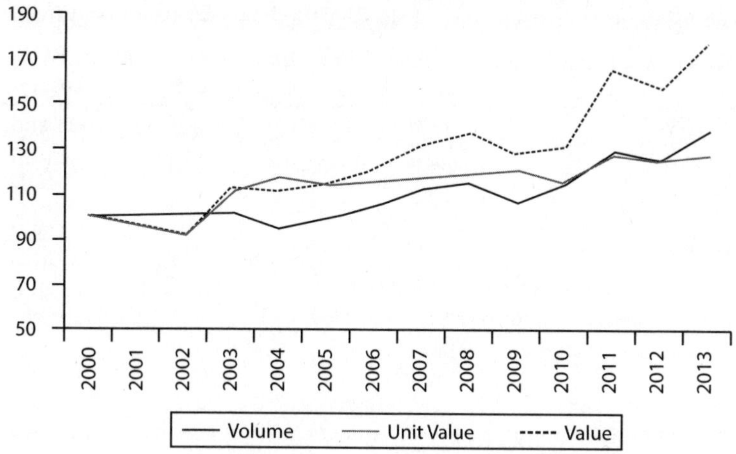

FIGURE 6.2 Volume, Unit Value, and Value Indices of Apparel Exports from Sri Lanka, 1985–2013 (1990 = 100)
Note: Value and unit value series are in US dollar (original series [in rupees] adjusted for changes in the average annual $/Re exchange rate).
Source: Based on data compiled from Central bank of Sri Lanka, *Annual Report* (various issues).

changes seem to have contributed to an increase in export value.[38] This pattern seems to mirror the structural shift in the commodity composition from basic products to fashion-basic (high-value) products. It seems that in the Sri Lankan case, the postulated price-lowering effect of quota removal has been counterbalanced by this structural shift in the commodity composition.

Another indicator of the upward shift in the product mix towards fast-replenishing apparel products is the share of air cargo in total exports (Table 6.7). Air shipment, which is far more costly compared to shipment by sea, is normally used in fashion-basic products which have a short replenishment cycle in order to mitigate competitive

[38] In a comparative study of export parlance, Tewari (2008b) has also found that unit values of export from Sri Lanka (and India's) to the EU remained high during the post MFA era compared to those of the other Asian competitor countries, including Bangladesh, Cambodia, PRC, Pakistan, and Viet Nam).

TABLE 6.7 The Share of Air Cargo in Total Clothing Exports from Sri Lanka (%)

	2000	2004	2008	2011
EU	23.2	18.4	26.4	26.4
Japan	30.1	23.4	23.1	25.2
US	26.8	21.6	39.3	42.3
World	21.0	20.4	32.1	33.7

Note: EU = European Union, US = United States.
Source: Compiled from customs records by mode of transport (accessed through Sri Lanka Export Development Board).

disadvantage arising from the distance to market (Evans and Harrigan 2005). These (in particular high-fashion lingerie) are also generally 'high-value-to-weight products' which permits absorbing the high transport cost into the production cost while maintaining a handsome profit margin. Between 2000 and 2004, the share of air cargo in total apparel exports from Sri Lanka remained virtually unchanged at about 20 per cent and increased to 33.6 per cent in 2011. Amongst the major markets, the share of air cargo in total export was much sharper, from 21.6 per cent in 2004 to 42.3 per cent in 2011. This pattern is consistent with the relatively higher share of fashion basic products (brassiere, in particular) in the composition of exports to the US.

Size Distribution

Data on the size distribution of exporting firms compiled from unpublished exporter/firm-level customs returns is summarized in Table 6.8. The data clearly shows that following MFA abolition, the Sri Lankan apparel industry has been in the process of settling into a smaller core of firms, which are well prepared to take advantage of changing future demand. During the MFA era, export quotas for a given country were set well below the supply potential of the country in a given product. At the same time the quota allocation mechanism at the country level was based on past export performance of manufacturing firms and at times bureaucratic discretion rather than on the export potential of firms. These constraints on the output expansion of firms have disappeared following MFA abolition. In a quota-free world, buyers have also

TABLE 6.8 Size Distribution of Clothing Exporting Firms in Sri Lanka

Cumulative Number of Firms in Ascending Order	Cumulative Export Share (%)			
	2000	2004	2008	2011
Top 3	13.0	13.4	21.8	35.2
Top 5	18.0	18.3	31.2	44.2
Top 10	26.0	27.0	45.2	55.5
Top 20	37.2	39.3	59.1	67.7
Top 30	44.6	48.4	67.4	74.6
Top 40	50.7	55.3	73.4	79.8
Top 50	55.9	60.6	78.1	84.0
Top 60	59.8	64.7	81.5	87.0
Top 70	63.4	68.5	84.6	89.6
Top 80	66.6	71.7	87.0	91.8
Top 90	69.6	74.5	89.1	93.5
Top 100	72.3	77.2	90.9	94.9
Top 150	82.4	87.2	96.2	98.5
Top 200	88.9	93.1	98.5	99.6
All	100	100	100	100
Memo items				
Number of firms	888	817	671	450
Total export ($ million)	2,685	2,762	3,433	4,212
Average export turnover ($ million) of				
top 3 firms	116	124	249	494
top 10 firms	70	75	155	234
top 20 firms	50	54	101	143

Note: Data compilation covered all customs entries with export values of $10,000 and above.

Source: Compiled from firm-level export records maintained by the Sri Lanka Customs (accessed through Sri Lanka Export Development Board).

started looking for competitive, large suppliers and forging long-term procumbent relations with them.

According to customs records, there were 817 exporting firms in 2004 (identified using $10,000 of exports as the minimum cut-off point). This number declined to 671 in 2008 and to 450 in 2011. The data clearly reveals the emergence of a size distribution of firms which is increasingly skewed to the right, with larger firms accounting for the bulk of exports (in value terms). At the upper end, the three largest firms accounted for over 35 per cent of total exports in 2011, up from 13.4 per cent in 2004. In 2011, over two-thirds of exports originated in the top 20 firms, compared to 39 per cent in 2004. At the lower end of size distribution, 250 firms accounted for a mere 3.4 per cent of total exports in 2011. According to information collected from the interviews, most of the small firms undertake subcontracting for the large firms. We found that even a firm which ranks itself within the top 10 firms in terms of the value of its own exports is a major subcontractor to one of the three largest firms. Thus, the trade data does not help in identifying the actual contribution of individual firms to the country's apparel exports. The data reported in Table 6.9, therefore, need to be interpreted as indicative of the increased concentration of 'apparel export trade' in a smaller core of firms. This emerging pattern of concentration would help the apparel industry to face highly competitive market conditions in the post-MFA era.

Direction of Trade

The geographic profile of apparel exports from Sri Lanka has undergone significant changes in the post-MFA period. From the beginning until about 2006, the US was the largest export destination, accounting for more than half to total annual exports. Since then the EU has become the largest export market (Table 6.9, Figure 6.3). Within the EU, the UK, Italy and France, in that order, have been the largest individual countries of destination.

What explains the shift in the relative positions of the US and EU as destinations of apparel exports from Sri Lanka? The popular explanation is the difference in tariff levels (Adhikari and Weeratunge 2007; IPS [Institute of Policy Studies] 2012). As already noted, Sri Lanka is eligible for EU-GSP and was also enjoying zero-duty market accession under GSP-plus during 2005–10. The GSP scheme of the US does not cover textile and apparel and exporters from Africa, Latin America and the Caribbean (which accounts for over 80 per cent of total apparel exports to the US) benefits from handsome tariff concession under various preferential trading arrangements.

Tariff differences may have played a role, but this explanation is not fully consistent with the available data. First, the decline in the share of apparel exports to the US started well before the introduction

Table 6.9 Geographic Profile of Clothing Exports from Sri Lanka, 1990–2012 (%)

	1990–2004	1995–2009	2000–04	2005–09	2010	2011	2012	2012	2013	2014
US	61.7	60.1	60.9	49.42	40.2	38.7	39.3	42.9	42.9	42.5
EU15	31.1	32.8	33.1	43.92	49.5	49	48.5	46.1	45.9	46.3
Belgium	0	1	1.9	2.08	2.9	3.3	3.2	3.7	3.7	3.5
France	4.5	2.9	1.7	1.86	1.9	2	2.4	2.7	2.7	3.5
Germany	10.6	7	3.7	4.74	5.9	5.9	5.6	4.4	4.4	3.9
Italy	1.4	1.2	2.3	8.06	10.6	11.6	10.5	9.6	9.6	10.7
UK	8.9	16.2	20.5	24.04	24.3	22.2	22.4	21.1	21.1	19.3
Canada	2.2	1.9	1.8	1.46	1.7	1.8	2.1	1.9	1.9	1.6
Switzerland	0.5	0.3	0.1	0.12	0.2	0.2	0.2	0.2	0.2	0.2
Japan	1.1	0.7	0.7	0.5	0.7	0.7	0.8	0.9	0.9	1.0
India	0	0.1	0.2	0.34	0.7	0.9	1.2	1.2	1.2	1.1
PRC	0	0	0	0.1	0.2	0.3	0.4	0.4	0.5	0.8
World	1,083[a]	1,881[a]	2,569[a]	3,150[a]	3,178	3,986	3,784	4,265	4,265	4,682

Note: US = United States, EU15 = Comprises the following 15 countries: Austria, Belgium, Denmark, Finland, France, Germany, Greece, Ireland, Italy, Luxembourg, Netherlands, Portugal, Spain, Sweden, United Kingdom, UK = United Kingdom, PRC = People's Republic of China.

[a] Annual average

Source: Compiled from US import records, UN Comtrade database and CBSL (2014).

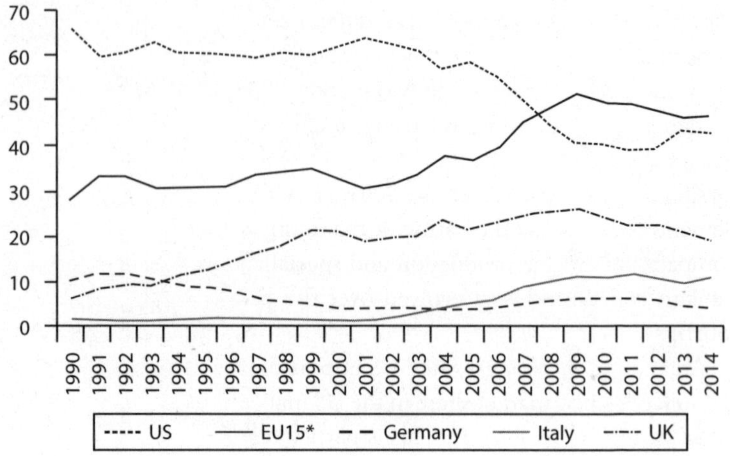

FIGURE 6.3 Direction of Apparel Exports from Sri Lanka, 1990–2014 (%)
Note: US = United States, EU15 = Comprises the following 15 countries: Austria, Belgium, Denmark, Finland, France, Germany, Greece, Ireland, Italy, Luxembourg, Netherlands, Portugal, Spain, Sweden, United Kingdom, UK = United Kingdom.
Source: Based on data compiled from UN Comtrade database.

of GSP+ which was the biggest source of tariff differential between the two destinations during 2005–10 (Figure 6.3). Second, as we have already discussed, the available data on GSP+ coverage and utilization patterns relating to Sri Lanka's exports to the EU suggest that tariff preferences could have had only a marginal impact on the expansion of exports to that market. Third, the data on the source country composition of imports to the US and the EU show that in both markets, a number of Asian exporting countries (which face similar import tariffs as Sri Lanka) have maintained and even gained market shares in the US market, whereas Mexico and a number of other countries in the US periphery lost market shares.

We believe that the major explanation for these market share shifts lies in a combination of the emerging patterns of commodity composition of Sri Lankan exports and differences in demand patterns in the two markets. There is evidence that the EU apparel market is much more heterogeneous: demand is more variable amongst various segments of the market, and hence order sizes are generally smaller compared to exports to the US market. These differences are also reflected in the importance of the type of retailers and international buyers involved in the value chain relating to the two markets. Speciality stores and brand marketers seem to play a relatively much more important role in the EU market compared to the US market which is dominated by large retail stores (Palpacuer et al. 2005; Tewari 2008a). The European demand patterns and the nature or marketing channels are much more compatible with the production and specialization patterns of the Sri Lankan apparel industry evolved over the past two decades (see the fourth section).

An analysis of disaggregated US import data[39] shows that Sri Lanka has in fact gained market share in the US in its top five apparel products (as identified in Tables 6.5). This is particularly the case with intimate wear, in which Sri Lanka accounts for over 15 per cent of total exports to the US, compared to a comparable figure of 8 per cent in the EU. Sri Lanka has lost market shares in various other product categories (mostly basic products) in which Sri Lanka no longer has a competitive advantage compared to the other low-cost Asian exporters such as PRC, Viet Nam, Bangladesh, and Cambodia.

Sri Lanka's market share gains in high value fashion goods in the US market runs counter to the prediction in previous studies that, given the buyers' increased preferences for 'fast fashion', geographic proximity (which underpins timeliness of delivery) would be a key determinant of export success in these products (Abernathy et al. 1999, 2006; Evans and Harrigan 2005). As noted before, the Sri Lankan exporters of high-value apparel products seem to rely heavily on air transport to mitigate the 'tyranny of distance'. Presumably factors such as local availability of fabric, supply chain management capabilities, and close links forged with buyers for over two decades would also have helped.

A related and overlapping reason in the difference between the US and EU relates to the FDI-trade nexus. A large number of firms from EU countries (in particular from UK, Italy, and Germany) have invested in Sri Lanka's apparel industry (Table 6.2) to produce specifically for their home markets. Firm-level data suggests that over 80 per cent of exports of these firms are destined for EU markets. In 2011–12 these

[39] Based on data compiled from the UN Comtrade database (not reported here for brevity).

firms accounted for 30 per cent of total exports to the EU. By contrast there is no significant presence of investors from the US in the Sri Lankan apparel industry, with the notable exception of the links forged by Mast Industries with MAS Holdings and Brandix.

* * *

Following the policy reforms initiated in the late 1970s, Sri Lanka has emerged as a successful participant in the global apparel value chain. The bulk of apparel exports from Sri Lanka are now by full package suppliers. Foreign buyers have played a pivotal role in linking Sri Lankan firms to the GVC and helping them in industrial upgrading, as predicted by the GVC approach. The process of industrial upgrading has unfolded in a distinct national context in which domestic human capital base and entrepreneurship, policy reforms, and proactive engagement of industry associations provide an enabling environment.

An important issue in the contemporary trade and industrial policy debate is whether an import-substitution phase is a precondition for successful transition of the economy to export orientation. In Sri Lanka the new local exporting firms (both those with FDI participation and purely local ones) developed initially following the reforms as exporting ventures independently of the industrial base developed during the import-substitution era. A few firms in the apparel industry established during the import substitution era have successfully ventured into the export business. However, their new operations were largely based on know-how and management inputs obtained though foreign collaboration and/or marketing links established with foreign buyers. Most of the firms, which were exporting to non-competitive Eastern European markets under bilateral trading agreements, disappeared under competitive market conditions after 1977. Moreover, unlike in some other countries, the import-substitution phase did not help the nascent apparel industry by providing the apparel with a competitive domestic fabric base. The domestic fabric base and other ancillary industries grew *following* the rapid expansion of the apparel industry. The recommendation by some 'economists' to develop domestic input linkages of the clothing industry through direct government intervention is not supported by the Sri Lankan experience. Domestic input linkages of the clothing industry should come naturally as part of the expansion of the latter through successful export expansion.

Growth and structural adjustment over three decades through engagement in apparel value change, in particular a niche carved out in high-end markets for intimate apparel (lingerie) and casualwear, seem to have helped the Sri Lankan apparel industry to face competitive market conditions following the termination of the MFA. The industry also has built a strong image of CSR, in particular relating to compliance with internationally agreed employment practices, and improved social and environmental standards. Improvement in the human capital base and design capabilities of the industry has enabled the industry to swiftly respond to buyers' quest for variety. These non-price factors seem to have played a pivotal role in securing export orders, even though Sri Lanka is no longer a low-cost production base compared to many other apparel producing countries in the region. Overall, the Sri Lankan experience demonstrates that apparel is a bundle of differentiated products, not a homogenous commodity as commonly assumed by the trade flow modellers, and individual exporting countries have room for specialization in specific products.

Appendices

Appendix 6A.1: Joint Apparel Association Forum

Following the decision made in 1995 under the Uruguay Round Agreement to phase out MFA, there was a fear that the garment industry in Sri Lanka would be hard hit by competition from the PRC and other low-cost sources. In 2002 leading apparel manufacturing firms joined hands to form the JAAF to prepare the industry to face the post-MFA challenges. It brought together the National Apparel Exporters Association, the Sri Lanka Garment Buying Office Association, the Sri Lanka Chamber of Garment Exporters and the Free Trade Zone Manufacturers Association, which had until then been pursuing their own agendas in an uncoordinated manner.

The JAAF joined hands with the government to formulate a 5-year strategy plan with the aim of consolidating and strengthening the industry. The plan, prepared by a group of leading players in the Apparel industry headed by Mahesh Amalean (CEO of MAS), came up with a road map for transforming the industry from being pure 'contract manufacturers' to providers of 'fully integrated services', encompassing activities across the entire clothing value chain. It emphasized the need to focus on exporting 'high-value' garments to premium markets as opposed to manufacturing low-cost garments for mass consumer markets. Based on an analysis of the past performance of the industry and on-going changes at the global stage, four product categories were earmarked as potential growth areas for Sri Lankan firms: active and sportswear, casual wear, children's clothing and intimate clothing (lingerie). The plan also emphasized the need to shift manufacturers' focus from production to marketing.

Nine committees were established to implement the strategic initiatives. These committees, led by industry pioneers, focused on key areas such as backward integration, human resource and technology advancement, trade, labour and SME initiatives, finance, logistics and infrastructure, and marketing and image building both locally and internationally. A secretariat (initially fully funded by a leading apparel exporting firm, Brandix) was established to coordinate to support the nine committees and oversee the implementation of the strategy. The JAAF strategic plan and policy reports prepared by the committees played a pivotal role in guiding individual firms to restructure their operation to face the post-MFA challenge. A second 5-year plan was issued in 2010. Based on an assessment of the emerging patterns of Sri Apparel exports during the post-MFA years, it focused on strategies for consolidating Sri Lanka's position as a high-value apparel hub in the region.

The JAAF achievements are particularly noteworthy in two main areas: skill development and promoting Sri Lanka's image as an ethical apparel producer. In the area of skill development, its achievements include launching a number of middle-level training programmes jointly with the Katubedda Technical University, establishing four training centres with financial and technical support from United States Agency for International Development (USAID) to train sewing machine operators, and inaugurating a certificate (diploma) course in marketing in collaboration with the Chartered Institute of Marketing, UK.

As part of its attempt to build Sri Lanka's image as an ethical apparel exporter, the JAFF launched a 'Garments without Guilt 'campaign in 2006. The campaign was launched based on market research, jointly funded by the government and the JAFF member companies, in the major export markets in the US and Europe. It placed particular attention on paying fair wages to workers, eliminating the 'sweat shop' image though workplace improvements, avoiding employment of child labour ('children have no business in our businesses'), and creating opportunities for worker education and personal growth. Firms were advised to communicate the new 'Garments without Guilt' image through packing material and corporate communication media such as company letterheads and company websites.

In order to provide third-party assurance of compliance by firms, the JAAF engaged the Swiss based SGS (Société Générale de Surveillance) Group—the world's largest organization in the field of inspection, verification, testing, and certification—to undertake 'Code of Conduct' audits. The top ten apparel-exporting firms and many other medium-sized firms in the Sri Lankan apparel industry are now 'SGS certified'. The JAAF has also been involved in encouraging/helping member firms to obtain Leadership in Energy and Environmental Design (LEED) certification, a third-party verification of energy and water efficient manufacturing environment, from the U.S. Green Building Council.

The JAAF is actively involved as an advisory body to the Sri Lankan government on international trade policy issues relating to apparel trade. It played a key role in GSP+ concessions from the European Union in 2005.

Appendix 6A.2: Profiles of Three Clothing Companies

MAS Holdings

The Amalean family—owners of MAS Holdings, the largest apparel firm in Sri Lanka—has a long history in the textile trading business in Colombo. The three Amalean brothers, Mahesh, Ajay and Sharad cut their teeth on apparel trade by working at a textile trading company founded by their grandfather in 1920. In 1984 they pooled \$10,000 to set up Sigma Industries with 26 Juki sewing machines to produce casual wear (Tafferta jackets) for Sears. Sigma Industries attracted the attention of Martin Trust, the president of Mast Industries, the sourcing arm of The Limited (the largest retailer of upmarket women's apparel in the US) who visited Colombo in November 1985. In 1986, a joint venture with Mast Industries, Unichela (coined from the Pali words of women and apparel) was established to manufacture women's dresses for The Limited (Trust 2007). MAS Holdings (named after the three brothers) was formed in 1987 as the umbrella company of Sigma and Unichela.

When women's dresses exports to the US market soon came under MFA quota restrictions, in 1987 Unichela moved onto production of brassieres, which was still a quota-free product without competition from any other local producer. Mahesh got the idea from a sales catalogue of Victoria's Secret (a newly established lingerie retailer taken over by The Limited a few years ago). He visited the PRC and Hong Kong, China to see how lingerie were made and then with the help of Martin Trust became a supplier to Victoria's Secret. The link forged with Victoria's Secret was the key to MAS's transition from a small venture to a global entity in the ensuing two decades. Following the initial success of Unichela's lingerie operation, Martin Trust helped MAS to form a large new firm in 1989, Shadowline, with MAS, Triumph International (a 100-year-old German lingerie company) and Mast as equal shareholders. This was followed by Bodyline, MAS's first fully-owned brassiere plant in 1992.

Until the early 1990s, MAS's exports were entirely to the US market, with Victoria's Secret accounting for over 80 per cent of total turnover. Diversification of exports to the UK and other EU countries began with the establishment of the Slimline plant in 1993, a joint venture with Courtaulds, a UK-based private label manufacturer (owned by Sara Lee, a US company) to produce briefs for Marks & Spencer. Diversification of the product mix from bras and panties to swimwear began in 2001, with the setting up of Linea Aqua, a joint venture with Speedo (UK) and Brandoit International (a new company formed by Martin Trust) to produce swimwear for Marks & Spencer and Victoria's Secret.

During the next two decades the customer list expanded to encompass a number of other prominent brand-owners including GAP, Triumph, Nike, Adidas, H&M, Ralph Lauren, Columbia, Soma, La Senza, Athleta, Land's End, Warnaco, DBA, and Lululemon. The highlights of its operation as a 'design-to-delivery solution provider' in the global apparel value chain include the 'Nike Revolutionary Sports Bra' (an ultra-lightweight sports bra adjustable three ways to ensure a personalized fit produced using no-sew (or bonded) technology), Fastskin11, a hydrodynamic swimsuit, produced jointly with Speedo for the 2004 Athens Olympics, and the FS Pro swimsuit for the 2008 Beijing

Olympics. In 2007 Victoria's Secret named MAS Holdings its top vendor in the world.

In the late 1990s, when lean retailing began to spread in developed country markets resulting in shortening the traditional fashion cycle from nine months to six weeks, MAS swiftly responded by restructuring its production plans. In 1997, it started two in-house IT consulting firms, one to manage their manufacturing and production information systems and the other to implement the business software solutions processes, 'Systems, Applications & Products' (SAP). MAS was the first Asian apparel company to embrace this new system, which ensured that the goods are ready for shipping within two weeks after receiving an order. SAP enables the foreign buyers to monitor the entire production process and change the order midstream (relating to the colour, size or the mode of delivery), depending on the sales patterns on the shop floor. In 2014 MAS acquired (at $20 million) Attune Consultancy, a well-established Sri Lankan IT firm (established in 2006) which offers SAP-based specialized consultancy in apparel and footwear industries. Attune has a branch network encompassing the US, UK, Germany, India, Sri Lanka, Italy, PRC, Hong Kong, China, and Australia.

After building a large customer base encompassing the US and European markets, in the late 1990s MAS embarked on backward integration within the apparel value chain by establishing input-supplying companies. Most of these new ventures were joint ventures set up with a number of foreign firms, which initially supplied fabric and clothing accessories. In 1995, Stretchline was set up jointly with Chamwood Elastics (UK) to manufacture elastic, a key input for intimate apparel. The other backward-liked ventures formed during the next decade included Linea Intimo, Sri Lanka's first seamless knit operation specializing in performing clothing; Textured Jersey, a joint-venture with Textured Jersey (UK) and Pacific Textiles (Hong Kong, China), to produce weft-knit fabrics; a joint venture with Noyon Dentelles de Calais of France to produce lace; Prym Industries Lanka, a joint venture with Prym Intimates Group in UK to produce bra accessories; Silueta a wholly owned by MAS, to manufacture laminated foam moulded bra cups; a joint venture with Dogi International (Spain) to produce warp-knit fabrics; and Text Print Lanka, a joint venture with Textprint S.A. (Spain) for fabric printing.

In 1996 MAS set up the first offshore apparel plant in Maldives. The Maldivian operation ended in 2005 following the abolition of the MFA.

However, the process of going global gained momentum following the post-MFA years. Intimate Clothing, a subsidiary of MAS Holdings has large production plants in Viet Nam and India. The two factories, in Chennai and Bengaluru, started operation in 2006, and currently employ over 1,500 and 1,300 workers, respectively. The MAS integrated fabric park in India, located in a 714 acre site in Chintavaram in Nellore District, Andhra Pradesh, started operation in 2007 with an initial investment of $200 million. It expects to generate $500 million export revenue and employ 30,000 workers at full capacity. The park is an integral part of MAS's global supply chain integration strategy, and is expected to attract investment in different stages of the manufacturing and finishing process of warp knit fabrics used in the production of corsetry, swimwear, and sportswear. MAS has already set up two joint-venture companies in the park, one with Dogi Spain and Elastic Fabric of the US and the other with Miami Exports (a Sri Lankan firm). A unique feature of the park is a training college, the Asian Institute of Management and Technology (AIMT), a knowledge centre for garment and textile technology, lean manufacturing and CSR and community development programmes.[40]

Stretchline Lanka, MAS's elastics producing subsidiary, has become a multinational in its own right with production plants in the PRC, Indonesia, Mexico, Honduras; sales offices in the UK, the US, and Hong Kong, China; and a research lab in UK jointly run with its parent company. Its UK affiliate, a joint venture with its initial UK partner, engages in R&D activities in addition to coordinating marketing in the UK and Europe. Stretchline is now a well-known provider of 'narrow fabric solutions' to some of the world's leading brands of intimate apparel.

In 2002 MAS became the first OMB apparel producer in Sri Lanka. That year, MAS launched in India a range of lingerie under its own brand name, *Amantē* (meaning 'the lover' in Italian). This brand was developed and designed in Sri Lanka for the premium segment of the lingerie market, to suit the South Asian climate and local taste in colour and print. Before designing it, MAS took measurements from 1,500 women across India because European or East Asian fits would not work in South Asia. After the initial launch in Chennai and Bengaluru, the

[40] Available at http://www.fibre2fashion.com/news/printStory.aspx?new_id=43172 (accessed on 1 October 2016).

Amantē range of lingerie is now sold in departmental stores and regional multi-brand outlets all over India. The range of *Amantē* brand sold in India was initially manufactured in Sri Lanka, but production shifted to the Chennai factory after 3 years. MAS has invested $10 million in the *Amantē* line with the aim of making the product a premier brand in the Asian region. By 2012 *Amantē* had already become 'a close third'(with a market share of 20 per cent) in the premium lingerie market in India, after Enamor and Triumph, which had entered the market a decade ago (Kulamannage 2012, p. 53). *Amantē* was successfully launched in Sri Lanka in October 2012, and MSA has plans to expand its distribution network to Pakistan and the Middle East in the near future.

The remarkable success of MAS has been built on unique management practices. The three brothers worked on the shop floor, supervizing production lines. Rather than treating the business as a source of family cash, the three bothers take salaries based on their title and responsibilities, like any other employee. Any other family members who worked for the company had to start on the shop floor and learn the business. MAS developed its leadership programme with the help of MDA Associates International with which it forged links through Victoria's Secret. Corporate hierarchy was abolished and all employees are encouraged to address one another by their first names. MAS managers eat in the same canteen and use the same restrooms as their workers.

MAS has played a pivotal role in building Sri Lanka's reputation as an ethical apparel producer through progressive human resources policies. From the mid-1980s when it started to become a major supplier to Victoria's Secret, the Amalean brothers have worked hard to reject every element of the sweatshop model; it embraced 'productivity is improved when the workplace is welcoming' as its management motto (Dinankar 2007).[41] MAS conducts English language classes, reproductive health workshops and leadership training programmes, organizes athletic and other social events, and provides maternity clinics, vaccinations, and personal hygiene programmes. In November 2003, MAS launched

[41] Thomas Friedman, who visited a garment factory of the MAS Holdings in 1999 wrote: 'In terms of working conditions, this factory was world-class. Wages aside, I would allow my own daughters work there' (Friedman 2000, p. 177)

a 'worker empowerment' programme called 'Women Go Beyond' in collaboration with Victoria's Secret and GAP. This programme has attracted worldwide attention as an example of ethical employment practice in the apparel industry (Watson 2007). According to MAS's estimates, the total cost of its worker-welfare programmes adds up to about 3-4 per cent of operational cost, but resulting improvement in worker's productivity could be as high as 5 per cent of the average productivity level in the industry (Dinakar 2007).[42]

In 2007, MAS inaugurated its own training school, the MAS Institute of Management and Technology (MIMT), to serve as a 'One Destination Solution' to training requirements in the apparel industry. Located in MAS Fabric Park, it offers a range of training facilities for its own employees and those from other apparel firms. Recently Nike joined hands with MAS to set up a global training facility, the Nike Apparel Innovation and Training Centre (Nike-AITC), at MIMT. Nike-AITC annually trains over 100 personnel from Nike vendors in 15 different countries.

After a quarter century of rapid expansion starting with a 26-machine CTM operation, MAS is now the largest intimate wear (lingerie, leisure-wear, and sportswear) producer in South Asia. In 2011 MAS's total sales touched $1 billion, accounting for nearly 10 per cent of the country's total merchandise exports. It employs over 55,000 in its worldwide operations, with a total employment of over 45,000 in Sri Lankan operations (one of the largest employers in the country).

Brandix Lanka

Brandix Lanka's history dates back to 1969, when the father of Ashrof Omer (the present owner-CEO of Brandix) set up a textile trading house (Firoze Ltd) in Colombo. In 1972 the Ashrof family ventured into apparel manufacturing by setting up Lux Shirts for commercial production of shirts for the domestic market. Following the liberalization reforms in 1977, Ashrof Omer expanded the family business by acquiring a number of sick companies which were not able to face the new competitive environment and restructuring them to undertake

[42] For a detailed account of MAS employment practices and worker-welfare programmes, see Watson (2006, 2010).

subcontracting for foreign buyers. In 1999 Phoenix Ventures was formed by amalgamating the various clothing firms.

The year 1986 was a watershed in the transformation of the family business as a complete service provider in the global apparel value chain. That year LM Apparel was formed as a joint venture of Phoenix and Mast Industries to produce casual wear for The Limited. Within the next decade the group diversified its product range and set up factories to specialize in different areas of apparel manufacturing. Casual wear continued to remain the core of the Brandix group of companies, but the product mix expanded during the past 10 years to encompass lingerie and sportswear. The list of customers expanded to cover well-known brand names including Victoria's Secret, Marks & Spencer, Nike, Speedo, Triumph, La Senza, GAP, DRA, H&M, Lululemon, Oysho and Athleta.

The process of supply chain integration by setting up firms to produce fabric and other accessories began in the mid-1990s. Key investments in the allied fields of dyeing, finishing and printing of textiles, manufacture of thread and apparel accessories, as well as a complete washing plant, enabled the group to provide total apparel solutions. As with the case of MAS these ventures were joint ventures with international firms with long-standing vendor relationships. These ventures include Quenby Lanka, a joint venture with Brandoit International (US) which provides rotary screen and digital printing facilities for both woven and knitted fabrics with a production capacity of 1.5m meters a month.; T & S Buttons Ltd, a joint venture with T & S Buttons (UK) the world's largest manufacturer of buttons, which produces a wide variety of button styles from a range of materials including imitation horn, wood, shell and pearl; Textured Jersey, producing knitted fabrics for the intimate apparel and sportswear industries; Ocean Lanka Ltd (joint venture with Hidramani Group and Fountain Set—the world's largest knit manufacturer headquartered in Hong Kong, China), is Sri Lanka's largest weft-knitted fabric manufacturer producing core products such as jersey, lycra, and fleece and terry towels; Stevenson Lanka, an exclusive garment dyeing facility (joint venture with Stevenson, UK); and A&E Brandix Hangers.

In March 2003 Brandix Lanka, a 'total apparel-solutions provider', was formed by merging Phoenix Ventures and Jewelknit Group (an apparel firm established in 1979 with capital contribution from Mast and a Hong Kong, China based investor) and acquiring the total equity interest of Mast industries. Brandix Lanka is structured into three sectors: Brandix Apparel, Brandix Textiles, and Brandix Investments. Brandix Apparel—the core of the group's business—focuses on product development, manufacturing and marketing of casualwear and intimate apparel. It has a marketing office in Hong Kong, China to coordinate its dealings with global buyers. Brandix Textiles produces fabric, thread, buttons, and hangers for Bradix's own apparel production and also for a number of other apparel producers in the country.

In 1996 the Phoenix College of Clothing Technology (later renamed The Brandix College of Clothing Technology, BCCT), the nation's first academic institution for apparel technology, was set up to train and produce textile and apparel technocrats for the company. BCCT offers tailor-made training programmes for Brandix employees from the grass roots level through to junior and middle level management.

The Brandix group took its first steps to establishing overseas production facilities with the setting up of Eden Fashions (Maldives) in 1996 to circumvent quota restrictions on exports from Sri Lanka. In subsequent years it set up production plants in India and Bangladesh. In 2006, Brandix started developing a 1000 acre vertically integrated textile and garment park ('Brandix India Apparel City', BIAC) in the port city of Visakhapatnam in India's Andhra Pradesh state. It was formally inaugurated in 2010. With an initial investment of $750 million, BIAC is so far the biggest foreign investment in the clothing industry in India. At full capacity, it expects to generate a turnover of $1.2 billion and employ over 60,000. Brandix Apparel Ltd was the first enterprise to start operations in BIAC. It currently employs 1,600 workers and has begun to supply fabric from the Indian base to Brandix apparel firms in Sri Lanka and Bangladesh. A number of other world-class companies involved in various layers of the global apparel supply chain (ranging from spinning, knitting and weaving, clothing accessories, apparel making and embellishment, store services and logistics) have either already set up operations in BIAC or made commitments to do so.

Brandix Casualwear Bangladesh Ltd, a state-of-the-art factory situated in Comilla, a free trade zone in Bangladesh, started operations in October 2010. The factory was designed as a lean manufacturing unit to produce woven bottoms for Marks & Spencer and GAP. With total force at full capacity of 2,800 workers, it is the first apparel firm in Bangladesh to receive 'Plan A' certification for environmentally friendly production from Marks & Spencer.

Brandix, together with MAS, Hidramani and other main apparel producers in the country, has played a pivotal role in promoting Sri Lanka's image as an ethical apparel producer. Over the past decade or so, meeting environmental standards has been a key priory in its factor expansion programme (environmentally friendly practices). In August 2008, Brandix Casualwear's Green Factory at Seeduwa was awarded the Platinum Certificate in the Leadership in Energy and Environmental Design rating system of the US Green Building Council. The Brandix Eco Centre, a converted 30-year old factory, is a lead manufacturing plant for Marks & Spencer. It was formally inaugurated in April 2008 by its CEO, Sir Stuart Rose. The plant's score of 76 of 85 points is the highest in the world by an apparel factory. Brandix Finishing has invested considerably in waste management and good environmental practices. It is the first company in Sri Lanka to achieve 'Deep Green Light' status, the highest rating from the Gap 2005 Global Water Program for meeting global water quality guidelines for vendor laundries. Some of the Brandix Finishing initiatives included wastewater treatment, stringent practice of cleaner production techniques (CPT), installation of a Reverse Osmosis Plant, minimizing water waste during production, installation of a cyclone collector, dust bag filter systems and fume extraction systems, eliminating dye reprocessing, solid waste disposal through re-use or recycling and implementing the Green Productivity Strategy.

The total turnover of Brandix group is rapidly approaching the $1 billion mark. It has a workforce of over 40,000, including 35,000 in 38 production plants in Sri Lanka.

Hidramani Group

The Hidramani Group has a history dating back to 1890 when Parmanand Hirdaramani set up a retail clothing store in Fort, Colombo. The store made a name by introducing the concept of same-day tailoring to passengers of cruise liners that docked at the Colombo Harbour. In 1954 Hidramani Industries was set up for commercial manufacturing of shirts and towels. A subsidiary of Hidramani Industries, Ceylon Knit Trend, was set up in 1974 to produce knitted garments for the export market. This is amongst the few apparel firms set up during the import-substitution era to thrive following the liberalization reforms in 1977.

During the post-reform years Hidramani group has set up over 25 production facilities the country, with a capacity of 13 million pieces per month and a workforce of over 30,000. A comprehensive Product Development Centre (located in Maharagama, a suburb of Colombo) provides design and consultation services for production plants within the group. The customers of the group include over 30 leading international brand owners such as Marks & Spencer, Tesco, True Religion, Levi's, Ralph Lauren, Tommy Hilfiger, Patagonia, Abercrombie and Fitch, and Nike. The group provides a complete product range of knit and woven garments from casual wear to jeans, sleepwear, lounge sportswear and underwear for women, men and children. It is the largest children's-wear producer in the country.

Hidramani Group was the first Sri Lankan apparel producer to set up a production plant overseas. In 1984 it established Comtextile Bangladesh, a joint venture with LT Apparel, a world leader in the children's wear industry. Its operations expanded in the mid-1990s by setting up more state-of-the-art factories (including a sophisticated washing plant, a reverse osmosis water treatment plant and an effluent treatment plant), which meet worker safety and environmental standards required by the buyers. It currently employs over 5,000 people. With a total workforce of over 5,000, Comtextile Bangladesh has also grown to become a large global sourcing company with offices in the US, Hong Kong, China, PRC, Indonesia, Viet Nam, Sri Lanka, India, and Bangladesh. It sources textiles, garments, and accessories for various US and European clients from over 50 factories in the region. Hidramani's Vietnamese venture, Fashion Garments Ltd., was set up in 2002. It is an integrated embroidery plant, with over 38 manufacturing lines and a production capacity of 1.25 million pieces a month.

Hidramani's supply chain integration strategy began with the establishment in 1996 of Ocean Lanka (Pvt) Ltd for producing knitted fabric, jointly with Fountain Set—the world's largest knit manufacturer headquartered in Hong Kong, China, and Brandix Lanka. Paxan Lanka, a joint venture with Paxan Corporation, (US), was set up in 1999, to produce apparel accessories. Hi Fashion (Pvt) Ltd (a fully owned subsidiary of Hirdaramani Group) was set up in 2005 to undertake graphic designing, colour development, and embellishments for its apparel firms.

A unique feature of the Hidramani group is its role as an apparel trading house, in addition to its core role as an apparel producer. Hirdaramani International Export (Pvt) Ltd. located in the Katunayake Export Processing Zone purchases products from local manufacturers for exporting to the US and EU markets.

Hidramani group is an active participant in the JAAF's 'Garments without Guilt' programme. Commitment to ethical employment practices, community development, and sustainable manufacturing have been integral parts of its business expansion strategy. It has developed a reputation amongst major global buyers as an environmental-friendly apparel producer. One of its newly-built factories ('Mihila' in Agalawatte) is the first carbon neutral apparel factory in Asia. Hidramani also produces apparel using fair-traded cotton for a number of leading brand owners.

References

Abayasekara, Ashani. 2013. 'GSP+ Removal and the Apparel Industry in Sri Lanka: Implications and Way Forward', *South Asia Economic Journal*, 14(2): 293–316.

Abernathy, Frederick H., John T. Dunlop, Janice H Hammond, and David Weil. 1999. *A Stich in Time: Lean Retailing and the Transformation of Manufacturing: Lessons from the Apparel and Textile Industries*. New York: Oxford University Press.

Abernathy Frederick H., A. Volpe, and David Weil. 2006. 'The Future of the Apparel and Textile Industries: Prospects and Choices for Public and Private Actors', *Environment and Planning A*, 38(12): 2207–32.

Adhikari, Ratnakar and Chatrini Weeratunge. 2007. 'Textiles and Clothing in South Asia Current Status and Future Potential', *South Asia Economic Journal*, 8(2): 171–203.

Arunatilake, Nisha, Priyanka Jayawardena, and Dushni Weerakook. 2011. 'Sri Lanka', in Saman Kelegama (ed.), *Migration, Remittances and Development in South Asia*, pp. 112–40. New Delhi: Sage.

Athukorala, Prema-chandra. 2012. 'Sri Lanka's Trade Policy: Reverting to Dirigisme?', *World Economy*, 35(12): 1662–86.

Athukorala, Prema-chandra and Sarath Rajapatirana. 2000. *Liberalization and Industrial Transformation: Sri Lanka in International Perspective*. Delhi: Oxford University Press.

Athukorala, Prema-chandra and Weligamage D. Lakshman. 1985. 'Activities of Transnational Trading Corporations in the Sri Lankan Economy',

Transnational Trading Corporations in Selected Asian and Pacific Countries, ESCAP/UNCTC, Bangkok, pp. 312–66.

Audet, Denis. 2007. 'Smooth as Silk? A First Look at the Post MFA Textiles and Clothing Landscape', *Journal of International Economic Law*, 10(2): 267–84.

Bair, Jennifer (ed.). 2009. *Frontiers of Value Chain Research*. California: Stanford.

Balassa, Bela. 1965. 'Trade Liberalisation and Revealed Comparative Advantage', *Manchester School*, 33(1): 99–123.

Bonacich, E., L. Cheng, N. Chinchilla, N. Hamilton, P. and Ong (eds). 1994. *The Garment Industry in the Restructuring Global Economy. Global Production: The Apparel Industry in the Pacific Rim*, 3–18.

CBSL. 2014. *Annual Report 2013*. Colombo.

Doner, Richard F. and Ansil Ramsey. 1984. 'Thailand in the Pacific Rim Garment Industry', in Edna Bonacich, Lucie Cheng, Nora Chinchilla, Norma Hamilton, and Paul Ong (eds), *Global Production: The Apparel Industry in the Pacific Rim*, pp. 180–96. Philadelphia: Temple University Press.

The Economist. 2008. 'Sri Lanka: Not Many Pleases', 14 August. Available at http:/www.economist.com/node/11921197 (accessed on 8 September 2016).

Evans, Carolyn L. and James Harrigan. 2005. 'Distance, Time, and Specialization: Lean Retailing in General Equilibrium', *American Economic Review*, 95(1): 292–313.

Feenstra, Robert C. and Gary Hamilton. 2006. *Emerging Economics, Divergent Paths*. Cambridge: Cambridge University Press.

Fernando, Mario and Shamika Almeida. 2012. 'The Organizational Virtuousness of Strategic Corporate Social Responsibility: A Case Study of the Sri Lankan Family-Owned Enterprise MAS Holdings', *European Management Journal*, 30(6): 564–76.

Friedman, Thomas L. 2000. *Lexus and the Olive Tree*. New York: Anchor Books.

Fung, Victor, William K. Fung, and Yoram Wind. 2007. *Competition in a Flat World: Building Enterprises for a Borderless World*. Upper Saddle River, New Jersey: Wharton School Publishing.

Gereffi, Gary. 1994. 'The Organization of Buyer-Driven Global Commodity Chains: How US Retailers Shape Overseas Production Networks', in Gary Gereffi and M. Korzeniewicz (eds), *Commodity Chains and Global Capitalism*, pp. 95–122. Westport, Connecticut: Preager.

———. 1999. 'International Trade and Industrial Upgrading in the Apparel Commodity Chain', *Journal of International Economics*, 48(1): 37–70.

Gereffi, Gary, John Humphrey, and Timothy Sturgeon. 2005. 'The Governance of Global Value Chain', *Review of International Political Economy*, 12(1): 78–104.

Gereffi, Gary and Stacey Frederick. 2010. 'The Global Apparel Value Chain, Trade and Crisis: Challenges and Opportunities for Developing Countries', in Oliver Cattaneo, Gary Gereffi, and Cornelia Staritz (eds), *Global Value Chain in a Post-Crisis World: A Development Perspective*, pp. 157–208. Washington, D.C.: World Bank.

Gunawardana, Samanthi. 2007. 'Struggle, Perseverence, and Organization in Sri Lanka's Export Processing Zones', in Kate Bronfenbrenuer (ed.), *Global Union: Challenging Transnational Capital through Cross-Border Campaigns*, pp. 78–98. Ithaca: Cornel University Press.

Hamilton, Gary G. and Gary Gereffi. 2009. 'Global Commodity Chains, Market Makers, and the Rise of Demand-Responsive Economies', in Jennifer Bair (ed.), *Frontiers of Commodity Chain Research*, pp. 136–61. Stanford, California: Stanford University Press.

Harrigan, James and Geoffrey Barrows. 2009. 'Testing the Theory of Trade Policy: Evidence from the Abrupt End of the Multifiber Arrangement', *Review of Economics and Statistics*, 91(2): 282–94.

Hale, Angela and Jane Wills. 2008. *Threads of Labour: Garment Industry Supply Chains from the Workers' Perspective*. New York: Wiley.

IPS. 2012. *Sri Lanka: State of the Economy 2012*. Colombo.

Irwin, Douglas A. 2009. *Free Trade under Fire*. Princeton New Jersey: Princeton University Press.

Jacob, Rahul. 2013. 'The Right Genes for Making Jeans', *Financial Times*, 22 January. http://www.ft.com/cms/s/0/d4191430-647b-11e2-934b-00144feab49a.html#axzz4Km6wisDL (accessed on 20 August 2013).

Iskyan, Kim. 2012. 'Bros Makes Bras', *Echelon*, Colombo, November, pp. 52–57.

Jassin-O'Rourke Group, LLC. 2008. 'Global Apparel Manufacturing Labour Cost Analysis 2008', http://www.nctextileconnect.com/documents/resources/GlobalApparelLaborCostSummary2008.pdf (accessed on 20 August 2013).

Joarder, Mohammad, Abdul Munim, A.K.M. Hossain, and Md Mahbubul Hakim. 2010. 'Post-MFA Performance of Bangladesh Apparel Sector', *International Review of Business Research Papers*, 6(4): 134–44.

Jones, Richard. 2006. *The Apparel Industry*. Oxford: Basil Blackwell.

Keesing, Donald B. and Martin Wolf. 1980. 'Textile Quota against Developing Countries', Thames Essay 23, London.

Kelegama, Saman. 2006. 'Ready-made Garment Industry: Preparing to Face the Challenge', in Saman Kelegama (ed.), *Development Under Stress: Sri Lankan Economy in Transition*, pp. 212–26. New Delhi: Sage Publications.

———. 2009. 'Ready-made Garment Exports from Sri Lanka', *Journal of Contemporary Asia*, 39(4): 579–96.

Kelegama, Saman and Fritz Foley. 1999. 'Impediments to Promoting Backward Linkages from the Garment Industry in Sri Lanka', *World Development*, 27(8): 1445–60.

Krishna, Kala M. and Ling Hui Tan. 2001. *Rags and Riches: Implementing Apparel Quotas under the Multi-Fibre Arrangement*. Ann Arbour: University of Michigan Press.

Kulamannage, Shamindra. 2012. 'Ajay Eyes Lankan Women after Indian Conquest', *Echelon*, Colombo, December, pp. 52–56.

Neidik, Binnur and Gary Gereffi. 2006. 'Explaining Turkey's Emergence and Sustained Competitiveness as a Full-Packaged Supplier of Apparel', *Environment and Planning A*, 36: 2285–303.

Nordås, Hildegunn Kyvik. 2003. 'The Impact of Trade Liberalization on Women's Job Opportunities and Earnings in Developing Countries', *World Trade Review*, 2(2): 221–31.

———. 2009. 'The Global Textile and Clothing Industry Post the Agreement on Textiles and Clothing', discussion paper no. 5, World Trade Organization (WTO), Geneva, Switzerland.

MAS Holdings. 2007. *20 Years Uncovered: The MAS Story*. Colombo: MAS Holdings.

McIntyre, Richard P. 2008. *Are Worker Rights, Human Rights*? Ann Arbour: University of Michigan Press.

Olson, Richard S. 1977. 'Expropriation and International Economic Coercion: Ceylon and the West, 1961-65', *Journal of Developing Areas*, 11(2): 205–26.

Perry, Patsy. 2012. 'Exploring the Influence of National Cultural Context on CSR Implementation', *Journal of Fashion Marketing and Management*, 16(2): 141–60.

Pickles, John and Adrian Smith. 2011. 'Delocalization and Persistence in the European Clothing Industry: The Reconfiguration of Trade and Production Networks', *Regional Studies*, 45(2): 67–185.

Pipkin, Seth. 2011. 'Local Means in Value Chain Ends: Dynamics of Product and Social Upgrading in Apparel Manufacturing in Guatemala and Colombia', *World Development*, 39(12): 2119–31.

Rhee, Yung Whee. 1990. 'The Catalyst Model of Development: Lessons from Bangladesh's Success with Garment Exports', *World Development*, 18(2): 333–46.

Ruwanpura, Kanchana N. and Neil Wrigley. 2011. 'The Costs of Compliance? Views of Sri Lankan Apparel Manufacturers in Times of Global Economic Crisis', *Journal of Economic*, 11(6): 1031–49.

Staritz, Cornelia. 2010. *Making the Cut? Low Income Countries and the Global Value Chain in Post-Quota and Post-Crisis World*. Washington, D.C.: World Bank.

Srinivasan, Thirukodikaval N. 1998. *Developing Countries and the Multilateral Trading System: From the GATT to the Uruguay Round and the Future*. Delhi: Oxford University Press.

Subramanian, Arvind and Devesh Ray. 2003. 'Who Can Explain the Mauritian Miracle?', in Dani Rodrik (ed.), *In Search of Prosperity: Analytical Narratives of Economic Growth*, pp. 205–43. Princeton, New Jersey: Princeton University Press.

Tewari, Meenu. 2008a. 'Varieties of Global Integration: Navigating Institutional Legacies and Global Networks in India's Garment Industry', *Competition and Change*, 12(1): 49–67.

———. 2008b. 'Deepening Interregional Trade and Investment in South Asia: The Case of the Textile and Clothing Industry', Working Paper No. 213, Indian Council for Research on International Economic Relations, New Delhi.

Tokatli, Nebahat, and Ömür Kızılgün. 2010. 'Coping with the Changing Rules of the Game in the Global Textiles and Apparel Industries: Evidence from Turkey and Morocco', *Journal of Economic Geography*, 10(2): 209–29.

Trust, Martin. 2007. *20 Years Uncovered: The MAS Story*. Colombo: MAS Holdings, 16–18, chapter 'Trust in MAS'.

USITC. 2011. *The Economic Effects of Significant U.S. Import Restraints* (Seventh Update). Washington, D.C.

Watson, Noshua. 2006. *MAS Holdings: Strategic Corporate Social Responsibility in the Apparel Industry*. Paris: Paris Business School (INSEAD). Available at www.thecasecentre.org/educators/products/view?id=68319 (accessed on 12 September 2016).

———. 2007. 'MAS and the Women Go Beyond Programme', in *Embedding Human Rights in Business Practice II* (United Nations Global Impact project), United Nations, Geneva, pp. 85–88.

Wijesiri, Janaka and Jagath Dissanayake. 2008. 'The Ending of the Multi-Fibre Agreement and Innovation in the Sri Lankan Textile and Clothing Industry', *OECD Journal: General Papers*, 8(4): 157–88.

7

RAJAT KATHURIA
MANSI KEDIA
UTTARA BALAKRISHNAN

Mapping the Future of High Value Manufacturing in India*

After Independence, the overarching objective of India's economic policy was to achieve self-sufficiency with state provision of the 'commanding heights' of the economy. Industrialization driven by the state was the preferred instrument to achieve multiple objectives including growth, equity, and jobs. In the decades immediately after Independence, India's industrial policy helped create a diversified and sophisticated export basket, establishing comparative advantage in 'core' products (metals, machinery, and chemicals) much more than was implied by India's prevailing per capita income (Felipe 2010).

Beginning in the 1990s, a services revolution gripped India. Services' contribution to gross domestic product (GDP) increased from 42 to 60 per cent between 1990 and 2014. A substantial amount of empirical literature cites several reasons for the growing ascendancy of services, such as splintering of industrial activity, rising demand for services exports, high income elasticity of demand, and the distinctive role of

* Opinions and recommendations in the chapter are exclusively of the author(s) and not of any other individual or institution including Indian Council for Research on International Economic Relations (ICRIER).

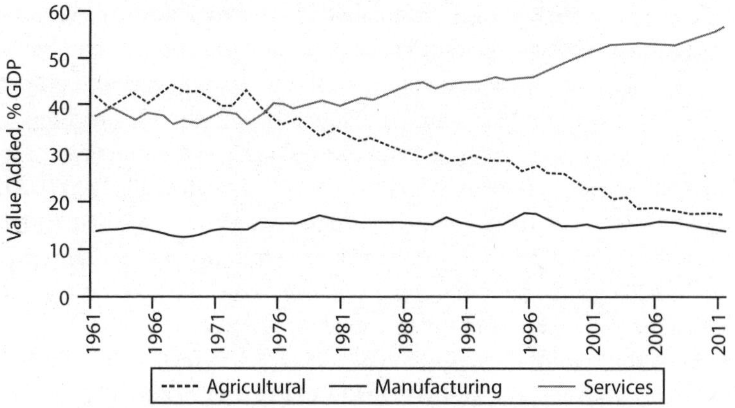

FIGURE 7.1 Value Added as a Percentage of Gross Domestic Product
Note: GDP = gross domestic product.
Source: World Bank Open Database, available at http://data.worldbank.org/ (accessed in 2013).

economic reforms in India (Gordon and Gupta 2004). At the same time, the share of manufacturing in GDP stagnated at around 15 per cent and has not recovered since. Figure 7.1 shows the sharp contrast in growth rates of agriculture, manufacturing, and services in the last five decades. According to India's recent National Manufacturing Policy (NMP, 2011), the contribution of manufacturing to India's GDP is 'much below potential'. The policy target is to reach an ambitious 25 per cent—comparable to other Asian economies that have consistently breached the 25 per cent mark.[1]

Growth driven by manufacturing finds widespread support for its ability to create scale, generate spillovers, engender technical progress, and induce overall productivity enhancements in the economy. India's structural transformation differs sharply from the traditional pattern. Recent research hints at the possibility of services emerging as the engine of growth for India by absorbing surplus labour from the agricultural sector (Eichengreen and Gupta 2011).

[1] According to National Manufacturing Policy, 2011, the share of manufacturing in GDP for both the People's Republic of China (PRC) and the Republic of Korea was 30 per cent in 2010.

However, questions over sustainability have meant that not everyone is as sanguine about services-led development. Moreover, the enormous labour pool and unrealized potential of the manufacturing sector in India does raise apprehensions of 'de-industrialization' from time to time.[2] Recent policy changes recognize the need to revive manufacturing from its stasis. The NMP and the Twelfth Five Year Plan (2012–17) acknowledge that there exists an urgent need to attain 'depth' and 'breadth' in manufacturing, implying a need for improving current production efficiency and underlining the importance of diversifying into more complex products in the manufacturing value chain.[3]

Since the seminal work of Kuznets (1971), the reallocation of economic activity across the three broad sectors (agriculture, manufacturing, and services) has generated significant interest both amongst scholars and policymakers. More recently, the literature on structural transformation examines its role in growth diagnostics and emphasizes the accumulation of complex capabilities such as in high value production.[4] As companies increasingly invest in improving technology and processes, hiring practices (especially in developed countries) have begun to favour high skills (McKinsey Global Institute 2012).

While the stagnation in manufacturing has attracted considerable research attention, India's conspicuous absence from high value manufacturing (HVM) is relatively uncharted terrain (Bardhan 2006; Mohan 2002; Nagaraj 2006; Panagariya 2008). One reason is the want of an internationally accepted definition of what constitutes 'high value'. This chapter attempts to bridge that gap and further uses the crafted methodology as the basis for an empirical evaluation of India's current capabilities (or lack thereof) as well as to draw comparisons with our chosen comparator countries, that is, the People's Republic of China (PRC), the Republic of Korea, and Japan. Finally, we analyse the opportunities for structural transformation towards high value products using Hausmann's Product Space framework.

[2] Felipe and Estrada (2008), using a logistic regression and controlling for income per capita, population and the share of trade in GDP, estimate a gap of about 5 percentage points in the share of India's manufacturing sector.

[3] Lack of depth manifests in two ways in India—(i) low level of value addition in manufacturing, and (ii) growing imports of capital equipment which are the building blocks of manufacturing competitiveness (Planning Commission 2011).

[4] We define 'high value' in the second section of the chapter.

To the best of our knowledge, this chapter represents the first attempt to define and investigate HVM in India. The rest of the chapter is organized as follows: the next section conceptualizes a definition for HVM along with the methodology and results. The second section after that introduces the concept of the product space and examines India's exports of HVM products and the potential for expanding these capabilities. The third section reviews the importance of industrial policy in economic development, especially with respect to high value production, and examines India's current industrial policy for those high value industries that constitute India's opportunity set. The fourth section concludes and offers policy recommendations based on extensive primary and secondary data analysis in the backdrop of the emerging economic environment.

Conceptualizing High Value Manufacturing

Arriving at a Definition of High Value Manufacturing

Manufacturing has undergone an interesting evolution. For much of the early twentieth century manufacturing largely focused on assembly line mass production where rolling out standardized products was the norm (Milgrom and Roberts 1991). In the latter half of the twentieth century, manufacturing began to be increasingly characterized by flexible processes and product differentiation (Hayes and Pisano 2000). Flexible manufacturing obviated the need for 'focused' factories. Since new technology could assist in easily and cheaply switching from one task to another, a firm could produce a wide variety of outputs in small batches. Flexible manufacturing enabled customization and allowed firms to exploit economies of scope for production of differentiated products (Eaton and Schmitt 1994).

In recent times, integration has paved the way for rise in global and regional production networks, necessitating a rethink in the competitive landscape of manufacturing.[5] Having failed to capitalize on the global value chain (GVC) phenomenon despite proximity to East Asia, India remains a small player in world manufacturing trade. Product categories such as electronics and electrical goods manufactures that are

[5] Available at http://www.globalvaluechains.org/concepts.html (accessed on 1 October 2016).

characterized by global production sharing comprise a very small share of India's exports.

Since modern manufacturing transcends mere production, there is need to develop a broader definition. Policy is currently designed based on the existing definition of manufacturing through the use of international industry codes[6] that view manufacturing and production as synonymous.[7] The Institute for Manufacturing, United Kingdom (UK) recognizes manufacturing as constituting the full cycle of activities from research and development (R&D), through design, production, logistics, and services to end-of-life management. Such an end-to-end approach implies that manufacturing *creates* value not just in production but through these other means as well. In other words, 'HVM' *cannot* simply include those industries which generate high revenue through their production activities. Recent attempts to arrive at what constitutes HVM include:

- The application of leading-edge technical knowledge and expertise to the creation of products, production processes, and associated services which have strong potential to bring sustainable growth and major economic benefits (Technology Strategy Board 2012).
- High value manufacturers can create value through unique production processes, high brand recognition, rapid delivery times, or highly customized services (Livesey 2006).
- High value manufacturers have strong financial performance, are strategically important to the regional and national economy, contribute to national R&D, and have positive social impact through environment performance, sourcing policies and community involvement (Institute for Manufacturing 2006).
- High value manufacturers are those that do not compete primarily on cost. Instead they deliver value for one or more of their *stake-*

[6] International industry classifications are of broadly three types: those that classify economic activities, products, and traded goods and services. The most commonly used classifications include the International Standard of Industrial Classification (ISIC); the Central Product Classification (CPC); and the Harmonized Commodity Description and Coding System (HS) and Standard International Trade Classification (SITC).

[7] See Appendix 7A for existing industry classifications and their shortfalls.

holder groups by contracting for capability, delivering product/service innovation, establishing process excellence, achieving high brand recognition, and/or contributing to a sustainable society. There are four pillars that help firms achieve these ends—products, manufacturing processes, service systems, and global value systems (Martinez et al. 2007).

The common characteristics in these definitions help us develop functional and estimable indicators of HVM in two ways—one based on outcomes (that is, outcome-related dimensions) and the other on enabling dimensions (see Table 7.1). Outcome-related dimensions measure the existence and extent of HVM and can be disaggregated into their financial, social, and strategic values.[8] The enabling dimensions focus on inputs and processes and can be categorized into high skill and high technology (HSHT), high capital intensity, and high process flexibility. These conform to the vision articulated in the NMP.[9]

Approaches Used to Identify High Value Manufacturing Industries

The ideal approach to arrive at an indicator for HVM would be to integrate both the *outcome-related* and the *enabling* dimensions. However, paucity of data constrains us. No single data source is able to provide information for all variables across countries and over time, with sufficient granularity. We, therefore, employ two different approaches to develop indicators for HVM industries and products. Both approaches are described as follows.

Approach I

This approach uses the outcome-related dimensions and provides a quantitative measure of how financial, social, and strategic values—

[8] This uses the definition of value employed by Livesey (2006).

[9] These include the acquisition of technological depth in manufacturing; creation of a strong indigenous value chain addition element; and creation of appropriate skill sets.

which are outcomes of the manufacturing process—are created. An index is developed using data at the 4-digit ISIC[10] level from United Nations Industrial Development Organization's (UNIDO's) Industrial Statistics INDSTAT4 Database for India and our comparator set—the Republic of Korea, PRC and Japan.[11] The methodology[12] is inspired by the one used to create the global innovation index (GII).[13]

Our index is a composite of three separate indices—financial, social, and strategic. Financial value is determined using value added,[14] social value is determined using wages and salaries,[15] and strategic value is determined using number of employees. Lack of sufficiently disaggregated data at the 6-digit level obliges us to conduct the analysis at the 4-digit level. The values are normalized in the [0, 100] range using the min-max method with higher scores representing better outcomes.[16] Following the normalization, we construct a combined HVM index by taking a simple average of the three separate indices. The advantage of the index is its simplicity, although this is perhaps also its primary weakness. While the variables measuring financial, social, and strategic value are potentially correlated, this does not bias the results since the index does not require individual variables to be independent. Assigning equal weight to each of the three sub-indices to arrive at our composite HVM index is at best a starting point. Besides, we are unable to identify an exact numerical point in the index to separate low, medium, and high values. Missing data is also a concern as country database often do not reflect newer industry groupings at the 4-digit level. Despite these shortcomings, the index does provide some interesting insights, discussed as follows.

[10] This refers to International Standard Industrial Classification

[11] The database contains data at the ISIC Rev 3 level

[12] The year used for all the variables was 2007, which was the latest year for which data was available for all four countries

[13] The GII is a composite index of two separate indices—the Innovation Input Sub-Index; and the Innovation Output Sub-Index. The GII is the simple average of these two indices. These indices are composed of pillars which are weighted averages of individual indicators.

[14] In the absence of better measures such as economic value added, we have used data on gross value added for the purpose of this analysis.

[15] Measured in $1,000 across countries.

[16] Actual Value–Minimum Value × 100

Maximum Value–Minimum Value

TABLE 7.1 Outcome and Enabling Dimensions of High Value Manufacturing

Outcome-Related Dimensions	Enabling Dimensions
Financial value: Financial value can be understood in terms of revenue. The most commonly used indicator in this regard is value added. Value added is generally defined as sales less the cost of bought-in materials, components, and services. It is the value generated of a product at each stage of production (Livesey 2006). The most reliable value-based measure is considered to be economic value added (EVA) which is the economic profit generated by a firm. **Social value:** While social value for a country would be a measure of minimal environmental impact, for a firm and its employees it would be wages and salaries. According to Milberg and Winkler (2010), social upgrading is based on the concept of 'decent work' developed by the International Labour Organization (ILO). Decent work accounts for four aspects—employment, social protection, workers' rights, and social dialogue. Wages and salaries is used a proxy for social value. **Strategic value:** Strategic value measures the spillover effects of industries on other components of economy that are of strategic importance including sustainable employment creation.	**Skill:** According to most empirical studies in trade economics, skill is measured using industry data on *production* versus *non-production* workers. However labour economists prefer using worker's education as a proxy for skill (Anderson, Robertson, and Smith 2001) **Technological intensity:** The OECD defines technologically intensive industries as those which spend a large proportion of their revenue on research and development (R&D). Moreover, products from these industries contain or embody technologies developed from R&D. **Capital intensity:** Capital intensity in its simplest form is the relative amount of capital used in production vis-à-vis other factors of production. Capital intensity is popularly measured using capital–labour ratio in production. Other measures include return on net assets. **Process flexibility:** Manufacturing flexibility is generally defined as the ability of a manufacturing system to respond efficiently, cost effectively, and do so in a time-bound manner to changing production needs and requirements (Kaschel and Bernal 2006).[17] The variables that can be used to measure process flexibility include delivery times, service response time, sales from new products, and lead time.

Note: EVA = economic value added, ILO = International Labour Organization, OECD = Organisation for Economic Co-operation and Development, R&D = research and development.

Source: Compiled by authors.

[17] According to Gerwin (1993), flexibility need not always be an adaptive response to environmental uncertainty. He claims that a firm can actively encourage flexibility by making customers see the benefit of new products, shorter lead time, amongst other factors.

RESULTS FROM APPROACH I

For India, textile fibre preparation and textile weaving achieve the highest value due to the labour-intensive nature of production (see Appendix Tables 7B.1–7B.4). Recall that large numbers employed in this sector leads to a high score on strategic value. The top ten industries are dominated by labour intensive and/or resource intensive industries. India's abundance of cheap labour drives the value of the index—pharmaceuticals and automobile parts are the only two high-value sectors not categorized as labour intensive.[18] Amongst the four nations, PRC achieves the highest index value of 68, almost double that of Japan at 37 and extraordinarily higher than the Republic of Korea and India that clock in at 12 and 7, respectively. The PRC's dominance is largely attributable to the strategic value index estimate. In addition, since growth in the PRC has been driven by the manufacturing sector, the financial value index is also high[19].

What is also striking is the presence of similar industries amongst the top ten for India and the PRC. Basic iron and steel, apparel, and textile fibre preparation are common to both countries. However, in products such as electronic valves and tubes and auto components that exhibit high index values, the PRC resembles the Republic of Korea and Japan much more than India. The PRC has also developed capabilities in office and computing machinery. The HVM index, while simple, offers insights into the existing levels of 'sophistication' in manufacturing across the four countries. The dominance of PRC and its imitation of the Republic of Korea and Japan in sectors of strategic and social

[18] The success of the Indian pharmaceutical industry in India is well documented. From 1972 to 2004, India's pharmaceutical industry has grown to be the fourth largest in the world in volume terms (Haley and Haley 2012). The size of the industry has exploded from Rs 100 million in 1947 to about Rs 500 billion in 2008. While foreign firms were the major players in the industry in 1950s and 1960s and drug prices were very high, the 1970s saw a process revolution with acquisition of technological capability helped in part by a weak patent regime. The Indian pharmaceutical industry embarked on the process of technological learning based on reverse engineering. This was facilitated by a policy environment that was very conducive and had a focused growth strategy for the industry. The fifth section explores the pharmaceutical industry in greater detail and provides case studies of companies and their growth stories which will provide us a perspective on the industry and its future growth prospects.

[19] Manufacturing value added for the PRC in 2010 was close to $1.1 trillion.

significance is palpable. However, since the index is driven by social and strategic values, the absence of technical and skill-related dimensions encourages us to explore a second approach that has technology and high skill as its core.

Approach II

The second approach is based on value-enabling dimensions—primarily, skills and technology. Since a large number of existing definitions for HVM emphasize skills and technology, this approach treats HSHT as synonymous with high value. We use United Nations Conference on Trade and Development's (UNCTAD's) classification at the 6-digit level[20] to identify HSHT-intensive manufactures that hereafter constitute our HVM group.[21] This method has been commonly applied to identify HVM *products* and differs from the aforementioned *industries* approach, in that it is employed at a disaggregated 6-digit level as opposed to the 4-digit level of Approach I.

Since technology and skills evolve only gradually, our data set of 2011 represents findings that have contemporary policy relevance. Of these, products that exhibit revealed comparative advantage (RCA) in the Balassa (1965)[22] tradition and contribute significantly to a country's exports are studied in greater detail to understand the underlying basis for their competitiveness. Data for computing RCA (based on the Ricardian concept of comparative advantage) and export shares have been extracted from the World Integrated Trade Solutions (WITS) database.

[20] The UNCTAD classification separates the products into the following categories: Non fuel primary commodities; Resource-intensive manufactures; Low skill- and technology intensive manufactures; Medium skill- and technology intensive manufactures; HSHT-intensive manufactures; and Mineral fuels.

[21] Available at http://www.unctad.info/en/Trade-Analysis-Branch/Data-And-Statistics/Other-Databases/(UNCTAD Basu forthcoming)

[22] In this study we employ Balassa's (1965) measure of relative export performance by country and commodity, defined as a country's share of world exports of a commodity divided by its share of total world exports. The index for country *i* and commodity *j* is: $RCA_{ij} = (X_{ij}/X_{wj})/\ (X_i/X_w)$. The RCA can take a value between 0 and $+\infty$. If the RCA>1, then the country has RCA in the particular product.

Results from Approach II[23]

Following the international trade literature, a product can be intensive in resource, skill, or technology.[24] In our group of comparator countries, Japan is the leader in HSHT products while resource-intensive goods that exhibit RCA form a larger share of exports for India and the PRC (compared to Japan and the Republic of Korea, Table 7.2). While the share of high value in total exports for India, PRC, and the Republic of Korea is similar—at around 20 per cent—the composition is quite different (see Appendix Tables 7B.9–7B.12). For example, in India HSHT mainly consists of chemicals, while the share of electronics, electrical apparatus, computers, and machinery is important for others. Moreover, the absolute value of HSHT exports from India is a fraction of that from Japan and the Republic of Korea. In addition, both India and the PRC record a small share of medium-skill and technologically intensive commodities (10 and 15 per cent, respectively) in total exports. For Japan and the Republic of Korea these numbers are higher at 31 and 22 per cent, respectively, reflecting the capability set developed by them to progressively move up the value chain, including institutional linkages and market integration. The emergence of industrial clusters (discussed later) is a driver of HVM in these countries.

Our results show that India has comparative advantages in 270 of the total 1024 HSHT products at the HS 6-digit level. The top 10 products in descending order of their RCAs are listed in Appendix Table 7B.5 (refer to Appendix Tables 7B.6–7B.8 for products in Japan, the PRC and the Republic of Korea). Interestingly, products with high RCAs are not necessarily those with high export shares (Appendix Table 7B.9). The *other organic compounds category* is an exception since export shares of commodities such as benzene, insecticides, and polypropylene are high due to the low world trade in these commodities. Pharmaceuticals, basic chemicals, and plastics are HSHT products exported from India with RCA. These products also have the highest share in total exports from India. Mapping these products to the ISIC code shows the corresponding industry category. Table 7.3 provides a summary of the top five industries (using ISIC codes).

[23] The analysis in this section uses data from 2011 which is the latest year for which data for all four countries is available.

[24] Factor intensity provides the relative proportion of the various factors of production used to make a given a product.

TABLE 7.2 Percentage Share of Exported Products with Comparative Advantage across Different Skill and Technology Categories (HS 6 digit)

Country	High Skill and Techno-logically Intensive	Medium Skill and Techno-logically Intensive	Low Skill and Techno-logically Intensive	Resource Intensive	Others
PRC	21	15	12	37	15
India	22	10	10	36	22
Japan	30	31	14	13	12
Korea, Republic of	24	22	17	19	18

Note: PRC = People's Republic of China.
Source: Author's calculations. Data extracted from the World Integrated Trade Solution (WITS) in 2013.

The PRC's high-value products comprise office, accounting and computing machinery, television and radio transmitters, apparatus for line telephony and line telegraph, electronic valves and tubes, and other electronic components which also represent the top HVM industries in both the Republic of Korea and Japan.[25] In addition, Japan and the Republic of Korea also show competitive advantage in television and

TABLE 7.3 Top Five International Standard of Industrial Classification Industry Categories Based on the Number of High-Skill and Technology-Intensive Commodities with RCA>1, India (2011)

Rank	ISIC Code	ISIC Industry Description
1	2411	Manufacture of basic chemicals, except fertilizers and nitrogen compounds
2	2423	Manufacture of pharmaceuticals, medicinal chemicals, and botanical products
3	2429	Manufacture of other chemical products not elsewhere classified
4	2413	Manufacture of plastic in primary forms and synthetic rubber
5	3330	Manufacture of watches and clocks

Source: Author's calculations. Data extracted from the World Integrated Trade Solution (WITS) in 2013.

[25] Section four talks about the policies that have facilitated this transition

radio receivers, sound/video recording and reproducing equipment. Arguably, this could be the result of industrial policy in the Republic of Korea and Japan that explicitly focused on the transition from low skill–low technology to high skill–high technology manufacturing. Data unambiguously shows that Japan and the Republic of Korea have stolen a march on the PRC and India, in that order, in the export of HSHT products. India thus falls short amongst the comparator group in this respect. What about India's prospects for HVM? The next section uses Hausmann's celebrated Product Space framework in an attempt to map India's opportunities in HVM, given the current capability set.

Product Space Analysis of India's Export Basket

According to the Hecksher-Ohlin (HO) theory, a country's exports are driven by its relative factor endowments such as land, labour, and capital (Krugman and Obstfed 1994). A country is said to have comparative advantage in products that use the abundant factor intensively. This fundamental insight is corroborated and extended by Hausmann, Hwang, and Rodrik in their work on production structures. They argue that specialization patterns are also, in part, shaped by exogenous elements and path dependencies. The nature of production matters for economic growth insofar as it is influenced by levels of 'sophistication' in a country's production. Countries that specialize in the production of more sophisticated goods are better placed to achieve higher growth. Hausmann, Hwang, and Rodrik (2005) calculate the incomes/productivities associated with each product (they call this index PRODY[26]) and the incomes/productivities associated with a country's export basket (they call this index EXPY[27]). Here, PRODY is effectively the 'sophistication' level of a product. Products with high values of

[26] PRODY provides a measure of the income content of a product. Let the per capita GDP of a country j be Y_j. Then the productivity level associated with product k is:

$$PRODY_k = \Sigma_j [(x_{jk}/X_j)/(\Sigma_j (x_{jk}/X_j)]^{*} Y_j$$

[27] EXPY is the productivity level of a country i's export basket. EXPY is the weighted average of the *PRODY* for a country where the weights are the value shares of the products in the country's total exports.

$$EXPY_i = \Sigma_l (x_{il}/X_i)^{*} PRODY_l$$

PRODY are complex and are placed higher in the manufacturing value chain. Estimated values for EXPY are highest for East Asian countries such as the Republic of Korea and the PRC given their dependence on exports and on goods with high productivity (Hausmann, Hwang, and Rodrik 2005).

The Product Space analysis—a theory of product relatedness—is an extension of this approach. Developed by Hausmann and Klinger in 2007, the theory emphasises the significance of the *initial* pattern of specialization. The location of products in a country's product space is a crucial determinant of its potential to develop comparative advantage in certain (related) products. Countries can progress by exploiting the relatedness of products requiring similar inputs including skills and technology, besides institutional and infrastructural needs. Thus, development is not merely advancement in general attributes such as education, health, rule of law, and infrastructure, but also the development of ancillary support systems and activities that are specific to an industry.[28]

A country's product space maps the character of its exports at a given point in time. It consists of a central dense core made up of machinery, metal products, chemicals, electronics, and capital-intensive goods with higher relatedness to other products. At the periphery are products such as petroleum, seafood, garments, and raw material products that are weakly related to other products. In general, products along the periphery are less sophisticated with lower income elasticity than those at the core (Abdon and Felipe 2011). The size of the product node represents the proportion of a good in the country's total exports and those with RCA are encircled in bold. Industries are differentiated by colours. The industry clusters are strikingly similar to the classification introduced by Leamer in 1984 (Leamer 1984). While all industry clusters are not of the same size, products belonging to the same industry have stronger links, that is, higher proximity.

The product space map is a useful tool to study a country's exports and the potential for increasing the corresponding levels of sophistication. Some examples of contemporary research in this area are Cruz and Riker's analysis of Brazil's exports using the Product Space Map

[28] Available at http://www.hks.harvard.edu/news-events/publications/insight/markets/ricardo-hausmann (accessed on 1 October 2016).

(2012), Abdon and Felipe's paper (2011) on opportunities for growth and structural transformation of Sub-Saharan Africa, Hamwey, Henrique, and Lucas (2013) on mapping green product spaces of nations, Bogetic, Pejović, and Osorio-Roddarte (2013) on expanding and diversifying Montenegro's Exports, Caglar (2011) on export promotion strategies in Turkey and the African Development Bank's (2012) study on comparative export policies in Egypt, Morocco, Tunisia, and the Republic of Korea. In 2011, a World Bank study by Mishra, Lundstrom, and Anand used the product space concept to study services export sophistication and economic growth.

India's current product space map represents a less dense core with a few chemical and metal products exhibiting RCA (Felipe, Kumar, and Abdon 2010). In the following section, we use the product space map to identify India's potential to develop HVM products.

Analysing India's Product Space Relative to the People's Republic of China, Japan, and the Republic of Korea

Comparison of the product space map across the four countries reinforces some of our earlier findings from the index approach. The product space maps of both India and the PRC show RCA for peripheral, low productivity, labour-intensive sectors such as textiles (represented by the dark green cluster). The PRC's RCA in electronics (represented by the blue cluster) demonstrates a superior ability to export complex products compared to India. While India shows competitiveness in chemical products (represented by the dark pink cluster), the PRC has accumulated complex capabilities within the core (as shown in Table 7.4). Arguably, the PRC's acquisition of more complex capabilities has been in large part policy driven (Abdon and Felipe 2011). Although India does manufacture some of these high-value products, these are not yet internationally competitive. A more detailed policy analysis is provided in the third section.

Japan and the Republic of Korea have evolved product spaces quite different from that of India. A significant portion of their exports originate from the core, namely, electronics, machinery, and chemical products, with large associated spillover benefits. The composition of HVM products exported by both countries is similar (details in Table 7.4), with Japan dominating in terms of the magnitudes of RCA.

TABLE 7.4 Cross-Country Analysis of High Value Manufacturing Exports at HS 4 Digit Level

Country	Number of HVM Products Exported (RCA>1)	Number of HVM Products Exported (RCA<1)	Description of Products with RCA>1
India	60	191	a) Products from chemical and allied industries b) Plastics and thereof c) Optical, photographic, cinematographic, measuring, checking, precision, medical or surgical instruments, and apparatus, parts and accessories thereof
PRC	104	148	a) Products from chemical and allied industries b) Plastics and parts thereof c) Machinery and mechanical appliances, electrical equipment, parts thereof, sound recorders and reproducers, television image and sound recorders and reproducers, and parts and accessories of such articles d) Optical, photographic, cinematographic, measuring, checking, precision, medical or surgical instruments and apparatus, parts and accessories thereof
Japan	103	148	a) Products from chemical and allied industries b) Plastics and thereof c) Machinery and mechanical appliances, electrical equipment, parts thereof, sound recorders and reproducers, television image and sound recorders and reproducers, and parts and accessories of such articles d) Aircraft, spacecraft, and parts thereof e) Optical, photographic, cinematographic, measuring, checking, precision, medical or surgical instruments and apparatus, parts and accessories thereof f) Clocks and watches and parts thereof

(Contd.)

Table 7.4 (*Contd.*)

Country	Number of HVM Products Exported (RCA>1)	Number of HVM Products Exported (RCA<1)	Description of Products with RCA>1
Korea, Republic of	60	189	a) Products from chemical and allied industries b) Plastics and parts thereof c) Machinery and mechanical appliances, electrical equipment, parts thereof, sound recorders and reproducers, television image and sound recorders and reproducers, and parts and accessories of such articles d) Optical, photographic, cinematographic, measuring, checking, precision, medical or surgical instruments and apparatus, parts and accessories thereof e) Clocks and watches and parts thereof

Note: PRC = People's Republic of China.
Source: Authors' calculations.

India (2010)

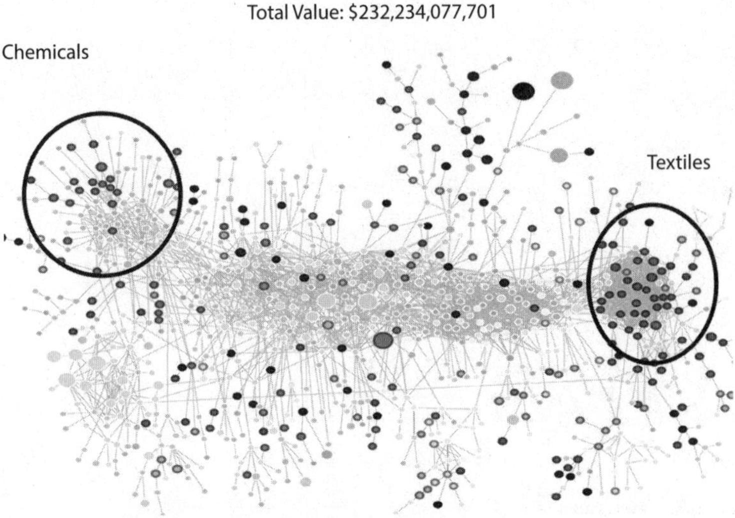

Japan (2010)

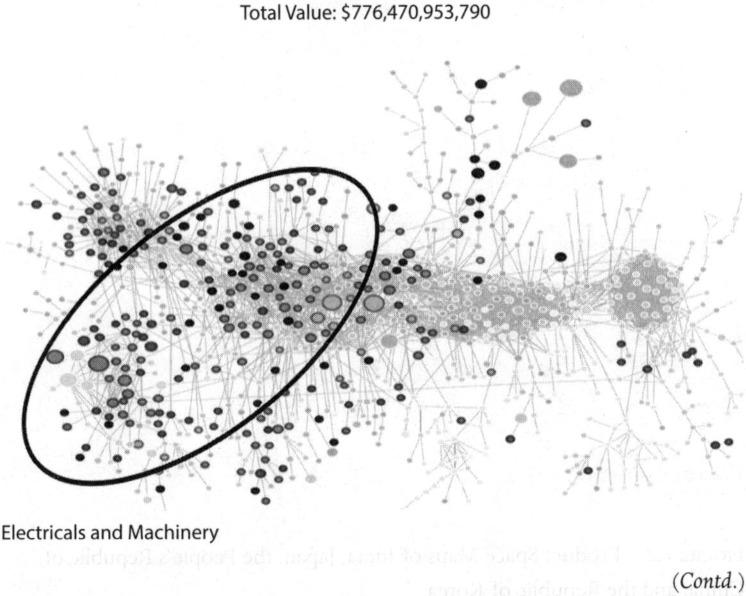

(*Contd.*)

People's Republic of PRC (2010)

Total Value: $745,120,532,941

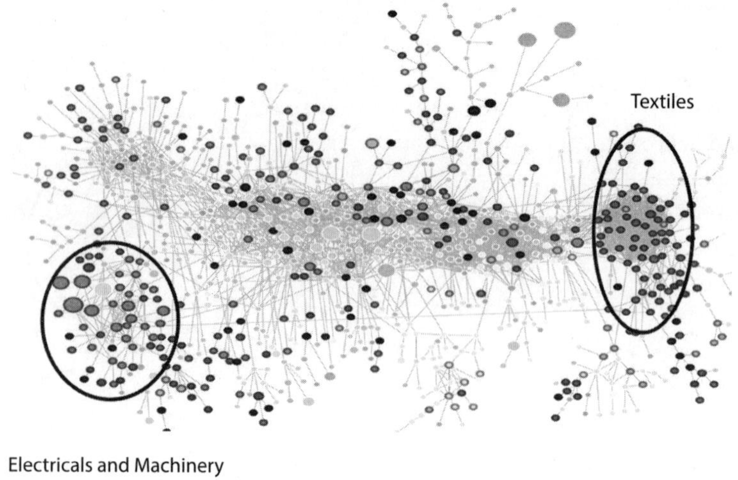

Republic of Korea (2010)

Total Value: $472,830,180,847

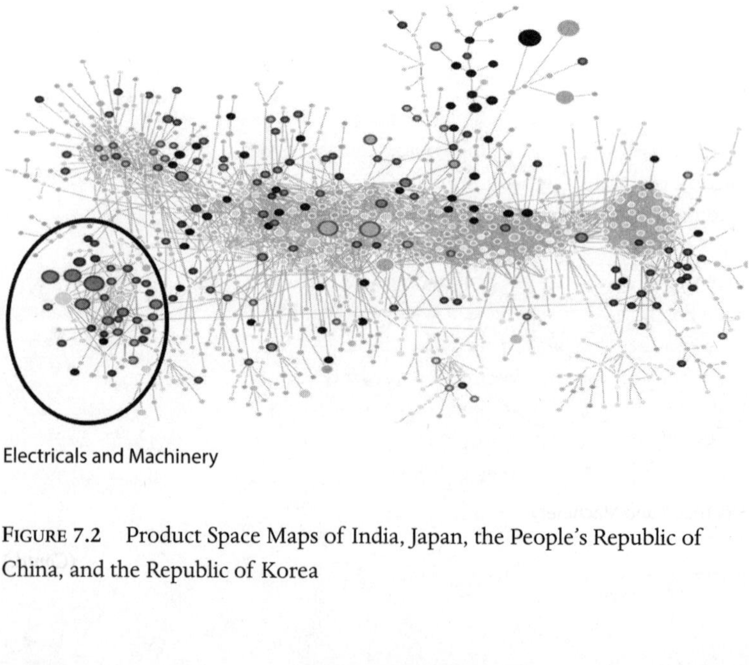

FIGURE 7.2 Product Space Maps of India, Japan, the People's Republic of China, and the Republic of Korea

Opportunities for Structural Transformation

As stated before, the network representation of the product space is a powerful tool for assessing potential for developing comparative advantages in exportables. The proximity matrix helps measure the probability that a country can develop capabilities for a new product given that it enjoys comparative advantage in a related product. According to Abdon and Felipe (2011) this depends on the existing *level of diversification*[29] of exports and the *distance* of the country's opportunity set to its current export basket. The 'distance' is defined in Hausmann and Klinger (2006) as the *density* which is a country-product level measure. The density of a product j not exported with comparative advantage is calculated as the sum of proximities between j and all those products the country exports with a comparative advantage scaled by the sum of all proximities leading to j:

$$densit_{cj} = \frac{\sum_i \phi_{ij} X_{ci}}{\sum_i \phi_{ij}}$$

where, $x_{ci} = 1$ if RCA ≥ 1 and is 0 otherwise and ϕ_{ij} denotes the proximity[30] between goods i and j.

The density of a product always lies between 0 and 1. The higher the estimated density, the easier it is for the country to develop export

[29] Export diversification can be horizontal, vertical, and even diagonal. Horizontal diversification is adding new products to existing ones, vertical diversification is moving from commodity to higher value added manufactures, and diagonal entails a shift from imported input into secondary and tertiary sectors.

[30] Proximity is calculated as the probability of exporting product A given that the country exports product B. The idea behind this conditional probability is that products use knowledge (capabilities) as input. The similarity between the capabilities required to produce two products is inferred by the probability of co-exporting them, that is, it is assumed that if two goods share a high number of common inputs (capabilities), the country that exports one of them will also export the other one; and vice versa, that is, products that share a few capabilities are less likely to be co-exported. For example, if 20 countries export computers (product A), 24 countries export wine (product B) and 8 export both, the *proximity* between computers and wine is 8/24=0.3 (we divide by 24 instead of 20 to minimize the number of false positives).

capabilities. The density is a proxy for the probability that a country successfully develops the capability to export a product with comparative advantage, given its current exports. For the purpose of this analysis, HVM products (identified on the basis of HSHT products) are separated into those exported with RCA>1, and those which are not (see Table 7.4). Densities have been calculated for all HVM products (at HS-4 digit level) that do not currently exhibit comparative advantage, that is, products with RCA<1. The products are then classified into three quartiles according to their densities. According to results in Table 7.5, about three quarters of HVM products in India have an average density of about 0.25. Moreover, the maximum density is 0.30 and the range of the density values is also low. This implies that within India's opportunity set, most HVM products are at a considerable 'distance' from products that are currently exported with comparative advantage. One consequence of this finding is that relative to East Asian countries, India might need a bigger policy push to move towards the core. Significantly, India has the highest number of products in its opportunity set of HVM products, followed closely by the Republic of Korea, and then Japan and the PRC. The PRC has the highest density of 0.547 along with the highest range of 0.236 amongst the four countries. This implies that the PRC has the most diversified product space amongst the four countries and the highest potential for developing capabilities amongst the

TABLE 7.5 Descriptive Statistics for Density Estimates for High Value Manufacturing Products with RCA<1 at HS 4 digit

	India	Korea, Republic of	PRC	Japan
Lower Quartile	0.219	0.181	0.371	0.260
Median	0.232	0.194	0.395	0.283
Upper Quartile	0.248	0.204	0.411	0.313
Minimum	0.189	0.160	0.311	0.175
Maximum	0.303	0.294	0.547	0.355
Range	0.113	0.134	0.236	0.179
Number of Observations	191	189	148	148

Note: PRC = People's Republic of China.

Source: Author's calculations. Data extracted from the World Integrated Trade Solution (WITS) in 2013.

comparator countries. This analysis does not include products that are completely absent from the country's export basket.

Products exhibiting high densities (top 10) for India have been ranked in Table 7.6. While products with potential to develop comparative advantage are within a narrow range, the corresponding level of sophistication as measured by PRODY (see under beginning of section titled 'Product Space Analysis of India's Export Basket') shows more variability with few sophisticated exportables. This implies that the potential for high-value exports from India exists only in islands. Table 7.7 lists the top 10 products (at the 4 digit level) with the highest levels of sophistication amongst India's potential HVM exportables and traces these back to their 4-digit product code. The two product categories amongst the top 10 products exhibiting both high levels of sophistication and high densities are 3103 and 2814. These belong to the chemical cluster in India's product space map. This should, however, not lead to policy incentives in favour of the chemicals cluster; all products estimated to have high PRODY (levels of sophistication) deserve attention because

TABLE 7.6 Top 10 Densities: India

Product Code (HS 4 digit)	Density	Product Description
3401	0.303	Soap; organic surface-active products in bars
3103	0.287	Mineral or chemical fertilizers, phosphatic
3105	0.285	Mineral or chemical fertilizers, not elsewhere classified; other fertilisers
2207	0.283	Ethyl alcohol, under-natured of >=80% alcohol, denatured of any strength
2834	0.279	Nitrites; nitrates
3201	0.271	Tanning extracts of vegetable origin; tannins and their salts; esthers and other derivatives
2814	0.269	Ammonia, anhydrous, or in aqueous solution
2841	0.268	Salts of oxometallic or peroxometallic acids
3805	0.267	Gum, wood or sulphate turpentine and other terpenic oils, sulphite turpentine and other crude paracymene
8469	0.266	Typewriters and word-processing machines

Source: Author's calculations. Data extracted from the World Integrated Trade Solution (WITS) in 2013.

TABLE 7.7 Top 10 Products by PRODY (India)

HS 4 digit Product Code	Product Description
3210	Other paints and varnishes
9007	Cinematographic cameras and projectors
3401	Organic surface-active products and preparations for use as soap
3501	Casein, caseinates, and other derivatives
2814	Ammonia, anhydrous, or in aqueous solution
9101	Wrist watches, pocket watches, and other watches
3103	Mineral or chemical fertilisers, phosphatic
3807	Wood tar, wood tar oil, wood cresote, wood naphtha, vegetable pitch and brewers pitch
2818	Artificial corundum, whether or not chemically defined
2851	Other inorganic compounds

Source: Author's calculations. Data extracted from the World Integrated Trade Solution (WITS) in 2013.

of their potential to create positive externalities. Additionally, there are several product categories (especially those at the core of the product space) that are not exported from India, and therefore do not feature in the analysis.

High value products exported from India, and those for which India appears to possess potential for comparative advantage are represented in the scatter plot in Figure 7.3 along the density and sophistication axes. Most products are tightly bunched together with few exceptions (such as paints and varnishes [3210], cinematographic cameras and projectors [9107] and products for soap preparation [3105]) that have either high levels of sophistication or high densities. While the new thinking on industrial policy is sympathetic to picking sectors/products that have strong externalities, it is also fraught with risk especially because of political economy considerations in India (Stiglitz, Lin, and Monga 2013). In the next section, we discuss enabling policies for manufacturing at the macro-level based on successful strategies adopted by comparator countries. Policies for specific industries or industry clusters need careful assessment especially when these are put in practice.

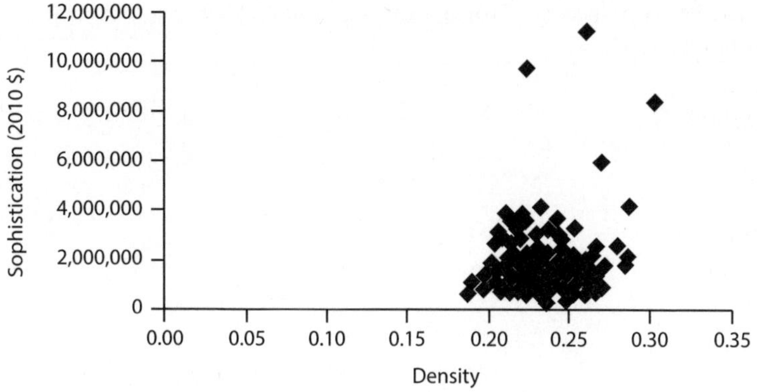

FIGURE 7.3 Scatter Plot for Sophistication and Density of High Value Manufacturing Products (4 digit), India

Policy Analysis

Lessons from East Asia

The role of government in inducing structural transformation, industrial upgradation, and economic growth cannot be overemphasized. This is especially relevant in the context of East Asian countries. Twenty three economies from the region grew faster than economies from any other region during 1965–90 (Page 1994). East Asian economies surpassed African nations and most Latin American countries that were richer in the 1960s (Table 7.8). The proximate causes lie in the careful integration of economic, political, and institutional policies which contain lessons for India (Stiglitz 2007).

Governments in East Asia facilitated structural transformation through policies that were outward oriented, while global integration was 'measured' and 'paced' (Stiglitz 2007). Focus on export-led growth did not imply a laissez faire economy. The respective governments carefully crafted an industrial policy of 'picking winners', identifying sectors with potential for high productivity, demand elasticity, and employment generation. Accordingly, investments were made in sectors such as electronics, computers, and computer chips. In Japan this policy was facilitated by the Ministry of International Trade and Industry (MITI) using instruments of trade protection, tax advantages, subsidies, and cheap credit. Private sector R&D was also actively promoted through

TABLE 7.8 Comparative Growth Experience, per Capita Gross Domestic Product (2005 $)

Country	1960	1985	1995	2011
Korea, Republic of	155	2,368	11,468	22,424
Japan	479	11,466	42,522	45,903
PRC	92	292	604	5,445
India	84	302	380	1,489
Brazil	208	1,636	4,751	12,594
Mexico	340	2,422	3,107	10,047
Ghana	18	350	380	1,570
Senegal	260	475	583	1,119

Note: PRC = People's Republic of China.
Source: World Bank (2013).

subsidies—one of the largest components of fiscal expenditure incurred by the Japanese government (Noland 2007). In the Republic of Korea, the 'picking winners' strategy saw deliberate creation of large conglomerate groups called *chaebols*.[31] Some examples include Daewoo, Samsung, and Hyundai. Operations of conglomerate groups were facilitated by controls on foreign investment inflows and proprietary technology. Unlike most developing countries which relied on private agents to promote industry in the post liberalization era, the Republic of Korea created public enterprises which became the launching pad for new industries.

More recently, the PRC's growth resembles this pattern. Industrial policy in the PRC was a combination of an 'open door' policy to attract foreign direct investment (FDI), the creation of Special Economic Zones (SEZs) to invite investments in low technology and light industry sectors, Open Port Cities (OPCs) to attract advanced technologies and promote industrial upgradation, and Free Trade Zones (FTZs) and High Technology Development Zones (HTDZs) for export promotion. These policies had knock-on effects on domestic research and development. Industrial upgrading within the Chinese economy is

[31] The *chaebols* are large, conglomerate family-controlled firms of the Republic of Korea characterized by strong ties with government agencies. For more on Chaebols see http://www.sjsu.edu/faculty/watkins/chaebol.htm (accessed on 1 October 2016).

apparent in its rapidly declining exports of labour-intensive products such as clothing, apparel, textiles, and footwear (from about 40 per cent in the early 1990s to less than 20 per cent in 2006). In contrast, exports of advanced manufactured products such as electronic equipment have grown (Yueh 2012).

Industrial Policy in India

According to Bardhan (2006), an incapacitating industrial policy and poor social and physical infrastructure constrained Indian manufacturing prior to the 1991 reforms. Private sector activity was restricted and public sector was handed an active role in industrial development.[32] Industrial and import licensing were two important instruments through which the government controlled the manufacturing sector. The policy however led to gross inefficiencies, misallocation of resources, and limited domestic and foreign competition.[33] The Monopolies and Restrictive Trade Practices (MRTP) Act, 1969 and the Foreign Exchange Regulation Act (FERA), 1973 constrained the expansion of business and discouraged foreign investment in the country. Post 1991, the New Industrial Policy addressed these concerns by promoting FDI, abolishing licenses in nearly all industries (barring some 18 industries), and ending most public sector monopolies. India developed capabilities in capital intensive and high-skill industries despite being a labour-abundant country (Felipe et al. 2010).

However, unlike East and South East Asia, India has never achieved 'miracle' growth rates of 10 per cent. For three decades between 1950 and 1980 India's economy grew steadily at the so-called 'Hindu rate of growth' of 3.5 per cent a year in real terms, and during the next two decades it grew at annual rates between 5 and 6 per cent (Panagariya 2004). After reform and during the golden period from 2003–04 to 2007–08, India grew at an unprecedented average of 9 per cent. The high growth has been attributed to vast private investment, open trade policies, and

[32] Key legislations included—Industrial Policy Resolution, 1948; Industries Development and Regulation Act, 1951; First and Second Five Year Plans; and Industrial Policy Resolution, 1956.

[33] For further reading on the license permit raj, see Ahluwalia 1991; Bhagwati and Srinivasan 1975; Joshi and Little 1994; Panagariya 2008, Felipe et al. 2010.

financial reforms that were periodically introduced. At the heart of the reform measures were the successful completion of several privatization initiatives (as distinct from disinvestment of minority stakes) and further relaxations in the FDI regime (Acharya 2001)

India's Current Policy Environment for Manufacturing

India's recent tryst with manufacturing can be traced to the creation of the National Manufacturing Competitive Council (NMCC) in 2004. The NMCC was set up to advise the government on industrial and sector-specific initiatives for enhancing competitiveness. However, it was only with the NMP, 2011 that some clarity emerged.[34] There are some important milestones in the NMP, 2011—to increase the share of manufacturing in GDP to 25 per cent within a decade and create 100 million new jobs. Importantly, the NMP, 2011 also recognized challenges, namely, the low levels of 'value-addition' in HSHT sectors and increasing dependence on imports for electronics and capital goods. The NMP, 2011 focuses on depth in manufacturing to help attain long-term competitiveness. The policy also emphasizes the need to build an indigenous value chain in sectors crucial to national security. National Investment and Manufacturing Zones (NIMZ) are at the core of the vision outlined in the NMP, 2011, which seeks to create massive industrial townships with world-class manufacturing activities. The Prime Minister's Make in India initiative (2014) is another comprehensive measure to facilitate manufacturing. Our research demonstrates a need to focus on formal manufacturing and within that on HVM—for in India 'unregistered' manufacturing that dominates the landscape has consistently been of low productivity. Accordingly, the transformational potential of manufacturing in India lies in manufacturing in general and in HVM in particular. Broad-based reforms under Make in India attempt to address this aspect by seeking to ameliorate infrastructure and labour market constraints, identifying and bridging skill gaps, strengthening innovation and the intellectual property rights regime and addressing delays in decision-making. The programme also emphasizes the need for sectoral focus, outside the gamut of horizontal reforms.

[34] Available at http://dipp.nic.in/English/policies/National_Manufacturing_Policy_25October2011.pdf (accessed on 1 October 2016).

While policies in India are quite well formulated and embedded in the local context, implementation continues to frustrate. The ability of the state to deliver on these several goals simultaneously depends on the quality of implementation, which is often politicized because of a variety of interests. Weak institutions and limited state capacity adds to the dilemma.

Recommendations

As a national goal, industrialization is important, alongside others such as redistribution, welfare, and sovereignty. India's federal structure makes policy formulation and implementation complex, and more often than not politicized, either because of centre–state conflicts or because the state is too weak to implement its own policies. Certain states have been relatively more successful in attracting investment but are not impervious to the criticism that weak institutions and an inability to pursue a cohesive development agenda detract from economic growth. For example, in West Bengal, the failure of Tata Motors to acquire land due to political conflict discouraged investors.[35] By contrast, Gujarat (where Tata Motors eventually invested) has pursued a pro-growth strategy with salutary results on investment, although social indicators have lagged behind.[36]At the centre, India has shifted from a reluctant pro-capitalist state with a socialist ideology, to an enthusiastic pro-capitalist state with a neo-liberal ideology (Kohli 2004). The shift however comes with its own set of concerns relating to institutional capacity, creating which has been challenging at best and at worst, a severe disappointment (Planning Commission of India). Unless India is able to create credible, conducive, capable, and transparent institutional structures across a wide range of state activity, the macroeconomic goal of high, stable, and inclusive growth will continue to suffer. For example, while judicial intervention into executive decisions ought to be a rare

[35] Available at http://in.news.yahoo.com/sc-notice-tata-motors-singur-land-065447558--finance.html (accessed on 1 October 2016)

[36] As per the *India Human Development Report* (2011). The Human Development Index (HDI) for Gujarat, in 2008, was 0.527 and it ranked 10th amongst Indian states. Kerala stood first (HDI: 0.790), Himachal Pradesh scored 0.652, Punjab 0.605, Maharashtra 0.572 and Haryana 0.552.

exception, of late it seems to have become routine[37]. At the same time, the pro-business tilt of government action has significant implications for the future of economic growth, including the possibility of developing and consolidating HVM in India. Box 7.1 highlights the success story of India's automobile industry in this regard.

Although the existing literature makes numerous references to 'high value', there is no single definition that captures it in its entirety. This study has attempted to conceptualize HVM from two different perspectives one that deals with value creation, including financial, social and strategic value and the other that focuses on enablers of value creation, namely, skill and technology. In the absence of adequate data on measures of value creation in India, we focused on enablers using UNCTAD's classification of products based on skill and technology intensity.

According to the secondary data analysis, HVM in India consists of pharmaceuticals, auto-components, and chemical industries. These islands of HVM activity highlight the role of innovation, skill, and technology in the transformation. Barring these fragmented success stories, India lacks the ecosystem for development of HVM. For example, despite the potential in electronics and information technology (IT) hardware, manufacturing is close to absent in India. Imports fill the breach, while the limited manufacturers of electronics and IT hardware in India deal with several business challenges, discouraging private enterprise. Most countries can reach the core only if they 'jump' over distances in the product space (Hidalgo et al. 2007). Industrial policy in both the Republic of Korea and Japan suggests that well-designed state interventions such as subsidies and other types of industry-specific assistance were responsible for promoting the cost-efficient and high-quality production that facilitated high-value exports (Chan Wai-keung 1999). Given the endemic market failures in technology development, private investors in India will need to be convinced that the government is serious about dealing with obstacles such as capital scarcity, infrastructure constraints, regulatory inconsistencies, and rigidities in labour markets. The need to create an environment for

[37] Recently (2014) India's Supreme Court cancelled all but four of the 218 coal block allocations declaring them illegal and arbitrary. In 2012, the Supreme Court also cancelled 122 telecom licenses. Such intervention by courts in executive decisions spells delays for economic growth

manufacturing to thrive, especially of high value products, cannot be over emphasized.

The product space analysis confirms India's poor performance in HVM compared to East Asian countries. According to the density analysis, India has the potential to rapidly develop comparative advantages in a few products (especially in chemicals and pharmaceuticals), which entail capabilities that already exist in India. However, there are product groups such as electronics and IT hardware that require serious

Box 7.1 The Success Story of the Indian Automobile Industry

Government facilitated the creation of an appropriate ecosystem for India's automobile industry. The industry was opened to foreign competition in the 1980s. The government formed a partnership with Suzuki in 1982, which led to setting up Maruti Udyog Limited. Private sector participation was restricted in the passenger car segment until the 1990s with only three major players—Maruti, Hindustan Motors, and Premier Automobiles Limited. However, the commercial vehicle segment was liberalized and saw the rise of joint ventures such as DCM–Toyota; Allwyn–Nissan, and Eicher-Mitsubishi. Government-funded training programmes and cluster building led to a change in supplier relations, enabling vendor development and effective supply chain management. Joint ventures with Japanese firms led to the creation of industrial agglomerations and adoption of Japanese practices such as cooperative agreements between suppliers and original equipment manufacturers.

Liberal policies allowed firms to invest in multiple product lines, which had been outlawed in the past by policy. Companies like Tata Motors introduced special purpose vehicles and platforms in order to enter the passenger car segment. Entry of new competitors led to spill-over benefits, especially on the technology side. This also led to increased expenditure on research and developement and a desire to innovate in order to distinguish products in the market. The time span between new products rapidly declined. Also, the institutional support for developing supplier capabilities led to the establishment of flexible supplier relationships which were very important. The industry benefitted immensely from innovation and its spillovers, brought out through inter-firm collaborations.

Source: Interview with Professor Pradeep Dutta, Indian Institute of Science and Saripalle (2012).

government intervention and policy incentives. India's absence from regional production networks in Asia is a manifestation of its inability to develop domestic manufacturing capabilities in electronics and IT hardware. The industry has therefore become a matter of serious concern for India—stated in several policies recently. The government has approved the proposal of two industry consortiums to set up semiconductor fabrication plants ('fabs') in India, reiterating the role of government intervention in promoting HVM in India. The performance of the electronics industry in India is in sharp contrast to that of auto and auto components, in which India has become significantly more competitive over the years. A wide range of factors inhibit electronics and IT hardware manufacturing, including lack of policy focus,[38] poor infrastructure, labour market rigidities, and the all-too-familiar bane of excessive red tape.

The HVM poses a serious challenge. A two-pronged strategy is called for horizontal reforms and sector-specific reforms. Evidence from comparator nations shows the importance of basic infrastructure facilities that drive manufacturing. Industrial research and skill enhancement are two other important factors that must be promoted across all industries. At the micro level, a policy to promote select HVM industries in clusters is a viable option. India's size and diversity make it impossible to scale up immediately. Even in the PRC, SEZs proved instrumental in accelerating economic development. While SEZs do exist in India, poor implementation has detracted from generating the desired impacts. Lessons from the SEZ experience will perhaps make the proposed NIMZs more successful. This chapter provides insight on which industry clusters are likely to generate the largest externalities immediately and in the long term.

Finally, a caveat to the findings from the product space analysis is the assumption that gross exports reflect a country's capabilities in manufacturing a product. Recent literature highlights the low levels of domestic value addition in certain country exports, suggesting that gross exports may overestimate a country's capability set. Appendix Table 7B.13 shows the total domestic value added in select industries

[38] The prevailing inverted duty structures in electronics manufacturing is one of the major cost drivers, rendering Indian manufacturing uncompetitive.

for Japan, the Republic of Korea, and the PRC from the World Input-Output Database (WIOD) database. According to these estimates, imported value in the PRC and the Republic of Korea's exports of electrical and optical equipment is 29 per cent and 37 per cent, respectively. These estimates reflect, on the one hand, the rise of 'global manufacturing' and on the other, the acute competition facing firms to move up the value chain. Although imported value in India's exports is much lower, the level of gross exports is miniscule compared to that for the PRC, Japan, and the Republic of Korea. Product space analysis using value added in exports could be the next step to this research. Though the results on industrial/manufacturing capabilities may be different due to emerging trends in global value chains, the broad conclusions on policy intervention to promote HVM in India will remain undisputed.

Appendix 7A: Existing Industry Classifications and Their Shortfalls

International industry classifications are of broadly three types: those that classify economic activities, products, and traded goods and services. The most commonly used classifications include the International Standard of Industrial Classification (ISIC); the Central Product Classification (CPC); and the Harmonized Commodity Description and Coding System (HS) and Standard International Trade Classification (SITC).

Existing internationally accepted industry classifications would be a natural starting point in assisting us in defining HVM. In fact, the International Standard of Industrial Classification (ISIC) which is maintained by the United Nations aims at providing a 'consistent classification structure of economic activities based on a set of internationally agreed concepts, definitions, principles and classification rules'. Currently in its fourth version, the ISIC attempts to constantly reflect the current structure of the world economy and the complexity and interconnectedness that have come to characterize it. The criteria that are used to define categories in the ISIC are based on the inputs of goods, service, and factors of production; the process and technology of production; the characteristics of outputs; and the use to which outputs are put. Moreover, these criteria are not watertight and a certain amount of flexibility is encouraged. At higher levels the characteristics of output and the use to which they are put become more important to create analytically useful aggregations.

Thus while current industry classifications, due to their frequent revisions, do take into account the changing nature and type of activities, they need to be supplemented for our purposes because the categories of the ISIC do not provide a basis for distinguishing which manufacturing industry and or/product can potentially be HVM since they say nothing about the different forms of *outcomes created* and the factors that enable the creation of these outcomes. In fact the ISIC defines manufacturing to be the 'physical or chemical transformation of materials, substances, or components into new products'.[39] Manufacturing, in other words, is equated to production. There is thus a need to evolve a supplemental set of parameters based on literature review that will enable us to identify which industries truly constitute HVM.

Appendix 7B

TABLE 7B.1 Top Ten International Standard of Industrial Classification Industries in Descending Order of High Value Manufacturing Index Value, India

S. No.	4-Digit ISIC Code	Description	HVM Index
1.	1711	Textile fibre preparation, textile weaving	7.20
2.	2710	Basic iron and steel	6.60
3.	1810	Wearing apparel, except fur apparel	5.00
4.	2423	Pharmaceuticals, medicinal chemicals, and botanical products	3.75
5.	3430	Parts/accessories for automobiles	3.26
6.	1600	Tobacco products	2.84
7.	1549	Other food products not elsewhere classified	2.67
8.	1542	Sugar	2.56
9.	1531	Grain mill products	2.14
10.	2520	Plastic products	1.93

Note: ISIC = International Standard of Industrial Classification, HVM = high value manufacturing.

Source: Author's calculations based on data from United Nations Industrial Development Organization's (UNIDO's) Industrial Statistics INDSTAT4 Database.

[39] The exception to this is the processing of waste which is classified separately in the ISIC.

TABLE 7B.2 Top Ten International Standard of Industrial Classification Industries in Descending Order of High Value Manufacturing Index Value, the People's Republic of China

S. No.	4-digit ISIC Code	Description	HVM Index
1.	2710	Basic iron and steel	67.95
2.	1810	Wearing apparel, except fur apparel	50.65
3.	3210	Electronic valves, tubes, and electronic components	33.58
4.	1711	Textile fibre preparation, textile weaving	30.65
5.	2520	Plastic products	21.11
6.	1920	Footwear	19.47
7.	2899	Other fabricated metal products not elsewhere classified	16.97
8.	3000	Office and computing machinery	16.39
9.	3430	Parts/accessories for automobiles	16.29
10.	2720	Basic precious and non-ferrous metals	15.87

Note: ISIC = International Standard of Industrial Classification, HVM = high value manufacturing.

Source: Author's calculations based on data from United Nations Industrial Development Organization's (UNIDO's) Industrial Statistics INDSTAT4 Database.

TABLE 7B.3 Top Ten International Standard of Industrial Classification Industries in Descending Order of High Value Manufacturing Index Value, Japan

S. No.	4-digit ISIC Code	Description	HVM Index
1.	3430	Parts/accessories for automobiles	36.93
2.	3210	Electronic valves, tubes, and electronic components	15.27
3.	2520	Plastic products	15.07
4.	3230	TV and radio receivers and associated goods	14.71
5.	3410	Motor vehicles	14.47
6.	1549	Other food products not elsewhere classified	11.99
7.	2710	Basic iron and steel	10.30
8.	2929	Other special purpose machinery	9.85
9.	2221	Printing	9.24
10.	2922	Machine tools	7.05

Note: ISIC = International Standard of Industrial Classification, HVM = high value manufacturing.

Source: Author's calculations based on data from United Nations Industrial Development Organization's (UNIDO's) Industrial Statistics INDSTAT4 Database.

TABLE 7B.4 Top Ten International Standard of Industrial Classification Industries in Descending Order of High Value Manufacturing Index Value, the Republic of Korea

S. No.	4-digit ISIC Code	Description	HVM Index
1.	3210	Electronic valves, tubes, and others	12.00
2.	3511	Building and repairing of ships and boats	8.08
3.	3430	Parts/accessories for automobiles	7.93
4.	3410	Motor vehicles	7.49
5.	2520	Plastics products	5.33
6.	2710	Basic iron and steel	4.78
7.	3220	TV/radio transmitters; line communication apparatus	4.12
8.	2929	Other special purpose machinery	3.54
9.	2915	Lifting and handling equipment	2.78
10.	3110	Electric motors, generators, and transformers	2.76

Note: ISIC = International Standard of Industrial Classification, HVM = high value manufacturing.

Source: Author's calculations based on data from United Nations Industrial Development Organization's (UNIDO's) Industrial Statistics INDSTAT4 Database.

Table 7B.5 Top Ten HS 6-Digit High Skill and Technology-Intensive Commodities in Descending Order of Revealed Comparative Advantages, India

Rank	HS 6-digit Code	RCA	Description	ISIC Industry Code	ISIC Industry Description
1	290362	48.42	Hexachlorobenzene and dichlorodiphenyltrichloroethane	2411	Manufacture of basic chemicals, except fertilizers and nitrogen compounds
2	290242	48.33	Xylenes -m-Xylene	2411	Manufacture of basic chemicals, except fertilizers and nitrogen compounds
3	294200	42.18	Cefadroxil and its salts, ibuprofane, nifedipine, ranitidine, danes salt of phenylglycine	2411	Manufacture of basic chemicals, except fertilizers and nitrogen compounds
4	330125	26.36	Of other mints	2429	Manufacture of other chemical products not elsewhere classified
5	290611	23.69	Cyclanic, cyclenic, or cycloterpenic: menthol	2411	Manufacture of basic chemicals, except fertilizers and nitrogen compounds
6	283190	22.70	Other Dithionites and sulphoxylates (excluding sodium)	2411	Manufacture of basic chemicals, except fertilizers and nitrogen compounds
7	293929	22.24	Other alkaloids of cinchona and their derivatives	2423	Manufacture of pharmaceuticals, medicinal chemicals, and botanical products
8	330190	19.85	Concentrates of essential oils in fats	2429	Manufacture of other chemical products not elsewhere classified
9	330124	18.77	Essential oil of pepper mint	2429	Manufacture of other chemical products not elsewhere classified
10	292142	18.69	Aniline derivatives and their salts	2411	Manufacture of basic chemicals, except fertilizers and nitrogen compounds

Note: RCA = Revealed Comparative Advantage, ISIC = International Standard of Industrial Classification.

Source: Author's calculations. Data extracted from the World Integrated Trade Solution (WITS) in 2013 and correspondence tables provided by United Nations Statistics Division.

TABLE 7B.6 Top Ten HS 6-digit High Skill and Technology-Intensive Commodities in Descending Order of Revealed Comparative Advantages, the People's Republic of China

Rank	HS 6-digit Code	RCA	Description	ISIC Industry Code	ISIC Industry Description
1	283660	7.57	Barium carbonate	2411	Manufacture of basic chemicals, except fertilizers and nitrogen compounds
2	360410	7.44	Fireworks	2429	Manufacture of other chemical products not elsewhere classified
3	282710	7.35	Ammonium chloride	2412	Manufacture of fertilizers and nitrogen compounds
4	284180	7.31	Tungstates (wolframates)	2411	Manufacture of basic chemicals, except fertilizers and nitrogen compounds
5	293221	7.27	Coumarin, methylcoumarins and ethylcoumarins	2411	Manufacture of basic chemicals, except fertilizers and nitrogen compounds
6	291421	7.17	Camphor	2411	Manufacture of basic chemicals, except fertilizers and nitrogen compounds
7	294140	7.05	Chloramphenicol and its derivatives	2423	Manufacture of pharmaceuticals, medicinal chemicals and botanical products
8	291461	6.85	Anthraquinone	2411	Manufacture of basic chemicals, except fertilizers and nitrogen compounds
9	293213	6.74	Furfuryl alcohol and tetrahydrofurfuryl alcohol	2411	Manufacture of basic chemicals, except fertilizers and nitrogen compounds
10	282919	6.72	Chlorates (excluding sodium)	2411	Manufacture of basic chemicals, except fertilizers and nitrogen compounds

Note: RCA = Revealed Comparative Advantage, ISIC = International Standard of Industrial Classification.

Source: Author's calculations. Data extracted from the World Integrated Trade Solution (WITS) in 2013 and correspondence tables provided by United Nations Statistics Division.

Table 7B.7 Top Ten HS 6-Digit High-Skill and Technology-Intensive Commodities in Descending Order of Revealed Comparative Advantage, Japan

Rank	HS 6-digit Code	RCA	Description	ISIC Industry Code	ISIC Industry Description
1	392073	18.61	Sheet of cellulose acetate, non-plasticized	2520	Manufacture of plastics products
2	290612	17.51	Cyclohexanol, methylcyclohexanols and dimethylc	2411	Manufacture of basic chemicals, except fertilizers and nitrogen compounds
3	370199	12.27	Photographic plates and film, in the flat (excluding paper, paperboard and textiles)	2429	Manufacture of other chemical products not elsewhere classified
4	370120	12.20	Instant print flat film, unexposed	2429	Manufacture of other chemical products not elsewhere classified
5	340540	10.92	Scouring pastes and powders and other scouring	2424	Manufacture of soap and detergents, cleaning and polishing preparations, perfumes and toilet preparations
6	910811	10.12	Watch movements, assembled, battery powered wit	3330	Manufacture of watches and clocks
7	320650	9.85	Inorganic products of a kind used as luminophor	2411	Manufacture of basic chemicals, except fertilizers and nitrogen compounds
8	391520	8.88	Waste, parings, and scrap of polymers of styrene	9999	Goods not elsewhere classified
9	290729	8.74	Other polyphenols, not elsewhere classified	2411	Manufacture of basic chemicals, except fertilizers and nitrogen compounds
10	370790	8.40	Chemical preparations for photographic use, not elsewhere classified	2429	Manufacture of other chemical products not elsewhere classified

Note: RCA = Revealed Comparative Advantage, ISIC = International Standard of Industrial Classification.

Source: Author's calculations. Data extracted from the World Integrated Trade Solution (WITS) in 2013 and correspondence tables provided by United Nations Statistics Division.

TABLE 7B.8 Top Ten HS 6-digit High Skill and Technology-Intensive Commodities in Descending Order of Revealed Comparative Advantage, the Republic of Korea

Rank	HS 6-digit Code	RCA	Description	ISIC Industry Code	ISIC Industry Description
1	283719	15.77	Cyanides, cyanide oxides (excluding sodium)	2411	Manufacture of basic chemicals, except fertilizers and nitrogen compounds
2	291732	12.81	Dioctyl orthophthalates	2411	Manufacture of basic chemicals, except fertilizers and nitrogen compounds
3	283711	10.64	Cyanides and cyanide oxides of sodium	2411	Manufacture of basic chemicals, except fertilizers and nitrogen compounds
4	901380	10.25	Optical devices, appliances and instruments, not elsewhere classified	3320	Manufacture of optical instruments and photographic equipment
5	290230	10.02	Toluene	2411	Manufacture of basic chemicals, except fertilizers and nitrogen compounds
6	291736	9.77	Terephthalic acid and its salts	2411	Manufacture of basic chemicals, except fertilizers and nitrogen compounds
7	291735	9.45	Phthalic anhydride	2411	Manufacture of basic chemicals, except fertilizers and nitrogen compounds
8	283640	8.37	Potassium carbonates	2411	Manufacture of basic chemicals, except fertilizers and nitrogen compounds
9	390330	8.03	Acrylonitrile-butadiene-styrene (ABS) copolymer	2413	Manufacture of plastics in primary forms and of synthetic rubber
10	281520	7.52	Potassium hydroxide (caustic potash)	2411	Manufacture of basic chemicals, except fertilizers and nitrogen compounds

Note: RCA = Revealed Comparative Advantage, ISIC = International Standard of Industrial Classification.

Source: Author's calculations. Data extracted from the World Integrated Trade Solution (WITS) in 2013 and correspondence tables provided by United Nations Statistics Division.

TABLE 7B.9 Top Ten High Skill and Technology-Intensive HS 6-Digit Products and Their Respective Parent International Standard of Industrial Classification Industry Categories, in Descending Order of Export Shares, India (2011)

Rank	HS 6-digit Code	Exports as a Percentage of Total Exports	Description	RCA	ISIC Industry Category
1	300490	1.75	Other medicaments of mixed or unmixed products	1.09	2423
2	852520	1.09	Transmission apparatus, for radio-telephony	1.12	3220
3	294200	0.85	Other organic compounds, not elsewhere classified	42.18	2411
4	880330	0.61	Aircraft parts not elsewhere classified	2.12	3530
5	390210	0.39	Polypropylene, in primary forms	3.16	2413
6	851790	0.31	Parts of electrical apparatus for line telephony	0.52	3220
7	300420	0.29	Cephalosporins and their derivatives	2.83	2423
8	290243	0.26	p-xylene	2.53	2411
9	380810	0.24	Insecticides, put up for retail sale	5.89	2421
10	290220	0.20	Benzene	4.08	2411

Note: RCA = Revealed Comparative Advantage, ISIC = International Standard of Industrial Classification.

Source: Author's calculations. Data extracted from the World Integrated Trade Solution (WITS) in 2013 and correspondence tables provided by United Nations Statistics Division.

Table 7B.10 Top Ten High Skill and Technologically Intensive HS 6-Digit Products and Their Respective Parent International Standard of Industrial Classification Industry Categories, in Descending Order of Export Shares, the People's Republic of China (2011)

Rank	HS 6-Digit Code	Export Shares	Description	RCA	ISIC Industry Category
1	847120	5.79	Digital auto data processing	6.20	3000
2	852520	3.33	Transmission apparatus, for radio telephony	3.45	3220
3	851790	2.01	Parts of electrical apparatus for line telephony	3.32	3220
4	847330	1.58	Parts and accessories of automatic data process	2.09	3000
5	901380	1.56	Optical devices, appliances and instruments	3.26	3320
6	854211	1.51	Monolithic integrated circuits, digital	1.03	3210
7	854140	1.47	Photosensitive semiconductor devices, photovoltaic	3.25	3210
8	851730	1.34	Telephonic or telegraphic switching apparatus	2.42	3220
9	852810	1.17	Television receivers including video monitors	2.06	3230
10	847193	0.84	Storage units	1.93	3000

Note: RCA = Revealed Comparative Advantage, ISIC = International Standard of Industrial Classification.

Source: Author's calculations. Data extracted from the World Integrated Trade Solution (WITS) in 2013 and correspondence tables provided by United Nations Statistics Division.

TABLE 7B.11 Top Ten High Skill and Technologically Intensive HS 6-Digit Products and Their Respective Parent International Standard of Industrial Classification Industry Categories, in Descending Order of Export Shares, the Republic of Korea (2011)

Rank	HS 6-Digit Code	Export Shares	Description	RCA	ISIC Industry Category
1	854211	6.73	Monolithic integrated circuits, digital	4.59	3210
2	901380	4.92	Optical devices, appliances and instruments, not elsewhere classified	10.24	3320
3	852520	2.72	Transmission apparatus, for radio telephony	2.81	3220
4	851790	1.61	Parts of electrical apparatus for line telephony	2.66	3220
5	852990	1.49	Other parts used solely or principally with apparatus of headings 8525 and 8528	4.35	3230
6	847330	0.90	Parts and accessories of automatic data process	1.19	3000
7	291736	0.81	Terephthalic acid and its salts	9.77	2411
8	854140	0.70	Photosensitive semiconductor devices, photovolta	1.54	3210
9	390330	0.50	Acrylonitrile-butadiene-styrene (ABS) copolymer	8.03	2413
10	290243	0.50	p-xylene	4.90	2411

Note: RCA = Revealed Comparative Advantage, ISIC = International Standard of Industrial Classification.

Source: Author's calculations. Data extracted from the World Integrated Trade Solution (WITS) in 2013 and correspondence tables provided by United Nations Statistics Division.

TABLE 7B.12 Top Ten High Skill and Technologically Intensive HS 6-Digit Products and Their Respective Parent International Standard of Industrial Classification Industry Categories, in Descending Order of Export Shares, Japan (2011)

Rank	HS 6-Digit Code	Export Shares	Description	RCA	ISIC Industry Category
1	854211	2.17	Monolithic integrated circuits, digital	1.48	3210
2	854219	1.38	Monolithic integrated circuits, not elsewhere classified	1.46	3210
3	852530	1.02	Television cameras	4.10	3220
4	901380	0.93	Optical devices, appliances and instruments, not elsewhere classified	1.95	3320
5	854140	0.80	Photosensitive semi-conductor devices, including photovoltaic cells whether or not assembled	1.77	3210
6	382390	0.62	Chemical products and residual products of chemicals	2.10	2429
7	852990	0.62	Other parts used solely or principally with apparatus of headings 8525 and 8528	1.80	3230
8	381800	0.47	Chemical elements and compounds doped for use in electronics, in the form of discs, wafers, cylinders, rods or similar forms	5.34	2429
9	290243	0.47	p-xylene	4.60	2411
10	900120	0.45	Sheets and plates of polarizing material	8.15	3320

Note: RCA = Revealed Comparative Advantage, ISIC = International Standard of Industrial Classification.

Source: Author's calculations. Data extracted from the World Integrated Trade Solution (WITS) in 2013 and correspondence tables provided by United Nations Statistics Division.

TABLE 7B.13 Percentage of Imported Value Add in a Country's Exports for Select Industries (million $)

Industry	Chemical and Chemical Products		Rubber and Plastics		Basic Metal and Fabricated Metal		Machinery		Electrical and Optical Equipment		Transport Equipment	
Country	Total Exports	Percentage of Imported Value Added	Total Exports	Percentage of Imported Value Added	Total Exports	Percentage of Imported Value Added	Total Exports	Percentage of Imported Value Added	Total Exports	Percentage of Imported Value Added	Total Exports	Percentage of Imported Value Added
PRC	89,736.3	0.22	54,324.7	0.22	99,319.8	0.25	118,000	0.21	638,982.3	0.29	79,335.7	0.21
Japan	57,476.4	0.18	29,188.1	0.15	102,658.6	0.21	81,753.3	0.14	162,860.6	0.15	174,328.5	0.14
Korea, Republic of	46,018	0.45	9,568	0.36	42,211.7	0.43	35,225.8	0.34	147,823.5	0.37	103,353	0.32
India	17,696.7	0.19	4,115.92	0.19	24,733.5	0.19	9,077.2	0.19	23,993.5	0.19	19,227.4	0.20

Source: Author's calculations based on data from the World Input Output Database (WIOD).

References

Abdon, A. and J. Felipe. 2011. 'The Product Space: What Does It Say About the Opportunities for Growth and Structural Transformation of Sub-Saharan Africa', Working Paper No. 670, Levy Economics Institute, USA.

African Development Bank. 2012. 'Comparative Study on Export Policies in Egypt, Morocco, Tunisia and South Korea', available at http://www.afdb.org/fileadmin/uploads/afdb/Documents/Project-and-Operations/Comparative%20Study%20on%20Export%20Policies%20in%20Egypt%20Morocco%20Tunisia%20and%20South%20Korea.pdf (accessed on 28 September 2016).

Anderson, M., R. Robertson, and S. Smith. 2001. 'Measuring Skill Intensity: Production Worker vs. Education Data in the NAFTA Countries', Office of Economics, U.S. International Trade Commission, USA.

Athukorala, P. 2013. 'How India Fits into Global Production Sharing: Experience, Prospects, and Policy Options', Paper for 10th Annual Policy Forum Workshop, New Delhi.

Balassa, B. 1965. 'Trade Liberalisation and Revealed Comparative Advantage,' *Manchester School*, 33: 99–123

Baldwin, R.E. and G.G. Cain. 2000. 'Shifts in US Relative Wages: The Role of Trade, Technology and Factor Endowments', *Review of Economics and Statistics*, 82(4): 580–95.

Bardhan, P. 2006. 'Awakening Giants, Feet of Clay: A Brief Assessment of the Rise of China and India', *Journal of South Asian Development*, April.

Basu, S. and M. Das. 2011. 'Export Structure and Economic Performance in Developing Countries: Evidence from Nonparametric Methodology', Study Series No. 48, UNCTAD.

Bhagwati and Srinivasan. 1975. "Trade and Poverty in the Poor Countries"

Bogetic, Zeljko, Igor Pejović, and Israel Osorio-Roddarte. 2013. 'Expanding and Diversifying Montenegro's Exports: A Product Space Analysis', *Journal of Central Banking Theory and Practice*, 2(2): 19–34.

Chan Wai-keung (Timothy). 1999. 'A Comparative Study on the Industrial Policy in Japan and South Korea', thesis, University of Hong Kong, Pokfulam, Hong Kong, China.

Cruz, J. and D. Riker. 2012. 'Product Space Analysis of the Exports of Brazil', Office of Economics Working Paper No. 2012-06A, U.S. International Trade Commission, USA.

Eaton, C. and N. Schmitt. 1991. 'Flexible Manufacturing and Market Structure', *American Economic Review*, 84(4): 875–88.

Eichengreen, B. and P. Gupta. 2011. 'The Service Sector as India's Road to Economic Growth', NBER Working Paper No. 16757.

Ernst, D. and L. Kim. 2002. 'Global Production Networks, Knowledge Diffusion, and Local Capability Formation, *Research Policy*, 31: 1417–1429.

Ettlie, J. and J.D. Penner-Hahn. 1994. 'Flexibility Ratios and Manufacturing Strategy', *Management Science*, 40(11): 1444–54.

Leamer, E. 1984. *Sources of Comparative Advantage: Theory and Evidence*. MIT Press: Cambridge, Massachusetts.

Felipe, J. and G. Estrada. 2008. 'Benchmarking Developing Asia's Manufacturing Sector', *International Journal of Development Issues*, 7(2): 97–119.

Felipe, J., U. Kumar, and A. Abdon. 2010. 'Exports, Capabilities and Industrial Policy in India', Working Paper No. 638, Levy Economics Institute.

Flynn, B. and J. Flynn. 2004. 'An Exploratory Study of the Nature of Cumulative Capabilities', *Journal of Operations Management*, 22(5): 439–57.

Hausmann, R. and B. Klinger. 2007. 'The Structure of the Product Space and the Evolution of Comparative Advantage', CID Working Paper No. 146, Harvard University.

Hausmann, R., J. Hwang, and D. Rodrik. 2005. 'What You Export Matters', CID Working Paper No. 123, Harvard University.

Hayes, R. and G. Pisano. 2000. 'Beyond World-Class: The New Manufacturing Strategy', *Harvard Business Review*, 72(1): 77–84.

Hamwey, Robert von, Henrique Pacini, and Lucas Assuncao. 2013. 'Mapping Green Product Spaces of Nations', *Journal of Environment and Development*, 20(10): 1–14.

Hidalgo, C. and R. Hausmann. 2009. 'The Building Blocks of Economic Complexity, Center for International Development and Harvard Kennedy School, Harvard University, Cambridge, Massachusetts.

Hidalgo, Klinger, Barabasi, and Hausmann. 2007. 'The Product Space Conditions the Development of Nations'.

Kaschel, H. and L. Bernal. 2006. 'Importance of Flexibility in Manufacturing Systems', *International Journal of Computers, Communications and Control*, 1(2): pp. 53–60.

Krugman, P.R. and Maurice Obstfed. 1994. *International Economics*, 3rd edition. New York: HarperCollins College.

Kuznets, Simo. 1971. *Economic Growth of Nations: Total Output and Production Structure*. Harvard University Press.

Leamer, E. 1984. *Sources of Comparative Advantage: Theory and Evidence*. Cambridge, Massachusetts: MIT Press.

Livesey, F. 2006. 'Defining HVM', Report for the Confederation of British Industry and the Department of Trade and Industry, January.

Martinez, V., A. Neely, G. Ren, and A. Smart. 2009. *HVM: Delivering on the Promise*. UK: Advanced Institute of Management Research, ESRC.

McKinsey Global Institute. 2012. 'Manufacturing the Future: The Next Era of Global Growth and Innovation.

Milberg, W. and D. Winkler. 2010. 'Economic and Social Upgrading in Global Production Networks: Problems of Theory and Measurement', Capturing the Gains Working Paper No. 2010/04.

Milgrom, Paul and Roberts, John. 1991. 'Adaptive and Sophisticated Learning in Normal Form Games', *Games and Economic Behavior*, 3(1): 82–100.

Mishra, Saurabh, Susanna Lundstrom, and Rahul Anand. 2011. 'Sophistication in Service Exports and Economic Growth', World Bank Economic Premise, No. 55, April.

Mohan, R. 2002. 'Small Scale Industrial Policy in India: A Critical Evaluation', in A.O. Krueger (ed.), *Economic Policy Reforms and the Indian Economy*, chapter 6. Chicago: University of Chicago Press.

Nagaraj, R. 2006. 'What Accounts for India's Undersized Industrial Sector? Can the Service Sector be the Engine of Growth?, paper presented at the conference Growth and Structural Change: Asia's Transformation and Future Growth Patterns, Beijing, PRC, 14–16 January.

Neely, A.D. 2008. 'The Servitization of Manufacturing: Further Evidence', 3rd World Conference on Production and Operations Management, Tokyo, Japan.

Noland, M. 2007. 'Industrial Policy, Innovation Policy and Japanese Competitiveness', Working Paper Series WP07-4, Peterson Institute for International Economics, Washington, D.C.

Page, J. 1994. 'The East Asian Miracle: Four Lessons for Development Policy', NBER Working Paper.

Panagariya, Arvind. 2004. 'India's Trade Reform: Progress, Reform and Future Strategy', in India Policy Forum, 2004, Columbia University, USA.

Planning Commission of India. 2011. 'Twelfth Five Year Plan', draft document, Government of India.

Planning Commission of India. n.d. *India Transport Report: Moving India to 2032*, Volume II Part I, Regulatory Issues: An Overall Approach. Government of India.

Saripalle, Madhuri. 2012. 'Learning and Capability Acquisition: A Case Study of the Indian Automobile Industry', Madras School of Economics Working Paper 65/2012.

Stiglitz, J. 2007. *Making Globalization Work*. W. W. Norton & Company.

Stiglitz, J., J.Y. Lin, and C. Monga. 2013. "The Rejuvenation of Industrial Policy', World Bank Policy Research Working Paper No. 6628, Washington, D.C.

Technology Strategy Board. 2012. 'A Landscape for the Future of High Value Manufacturing in the UK', available at http://www.nibec.ulster.ac.uk/uploads/documents/tsb_ifm_highvaluemanufacturingt12_009_final.pdf (accessed on 28 September 2016).

Venanzi, D. 2012. *Financial Performance Measures and Value Creation: The State of the Art*. Springer Publications.

Yueh, L. 2012. 'Why China Must Continue to Reform', *European Financial Review*, February–March: 54–57.

8

MEENU TEWARI
C. VEERAMANI
MANJEETA SINGH

Indian Manufacturing in Asian Production Networks

Patterns and Prospects of Deeper Regional Integration*

Global production networks and value chains are the defining organizational features of trade today. The central feature of this way of organizing trade is the unbundling of parts and components that go into a finished product and the spatial dispersal of these value-adding activities across the globe. Independent suppliers produce these fragmented components, moving them across global sites to assemblers and lead

* The authors would like to thank the Asian Development Bank (ADB) for financial support for the larger research on which this chapter is based. We thank T.N. Srinivasan and B.N. Goldar for very useful comments on previous drafts of the chapter. We also benefitted from comments at ADB's conference on production networks where this work was presented. We are grateful to Madhuri Saripalle for helping us establish interview contacts in Chennai, India. Vidhya Unnikrishnan provided able research assistance. A different version of this text was published in *Global Economy Journal* in June 2016. All errors of fact and interpretation are our responsibility.

firms that drive these chains. Consequently, today, trade involves the exchange not only of end products, but of the parts and components that go into making them (Feenstra 1998; Gereffi 1994, 1999; Kemeny and Rigby 2010).

A growing new literature seeks to understand these vertically disintegrated trade flows and measure the complex ways in which value is added as a product moves across space along spatially dispersed production networks (Athukorala 2010; Gereffi et al. 2013; Hummels, Ishii, and Yi 2001; Koopman et al. 2011). This literature also seeks to examine how participation in regional and global production networks is linked to economic development and industrial upgrading (Gereffi 1999). It is to this body of work that this chapter contributes a case study of India–Association of Southeast Asian Nations (ASEAN) trade relations, asking why India's integration in regional markets has not been deeper in an age when vertically specialized trade through production networks is resurgent.

There is ample evidence that in the past 30 years, parts and components (P&C) trade has grown much faster than total manufacturing and has played an important role in the expansion of manufacturing-led development in many countries (Feenstra 1998; Gereffi 1999; Grossman and Rossi-Hansberg 2008; Jiang and Milberg 2012). During 1992/93–2006/07, world manufacturing exports increased three-fold from $2,651 billion to $8,892 billion, while world exports of P&C rose five-fold from $511 billion to $2,405 billion. This resulted in a substantial increase in the share of P&C in total manufacturing exports from around 19 per cent to 27 per cent during the same period (Athukorala 2011). By 2007, trade in intermediates accounted for nearly 60 per cent of world trade in manufacturing compared to just over 50 per cent in 1990. For services, trade in intermediates stood at nearly 70 per cent in 2007 (Jiang and Milberg 2012; Miroudot et al. 2009).

In the last two decades, East Asia has been one of the fastest growing economic regions in the world, with the People's Republic of China (PRC) as the region's most dynamic economy. East Asia's share in world manufacturing trade increased from about 28 per cent in 1992–93 to 34 per cent in 2006–07 and since then has not only grown but transformed with the rise of an increasingly sophisticated product mix in the region's manufacturing and export basket. Much of the region's trade in manufactures, however, is intra-regional due largely to the predominance of production networks across the subregion. This is evidenced by data that shows that the share of intra-regional exports of P&C increased at a rate higher than that of global exports of P&C of the subregion, from 23.6 to 47.6 per cent during 1992–93 to 2006–07, a trend that has since only grown (Athukorala 2011).

India, by contrast, has largely remained outside the mainstream of industrial development in the region, especially with respect to integration within Asia's burgeoning production networks. In 2006–07, India's share in world exports of P&C was only 0.4 per cent, far less than most other developing economies in East Asia such as PRC, Philippines, Indonesia, Malaysia, and Thailand. Parts and components accounted for 31 per cent of PRC's non-fuel merchandize imports and 15 per cent of its exports soon after it joined the World Trade Organization (WTO), compared to only 12 and 6 per cent for India, respectively, during that time (Dimaranan et al. 2004).

This chapter analyses Indo-ASEAN trade to investigate why India has stayed on the margins of regional trade networks. India and ASEAN signed a wide-ranging free-trade agreement (the ASEAN–India Free Trade Area [AIFTA]) in 2009, creating the potential for a possible opening towards production sharing, but this has yet to generate significant embeddedness of Indian manufacturing within other parts of Asia. An understanding of the dynamics of vertically specialized trade between India and ASEAN can help shed light on the emerging ties between Indian and East Asian production networks and on implications for India's own industrial development, job creation, and capability formation.

A secondary concern of the chapter is the low employment intensity of Indian manufacturing, particularly in light of several rounds of policy reforms that have taken place since 1991–92 and the rapid growth of demand in the domestic market. Some of the standard factors assumed to inhibit the global competitiveness of Indian manufacturing are well known—for example, inadequacy in a wide range of supply-side factors such as underdeveloped physical infrastructure, poor quality power supply, complexity of internal taxation, land cost, skill deficit, and a plethora of behind-the-border factors that increase transaction cost. Despite these well-known problems, are there sectors that have been able to break these bottlenecks and enhance global production sharing in their value chains? If so what explains their performance and what are the conditions that set them apart from sectors that have done less well in this regard? In addressing these issues, the chapter deals mainly with the behind-the-border situation within India.

Methodology

The study uses mixed methods to address these questions, involving both quantitative (trade data analysis) and qualitative techniques (interviews). The quantitative analysis identifies the patterns of manufacturing trade between India and ASEAN at multiple levels of disaggregation over a 10-year period from 2000 to 2011. It also identifies the product categories where India has the highest potential for vertically specialized trade with ASEAN and vice versa. This analysis forms the basis of the interviews that were conducted with a purposive sample of 21 firms, industry actors, and government officials.

We identify five product categories where India has the highest intermediates trade with ASEAN. These include (i) machinery, transport equipment and scientific instruments (comprised of HS 84, 85, 87, and 90); (ii) basic metals and products (HS [harmonized system] 72, 73, 74, 76, and 80); (iii) chemicals (including HS 29, 32, and 38); (iv) plastics and rubber (HS 39 and 40), and (v) other (a miscellaneous list of HS groupings). Within these categories we conduct a more detailed analysis at 4- and 6-digit HS levels and identify: (i) high-performing sectors where vertically specialized trade has experienced high rates of growth during the past decade; (ii) depressed/stagnant sectors where growth rates and shares have fallen over the same period; and (iii) sectors with high potential for integration where multilateral imports into ASEAN are high, but imports from India are low. The firms we interviewed fall within these three groupings. We identify another striking pattern of India–ASEAN trade. India's share of trade in assembled products (network trade) was higher than trade in parts and services.

Organization of the Chapter

The rest of the chapter is organized as follows. Following a brief review of the theoretical literature on vertically specialized (see the second section), we report on the dataset we built and the trade data analysis we carried out for ASEAN and India at the world and bilateral levels (third section). The fourth section discusses the main findings from our field-based interviews with Indian firms and the fifth section concludes.

Measuring International Fragmentation and Vertical Specialization

A singular feature of global trade over the last quarter century is that trade in P&C trade has risen faster than finished goods trade. Much of the trade in intermediates is the result of global production networks and value chains created by multinational firms as they locate input processing in foreign affiliates (Gereffi 1999). Helleiner (1981) was one of the first to study fragmentation from the perspective of transnational corporations and intra-firm trade. This approach, however, does not capture arm's length transactions between unrelated firms and hence underestimates the magnitude of fragmentation. This is a major lacuna given that international outsourcing to external suppliers has increased faster than intra-firm trade in intermediates (Antras and Helpman 2004).

Some studies therefore have used highly disaggregated trade data to separate trade in P&C from final goods trade (see, for example, Athukorala 2005, 2011; Athukorala and Menon 2010; Kimura 2006; Ng and Yeats 2003; Yeats 2001). A majority of existing studies have used disaggregated data based on the Standard International Trade Classification (SITC Rev 2). The SITC Rev 2 system identifies about 60 product groups, at the lowest (5-digit) level, as representing P&C. The newer HS of trade classification expands this coverage to 200 product groups as representing P&C. Another approach involves the computation of intra-industry trade (IIT) in intermediate inputs (for example, Fukao et al. 2003; Kierzkowski 2001; Kimura 2006). The well-known index suggested by Grubel and Lloyd (1975) is generally used to measure the intensity of IIT in an industry.

The field however has come to follow Hummels, Ishii, and Yi (2001) who proposed an index of vertical specialization using input–output tables. This approach was refined by Koopman et al. (2011) who proposed a framework for measuring the foreign value added share of a country's exports taking into account the trade of intermediates across multiple borders. This method has been augmented by work on input–output accounts such as that of De Backer and Miroudot (2012), who have applied this analysis using World Input-Output Database (WIOD) data covering 56 countries and 37 industries.

Against the background of the approaches that scholars have used to measure vertically specialized trade, we turn towards building our own dataset to examine the patterns of vertically specialized trade between India and ASEAN.

Trade Data Analysis: Trends and Patterns in Vertically Specialized Trade between India and Association of Southeast Asian Nations

The emergence of AIFTA in 2010 opened up new possibilities for India and ASEAN to engage in production-sharing activities. As part of AIFTA, India and ASEAN agreed to reduce or eliminate import tariffs for about 80 per cent of mutually traded goods. Based on an empirical analysis of current trends and patterns in fragmentation-based trade between India and ASEAN for the period 2000–11,[1] the chapter assesses the potential for and obstacles to greater cross-border production sharing between the two regional economies.

Data and Methods

It is not easy to construct direct measures using published sources, as trade data is usually collected and reported as gross flows at each border crossing rather than the net value added between border crossings. The main task is to find credible ways to separate trade in P&C from end products trade (see, for example, Athukorala 2005, 2011; Athukorala and Menon 2010; Kimura 2006; Ng and Yeats 2003; Yeats 2001). For example, it is important to distinguish primary and conventional intermediate commodities and inputs (such as coal, timber, iron ore, iron and steel, rubber, primary chemicals, amongst others) from fragmentation-based P&C (see Hummels 2002 for this distinction).

[1] Within the ASEAN group, only the largest six countries—Indonesia, Malaysia, the Philippines, Thailand, Singapore, and Viet Nam—are covered in the analysis. Other smaller economies—Brunei, Cambodia, Lao PDR, and Myanmar—are excluded due to the paucity of data.

The latter appear further along the production chain and form a layer between primary inputs and final consumer goods. Unlike in the case of primary and conventional intermediate inputs, international exchange of fragmentation-based P&C does not occur in organized markets. Trade in fragmentation-based P&C generally takes place through a network of intra- and inter-firm relations rather than in an arms-length manner.

The customs classification, however, does not give us a straightforward way of partitioning the trade data on the basis of the conceptual categories mentioned here. Athukorala (2011) points out that the only practical way of addressing the issue is to focus on the specific product categories in which fragmentation trade is heavily concentrated. Based on the available literature on production sharing, he identified seven product categories: office machines and automatic data processing machines (SITC 75), telecommunication and sound recording equipment (SITC 76), electrical machinery (SITC 77), road vehicles (SITC 78), professional and scientific equipment (SITC 87), and photographic apparatus (SITC 88). Athukorala argues that these product groups, referred to as 'network products', generally do not contain any end product produced from start to finish in a given country.

We follow this approach to build a disaggregated dataset using the United Nations (UN) Comtrade database concorded with the Broad Economic Categories (BEC) system to identify trade in manufactured P&C. We begin with collating trade data for India and ASEAN at the 6-digit level of the HS of trade classification. This yielded a total of 5,017 product codes at the 6-digit HS level. This was concorded with the Standard International Trade Classification (SITC) revision 3 to identify and extract all the manufacturing product codes. Consistent with standard practice, this gave us a list of manufacturing codes at the 6-digit HS level that corresponded with SITC 5 (chemicals), SITC 6 (manufactured materials), SITC 7 (machinery and transport equipment), and SITC 8 (miscellaneous manufactured articles). We then parsed out the codes related to P&C within manufacturing using the BEC system of classification to generate 4,185 HS product codes at the 6-digit level, of which more than half (2,518) were P&C. Next, we identified network products which comprise 'assembled end products' and 'P&C' (576 codes at the 6-digit HS level belonged to the group of network products, of which 241 are P&C). The value of 'assembly trade' was measured as the difference between the total value of trade in network products and the value of trade in P&C within this category.

India and ASEAN's Network Trade with the World

A striking finding here was the rising importance of assembled network trade in India's export basket. In the decade between 2000 and 2011, India's total manufactured exports, in current US dollars, registered a robust growth rate of about 17.7 per cent per annum with a share of P&C in total manufactured exports at about 58 per cent during the period (Table 8.1). By contrast, in keeping with East Asia's well-integrated regional trade networks, ASEAN member states had a much higher share of P&C in their export as well as import baskets. The ASEAN's share of P&C in total manufactured exports actually increased from 60.5 per cent in 2000 to 65.4 per cent in 2011. However, India's exports of network products[2] recorded significantly higher growth rates between 2000 and 2011 (24.8 per cent per year) relative to aggregate manufacturing exports as a whole, to the extent that the share of network products in India's total manufactured products doubled over the past decade (6 per cent in 2000 to 12 per cent in 2011). The ASEAN always had a high share in total exports—a hefty 65 per cent of manufactured exports in 2000, which declined to about 48 per cent in 2011 from this high base.

The role of network products in India's exports was the result of strong exports in a variety of assembled end products, such as automobiles. Assembled products in India's export basket of network products had risen to a striking 60 per cent in 2011 (up from 44 per cent in 2000). This rests largely on India's growth in the export of 'road vehicles' (STIC 78, which correlates with HS 87 after concordance) and more recently, by 'telecommunication and sound recording equipment' (SITC 76, or HS 85, electrical machinery and parts thereof after concordance). Cars, motorbikes, or generator sets are assembled

[2] Note that network products refer to finished goods that are largely assembled involving inputs made globally—that is, products that are not made in one country from start to finish. Network trade includes these assembled goods and the P&C involved in them. This is distinct from the overall category of P&C.

Table 8.1 Average Annual Growth Rates of Trade, 2000–11

	Multilateral Trade				India's Bilateral Trade with ASEAN	
	ASEAN		India			
	Exports	Imports	Exports	Imports	Exports	Imports
Manufactured products, all	8.7	9.5	17.7	23.8	20.9	20.6
Manufactured products, parts and components	9.3	9.2	17.6	25.9	17.4	20.2
Manufactured products, end products	7.7	10.2	17.7	20.7	28.5	21.4
Network products, all	5.7	6.5	24.8	23.5	23.8	17.0
Network products, parts and components	5.8	5.5	20.1	21.8	13.7	14.9
Network products, assembled products	5.3	9.2	29.1	25.2	34.6	19.3

Note: Growth rates are calculated using semi-logarithmic regressions. ASEAN = Association of Southeast Asian Nations.

Source: Estimated using UN Comtrade database (accessed via the World Bank's WITS server), available at http://wits.worldbank.org/ (accessed on 7 November 2016).

TABLE 8.2 India's Exports of Intermediate Manufactured Products to the World (top 20 product groups)

Product Code	Product Description	India's Exports to World					
		2000–01	2004–05	2010–11	2000–01	2004–05	2010–11
		Value ($ million)			% share		
I	**Machinery, transport equipment and scientific instruments**						
84	Nuclear reactors, boilers, machinery and mechanical appliances	506,885	1,497,903	4,295,950	2.8	4.1	4.6
85	Electrical machinery equipment and parts thereof	774,583	1,248,937	4,261,993	4.3	3.4	4.6
87	Vehicles other than railway or tramway rolling stock and parts	480,750	1,069,756	2,711,953	2.7	2.9	2.9
II	**Basic metals and products**						
72	Iron and steel	1,044,615	3,910,977	7,449,090	5.9	10.8	8.1
73	Articles of iron or steel	647,324	1,924,374	5,692,715	3.6	5.3	6.2
74	Copper and articles thereof	150,258	1,047,212	4,141,717	0.8	2.9	4.5
76	Aluminium and articles thereof	277,158	488,348	1,267,431	1.6	1.3	1.4
79	Zinc and articles thereof	4,717	35,994	729,697	0.0	0.1	0.8
III	**Chemicals**						
29	Organic chemicals	1,620,793	3,864,108	9,869,301	9.1	10.6	10.7
28	Inorganic chemicals; compounds of precious metals	201,666	347,549	1,038,801	1.1	1.0	1.1

32	Tanning or dyeing extracts; tannins and their derivatives, dyes, pigments and other colouring matter	504,405	751,696	1,756,165	2.8	2.1	1.9
38	Miscellaneous chemical products	163,506	302,714	930,482	0.9	0.8	1.0
30	Pharmaceutical products	246,764	374,276	1,046,964	1.4	1.0	1.1
IV	**Plastics and rubber**						
39	Plastics and articles thereof	609,559	1,905,343	4,104,410	3.4	5.2	4.4
40	Rubber and articles thereof	303,881	682,072	1,797,853	1.7	1.9	1.9
V	**Other products**						
71	Natural/cultured pearls, precious stone	6,386,487	10,724,988	27,619,522	35.9	29.5	29.9
54	Man-made filaments	505,440	954,430	2,411,800	2.8	2.6	2.6
52	Cotton	951,555	1,018,058	2,173,906	5.3	2.8	2.3
55	Man-made staple fibres	419,381	696,358	1,425,362	2.4	1.9	1.5
68	Articles of stone, plaster, cement, asbestos, mica, or similar materials	299,469	505,259	1,001,569	1.7	1.4	1.1
	Total	16,099,196	33,350,352	85,726,681	90.2	91.6	92.6
	Grand total	17,808,437	36,356,513	92,517,082	100	100	100

Source: Estimated using UN Comtrade database (accessed via the World Bank's WITS server), available at http://wits.worldbank.org/ (accessed on 7 November 2016).

products and are distinct from P&C such as brake linings, transmission systems, headlights, gearboxes and so on, which grew more slowly in India. Over the 10-year period between 2000 and 2011, the share of road vehicles in India's manufactured exports rose from 2.4 per cent in 2000 to 5.3 per cent in 2011. Within this, exports of assembled vehicles saw their share in manufactured exports rise four-fold, from less than 1 per cent to nearly 4 per cent during this period.[3] Similar changes were seen in the latter half of the 2000s in the rise of the export of telephones (mobile phones) brought about by the rising share of transmission apparatus for radio telephony incorporating reception apparatus,[4] whose share in India's total manufactured exports increased rapidly.[5]

The ASEAN's and India's export composition has also undergone changes in recent years. For example, electrical machinery equipment and parts (HS 85) constituted more than half of ASEAN's intermediate exports in 2000, but its share has declined drastically to 23 per cent in 2011. Thus, the decline in the share of network products in ASEAN's export basket, as seen before in this chapter, is primarily driven by electrical machinery. By contrast, the export shares of most other products have increased over time. This suggests a shift of ASEAN's basket of exports away from its traditional domain of electrical machinery to other products that are gaining prominence, or an exit of some electrical machinery parts manufacture to other lower cost countries. The declining importance of electrical machinery for ASEAN may imply that countries like India can potentially emerge as a hub for electrical machinery manufacturing and assembly.

Similarly, as can be seen in Table 8.2, the composition of India's manufactured intermediate exports has changed with a growing shift towards more resource- and capital-intensive products (chemicals, metals, rubber and machinery, transport equipment and scientific instruments respectively). This has been associated with a decline in labour-intensive manufactured products (gems and jewellery, footwear, garments and so on). The product groups that have gained in shares

[3] 6-digit level reveals that this increase has been driven by small cars and motorcycles of a wide range—from 50cc mopeds to 250cc motorbikes where exports very likely embody imported parts.

[4] HS 852520

[5] From a negligible 0.02 per cent in 2000 to as high as 1.7 per cent in 2011.

include 'nuclear reactors, boilers etc.' (HS 84), various basic metals and products thereof (iron and steel, copper and zinc), organic chemicals (HS 29), and plastics and articles thereof (HS 39).[6]

Imports: Parts and Components Imports Grow Faster than Imports of Finished Goods

The patterns of exports and imports noted here suggest that there has been some expansion of assembly activity in India in the recent past. The share of P&C in India's manufactured imports has increased significantly (see Table 8.3). However, the share of final products in India's total manufacturing exports remained broadly constant, which may imply that most of the assembly activities in manufacturing are oriented towards the domestic market in India rather than the export market. A major exception to this is 'network products' where we noted a significant increase in the share of assembled products in the export basket.[7]

Despite this modest expansion of export-oriented assembly activity in recent years, India remains a net importer of assembled network products. The growth in assembly-related exports are largely confined to 'road vehicles' and 'telecommunication equipment'. Evidence suggests that ASEAN is losing its competitive advantage in some product lines within 'electrical machinery'. This, in turn, points to the existence of significant potential for India to expand assembly-related export activities in this important sector. To this end, India can develop strong synergies with ASEAN, exploiting the latter's competitive advantage in P&C production of electrical machinery. India's potential for expansion of assembly activities exists also in other categories of network

[6] The product groups that have lost share over the past decade include traditional labour-intensive products such as natural and cultured pearls and precious stones, amongst others (HS 71) and cotton (HS 52).

[7] India's growth rate of manufactured P&C imports was higher than that of manufactured end products (26 per cent per year relative to 21 per cent). The share of P&C in India's imports of manufactured goods thus increased from 54 per cent in 2000 to 65 per cent in 2011. In general, P&C accounts for a larger share in India's manufactured imports (65 per cent in 2011) than exports (57 per cent in 2011). For ASEAN, components feature prominently in both export and import shares.

products, professional and scientific equipment (SITC 87), telecommunications and sound recording equipment (SITC 76), office machines and automatic data-processing machines (SITC 75), and of course road vehicles (SITC 78).

Bilateral Trade between India and Association of Southeast Asian Nations

It is evident from Table 8.1 that ASEAN's imports from India have grown significantly faster than its imports from the rest of the world. Thus, India's market share in ASEAN (that is, India's share in ASEAN's imports from the world) has steadily increased (from less than 0.5 per cent to nearly 2 per cent). The growth in market share has been sharpest for manufactured end products (nearly 3.5 per cent) and assembled network products (about 2 per cent—see Tables 8.1 and 8.4 for details).[8]

Within network products, the specific product groups that have contributed most to India's high export growth in the ASEAN market are not different from those that have driven India's overall export growth in these categories globally. As Table 8.4 shows, as in the case of India's multilateral exports, the product groups that have recorded the fastest export growth in ASEAN are 'road vehicles' (STIC 78) and 'telecommunication and sound recording equipment' (SITC 76). The share of road vehicles increased quite dramatically from 1.7 per cent in 2000 to 6.5 per cent in 2011. Further, much of this increase was due to the rise in the export of *assembled* road vehicles, whose share in manufactured exports increased from less than 1 per cent to above 4 per cent during this period. The overall pattern of India's export of 'road vehicles' parts and assemblies to ASEAN does not look very different from its exports in this area overall.

[8] India's exports of aggregate manufactured products to ASEAN grew at the rate of about 21 per cent per year during 2000–11, which is higher than India's multilateral export growth (17.7 per cent) during the same period in manufacturing (Table 8.1). India's better performance in the ASEAN market compared to its global average is entirely driven by the export of manufactured end products rather than of P&C. In particular, India's exports of assembled network products to ASEAN grew at a faster pace (35 per cent per year) than its exports to the rest of the world (29 per cent per year).

Table 8.3 India's Imports of Intermediate Manufactured Products from the World (top 20 product groups)

Product Code	Product Description	World Exports to India					
		2000–01	2004–05	2010–11	2000–01	2004–05	2010–11
		Value ($ million)			% share		
I	**Machinery, transport equipment and scientific instruments**						
84	Nuclear reactors, boilers, machinery and mechanical appliances	1,945,008	3,542,778	13,807,623	11.6	9.1	12.2
85	Electrical machinery equipment and parts thereof	1,765,426	3,530,959	10,951,745	10.6	9.0	9.7
87	Vehicles other than railway or tramway rolling stock and parts	420,459	1,004,673	4,152,321	2.5	2.6	3.7
90	Optical, photo, technical, medical, etc apparatus	348,819	540,399	1,272,270	2.1	1.4	1.1
II	**Basic metals and products**						
72	Iron and steel	627,216	2,674,321	8,594,728	3.8	6.8	7.6
73	Articles of iron or steel	302,428	1,059,980	4,082,351	1.8	2.7	3.6
76	Aluminium and articles thereof	126,104	375,354	1,353,973	0.8	1.0	1.2
74	Copper and articles thereof	128,190	438,651	1,103,690	0.8	1.1	1.0
III	**Chemicals**						
29	Organic chemicals	1,633,304	3,823,571	11,059,727	9.8	9.8	9.8
31	Fertilizers	326,778	805,638	8,304,806	2.0	2.1	7.3
28	Inorganic chemicals; compounds of precious metals	675,369	1,586,260	3,243,637	4.0	4.1	2.9

(Contd.)

Table 8.3 (*Contd.*)

Product Code	Product Description	World Exports to India					
		2000–01	2004–05	2010–11	2000–01	2004–05	2010–11
38	Miscellaneous chemical products	372,438	693,380	2,185,606	2.2	1.8	1.9
32	Tanning or dyeing extracts; tannins and their derivatives, dyes, pigments and other colouring matter	236,303	487,494	1,162,032	1.4	1.2	1.0
30	Pharmaceutical products	109,291	208,072	735,443	0.7	0.5	0.6
IV	**Plastics and rubber**						
39	Plastics and articles thereof	632,341	1,766,736	5,947,310	3.8	4.5	5.2
40	Rubber and articles thereof	117,821	241,575	1,037,741	0.7	0.6	0.9
V	**Other products**						
71	Natural/cultured pearls, precious stone	4,669,126	11,460,725	22,682,411	28.0	29.3	20.0
48	Paper & paperboard, articles of pulp, paper and board	267,422	480,624	1,160,504	1.6	1.2	1.0
59	Impregnated, coated, cover/laminate	126,441	358,828	1,010,540	0.8	0.9	0.9
54	Man-made filaments	239,431	509,079	833,351	1.4	1.3	0.7
	Total	15,069,715	35,589,097	104,681,809	90.4	91	92.3
	Grand Total	16,695,379	39,055,633	113,363,719	100	100	100

Source: Estimated by the authors from the dataset we constructed from the UN Comtrade-WITS database.

TABLE 8.4 Percentage Share of Network Products in India's Total Exports of Manufactured Products to the Association of Southeast Asian Nations

	Parts and Components			Assembled Products			Total		
	2000/01	2004/05	2010/11	2000/01	2004/05	2010/11	2000/01	2004/05	2010/11
Office machines and automatic data processing machines (SITC 75)	6.49	1.28	0.47	1.31	0.66	0.90	7.79	1.94	1.37
Telecommunication and sound recording equipment (SITC 76)	0.17	0.11	0.12	0.37	0.24	2.40	0.54	0.35	2.53
Electrical machinery (SITC 77)	1.96	1.39	1.73	0.99	1.24	1.46	2.95	2.63	3.19
Road vehicles (SITC 78)	1.19	1.69	2.14	0.55	0.49	4.33	1.74	2.18	6.47
Professional and scientific equipment (SITC 87)	0.07	0.11	0.49	0.40	0.45	0.79	0.47	0.56	1.28
Photographic apparatus (SITC 88)	0.20	0.15	0.11	0.10	0.10	0.09	0.31	0.24	0.20
Total Network Products	10.08	4.73	5.07	3.73	3.18	9.97	13.81	7.91	15.04

Note: These shares are averages for the given 2 years. ASEAN = Association of Southeast Asian Nations.

Source: Estimated using UN Comtrade database (accessed via the World Bank's WITS server). Available at http://wits.worldbank.org/ (accessed on 29 September 2016).

Most recently, exports of assembled products in the telecommunications equipment area (within SITC 76 or HS 85) have registered gains in the ASEAN market, pushing up India's share of this category to ASEAN from a mere 0.2 per cent in 2004/05 to nearly 2.4 per cent in 2010–11. This increase has been almost entirely driven by transmission equipment and mobile phone-related components, specially 'transmission apparatus for radio telephony incorporating reception apparatus' (HS 852520), whose share increased from a negligible 0.04 per cent in 2000 to as high as 2.2 per cent in 2011. This pattern within SITC 76 (or HS 85) is very similar to the pattern of India's overall multilateral exports, signifying that India's improved performance in ASEAN is part of the overall evolution of India's vehicle and telecommunications sectors and its growing competence in this area, rather than shifts induced by trade agreements.

The Skill in India's Exports

Using the factor-intensity classification of the International Trade Centre (ITC), adapted by Hinloopen and van Marrewijk (2008), we classify India's traded intermediate products into four specific categories: natural resource-intensive, unskilled labour-intensive, human capital-intensive and technology-intensive. This classification makes use of data disaggregated at the 3-digit level of SITC (Rev 2).[9] Calculations are done after mapping HS 6-digit codes on to SITC (Rev 2) 3-digit codes. Consistent with the pattern observed for India's overall multilateral exports, the product groups that have gained export share in the ASEAN region are capital-intensive while the groups that had experienced a decline are traditional, labour-intensive products. As can be seen in Table 8.5, a majority of the sectors where India's exports have grown and gained share between 2000 and 2011 fall under the category of medium-high

[9] The classification is available at http://www2.econ.uu.nl/users/marrewijk/eta/intensity.htm (accessed on 14 October 2016). A total number of 240 items, at the 3-digit SITC level, have been grouped into five categories (number of items in each category in parentheses): primary (83), natural-resource intensive (21), unskilled-labor intensive (26), human capital-intensive (43), technology-intensive (62), and unclassified (5). For our purpose, we define an additional category, called capital-intensive category, by adding human capital-intensive and technology-intensive categories.

technology industries (for example, HS 84, 87, 29) or high technology industries (HS 30, 90 and some categories of HS 85 such as transmission and recording equipment and optical equipment). It is evident that the share of capital-intensive products in India's exports to ASEAN has increased significantly from about 61 per cent in 2000/01 to 75 per cent in 2011.

Within capital-intensive products, both human capital-intensive and technology-intensive increased their shares, though the increase is more pronounced for technology-intensive products. In contrast, the shares of natural-resource intensive and unskilled labour-intensive products have declined significantly. A similar trend can be observed in India's overall exports to the world (Table 8.2).[10] This then is worrisome from the perspective of job creation for India's growing workforce. How will this shift away from labour-intensive jobs and the rise of capital- and technology-intensive work help accommodate the nearly million people that enter India's labour market each month?

Export Intensities

Is India supplying in categories that are important to ASEAN, and are there opportunities that India is missing and can potentially grow into? The analysis in this section suggests that India has a significant potential to expand its ASEAN export share in the machinery sector, while also building on its existing strength in the chemicals sector to expand more fully in the ASEAN market. Comparison shows that India's shares (reported in Table 8.5) in almost all the production categories related to machinery, transport equipment, and scientific equipment (Category I in the given scheme) are considerably lower than ASEAN's corresponding import shares from the world. By contrast, India's shares are higher than world shares for products grouped under Category III (chemicals), particularly in 'organic chemicals' (HS 29). In 2010/11, 'organic chemicals' accounted for more than 20 per cent of ASEAN's imports from India while its share in ASEAN's imports from the world is only 6 per cent.

We estimated India's export intensity in the ASEAN market by dividing India's export shares reported in Table 8.5 by the correspond-

[10] In 2010/11, 54 per cent of India's manufactured intermediate exports fell into the capital intensive category, up from 42 per cent in 2000/01.

TABLE 8.5 India's Exports of Intermediate Products to the Association of Southeast Asian Nations (top 20 product groups)

HS Code	Product Group	Values ($ million)			Percentage Shares		
		2000/01	2004/05	2010/11	2000/01	2004/05	2010/11
I	**Machinery, transport equipment, and scientific instruments**						
84	Nuclear reactors, boilers	35	118	498	3	3	7
85	Electrical machinery equipment and parts	113	105	198	8	3	3
90	Optical, photo, technical, medical, etc. apparatus	4	15	95	0	0	1
87	Vehicles other than railway or tramway rolling stock and parts	26	92	283	2	2	4
II	**Basic metals and products**						
72	Iron and steel	107	486	521	8	13	8
74	Copper and articles thereof	13	225	376	1	6	6
76	Aluminium and articles	124	154	286	9	4	4
79	Zinc and articles thereof	0	4	228	0	0	3
73	Articles of iron or steel	37	69	225	3	2	3
III	**Chemicals**						
29	Organic chemicals	168	621	1389	13	16	21
38	Miscellaneous chemicals	24	65	181	2	2	3
32	Tanning/dyeing extract	42	68	174	3	2	3
28	Inorganic chemicals	25	75	160	2	2	2

IV	**Plastics and rubber**						
39	Plastics and articles thereof	72	159	316	5	4	5
40	Rubber and articles thereof	35	56	213	3	1	3
V	**Other products**						
71	Natural/cultured pearls	306	1151	723	23	30	11
54	Man-made filaments	50	108	152	4	3	2
52	Cotton	33	35	89	2	1	1
30	Pharmaceutical products	15	18	75	1	0	1
55	Man-made staple fibres	17	25	64	1	1	1
	Total	1,246	3,646	6,246	93	95	93
	Grand Total	1,336	3,843	6,728	100	100	100

Source: Estimated using UN Comtrade database (accessed via the World Bank's WITS server). Available at http://wits.worldbank.org/ (accessed on 29 September 2016).

TABLE 8.6 India's Imports of Intermediate Products from the Association of Southeast Asian Nations (top 20 product groups)

HS Code	Product Group	Values ($ million)			% Share		
		2000/01	2004/05	2010/11	2000/01	2004/05	2010/11
I	**Machinery, transport equipment, and scientific instruments**						
85	Electrical machinery equipment, and parts	422	622	1547	22.1	17.1	14.2
84	Nuclear reactors, boilers	156	358	1426	8.1	9.8	13.0
87	Vehicles other than railway or tramway rolling stock and parts	46	89	189	2.4	2.4	1.7
90	Optical, photo, technical, medical, and other apparatus	35	116	353	1.8	3.2	3.2
II	**Basic metals and products**						
73	Articles of iron or steel	22	65	304	1.1	1.8	2.8
72	Iron and steel	25	117	294	1.3	3.2	2.7
74	Copper and articles thereof	23	57	218	1.2	1.6	2.0
76	Aluminium and articles thereof	28	62	206	1.5	1.7	1.9
75	Nickel and articles thereof	31	45	188	1.6	1.2	1.7
80	Tin and articles thereof	14	35	161	0.7	1.0	1.5
III	**Chemicals**						
29	Organic chemicals	253	713	2256	13.2	19.6	20.6
38	Miscellaneous chemical products	91	82	287	4.8	2.3	2.6
32	Tanning/dyeing extract; tannins	52	126	192	2.7	3.4	1.8
28	Inorganic chemicals	60	65	159	3.1	1.8	1.5

30	Pharmaceutical products	3	4	77	0.2	0.1	0.7
IV	**Plastics and rubber**						
39	Plastics and articles thereof	139	396	1404	7.3	10.9	12.8
40	Rubber and articles thereof	14	35	145	0.7	1.0	1.3
V	**Other products**						
49	Printed books, newspapers	34	84	343	1.8	2.3	3.1
71	Natural/cultured pearls	86	46	236	4.5	1.3	2.2
54	Man-made filaments	118	153	113	6.2	4.2	1.0
	Total	1,651	3,270	10,098	86.4	89.7	92.4
	Grand Total	1,911	3,644	10,933	100	100	100

Source: Estimated using UN Comtrade database (accessed via the World Bank's WITS server). Available at http://wits.worldbank.org/ (accessed on 29 September 2016).

TABLE 8.7 Export Intensity of the Association of Southeast Asian Nations in the Indian Market

		S_{aw}	EI_1			EI_2		
		2010/11	2000/01	2004/05	2010/11	2000/01	2004/05	2010/11
I	**Machinery, transport equipment and scientific instruments**							
85	Electrical machinery equipment parts	23.1	2.1	1.9	1.5	0.4	0.5	0.6
84	Nuclear reactors, boilers	11.8	0.7	1.1	1.1	1.7	1.3	1.1
87	Vehicles other than railway or tramway rolling stock and parts	3.3	1.1	1.8	1.5	1.1	0.9	0.5
90	Optical, photo, technical, medical, and other apparatus	3.8	0.7	1.2	0.9	1.0	1.0	0.9
II	**Basic metals and products**							
73	Articles of iron or steel	3.6	0.6	0.7	0.8	0.6	0.6	0.8
74	Copper and articles thereof	2.8	1.5	1.4	2.0	0.9	0.9	0.7
72	Iron and steel	2.4	0.4	0.5	0.4	1.1	1.3	1.1
80	Tin and articles thereof	1.6	5.7	8.2	8.8	1.3	0.9	0.9
76	Aluminium and articles thereof	1.4	2.0	1.8	1.6	1.5	1.4	1.4
82	Tool, implement, cutlery, spoon	0.5	1.0	1.6	1.7	1.6	1.6	1.4
III	**Chemicals**							
29	Organic chemicals	10.9	1.4	2.0	2.1	2.4	1.8	1.9
38	Miscellaneous chemicals	2.8	2.1	1.3	1.4	3.1	1.2	0.9

32	Tanning/dyeing extract	0.9	1.9	2.8	1.7	2.4	2.9	1.9
28	Inorganic chemicals	0.9	0.8	0.4	0.5	6.7	2.9	1.6
30	Pharmaceutical products	0.6	0.2	0.2	1.1	0.8	0.4	1.2
33	Essential oils and resinoids	0.6	1.1	1.2	2.6	1.2	0.8	0.7
34	Soap, organic surface-active	0.5	0.7	1.2	1.5	1.2	1.2	1.0
IV	**Plastics and rubber**							
39	Plastics and articles thereof	10.6	1.9	2.4	2.4	1.1	1.2	1.2
40	Rubber and articles thereof	4.3	1.0	1.5	1.5	0.4	0.4	0.3
V	**Other products**							
44	Wood and articles of wood	1.7	4.7	2.1	4.4	0.2	0.1	0.4
49	Printed books, newspapers	1.4	5.0	4.8	7.4	11.2	13.4	2.2
54	Man-made filaments	1.2	4.3	3.2	1.4	3.2	2.8	0.9
71	Natural/cultured pearls	1.1	0.2	0.0	0.1	5.4	1.0	2.0
55	Man-made staple fibres	1.0	1.9	1.5	1.1	0.3	0.3	0.3
70	Glass and glassware	1.0	1.7	2.0	0.9	1.9	1.5	0.5
48	Paper and paperboard	0.9	1.1	0.9	0.6	1.4	1.6	0.7

Source: Estimated using UN Comtrade database (accessed via the World Bank's WITS server). Available at http://wits.worldbank.org/ (accessed on 29 September 2016).

ing world export shares. We compute two separate indices of export intensity as follows.

$$EI_1 = \frac{S_{ia}}{S_{wa}} \text{ and } EI_2 = \frac{S_{ia}}{S_{iw}}$$

where S_{ia} represents the share of a product group in India's (i) total exports of intermediates to ASEAN (a); S_{wa} denotes the share of the same product group in the world's (w) total exports of intermediates to ASEAN; and S_{iw} is the given product group's share in India's exports to the world. The export intensity indices are the ratios of the two shares. The value of EI_1 index indicates whether or not India's export basket is overrepresented or 'biased' towards ASEAN in those categories than exports from the world to ASEAN on average. Similarly, the value of EI_2 shows whether or not India's export basket shows a bias towards ASEAN relative to India's exports in those categories to the world as a whole. A value greater than 1 for EI_1 indicates that India's export share in those categories is larger than the world's share to ASEAN; and a greater than 1 value for EI_2 implies that in those categories ASEAN is a particularly important market for India relative to the world.

Values for the EI_1 index indicate that India has a high export intensity in ASEAN for most chemicals, some basic metals (iron and steel, copper, and aluminium) and most of India's traditional export items (gems and jewellery, man-made filaments, cotton, and man-made staple fibre). There is a disproportionate presence of these product groups in India's export basket to ASEAN.[11] The product groups with low EI_1 values include most of the machinery items, articles of iron and steel, and plastic. The ASEAN prefers to import these intermediate goods from other countries than India. While the EI_1 index may indicate India's general bias towards or against a particular product group, the EI_2 measures India's specific bias in the given product group towards ASEAN relative to other markets. The values of EI_2 index show a somewhat different picture of India's export intensity with ASEAN, particularly in the machinery sector (intermediates related to the machinery sector). With the notable exception of 'electrical machinery equipment

[11] Of course, this bias may be present in India's exports to other trading partners as well, not just in the case of ASEAN. Our second measure of export intensity (EI_2) shows the bias specifically towards ASEAN as compared to other markets.

and parts', the values of the EI_2 index show a significant increase for all product groups under Category I. This indicates India's growing export orientation towards the ASEAN market in these products. In fact, over the last 10-year period this trend has intensified, and by 2010/11, the values of the EI_2 index had risen significantly above 1 in many of these categories.

The surprising finding is that India's export orientation towards the ASEAN market shows a steady decline in the case of 'electrical machinery equipment and parts'. This is a matter of concern given that this product group continues to hold the top position in ASEAN's multilateral trade (both imports and exports) despite its declining share over the past decade. It is clearly a potential area for India to do better.

We can thus conclude that there is a significant potential for India to increase its vertically specialized export to ASEAN in the following three product spaces: (i) 'electrical machinery equipment and parts' (HS 85); (ii) articles of iron and steel (73); (iii) all product groups under category V (that is India's more traditional products such as gems and jewellery and textiles (particularly man-made filaments, cotton and man-made staple fibres). In addition, based on an examination of export intensities at the 6-digit HS level, we can identify two major products within HS 84 where India holds an unexploited potential in the ASEAN market. These are: 'parts for diesel and semi-diesel engines' (HS 840999) and 'parts for spark-ignition type engines nes' (HS 840991). Similarly, India's EI_2 values are very low for most of the products within HS 85, which implies that there is a significant potential to expand Indian exports in this group.[12]

With respect to bilateral imports, there is clearly an imbalance (Table 8.1). India's low import growth from ASEAN compared to that from the world is a direct result of manufactured parts and components that grew at a lower growth rate of 20.2 per cent per year in the bilateral

[12] Export growth within HS 87 has been driven by 'motor vehicle parts nes' (HS 870899), and 'transmissions for motor vehicles' (HS 870840). The EI_2 values of these fast growing products have increased significantly. It may also be noted that one product within HS 84—'parts and accessories of automatic data process' (847330)—has recorded a significant decline in its share of exports to ASEAN from as high as 8.5 per cent in 2000/01 to as low as 0.8 per cent in 2010/11. At the same time, the share of 'aircraft parts nes' (HS 880330) has increased from 0.5 per cent to 2.3 per cent during the same period.

case (as opposed to 25.9 per cent in the multilateral case). India's import growth for network products from ASEAN is miniscule compared to India's overall import growth. The bias against ASEAN, moreover, can be seen also for assembled network products. Within network products, P&C imports from ASEAN grew at 14.9 per cent per year compared to a much larger growth rate of 21.8 per cent from the world. India's slow growth of P&C imports from ASEAN could be attributed to the lackluster performance of the former in electrical machinery assembly. For India's imports of intermediate products from ASEAN, see Table 8.6. Table 8.7 reports ASEAN's export intensity in the Indian market.

We employ the Grubel-Lloyd index to measure the extent of IIT in intermediate products between India and ASEAN—that is, the simultaneous occurrence of exports and imports within the same industry. The index of IIT in industry *j* and year *t* in trade of the country under consideration is defined as:

$$IIT_{jt} = \frac{(X_{jt} + M_{jt}) - \left|X_{jt} + M_{jt}\right|}{(X_{jt} + M_{jt})}$$

where: X_{jt} = value of exports from India to ASEAN in industry *j* and year *t*
M_{jt} = value of imports to India from ASEAN in industry *j* and year *t*

While IIT_{jt} measures IIT in a specific industry (that is, within each HS 6-digit product), its trade-weighted average can be used to measure IIT in the aggregate groups of industries and in the entire manufacturing sector.

Trade-weighted averages for different product groups at the HS 2-digit level and the overall index suggests that for the year 2000, about 26 per cent of India's bilateral trade with ASEAN in manufactured intermediates was IIT. This share had fallen to 21 per cent in 2005 but then registered an increase to 29 per cent in 2011. Between 2000 and 2011, the individual products that have recorded an increase in the value of the IIT index include 'vehicles' (HS 87), 'electrical machinery equipment and parts' (HS 85), and 'optical, photo, cine, measuring, checking precision, medical or surgical instruments and apparatus parts and accessories thereof' (HS 90). All these product groups belong to our Category I (machinery, transport equipment and scientific instruments). It is particularly striking that the IIT index in HS 87 increased steadily from 27 per cent in 2000 to 64 per cent in 2005 and to as high as 74 per cent in 2011.

In most cases, the unit values of products exported by India are generally lower than that of its imports. Significant potential for regional integration for India in ASEAN's manufacturing networks exists in the expansion and deepening of HS 85, electrical machinery, electronics and other product categories such as basic metals, chemicals, and plastics and rubber.[13]

View from the Field: Firm-Level Analysis

In this section we report on findings from 20 semi-structured open-ended interviews that we conducted with a purposively drawn sample of firms and industry associations in product categories that are important for India's vertically specialized trade with ASEAN (and the globe). We spoke with firms in sectors where such trade is high, as well as with those where significant potential exists for India in the ASEAN market but where current growth is low. In the former category we interviewed firms in the road vehicles or automotive and auto components sector (HS 87) and in the chemicals and organic chemicals (HS 29) sector that the data shows are particularly important categories for India in the ASEAN market. In terms of sectors where there is significant under-exploited potential we interviewed firms in the electrical machinery, equipment, and parts sector (HS 85) and non-electrical machine tools (HS 84). In addition to firms, we interviewed government officials and leading industry associations in each sector. These interviews shed light on how specific (leading) firms view their own participation and performance in production networks, why they participate (or do not) in these networks, what drives vertical specialization where it does occur, and what are some bottlenecks to wider integration of Indian firms in production networks, as well as to industrial upgrading.

As demonstrated by our trade data analysis, the interviews also reveal that India's trade with ASEAN has seen the most growth in relatively capital-intensive product categories. By contrast the share of trade in more labour-intensive product groups (textiles, leather, gems, and jewellery) have declined during this same period. The picture on

[13] In general, the product groups within Category I record higher levels of IIT compared to the product groups belonging to other categories. A major exception is HS 85, where the IIT index is relatively low.

the import side is mixed and varies by sector. The interviews also show that India imports higher value and more technologically advanced P&C than it exports. Finally, Indian firms see ASEAN as an important potential market, especially after AIFTA, India–Japan Comprehensive Economic Partnership Agreement (CEPA), India–Republic of Korea CEPA, and India–Malaysia Comprehensive Economic Cooperation Agreement (CECA) were signed. At the same time they point to the difficulty of deepening production and trade ties with ASEAN, despite the FTA, given ASEAN's long-standing and deep linkages with PRC, which is far more competitive in the region relative to India.

Why has India's integration in global markets been slow even after 25 years of liberalization and economic reforms of the early 1990s? Scholars have identified several factors that determine vertical specialization and production sharing within global or regional networks. Some of these factors include trade costs, export-oriented FDI, locational advantages and 'service link' costs. Tariffs are important, but the presence of export-processing zones, duty suspension, and drawback facilities for export-oriented production activities, as well as FTAs mitigate their direct impact. Others have shown that structural factors in the home country, such as access to finance and intra-period credit, quality of infrastructure, skill levels, governance, and political stability, are important. Yet others have spoken of scale and scope economies and capacity to deliver on time are equally important so as not to disrupt production plans for the entire production chain.

Our findings show that several of the factors that drive a potentially more efficient and quality-enhancing growth are missing in Indian manufacturing: very high service costs, high interest rates, poor credit markets, and very poor infrastructure and logistics support, topped by severe shortages of reliable power supply, all of which undermine the capacity of firms to deliver to quality and on time have hampered India's trade reliability and integration in Asian and global markets. Land costs and land-acquisition complexities add to project uncertainty. Low levels of research and development (R&D) further complicate efforts at upgrading. On the face of it, therefore, there is good reason for poor global integration of India's manufacturing sector.

Keeping the obvious lacks in mind, we take a closer look at what specifically emerged from our interviews about processes that constrain firms and what are ways to get past them.

Power Sector Subsidies, Price-Pressured End-Users and Their Innovation-Dampening Effects

The electrical machinery sector in India is currently focused primarily on the large domestic market. Only 18 per cent of the sector's $22 billion worth of output is exported. The bulk of its output of boilers, generators, transmission, and distribution equipment is oriented towards public sector utilities and power companies (IEEMA Interview, 2013). Given the vast demand for power in India, the large size of the domestic market could be an important source of scale and stability that can foster growth, development, and upgrading in the sector, but the opposite is the case. Save some exceptions, the industry has very low levels of value addition and stagnant technology. Indian firms cannot compete with the global competition in many key subsegments and imports have been growing. For example, there is significant import of boiler turbine generator (BTG) equipment (at about 13 per cent) in the boiler segment, which constitutes a major share of the sector. Imports are predominantly from countries such as PRC and the Republic of Korea. Due to the emergence of new technologies, such as supercritical technology, the market share of foreign BTG players has been rising in the total orders placed (*Annual Report* 2012–12, p. 27). More than 80 GW of supercritical BTG sets have been awarded by India so far, of which more than 68 GW (85 per cent) have been awarded to foreign players, with Chinese players capturing more than 80 per cent of the overseas orders. Domestic players significantly lag behind their global peers in adding BTG capacity in the supercritical boiler and turbine segments, as also in other key technologically advanced components (Ministry of Heavy Industries and Public Enterprises 2011, p. 28).[14]

In our interviews respondents repeatedly attributed the sector's lagging technology to the fact that their main clients are utilities and power companies whose primary concern is low costs and low-end prices. They were quick to point out exceptions and instances of upgrading in other product segments: for example, transmission is now being done through smart grids, ABB (ASEA Brown Boveri) produces circuit breakers in India for global exports, transformers produced in

[14] For more details, see Ministry of Heavy Industries and Public Enterprises (2011).

India are exported to the West, and BHEL (Bharat Heavy Electricals Limited) and Siemens are collaborating to produce supercritical sets. However, overall, the lagging technology in the vast power generation and distribution sector has kept the industry bogged down.

As is the case with all public sector companies, the utilities award projects through a tendering system and applicants are judged at two levels. They are first required to meet a set of technical standards, which according to the respondents are quite basic—adequate but rudimentary. Once a bidder qualifies on technical grounds they are evaluated on their financial offer with the contract going to the lowest bidder. If any company comes up with a technically better product or an innovative technical process, it is out-bid on price. The main objective of the companies therefore becomes to just meet the basic parameters rather than to propose new things or new ways of doing things. This least-common-denominator approach to technical standards eliminates incentive on the part of the supplier firms to innovate or move towards the industry frontier. 'If [the government's] technical standards are higher and the norms more stringent, then better products will come up' (IEEMA Pandit Interview, March 2013).

A second key issue that reinforces this low-level equilibrium trap is India's electric power subsidies. On the face of it, the utilities' use of a no-frills bidding process to keep prices down is not unusual—it happens all around the world. But steep power sector subsidies create an added negative feedback loop that further retards the sector's technical growth (IEEMA Interview, March 2013). The politics around power prices is well known. They keep electricity prices artificially low which has a ripple effect throughout the value chain from generation to transmission to distribution. Since power companies have to provide electricity at a low price, they have to produce it at an even lower price. This leads to 'cutting down project costs by the use of cheap products, or inferior quality equipment' which eventually traps the system in a low-technology, low-efficiency, low-productivity cycle (Pandit Interview, March 2013).

When asked about cutting costs through upgrading or innovation, the response was that most generation and distribution companies have low profit margins to begin with. Given the unsustainably low prices at which they have to deliver power, and the losses they have to deal with, many are in the red: 'there is no money to make new investments and [firms] are not interested in upgrading' (IEEMA Interview, March 2013).

As a consequence the price pressures that cascade down the chain have an adverse effect on innovation and R&D, creating long-term sector-wide weaknesses that saddle the industry with obsolete and lagging technology.

The irony is that in reality the purported cost-saving wrested from squeezing prices and imposing just-acceptable, minimal technical standards at the front end, prove illusionary and end up only hurting the sector. They add to costs rather than saving them. They add to costs, first, by discouraging modernization that keeps high-cost system-wide inefficiencies locked in. Second, the low technical standards to which the sector is held and the 'fixes' adopted by firms to cut costs, can lead to more frequent breakdowns, work-stoppages, and productivity losses which end up adding to costs over time rather than cutting them. By contrast, a lifecycle view of costs—unit costs and efficiencies over time—would reveal that fostering continuous innovation, learning, and upgrading within the sector by incrementally ratcheting up standards in gradual congruence with global norms would lead to greater cost savings from the better performance of the equipment and the higher productivity of the system as a whole. These benefits could be passed on to the consumer or invested in R&D. Some policymakers and government officials are beginning to look at lifecycle costs and are of the view that if a product is priced higher but has a longer and trouble-free lifecycle, it should be preferred over lowest cost (IEEMA Interview, March 2013).

Thus a product's primary end-users can powerfully shape its prospects for upgrading. In this case, where public parastatals and power companies dominate, the government could leverage its presence strategically, as a demanding buyer, to foster innovation and help raise standards in the industry, rather than keeping them down.

Policy Costs

It is striking that in the face of vast demand—which has to be met by imports because domestic capacity cannot keep up with it—there are currently tremendous unused capacities in the electrical machinery sector (IEEMA Interview, BHEL Interview, March 2013). This underutilization of capacity is due to a slowdown in the expansion of the domestic power sector, a slowdown that is serious enough to have pushed domestic equipment suppliers to look towards export markets, alongside rising pressure of imports from the PRC (BHEL Interview, March 2013).

The power sector slowdown, according to the firms we interviewed, is on account of a set of policy issues related to land acquisition, environmental clearance procedures, and the government's coal-linkages policy which have delayed companies' expansion plans, suspended already commissioned operations, and, in some cases, disrupted ongoing operations. Land acquisition problems have put several new power projects on hold, caused other plants to postpone capacity expansions, and adversely impacted the orders of firms in the electrical machinery sector. Several other projects have been delayed due to complications with environmental clearances. Similarly, coal shortages and the inability of many thermal power projects to get on to the government's coal linkage list have produced the same outcome—of delaying power projects and affecting orders for machinery and equipment makers. As recently as April 2013, the coal ministry said that due to coal shortages it would not be able to meet the coal demand of several 16,000 MW power plants that were planning to come on board in 2014–15 as it was already committed to honouring 143 coal-linkage commitments for larger power plants (60,000 MW and higher) during the Twelfth Plan (PTI 10 April 2013). As a general manager at BHEL put it, these issues slow down production in the power sector, and consequently demand for products produced by BHEL suffers. 'Policies like land acquisition and coal linkages seriously affect BHEL's order books', and they hit private sector companies even harder (BHEL Interview, April 2013).

High costs of land acquisition, along with high levels of taxation, lack of reliable power supply rising input costs as well as a lack of local capabilities have pushed firms in several sectors to locate plants overseas. A leading automotive company that has amongst the highest market shares in the country spoke about their growing overseas investments: 'Just within the last decade, land prices in India have increased ten-fold and the cost of energy and inputs has trippled.' Potential high-quality steel projects (inputs that can help make cars lighter) like POSCO (Pohang Iron and Steel Company) are still in limbo. 'High levels of excise duties and cascading taxation policies hinder [our] competitiveness. With excise duties, value added tax (VAT) and octroi, a small car is taxed at 53 per cent and a larger one at 83 per cent—charges that are approximately equivalent to tobacco taxes.[15] This consistent inflation of cost has forced [us] to set up plants in countries such as Poland, the Czech Republic, Viet Nam, Turkey, Thailand, Indonesia and PRC where land and energy prices are relatively cheaper' (Maruti Suzuki Interview, April 2013). Maruti Suzuki's other plants are in Japan and Pakistan.

A third issue concerned the inverted duty structure in the sector that firms believed hampered component imports and militated against the localization of the value chain. Several firms felt that the imports of finished products had 'increased by leaps and bounds' over component imports after recent FTAs were signed with ASEAN, the Republic of Korea, and Thailand, for example. This, they argue, is primarily because duties on final goods have come down to zero or near-zero levels post the FTAs, while some inputs carry relatively higher duties. (Compared to this, in the auto sector, imports of finished cars carry 60–70 per cent duties.) Others pointed out that even though electronic components are supposed to have zero duty under the WTO enforced Information Technology Agreement (ITA)-I, quite a number of the same inputs in fact attract import duties of 5–10 per cent for consumer electronics (ELCINA [Electronic Industries Association of India] n.d.). In a survey carried out in August 2012, the Federation of Indian Chambers of Commerce and Industry (FICCI) found that seven product areas were strongly impacted by the inverted duty structure: pumps, tyres, electronic hardware, electrical equipment, medical devices/instruments, aluminum and articles thereof, and technical textiles (FICCI 2012).

Under these conditions, 'it makes business sense to import final goods and sell them here rather than produce them locally' (CEAMA [Consumer Electronics and Appliances Manufacturers Association] Interview, April 2013). According to this respondent, imports such as this neither create the linkages with global production networks that help one learn nor foster the creation of domestic capacities. They simply encourage trading companies (importers) to set up shop. Firms feel that the lack of scrutiny over whether rules of origin are actually being followed in context of the various FTAs that the government has signed exacerbates this problem. Given that the component base is already

[15] Apart from taxes, the absence of good infrastructure, lack of reliable power supply, high cost of land, and an unstable policy environment have undermined manufacturing performance (Maruti interview, April 2013).

weak in India, and the inverted duty structure further undermines the development of local capabilities, the industry associations (for example, CEAMA) have protested against this to the government, but so far with little success. From the interviews we conducted, it is unclear what other factors might be at play here but the point was echoed by several respondents in the electronics sector. The chemical industry had the same lament about inverted duty structure.

Other factors named by firms that add to production costs include high landed costs, poor infrastructure, high interest rates, high transactions costs ('every interaction with the government adds to your costs') and high costs of serviced land. As one respondent said, the logistics costs of moving goods from Delhi to Mumbai, Kolkata, or Chennai is so high (due to 'numerous checkpoints, poor infrastructure, high transactions costs') that it is easier to bring in the goods from Thailand' (Khanna Interview, March 2013).

The government is well aware of these 'policy costs' and how high interest rates, bad infrastructure, problems of port congestion, and so on restrict manufacturing growth in India. But the reason some officials counter that part of the problem also is that many firms are 'happy with the status-quo and not interested in doing something new'. They argue that the domestic market is large and moving beyond it requires taking risks which many are averse to. 'Most companies are interested in business returns of 5-10-15 per cent, and the large domestic market allows them to get those returns with whatever they are doing' (Interview, 16 April 2013). Pointing to the success of the automotive and auto parts sector they argue that stagnation is not inevitable and these bottlenecks can be gotten around. Even so, the government is focused on introducing new plans, policies, and incentives to break the infrastructure bottlenecks and ease other supply (Interview, April 2013).

Upgrading within Global Production Networks

Finally, a common theme that emerged from our interviews with government officials was the concern about upgrading within global production networks. The general discomfort with participating in global production networks and value chains was the fear that firms from low-income countries can get easily trapped at the bottom global value chains while higher value production, profits, and technologies remain in the hands of lead firms from advanced economies who drive these chains (Ministry of Heavy Industries and Public Enterprises interviews, March and April 2013). So what are the conditions under which economic upgrading can occur in value chains, in the face of intensified global competition from low- and high-cost players?

A striking example of the challenges of upgrading in global value chains and how it may occur comes from the automotive industry—a sector that has a better record of performance than many others and one that is much more inserted in global production networks than other sectors we interviewed. About a decade ago, a leading domestic components supplier—the TVS group's (TV Sundaram Iyengar Motor Company's) Sundaram Fasteners Ltd. (SF)—became the preferred supplier of high-tensile radiator caps for General Motors' (GM's) global platform. In this case, SF set up a separate dedicated plant for the caps and established a just-in-time supply chain from India to the US. Within a short time it went on to win nearly 80 per cent of GM's global business in high tensile radiator caps (of a certain size) and won supplier of the year awards from GM 5 years in a row. The component they supplied was no doubt a low value, non-critical part, costing $0.86 per unit, but it was very significant that this contract made SF one of the first Indian auto-component suppliers to successfully penetrate a leading manufacturer's global supply platform, and it generated a lot of learning for the company (G.P. Interview, March 2013). However, this changed in 2011. Just as SF was negotiating with GM to revise the price of the caps they produced up to $1.03, given the rising input and production costs, they were outbid by a global competitor who was able to supply the same part to GM for $0.43, or 60 per cent less than the cost SF was quoting. By the end of 2011, SF's orders fell to less than a third of previous levels (SF Interview, March 2013).

The surprise was that SF was outbid on price not by a lower cost manufacturer from PRC, Viet Nam, or some other low-cost emerging economy, but by an Austrian firm. The Austrian company, which entered into the radiator cap business in 2010 in the wake of the recession in Europe, was able to supply the caps at less than half the cost of SF because it had opted for a fully automated production process. This generated a lower cost product of greater precision, more consistent quality, and shorter turn-around times (SF Interview, March 2013). By contrast, SF had been struggling with delays and higher input and production costs due to a range of factors. Sixty per cent of the value of their product is outsourced to small- and medium-sized producers in Tamil Nadu. Given the dismal power situation in Tamil Nadu where power supply to industry is available only for a few hours a day, firms routinely have to rely on costly back-up generators. Though it adds to costs, for larger firms generators or captive power plants have become a routine investment. But for many of SF's smaller suppliers who have to borrow at high interest rates to invest in back-up generation, the costs are too high. The worsening power problem, escalating input costs, and high interest rates had combined to drive up SF's costs, and ironically it lost out on a relatively low-value component to a high-wage competitor.

When asked how SF had responded, the company said it had found substitute global buyers for now (Ford), gotten alternative orders for other parts from GM, but eventually would have to find ways to cut costs to compete with the Austrian firm. About 2 years after the shock of loss, and a wide-ranging analysis of their situation, the company had come to the conclusion that it would have to compete by also automating. Given the high capital cost of the multiform precision equipment required to produce the caps with 100 per cent automation, India's high interest rates would make it prohibitively expensive to automate domestically. Its plans are to set up plants outside the country to take on the Austrian competitor (SF Interview, March 2013).

Many critics of global production networks and the unequal power embodied in these networks could very well point to SF's decision to get into the production of relatively low-value radiator caps for lead auto assemblers (GM, Rolls Royce) as an example of how Indian firms remain trapped at the bottom of global value chains. '[Many firms] are happy with the status quo and not interested in doing something new' (Ministry of Heavy Industries and Public Enterprises Interview, April 2013). At first glance that may seem like a valid observation. In an interview that one of the authors of this chapter had conducted with SF in the early 2000s, when they were just getting established as GM's lead supplier of radiator caps, a similar question had been asked. Is this an example of upgrading or downgrading? The response then was that the experience had already generated knowledge about what it takes to be a first-tier supplier on a global platform and consistently produce significant quantities of output global quality standards. Even if the product was simple, tremendous learning had taken place (Tewari 2005).

In a recent interview, SF echoed this view. While on the face of it GM's decision to switch to the lower cost Austrian firm seems to suggest that a decade-plus buyer–supplier relationship between SF as GM's top supplier of this product came to naught as it was so easily wiped out by price. Underneath the surface, however, things are more complex. GM and SF still have a strong relationship and SF still supplies a third of GM's demand for radiator caps. Besides, GM exchanged information with SF about cost cutting before shifting the order and gave them time to adjust and participated in the discussions.

When it became clear that under present manufacturing conditions in India cutting costs by the order of magnitude required was not possible, GM shifted the order; at the same time, it negotiated with SF to move to an alternative product: a \$6.00 shifter. This is a more technically complex sub-assembly and although it is not a critical component, it is more advanced than the radiator cap. GM has been producing it for the past 2 years and is moving into other similarly higher value products. Meanwhile, other global buyers, like Ford, approached SF to supply radiator caps for them, and so SF's radiator business is still running at near-full capacity. But the important point is that GM did not simply drop SF. Instead, SF diversified, and moved up the value chain a notch, to a \$6 component instead of a \$0.86 component (Interview, March 2013). TVS as a whole has redoubled its efforts to manage logistics and the company in a more focused way through its separate dedicated logistics firm in the automotive vertical, TVS Logistics, which now has offices around the globe and has entered into key joint ventures (Interview, March 2013). In the wake of the crisis then, industrial upgrading did take place and was accompanied by a deepening of the firm's place within global networks, not a withdrawal.

Two insights emerge from the firm-level cases discussed here. First, the examples raise stark questions about the employment-generation ability of the domestic manufacturing sector given its current status. The government has made job generation a priority in the manufacturing and services sectors. The SF example given in this chapter, however, shows how pressures of global competition combined with a deeply disabling set of domestic institutional deficits (high interest rates, a ruinous power situation, near total lack of quality inputs, quality hardware, and reliable logistics) are together pushing firms towards automation and outward investment. This push towards automation, moreover, is occurring not in high-tech, cutting-edge advanced manufacturing sectors where domestic capabilities do not exist, but in relatively low-value manufacturing that one assumes there is domestic capability for. If more and more firms choose this capital-intensive route to leapfrogging over domestic bottlenecks, then policymakers need to worry about where the entry level and skilled manufacturing jobs that carry the potential of a pathway towards upward mobility will come from.

Second, it points to the fact that there is competition from both the high and low end (industrial and low-income countries) even in low-value products with relatively low margins. Domestic producers are thus squeezed in the middle by pressure, on the one hand, from efficient low-cost producers in countries like PRC, and on the other from deep-pocketed competitors from advanced economies who use automation to overcome low-income economies' cost advantages. We heard about this dual competition from firms in many sectors. The key variable with respect to upgrading, therefore, is not low wages, but *costs per unit* of output (Berger 2005). The Austrian firm that outbid SF operated in a high-wage context, but due to other factors, such as automation, had much lower unit costs than SF which operated in an environment where even with much lower wages, it was not possible to match its competitor's cost advantages. In light of the ongoing obsession in Indian policy circles about the rigidity of the labour market and labour cost, it was striking that in our interviews with firms, associations, and government officials, no one, except one firm, brought up the issue of labour laws or wages as an impediment to their competitiveness. The main issue about labour that emerged was about some skill shortages and the critical need for skill development.

* * *

This chapter constructed a highly disaggregated trade dataset to distinguish between parts and components, and assembled end products, in India's trade with ASEAN and the world. We found evidence of a steady growth in India's integration with global production networks. India's intermediates exports grew much faster (25 per cent per year) than its aggregate manufactured exports (18 per cent per year) during the 10-year period we studied, and India's share of 'network' exports (assembled end products) doubled during this period. Imports showed a similar trend. By 2011, P&C comprised 65 per cent of India's manufactured imports (up from 54 per cent in 2000), and 58 per cent of its manufactured exports. India's engagement with ASEAN grew at a faster pace than multilateral trade during this period, led by exports, which grew at an impressive 35 per cent a year (relative to 29 per cent a year for the world) during this period.

The worrisome finding is that Indian exports to ASEAN show a growing bias towards more capital-intensive and natural resource–intensive products (machinery, transport equipment and instruments, and chemicals, metal and rubber, respectively) at the expense of traditional, labour-intensive manufactured exports. There is also evidence of an increasing bias in favour of final goods (including assembled goods) rather than P&C. The skill composition of India's exports also reflects a dominance of capital-intensive intermediate and network exports from India. Human capital-intensive and technology-intensive exports increased their shares, with technology-intensive product shares rising fastest. The shares of natural resource–intensive and unskilled labour-intensive products declined significantly. This has important implications for the employment potential of India's emerging export patterns, a worrisome trend given the large projected increases in working age youth that will be added to the labour market in the coming decades.

A crucial finding, however, is that India has been a fast-growing market from the point of view of ASEAN's exports, and vice versa. There is significant potential for growth in India's insertion in production networks in ASEAN by expanding its intermediates exports in the machinery sector, building on its strong performance in the chemicals sector by expanding the export of higher value specialty chemicals, and in general attempting to move up the value chain in the parts, components, and assembled goods exported in the (electrical and non-electrical) machinery, telecommunications, and transport equipment product categories. There is tremendous underexploited potential for growth in electronics and related equipment categories (HS 85). The data also suggests that there is significant potential for India to expand assembly-related export activities in certain categories of network products, such as electrical machinery (SITC 77), professional and scientific equipment (SITC 87), telecommunications and sound recording equipment (SITC 76), office machines and automatic data processing machines (SITC 75), and, of course, road vehicles (SITC 78).

Our field-level interviews bore out some of these emerging trends. and showed that while East Asia and ASEAN are seen as important destinations for Indian exports, deeper integration is affected by three factors: (i) Indian firms' preoccupation with the large domestic market over exports; (ii) the low-value addition in Indian manufacturing which translates into low-value component exports and a high degree of reliance on expensive imports; and (iii) a variety of impediments that add to production costs, such as suboptimal scales of production in key intermediate sectors, a near total lack of quality inputs (high-quality steel, electronics, quality plastics), precision and high-quality tooling, the complete absence of the electronics hardware sector (including semiconductor devices), and a lack of serious R&D or skill development. These structural deficits are compounded by policy costs imposed on firms by the disabling lack of reliable power supply, inadequate infrastructure and logistics, high interest rates and land costs, and an unstable policy environment. Although some firms have found innovative ways to cope, the costs are high.

The broader points this raises is that participating in regional and/or global production networks in any meaningful way—such that upgrading occurs and firms do not remain trapped at the base of the value chain—requires the building of local/domestic capabilities. This requires mitigating not only supply-side initiatives and fixing the many behind the border factors such as poor power and infrastructure and high interest rates, a myriad interstate taxes, and so on. Equally important are *demand-side factors* and policy inducements that can ratchet up production quality and standards, and deepen collaborative and competitive capabilities as well as learning from an institutional perspective, as the power-sector cases show. In sum then, at the current time, meaningful participation in global networks requires not only strategic trade in tasks—or bundles of capabilities—but also linkages with a steadily growing domestic market.

To strengthen India's participation in global production networks, then, low service link costs will be very important. This is important because the mere presence of multinational enterprises and global firms does not ensure that India is automatically part of GPNs. Multinational enterprises come with different objectives—they can be market seeking, efficiency seeking, resource seeking, and so on. Evidence shows that the bulk of inward FDI in India is market seeking, in part because of the high costs of trading across borders. In order to strengthen India's participation in GPNs, it would be important to make it attractive for MNEs to use India as a manufacturing hub for export production.

References

Antras, P. and E. Helpman. 2004. 'Global Sourcing', *Journal of Political Economy*, 112(3): 552–80.

Athukorala, P. 2005. 'Product Fragmentation and Trade Patterns in East Asia', *Asian Economic Papers* 4(3): 1–27.

Athukorala, P. 2011. 'Production Networks and Trade Patterns in East Asia: Regionalization or Globalization?' *Asian Economic Papers*, 10(1): 65–95.

ELCINA. n.d. *Pre-Budget Recommendations, 2013–14*. India.

Feenstra, R.C. 1998. 'Integration of Trade and Disintegration of Production in the Global Economy,' *Journal of Economic Perspectives*, 12(4): 31–50.

Fukao, K., H. Ishido, and K. Ito. 2003. 'Vertical Intra-Industry Trade and Foreign Direct Investment in East Asia', *Journal of the Japanese and International Economies*, 17(4): 468–506.

FICCI. 2012. 'FICCI Survey on Inverted Duty Structure in Indian Manufacturing', mimeo.

Gereffi, G. 1999. 'International Trade and Industrial Upgrading in the Apparel Commodity Chain', *Journal of International Economics*, 48(1): 37–70.

Gorg, H. 2000. 'Fragmentation and Trade: US Inward Processing Trade in the EU', *Weltwirtschaftliches Archiv*, 136(3): 403–22.

Grossman, G.M. and E.R. Hansberg. 2008. 'Trading Tasks: A Simple Theory of Offshoring', *American Economic Review*, 98(5): 1978–97.

Grubel, H.G. and P.J. Lloyd. 1975. *Intra-Industry Trade*. London: Macmillan.

Helleiner, G. 1981. *Intra-firm Trade and the Developing Countries*. London: Macmillan Press.

Hinloopen, J. and C. van Marrewijk. 2008. 'Empirical Relevance of the Hillman Condition for Revealed Comparative Advantage: 10 Stylized Facts' *Applied Economics*, 40 (18); 2313–28.

Hummels, David, Jun Ishii, and Kei-Mu Yi. 2001. 'The Nature and Growth of Vertical Specialization in World Trade', *Journal of International Economics*, 54(1): 75–96.

Jiang, Xiao and William Milberg. 2012. 'Vertical Specialization and Industrial Upgrading: A Preliminary Note', Working Paper 10, 'Capturing the Gains', University of Manchester, UK.

Kemeny, Thomas and David Rigby. 2010. 'Trading Away What Kind of Jobs? Globalisation, Trade and Tasks in the US Economy', PWP-CCPR 2010-007,

California Center for Population Research, University of California, Los Angeles, USA.

Kierzkowski, H. 2001. 'Joining the Global Economy: Experience and Prospects of the Transition Economies', in S.W. Arndt and H. Kierzkowski (eds.), *Fragmentation: New Production Patterns in the World Economy*. New York: Oxford University Press.

Kimura, F. 2006. 'International Production and Distribution Networks in East Asia: 18.

Facts, Mechanics, and Policy Implications', *Asian Economic Policy Review*, 1(1): 346–47.

Koopman, R., W. Powers, Z. Wang, and S. Wei. 2011. 'Give Credit where Credit is Due: Tracing Value Added in Global Production Chains', NBER Working Paper 16426, September 2010, Revised September 2011. Available at www.nber.org/papers/w16426 (accessed on 14 October 2016).

Ministry of Heavy Industries and Public Enterprises. 2011. *Indian Electrical Equipment Industry Mission Plan 2012–2022: Base Document*. Government of India.

Miroudot, S., R. Lanz, and A. Ragoussis. 2009. 'Trade in Intermediate Goods and Services', OECD Trade Policy Working Paper No. 93, Paris, France.

Ng, F. and A. Yeats. 2003. 'Major Trade Trends in East Asia: What Are Their Implications for Regional Cooperation and Growth?', Policy Research Working Paper No. 3084, World Bank, Washington, D.C.

Yeats, A.J. 2001. 'Just How Big is Production Sharing?', in S.W. Arndt and H. Kierzkowski (eds), *Fragmentation: New Production Patterns in the World Economy*. New York: Oxford University Press.

9

ANWARUL HODA
DURGESH KUMAR RAI

Trade and Investment Barriers Affecting International Production Networks in India

Global production-sharing arrangements, particularly in manufacturing, have been a prominent feature of the integration of world economy over the past few decades. Such arrangements involve the segmentation of production processes in both goods and services and the dispersal of the segments over an international network. International production networks have been facilitated by the steep declines in tariff and non-tariff barriers (multilaterally as well as in regional agreements), reduction in the time taken for transporting goods from one country to another and advances in communication technologies (radio frequency identification tags, the Internet, and transponders) that have made it possible to track, monitor, and control production taking place in different locations.

Existing studies (Gaulier, Lemoine, and Ünal-Kesenci 2005; Sen and Srivastava 2011; United Nations Conference on Trade and Development [UNCTAD] 2013; World Bank 2005) strongly suggest that foreign direct investment (FDI) plays a key role in international production networks. Whether by production through affiliates (offshoring) or procurement of inputs through arm's length transactions (outsourcing), multinational firms are the main coordinating agents in international production networks.

As other authors (Athukorala 2010; Athukorala and Menon 2010; Rajan 2003; Kimura and Obashi 2010, 2011; Sen and Srivastav 2011) have pointed out, India has the lowest participation in international production networks amongst Asian countries. While large economies with a diversified industrial structure may not need to depend on such networks for industrial growth to the same extent as smaller economies, it is a supplementary strategy that India must consider if it wants the share of manufacturing in gross domestic product (GDP) to increase from the 15 per cent level[1] it has remained stuck in for more than a decade. As India looks for ways to significantly step up its GDP growth rate, as it must in order to eradicate poverty and raise the standard of living of its peole to a decent level, reviving manufacturing has to be on top of the agenda. In 2011, the Government of India had already brought manufacturing to the forefront and enunciated the National Manufacturing Policy (NMP). The Prime Minister's 'Make in India' initiative in 2014 seeks to give a further fillip to the sector.

The NMP is overly ambitious in aiming to increase the share of manufacturing in GDP from 15 to 25 per cent by the year 2025 and in setting a target of 100 million jobs in manufacturing in the next decade. However, even modest progress in achieving these targets is not conceivable without a new initiative to accelerate the growth of manufacturing. The People's Republic of China (PRC), Malaysia, and Thailand have all achieved impressive growth in manufacturing by encouraging regional and global production networks, particularly in the last two decades. The issue before India is whether providing policy stimuli to increase India's participation in international production networks can be the new initiative needed to propel manufacturing forward.

In the second section, we explain the objective and methodology of the study. In the third section of the chapter, we look at the latest

[1] In January 2015, the Central Statistics Office (CSO) changed the base year from 2004–05 to 2011–12 and introduced a number of methodological improvements. In the new series, the share of manufacturing was 18.1, 17.9, and 17.3 per cent in 2011–12, 2012–13 and 2013–14 respectively. For the earlier years, the data calculated on the basis of the new methodology have not yet been made available.

picture of India's participation in global as well as regional production networks. We also describe briefly the trends in FDI inflows into India in view of the key role that such inflows play in international production networks. The fourth section is devoted to trade barriers and the gateway infrastructure and logistics costs on which international production networks are critically dependent. In the fifth section, we analyse the behind-the-border investment environment that influences investment, including FDI, in manufacturing enterprises. In the sixth section, we make recommendations to improve the investment climate and adjust the policy framework to quicken the pace of development of manufacturing by expanding Indian participation in international production networks. The seventh section concludes.

Objective and Methodology of Study

The starting point for this chapter is that India is an outlier in the development of international production networks, which is both a global and regional phenomenon. India needs to expand manufacturing in order to provide employment to the millions of people being added every year to the job market, but it has been unable to seize the opportunity provided by production-sharing networks to meet this objective. What should make this route attractive for the country is that it offers a quicker route to expand manufacturing than the alternative of building productive capacity covering all stages of production. In any case, the strategy needs to be only to supplement, not supplant, more comprehensive industrialization.

The objective of this study is to investigate the reasons for India's poor participation in production-sharing networks and to make recommendations to improve the position. The approach that we adopt is of analysis and comparison and we have selected three comparator countries in the region that have been successful in production-sharing arrangements as well as in industrial growth, namely, the PRC, Malaysia, and Thailand. An important aim of the study is to delineate and measure the gap between India and the comparator countries in respect of each of the factors that we identify as responsible for India falling well behind them in international production networks. The methodology includes both desk work and field surveys/interviews. A significant part of our field work was interviews with senior representatives of multinational firms that are manufacturers of original equipment (OEMs) in the Asian region and have a substantial presence in regional production networks, and consultations with industry associations. An examination of the gateway infrastructure and logistics costs occupies a central place in our study on account of its importance for the location of manufacturing enterprises participating in international production networks. During the field work on this aspect, the research team interacted with representatives of freight forwarders and express delivery providers in five ports (Chennai, Mumbai, Port Klang, Laem Chabang, and Shanghai) and two airports (Delhi and Beijing). Discussions were also held with associations of freight forwarders, logistics service providers (LSPs) and customs house agents, and with port authorities. The list of entities with whom discussions/consultations were held is given in Annexure 9A.

India's Participation in International Production Networks

Before undertaking an analysis of the underlying reasons for India being left out of the mainstream in the worldwide development of international production networks, we check the current position in this regard.

Manufacturing Sector in India

India's lack of success in participation in international production networks is interlinked with the wider phenomenon of the lack of dynamism in India's manufacturing sector. As alluded to earlier, the share of manufacturing in GDP has hovered around 15 per cent in India for more than two decades, while according to World Development Indicators (WDI) of the World Bank, in 2011, it was 31.8 per cent in the PRC, 14.7 per cent in India, 24.3 per cent in Malaysia, and 34.0 per cent in Thailand, as shown in Figure 9.1.

In the last two decades, world trade in manufactures has risen sharply from $5.4 to $23.4 trillion. In 1992, India was behind not only the PRC but even the comparatively small economies of Malaysia and Thailand in terms of its international trade share in manufactures. By 2011, the PRC had made impressive strides in manufacturing to raise its share

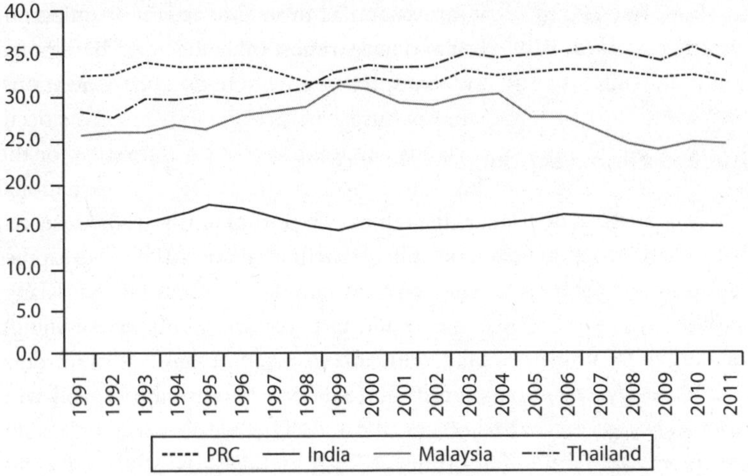

FIGURE 9.1 Share (%) of Manufacturing in Gross Domestic Product
Note: PRC = People's Republic of China.
Source: World Bank, *World Development Indicators*, available at http://data.worldbank.org/ (accessed on 29 September 2016).

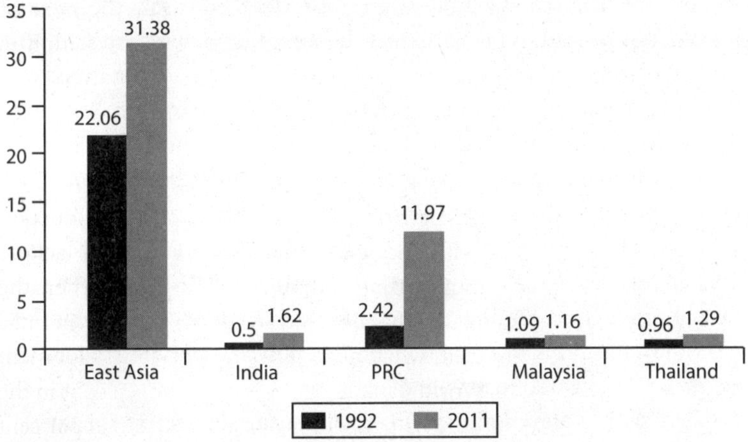

FIGURE 9.2 Share (%) of India and Comparator Countries in World Trade of Manufactures
Note: PRC = People's Republic of China.
Source: World Trade Organization (WTO), *Statistics database*, available at http://stat.wto.org/Home/WSDBHome.aspx?Language=E (accessed on 29 September 2016).

to about one-eighth of world trade and push East Asia's[2] share up to almost one-third. While India has edged past Malaysia and Thailand, it trails far behind the PRC, with a share of a meagre 1.62 per cent.

India in Global Production Networks

There are two main alternative approaches to quantify trade in international production networks. The conventional approach relies on the input-output database developed from national sources but we adopt another approach, which uses trade in parts and components (P&C) as a proxy for international production sharing in manufacturing. This methodology was pioneered by Yeats (1998) to estimate the relative importance of trade in P&C in the OECD trade in machinery and transportation equipment group (SITC 7) and used by Athukorala and Yamashita (2007). Athukorala (2010) developed it further, drawing up a comprehensive list, which expanded the coverage of P&C beyond SITC 7 and included assembled goods as well. Assembled goods do not necessarily enter international trade but varying proportions of such goods produced from internationally traded P&C are absorbed within the country in which the assembly takes place. For this reason, the growth of P&C can be said to better reflect the intensity of international production sharing and we consider trade in P&C only in our analysis.

International trade in P&C has risen even faster than in manufacturing with the result that its share in world trade in manufactures in 2011 was higher than in 1992, moving up from 15.47 to 24.08 per cent. This reflects the rapid rise of global production sharing. Global production sharing has been most active in electrical goods, including semiconductores and its devices, as can be seen in Figure 9.3. There has been substantial production sharing in four other areas, namely, road vehicles, telecommunications and sound recording, power-generating machines, and general industrial machinery.

East Asia has played a major role, increasing its already substantial share of 28 per cent to 38 per cent during the period, as shown in Figure 9.4. The increasing dominance of East Asia is due prinicipally to the

[2] In this chapter, East Asia includes 6 ASEAN economies (Indonesia, Malaysia, Philippines, Singapore, Thailand, and Viet Nam) and 5 major economies of the region (PRC, Hong Kong, China, India, Japan and Republic of Korea).

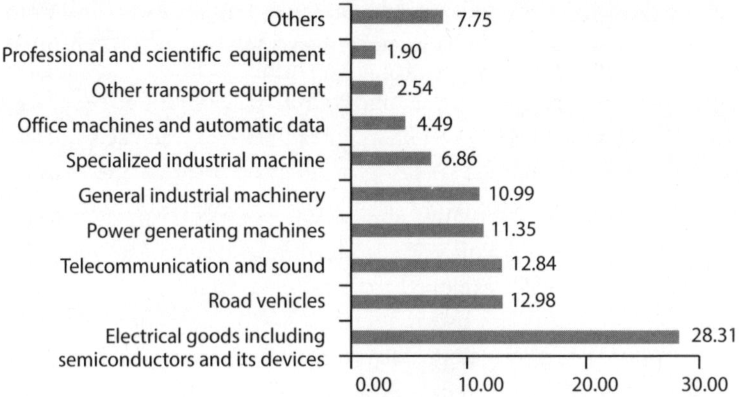

FIGURE 9.3 Sectoral Share (%) of World Trade in Parts and Components, 2011
Source: Authors' calculation from UN Comtrade data (obtained through World Integrated Trade Solution (WITS) software).

impressive performance of the PRC. Malaysia and Thailand have not been able to retain the relatively large shares that they had already secured 20 years ago, India is slowly increasing its share from a very low base level, but it remains the smallest player amongst comparator countries in 2011.

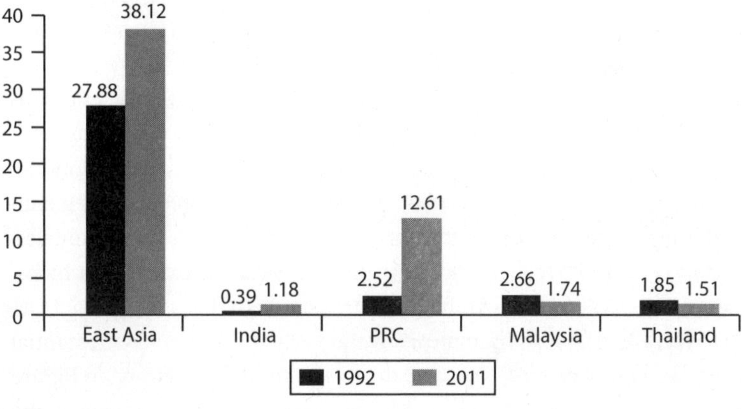

FIGURE 9.4 Share (%) of India and Comparator Countries in Global Trade of Parts and Components
Note: PRC = People's Republic of China.
Source: Authors' calculation from UN Comtrade data (obtained through World Integrated Trade Solution (WITS) software).

India in Regional Production-Sharing Arrangements

Statistics of intra-regional P&C trade also bring out the fact that regional production sharing is more significant in East Asia. Out of East Asia's global P&C trade of $2,151.6 billion, intra-East Asia trade accounts for $1,254.5 billion or about 58.3 per cent. Figure 9.5 shows the share of India and the comparator countries in intra-regional P&C trade.

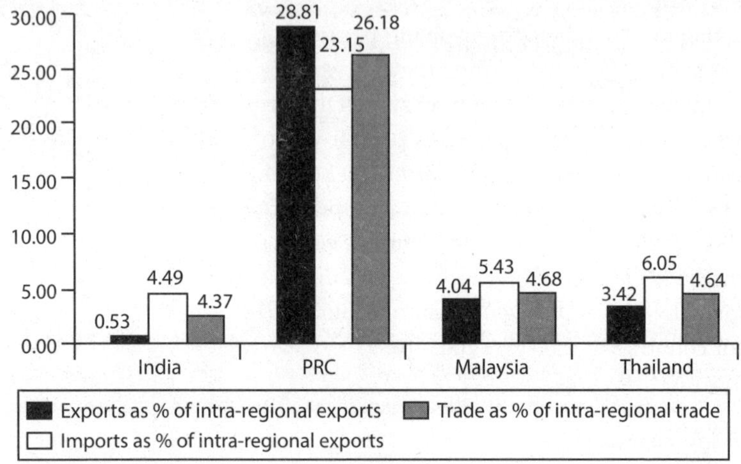

FIGURE **9.5** Share (%) of India and Comparator Countries in East Asia Intra-regional Parts and Components Trade, 2011
Note: PRC = People's Republic of China.
Source: Authors' calculation from UN Comtrade data (obtained through World Integrated Trade Solution (WITS) software).

In intra-regional trade in P&C, the PRC is once again the dominant and India the smallest player. India's share is about half even compared to Malaysia and Thailand. What is even more significant is that India's exports of P&C are a fraction of 1 per cent against 4.04 and 3.42 per cent for Malaysia and Thailand, respectively.

Foreign Direct Investment in India's Manufacturing Sector

If India has had a low participation in international production networks, it is principally on account of very limited stock of FDI in India's manufacturing sector. Until the economic reforms of 1991–92, India's external economic policy was biased against FDI and foreign equity in industrial ventures could not be above 40 per cent, except with the express permission of the central government, which was given only in limited cases involving transfer of technology, and that too with strict conditions. Even after the introduction of economic reforms, foreign equity was allowed only up to 51 per cent to start with and was increased gradually to 100 per cent in most manufacturing activities only at a later stage.

Figure 9.6 shows the evolving position of FDI stock in India and comparator countries during the last two decades.

India was a late starter in seeking FDI and the comparator countries were well ahead of India up to 2000. It was only around 2007 that the annual inflows of total FDI into India became substantial, but a point of significance was that while a major proportion of FDI inflows in the PRC, as also in Malaysia and Thailand, was in the manufacturing sector, the bulk of FDI inflows in India was in the services sector. Table 9.1 gives the figures of FDI flows into manufacturing in India and comparator countries in the years 2003–10.

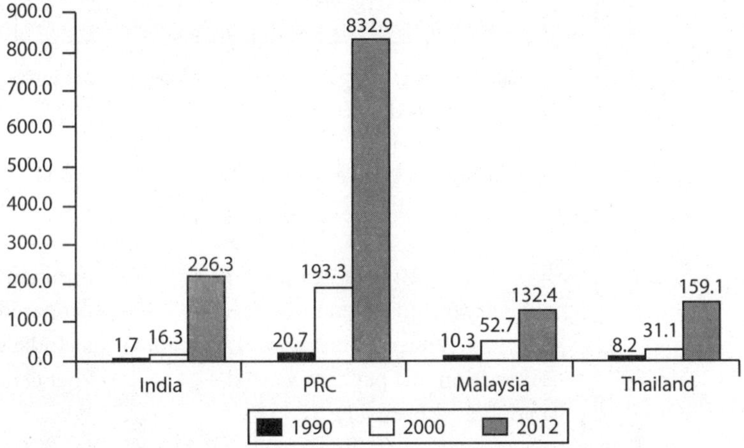

FIGURE 9.6 Inward Foreign Direct Investment Stock in India and Comparator Countries ($ billion)

Note: PRC = People's Republic of China.

Source: UNCTAD, *UNCTADstat*, available at *http://unctadstat.unctad.org/wds/ReportFolders/reportFolders.aspx* (accessed on 29 September 2016).

TABLE 9.1 Annual Foreign Direct Investment Inflow in Manufacturing ($ billion) and Its Share (%) in Total Foreign Direct Investment

	2003	2004	2005	2006	2007	2008	2009	2010	Cumulative 2003–10
India	0.8	1.5	2.1	2.3	4.8	6.2	7.2	7.5	32.4 (16.9%)
PRC	36.9	43	42.5	40.1	40.9	49.9	46.8	49.6	349.7 (58.3%)
Malaysia	1.4	3.5	1.8	1.3	3.2	3.7	-0.7	5	19.2 (44.0%)
Thailand	2.4	3.8	3	4.1	3.7	5.7	3.7	3.4	29.8 (49.9%)

Note: All the figures for India are for financial years from 1 April to 31 March. The Reserve Bank of India data on manufacturing does not include reinvestment. The reinvestment amount is projected on the basis of the share of reinvestment in total FDI in India shown in Department of Industrial Policy and Promotion data. PRC = People's Republic of China.

Source: For India, Department of Industrial Policy and Promotion, *FDI Statistics*, Ministry of Commerce and Industry, online version (http://dipp.nic.in/English/Publications/FDI_Statistics/FDI_Statistics.aspx) and Reserve Bank of India, *Database On Indian Economy,* online version (https://dbie.rbi.org.in/DBIE/dbie.rbi?site=home). In case of PRC, National Bureau of Statistics, *Statistical Database,* available at *http://www.stats.gov.cn/english/*) and ASEAN Investment Report 2011, available at *http://investasean.asean.org/files/upload/ASEAN%20 Investment%20Report%202010-2011.pdf*, for Malaysia and Thailand.

While India caught up with Thailand and Malaysia and even outstripped them during this period, the cumulative FDI inflow in the PRC was more than 10 times that in India.

The foregoing analysis shows that India's participation in international production-sharing arrangements is very low in comparison with other developing countries in the region and that there is a close correspondence between such participation and FDI inflows into manufacturing. In the third and fourth sections, we look closely at the trade barriers and logistics situation in India and examine various facets of the domestic investment environment in order to determine the contributory factors for the meagre FDI inflows into India and the poor participation of the country in international production networks.

Trade Barriers and Logistics in India

We have noted earlier that one of the factors that led to global production-sharing in the post-1980 phase of globalization was a reduction in trade barriers. In this section, we look at the trade barriers in India vis-à-vis the comparator countries.

Evolution of India's Trade Policy

There has been a transformation in India's trade policy after the economic reforms of 1991–92. Quantitative restrictions on imports have been eliminated except for reasons explicitly permitted in General Agreement on Tariffs and Trade (GATT) 1994. Non-agricultural import tariffs have come down from 150 per cent or more to a peak level of 10 per cent, except for a handful of tariff lines. While the country has lagged behind in undertaking multilateral commitments for binding tariffs at reduced levels, the applied levels have remained stable after reduction.

Current Level of Most Favoured Nation Tariff

In terms of the simple average of applied most favoured nation (MFN) tariffs, India is not out of line with the comparator countries. According to the World Trade Organization (WTO) Secretariat's Integrated Data Base (IDB), the latest available simple averages in ad valorem percentage are India: 9.8 (2010); the PRC: 8.7 (2009); Thailand: 8.0 (2011); and Malaysia: 5.8 (2010).

Simple averages do not reflect the full picture as we must also take the peak tariffs into account. In Table 9.2, we take six P&C product groups in which international production sharing is common and compare not only the simple averages but also the peak duties.

India's MFN tariff profile is comparable to that of the three countries included in our analysis, even when both the simple average and peak tariffs are taken into consideration. If Malaysia scores over India in respect of the simple average, India looks more liberal if we take into consideration the lower incidence of tariff peaks.

Deficiencies in India's Tariff Structure

While the current levels of non-agricultural tariffs in India are broadly comparable with those prevalent in comparator countries, the country's tariff structure has some deficiencies that tend to impede global production sharing. First, in the regional preferential arrangements, there are instances of import duty being eliminated on the finished products while being retained on P&C, thereby creating an inverted duty structure. Egregious cases are of Liquid Crystal Display and Light Emitting Diode televisions (below 19 inches), refrigerators, air conditioners, washing machines, and microwave ovens.[3] The Information

[3] India–Thailand FTA allows imports of certain finished products, namely, LCD/LED TV, refrigerators, air-conditioners, washing machines and microwaves on a duty free basis. The MFN duty on flat panel displays (FPD) of less than 19", which the most important part of LCD/LED TVs, is 10 per cent. Similarly, in respect of other products, MFN duties apply on important parts and components, for example, 10 per cent on clutch assembly for washing machines, 7.5 per cent on motor for refrigerator and air-conditioners and 10 per cent on magnetrons for microwave ovens. There is an exemption notification for magnetron under Customs (Import of Goods at Concessional Rate of Duty for Manufacture of Excisable Goods) Rules, 1996, but the manufacturers are unable to comply with the condition that the manufacture must take place in their factory, as they generally outsource the assembly stage. As tariffs on some of the parts are scheduled to be progressively reduced in the FTA agreements with ASEAN, the Republic of Korea and Japan, the problem of inverted duty structure will become less severe. It must be noted, however, that FPD and motor for refrigerator and air conditioners are excluded from all the FTA agreements currently in force.

TABLE 9.2 Comparative Picture of Import Tariffs in India, the People's Republic of China, Thailand, and Malaysia in Groups of Products in Which International Production Sharing Is Common

Country	Tariffs	Power Generating Equipments	Office Machine and Automatic Data Processing Machine	Telecom and Sound Recording Equipments	Semiconductors and Semiconductor Devices	Electrical Goods	Road Vehicles and Other Transport Equipments
India	Simple average	6.84	0.63	7.28	5.25	7.32	9.45
	Peak tariff	8.8	10	10.0	10.0	10.0	10.0
PRC	Simple average	7.16	1.54	13.25	5.66	7.73	8.89
	Peak tariff	7.16	24.5	35.0	18.0	24.5	30
Malaysia	Simple average	2.90	0.0	6.60	3.07	4.05	11.23
	Peak tariff	25	21.7	20.0	15.0	21.7	30
Thailand	Simple average	4.62	1.67	9.18	3.79	6.97	17.23
	Peak tariff	10.0	30	30.0	10.0	30	80

Note: The data year for India and Malaysia is 2010, for Thailand 2011, and for PRC 2009. PRC = People's Republic of China.

Source: World Trade Organization (WTO), *Integrated Data Base (IDB) and Consolidated Tariff Schedules (CTS) database*, available at *https://tao.wto.org/welcome.aspx?ReturnUrl=%2f%3fui%3d1&ui=1* (accessed on 29 September 2016).

Technology Agreement (ITA) has also resulted in a similar situation, since the ITA products have been made duty free while some materials that go into its production such as plastics, copper, and aluminium attract varying levels of duty. Second, there are instances in the automobile sector of the opposite kind, in which the finished products attract high levels of duty while much lower import duties apply to P&C, resulting in a high effective rate of protection in automobiles. This may have stimulated market-seeking rather than efficiency-seeking investment inflows, constraining rather than promoting international production-sharing arrangements. Third, India's higher tariffs on capital goods lowers its competitiveness as the duty on capital goods cannot be exempted or rebated consistently with WTO obligations when the goods produced from these goods are exported.

Gap between Applied and Bound Duty Levels

The simple averages of bound and applied non-agricultural tariffs respectively in per cent ad valorem are 34.5 and 10.4 for India, 9.1 and 8.7 for the PRC, 14.9 and 5.8 for Malaysia, and 25.4 and 8.0 for Thailand (WTO n.d., 'Tariff Profiles'). In the PRC the bound and applied levels are nearly the same, but there are large gaps in other countries. In India, these levels are farthest apart, mainly because of unilateral liberalization after the Uruguay Round.

The economic policies of successive governments during the last two decades seem to suggest that lowered import tariffs are irreversible in practical terms. For this reason, potential foreign investors have not expressed any concern regarding the gap between applied and bound rates. Even so, binding of tariffs nearer the applied levels would increase the confidence amongst investors that tariffs would not be raised.

Logistics

International production sharing involves large volumes of exports and imports in P&C and, in some cases, these traverse borders several times. Imported P&Cs may be exported again after further processing or they may be used along with domestically produced P&Cs for the assembly of the final goods. The final goods may be either sold for consumption within the country or again exported to destinations outside the country. With the fall in the traditional barriers to trade, such as tariffs and quantitative restrictions amongst non-tariff barriers, the importance of logistics has increased as a determinant of trade flows between countries. Logistics cover freight transportation, loading and unloading, border clearance, payment systems, warehousing, and a host of other functions.

Since more than 80 per cent of merchandise is transported by sea, the availability and quality of shipping services and port facilities is critical for international production sharing. The need to save on the time taken in transportation has led to the adoption of such business models as just-in-time manufacturing and has increased freight transportation by air also in international production sharing, even though air freight cost is 12–16 times the sea transport cost (World Bank 2009).

We have three international indices that have a bearing on logistics efficiency of individual countries, namely, the World Bank's logistics performance index (LPI), the UNCTAD's Liner Shipping Connectivity Index, and the World Bank's Air Connectivity Index.

India's standing in overall logistics efficiency vis-à-vis comparator countries in mirrored in its rankings in these three indices, which are shown in Table 9.3.

India's rank is lower than that of the comparator countries in virtually all the indices. The feedback from representatives of OEMs during the fieldwork was that India needed to benchmark its port infrastructure with countries like the PRC, Malaysia, and Thailand. In light of this,

TABLE 9.3 Comparative Overall Position of India on Logistics, Liner Shipping, and Air Connectivity

Country	Position in World Bank's LPI, 2012	Position in UNCTAD'S Liner Shipping Connectivity Index, 2011	Position in World Bank's Air Connectivity Index, 2007
PRC	26	1	46
Malaysia	29	7	83
Thailand	38	28	75
India	46	22	88

Note: PRC = People's Republic of China, LPI = Logistics Performance Index.
Source: World Bank (2011, 2012) and UNCTAD (2011).

ICRIER research teams visited Jawaharlal National Port Trust (JNPT) and Chennai in India, Shanghai in PRC, Westport Klang in Malaysia, and Laem Chabang in Thailand, and interacted with freight forwarders and express-delivery service providers to understand the reasons for India's low rank in logistics performance. The airports included in the survey were New Delhi in India and Beijing in PRC.

The comparator countries do not suffer from inadequacies in transport infrastructure and inefficiencies in the logistics processes at the gateways, which reduce India's competitiveness in manufacturing and lower its attractiveness as a destination for FDI. The comparative position is described in Box 9.1.

Box 9.1 Transport Infrastructure and Logistics Processes in India and Comparator Countries

- While a number of private ports are making notable progress in the country, India's 12 major ports are congested and, unlike in comparator countries, port capacity is constrained due to the lack of a cushion between installed capacity and actual traffic. The field survey by the Indian Council for Research on International Economic Relations (ICRIER) revealed a large gap in the vessel turnaround time (in hours) between Indian and comparator ports (JNPT, India-31; Chennai, India-40; Shanghai, the People's Republic of China (PRC) 19; Laem Chabang, Thailand-12; and Port Klang, Malaysia-12).
- Inadequate draft in the channels and harbours result in Indian ports, particularly those on the Eastern seaboard, being ignored by liner vessels and figuring lower in the connectivity index. Inadequacies of draft are unknown in comparator countries. Indian ports suffer also from inadequate road and rail connectivity with the hinterland and long queues of both incoming and outgoing vehicles are common. There is absence of a world class, access-controlled expressways such as those in PRC and Malaysia or of high quality dual carriageway as in Thailand. Railways suffer from congestion in the corridors linking industrial centres, making freight transport by rail unreliable in terms of timeliness of delivery. Dedicated freight corridors being constructed by Indian Railways will alleviate the situation but the country has no credible plans to build access controlled expressways. In India, air cargo transportation received a boost from the adoption by government of 'Air Cargo Open Sky Policy' and the abolition of

(*Contd.*)

Box 9.1 (*Contd.*)

the regulatory regime over cargo rates for major export commodities. However, there is scarcity of space in Indian airports, which translates itself into a dearth of storage facilities for perishable cargo, shortage of landside truck docks, and an inadequate number of dedicated bays for freighter traffic. On the other hand, there is no dearth of space in airports in comparator countries.

- A risk management system (RMS) was introduced in India in December 2005 for imports, and in October 2013 for exports, but the assessment is that up to 10 per cent, and sometimes even more, of consignments are still physically checked. In PRC, it is 3 per cent, in Malaysia 1 per cent, and in Thailand even less. The Indian Customs Electronic Data Interchange (EDI) System (ICES) has been operational for many years. However, the main objective of enabling the customs clearance process through a single window without face-to-face contact with officials has not been achieved. For a large number of processes for both export and import, paper copies and signature endorsement of customs officials on them are still required. During interactions with the ICRIER's survey teams the freight forwarders and express delivery service providers in the Shanghai, Laem Chabang, and Port Klang expressed great satisfaction with the functioning of the EDI system, which they regard as smooth, efficient, and standardized.
- Some of the eligibility criteria for admitting entities into the Accredited Clients Programme (ACP) are very stringent, for example, they should have no cases (including a show cause notice) of customs, central excise, or services tax booked against them in the previous three financial years. This has severely restricted access to the programme.

Source: The observations in the box are based either on widely known general information or information gathered during field surveys.

The deficiencies in physical infrastructure in ports and airports and the shortcomings in processes adopted for border controls get reflected in the dwell time of both import and export cargo. The comparative position in respect of dwell time in ports in India and comparator countries is given in Table 9.4.

TABLE 9.4 Dwell Time for Import and Export Cargo at Ports (in days)

Name of Port	Total Dwell Time on Import	Time Taken in Customs on Imports	Total Dwell Time on Exports	Time Taken in Customs on Exports
Indian ports	9–10	3½	9-10	3½
Shanghai	2–3	2	1–2	1
Port Klang	2	¾	1	½
Laem Chabang	2–3	Very little	1–1½	Very little

Source: Data for India ports is obtained from Centre for WTO Studies, 2012 and Indian Council for Research on International Economic Relations field survey for other countries.

It is seen from Table 9.3 that other parties (port authority, terminal operator, and the shippers) contribute more to the cargo dwell time than customs. One major cause of delay is the pre-berthing detention of ships due to insufficient cargo handling capacity and congestion in ports. The time taken for unloading or loading the cargo adds to the dwell time and finally there is the factor of the shipper using ports as storage location because of the free storage time.

The regulatory environment related to logistics services in India is pro-competitive on the whole. Importers and exporters have complete freedom to access the most efficient shipping service for seaborne trade, irrespective of the flag of vessel. The UNCTAD Code on Liner Conferences envisaging cargo sharing on a 40:40:20 basis and the bilateral shipping agreements with some countries on equality of freight lifting have remained a dead letter in actual practice. The only exception is government cargo, for carrying which the first right of refusal is given to Indian flag ships. In accordance with international practice, foreign flag ships are also not permitted to carry domestic traffic. The cabotage restriction has, however, been relaxed to enable transhipment of containers for export and import through the International Container Transhipment Terminal, Vallarpadam, Kochi.

Foreign direct investment up to 100 per cent is allowed in shipping companies but only vessels registered in the country can fly the Indian flag and are eligible to carry government cargo to and from foreign countries or to carry coastal cargo. Foreign flag vessels can carry coastal cargo only when no Indian flag vessel is available.

An open skies policy for cargo has also prevailed in the country for many years, enabling airborne freight traffic to have access to the most efficient air-freight service provider. As with seaborne trade, the policy applies only to import and export and not to domestic traffic. Foreign equity up to 74 per cent and non-resident Indian (NRI) investment up to 100 per cent is allowed for cargo airlines through the automatic route.

There are no regulatory restrictions on foreign road transport service providers and 100 per cent equity is allowed through the automatic route. However, railways are a public monopoly, except for the permission given to a number of private operators to move container trains on the network provided by the monopoly.

Several auxiliary services related to all modes of transport, such as warehousing, ground handling, and freight forwarding have also been liberalised and 100 per cent foreign equity has been allowed through the automatic route.

In the comparator countries, the general pattern of regulations of LSPs is the same as in India, particularly in relation to cargo reservation and cabotage in shipping services and open skies policy on air freight with respect to international cargo. Overall, the regulatory environment in India for LSPs is comparable with that in the comparator countries, even though there are deviations in practice on some aspects. Hollweg and Wong (2009) have come to the conclusion that for foreign LSPs, the restrictions in the PRC and Malaysia are marginally higher than in India and Thailand, which are broadly at the same level. The position is different in respect of domestic LSPs, the PRC being the least restrictive and India the most, with Malaysia and Thailand in between, although the distances amongst them are small.

Domestic Investment Environment

Labour Laws

During interactions and consultation, the representatives of OEMs and business associations in FDI-source countries emphasized that Indian labour laws were too protective of workers and unfriendly to investors. They observed that laws that made downsizing difficult were out of tune with the globalized world of manufacturing. Three statutes were mentioned as particularly important in this connection, namely, the Industrial Disputes Act, 1947, the Contract Labour Regulation and Prohibition Act, 1970, and the Trade Unions Act, 1926.

Industrial Disputes Act, 1947

The Industrial Disputes Act, 1947 lays down the procedures for the settlement of industrial disputes. In 1976, Chapter VB was introduced through an amendment, whereby employers were restrained from laying-off or retrenching workmen or even closing down factories without prior permission of government, if the number of employees is more than 300, and this threshold was lowered to 100 through another amendment in 1982. Although permissions have been given for lay-off, retrenchment, and closure, the important point is that no objective rules are laid down in the law on the basis of which such permission would be given. The requirement for compensation in the event of retrenchment or closure is relatively mild: 15 days' average pay has to be paid for every completed year of continuous service.

Under Chapter VC of the Industrial Disputes Act, 1947, it is an unfair labour practice (punishable with a jail sentence of up to six months) for the employer to keep a worker temporary for years with a view to depriving him of the privileges of permanent workmen. In this context it is also relevant to mention that by virtue of the Industrial Standing Orders Act, 1946, workmen become permanent after a probation of three months.

The cumulative effect of these provisions is to grant total job security to workmen, who have a virtual guarantee against being laid-off or retrenched. Not only downsizing but even closure of loss-making industrial undertakings is made difficult. This creates a sense of uncertainty amongst entrepreneurs and inhibits investment, as they are reluctant to expose themselves to the risk of indefinite liability. Alternatively, employers adapt to the situation by making their investment capital intensive. India's comparative advantage lies in having competitively priced semi-skilled and skilled labour but Chapter VB of the Industrial Disputes Act, 1947 substantially neutralizes the advantage. Another effect of the rigidity in labour laws is that the growth of industry is taking place in the unorganized sector, with lower pay and benefits for workers.

Contract Labour (Regulation and Abolition) Act, 1970

The Contract Labour (Regulation and Abolition) Act, 1970 gives the central and state governments authority to abolish contract labour in respect of jobs of a perennial nature and to regulate the service conditions of contract labour in other cases. Clearly, the intention is to disallow the employment of contract labour in mainline production functions or core activities and allow but regulate their employment in non-core activities. However, the actual position in the country is widely at variance with the intention behind extant laws. Due to ambiguities in the laws at the state level and lack of rigour in enforcement even where such laws exist, contract labour is being widely used in mainline production functions by manufacturers and other employers in the country. A grey-area practice has developed whereby manufacturers and other employers in India are outsourcing jobs to private placement agencies, and it is these agencies that are the primary employers of temporary contract workers in factories and other establishments (New York Times, 30 November 2011). A fallout of the practice has been that a wide gap separates the levels of wages and job security of the regular and contract workers in the same enterprise and this has become a new focal point of industrial unrest in the country.

A related deficiency in the Indian labour laws is that direct employment on fixed-term contracts is not recognized. The model standing orders at Schedule I to the Industrial Employment (Standing Orders) Central Rules, 1946 classifies workmen as permanent, probationers, badlis, temporary, casual, and apprentice and there is no mention of employees on fixed-term contracts. One suggestion made by industry is that an amendment should be introduced so that employment under fixed-term contracts becomes generally permissible. Even though the restriction on employing contract labour for jobs of a perennial nature is hardly being enforced, employers would have a preference for employing workers with fixed-term contracts directly under a law explicitly allowing such employment. A clear enabling provision would give them immunity from adverse court interpretations in future as well as from harassment by labour inspectors.

Trade Unions Act, 1926

The multiplicity of trade unions in India permitted by the Trade Unions Act, 1926 is a fundamental weakness as it impairs the process of collective bargaining. Any combination of workmen having a membership of seven persons (10 in the case of enterprises with 100 or more workers) can apply for registration, although registration is not mandatory. The position becomes even more anomalous by virtue of the fact that there is no obligation on the employer to recognize any registered trade union. Collective bargaining settlements can be arrived at even by unrecognized unions but such settlements are binding only on the participating unions. Other trade unions are free to raise the same issues, with the result that there is competition amongst unions to ask for greater benefits.

Two other aspects of the trade union law in India must be mentioned. First, the Trade Unions Act expressly permits admission of non-workers to trade unions, under the guise of honorary or temporary members. Second, the law does not provide anywhere for election or secret ballot to elect representatives of workers or to take a decision on such matters as going on strike. Entry of outsiders into trade unions or the appointment of office bearers without election or the taking of decisions to strike and other important matters without endorsement of a majority are against the interests of not only employers but also of workers (Nath 2005). Although the law, as it stands today, puts a limit of one-third or five office-bearers in the union that outsiders can hold, it still allows them to corner the important posts of president as well as general secretary, thus marginalizing workers by leaving only the less important posts for them.

In sum, the rigidities in Indian labour laws inhibit the creation of regular jobs by enterprises, induce informalization, discourage labour-intensive investment, and do not foster the maintenance of harmonious industrial relations. The labour laws in comparator countries are geared more towards meeting the exigencies of a globalized world and at the same time are more conducive to maintaining harmonious industrial relations. A snapshot of the comparative position in labour laws in the four countries is given in Box 9.2.

Box 9.2 Labour Laws in India and Comparator Countries

- The laws of the People's Republic of China (PRC), Thailand, and Malaysia specifically allow employment contracts for a fixed term, giving flexibility to investors to vary the number of employees in order to respond to changing market conditions (Labour Contract Law of the PRC, 2007; Labour Protection Act, 1998 and Labour Protection Act, 2008, Thailand; Employment Act, 1955 Malaysia). In India, labour laws do not envisage fixed-term employment directly by the principal employers.
- In PRC, Malaysia and Thailand, the ultimate decision on the matter of reducing the labour force is left with the employer. In India, the Industrial Disputes Act, 1947 mandates companies with 100 or more workmen to obtain express permission of government authorities for lay-off, retrenchment, and closure.
- The central objective of the Contract Labour (Abolition and Regulation) Act, 1970 is to abolish contract labour for jobs of a perennial nature. However, the de facto situation in respect of contract labour in India is widely at variance with the de jure position and there is widespread use in the country of contract labour supplied by placement agencies even for jobs of a perennial nature. This practice serves to alleviate to some extent the problem of labour rigidity created by the Industrial Disputes Act but a fallout of the practice has been that a wide gulf has developed in the levels of wages and job security between regular and contract workers in the same enterprise. This difference has become a new source of industrial unrest in the country.
- In PRC, trade unions occupy a unique position as employers finance them through a 2 per cent union levy on the payroll and there is no effective separation between the management and workers (Ministry of Commerce, PRC 2007). In Thailand and Malaysia, laws relating to the functioning of trade unions make them better suited for collective bargaining. Registration of trade unions is compulsory and collective bargaining takes place only with recognized unions. Decisions on strikes have to be taken through a democratic process (Malaysia's Trade Union Act, 1959; Thailand's Labour Relations Act 1975). In India, registration of trade unions is not compulsory and even recognition is not required for participation in dispute settlement or collective bargaining. Industrial peace is disturbed when rival unions vie with each other in demanding better terms from the management. The fact that non-workers and outsiders can be office-bearers

(Contd.)

Box 9.2 (*Contd.*)

of trade unions and they do not always have the welfare of workers in mind exacerbates the uneasy situation in industrial relations. Since the law does not require that office bearers be elected or that decisions on strikes must be taken by the full membership through secret ballot, the situation gets aggravated further.

Source: Authors' elaboration based on the text of the statutes referred to in the box.

Power Supply

Uninterrupted supply of good quality power is one of the prerequisites for the efficient functioning of modern manufacturing units. Unreliable supply due to frequent power failures and uneven quality on account of voltage fluctuation seriously affect India's ability to attract FDI in manufacturing and hamper even domestic investment. In fact, the problem is felt more acutely by small and medium manufacturers as the only option for them is to invest in small captive power generation units, which substantially increases their operational cost. Uninterrupted and good quality supplies are particularly critical for manufacturing units in the information and communication technology (ICT) sector as an interruption affects the quality of output in the entire production cycle.

The current power scenario in the country from the perspective of industry has been very well analysed in a report (Federation of Indian Chambers of Commerce and Industry [FICCI] 2012) on a survey of industrial units published in late 2012.

The survey revealed that the international competitiveness of manufacturing units was eroded by power cuts that extended in some states to 30 hours a week, unscheduled load-shedding, cost escalation up to 30 per cent on account of use of standby generators, and substantial losses on account of voltage fluctuation.

The power supply situation for industries is clearly a major factor driving down India's competitiveness in manufacturing and discouraging investments in the sector. The situation in comparator countries is far better than that in India as can be seen from the comparative picture given in Box 9.3.

Box 9.3 Power Supply Situation in India and Comparator Countries

- During the last 10 years, India has consistently experienced energy shortages of 7–11 per cent and a peak deficit of 10–17 per cent (Ministry of Power 2012). In Malaysia and Thailand, a reserve margin of 30–50 per cent has ensured that there is no gap between installed capacity and maximum demand (Electricity Generation Authority of Thailand and Energy Commission of Malaysia, various reports).
- Interruptions in power supply occur in other countries also, arising from myriad causes including natural disasters, but their frequency and duration are very small when compared to the situation in India. Against interruptions extending to 30 hours a week in some industrial units in Andhra and Tamil Nadu, the average interruption duration was less than two hours for the whole year in Peninsular Malaysia, just more than one hour in metropolitan areas in Thailand and about six hours per year in the provincial areas of Thailand (Energy Commission, Malaysia 2012 and Metropolitan Electricity Authority, Thailand 2013).
- The share of firms that own generators, according to a World Bank Report of June 2008, was 8.3 per cent in Thailand, 18.3 per cent in PRC and as much as 63.6 per cent in India. The percentage of power consumption from own generator was 11.2 per cent in Thailand 1.5 per cent in PRC and 19.1 per cent in India (World Bank 2008).

Taxation and Incentives for Investment

The corporate tax rate in India is 30 per cent for domestic companies plus education cess of 3 per cent. In addition, there is a surcharge of 7 per cent if the taxable income exceeds Rs 10 million ($159,681)[4] and of 12 per cent if it exceeds Rs 100 million ($1.59 million). Domestic companies with taxable income of less than Rs 10 million are exempt from the surcharge. Thus, the total corporate income tax rate on domestic companies with a taxable income of less than Rs 10 million ($159,681) is 30.9 per cent, for those with taxable income of more than Rs 10

[4] Converted at the exchange rate of $1 = Rs 62.6250, as per RBI on 18 November 2013.

million ($159,681) is 33.06 per cent and for those with a taxable income of Rs 100 million ($1.59 million) or more is 34.61 per cent.

An important announcement in the budget speech for the year 2015–16 was that it is the intention of the government to reduce the corporate tax rate for domestic enterprises from 30 to 25 per cent in 4 years beginning with 2016–17 (Speech of Finance Minister, 2015–16 Budget). For 2015–16, the rate remains unchanged. In fact, with the increase in surcharge, it goes up marginally, as mentioned earlier.

For foreign companies, the basic income tax rate is substantially higher at 40 per cent. The rates of surcharge are, however, lower at 2 per cent if the taxable income exceeds Rs 10 million ($159,681) and 5 per cent if it is more than Rs 100 million ($1.59 million). Foreign companies with taxable income of less than Rs 10 million are exempt from the surcharge. Inclusive of education cess, the total income tax on foreign companies in the three slabs outlined here works out to 41.2/42.02/43.26 respectively.

There are significant direct tax benefits for Special Economic Zones (SEZs). Units in the SEZs are eligible for exemption from income tax at the rate of 100 per cent of the profits derived from exports for the first 5 years and 50 per cent for the next 5 years. For the subsequent period of 5 consecutive years, the exemption of profits from exports is conditional on the entire amount being ploughed back for investment in the unit. The developers of SEZs have also been allowed exemption of 100 per cent profits for 10 years.

When the new scheme for SEZs was launched in 2005, SEZ units as well as developers were also exempted from the levy of Minimum Alternate Tax (MAT) leviable on zero tax companies, that is companies which were not liable to pay taxes despite book profits on account of various allowances available in the Income Tax Act. The SEZ developers were further exempted from payment of Dividend Distribution Tax (DDT). In 2011–12, in a significant move, the finance minister made MAT applicable to SEZs , thereby subjecting them to a levy of 18.5 per cent plus an education cess of 3 per cent, considerably eroding the tax incentive for SEZ units. The exemption of developers from DDT was also withdrawn.

In the budget for 2013–14, a new incentive has been introduced for 15 per cent investment deduction allowance for the period 2013–15 for a minimum investment of Rs 1 billion ($15.97 million).

Taxation Environment

Investor feedback suggests that the tax environment is high on the list of disincentives for FDI in India. Apart from high corporate tax rates in comparison with Asian countries, a complicated taxation structure and unclear rules lead to harassment of companies by tax officials. There is a general complaint that in India, the transfer pricing regime is not applied in a consistent manner to taxpayers. Foreign enterprises have been requesting for the establishment of a fair and transparent regime, which could prevent the use of transfer pricing rules as a selective mechanism for raising revenue. Further, foreign investors have baulked at the introduction in 2012 of the General Anti-Avoidance Rules (GAAR) and certain retrospective changes in tax laws. Although the introduction of GAAR has now been deferred to 2016, the tendency to give retrospective effect to changes in tax laws constitutes a disincentive for companies proposing to invest in India. In September 2013, the Ministry of Finance has taken a step forward to clear the air on transfer pricing and also issued revised safe harbour rules after consultations with the stakeholders. These steps may help to improve the taxation environment to some extent.

The level of corporate taxation, particularly the higher rate applicable to foreign enterprises, taken together with an unpredictable tax environment dissuades these enterprises from investing in India. The corporate tax rate is lower in the comparator countries and is sweetened further through long-standing investment incentives as reflected in Box 9.4.

Box 9.4 Taxation and Tax Incentives in India and Comparator Countries

In a globalized world in which Foreign Direct Investment (FDI) flows freely across borders and investors want to maximize their post-tax earnings, the following factors make India less attractive as a destination for FDI:

- As compared to the comparator countries (People's Republic of China [PRC]: 25 per cent, Malaysia: 25 per cent, and Thailand: 20 per cent), India's rate of corporate tax for the highest slab of taxable income is well above the rest at 34.61 per cent for domestic companies and

(Contd.)

Box 9.4 (*Contd.*)

43.26 per cent for foreign companies in 2015 (Klynveld Peat Marwick Goerdeler [KPMG] 2015). As the plan to reduce the basic corporate tax to 25 per cent is implemented, the differential in the tax rate vis-à-vis comparator countries will be narrowed down.

- Until recently, PRC had encouraged FDI through a lower rate of corporate tax for foreign enterprises and it was only in 2008 that the preferential taxes for such enterprises were given up (Jade & Fountain: PRC Lawyers). India, on the other hand, levies a higher rate of tax on foreign enterprises (KPMG 2015).The difference will increase in future as the rate for domestic companies is phased down.
- Thailand and Malaysia have long-standing incentives for new investments in industries (Pannell Kerr Forster [PKF] 2013 and PricewaterhouseCoopers [PWC] 2013a). India has recently introduced 15 per cent investment deduction allowance on a temporary basis for 2013–15 for a minimum investment of Rs 1 billion (PWC 2013b).
- High-technology industries have been getting substantial incentives, including reduced corporate taxes in all three comparator countries. In 2012, a new scheme was announced for capital subsidy and reimbursement of central taxes (Department of Electronics and Information Technology 2012).
- India's effective corporate tax rate, after taking the incentives into account, is even less attractive for foreign investors relative to the comparator countries. It has been estimated that the 2014–15 'Indian tax rate of 29 per cent is a full 11 percentage points higher than most of our East Asian competitors' (Bhalla 2014).
- The tax environment in India has been vitiated by lack of stability in the taxation regime, retrospective changes in tax laws, introduction of GAAR, and arbitrariness and lack of transparency in tax laws (particularly on transfer pricing).

Internal Taxation

Complexities in the internal taxation system are a constraint on manufacturing in India. One of the main reasons for this is that the authority to collect indirect taxes has been split under the Indian Constitution between the central government and the state governments (and six union territories). The centre collects service tax, excise duty, and customs duty while the states (and union territories) collect sales tax on all goods. There is also a central sales tax (CST) on interstate transaction, which is collected by the states.

Deficiencies in the Current Internal Taxation Regime in India

Before 2005, the taxation system was even more flawed than it is today. However, the introduction of central value added tax (CENVAT) at the centre and value added tax (VAT) in the states improved the situation by considerably whittling down the cascading effect of taxes on inputs at prior stages in the production process and by bringing a modicum of uniformity in the rates of taxes. But the system needs more reform to eliminate impediments to business and bring it at par with developed and emerging economies.

The CST on interstate transactions, levied earlier at the rate of 4 per cent but reduced to 2 per cent a few years back, constitutes a major barrier in internal trade as it is an 'export tax' on goods moving out of a state and entry tax and octroi are 'import taxes' on goods moving into a local area. The imposition of these taxes requires the erection of check posts at inter-state borders and at the gateways of cities imposing local area taxes and stoppages at the check posts increase the logistics component of the cost of manufacturing. Moreover, neither the CST nor entry taxes into local areas is integrated with the value added tax system and is not eligible as a credit in the imposition of VAT in downstream industries. The feedback on CST from investors is that it substantially increases the cost of manufacturing.

The CENVAT and state VAT as levied at present have not succeeded in eliminating the cascading effect of taxation in the country, as several taxes collected at the central level (such as additional customs duty collected on imported goods in lieu of excise duty and service tax) and state level (such as luxury tax and entertainment tax) remain out of their purview. Differential treatment of goods and services is also becoming problematic as advances in digital technology are blurring the distinction between goods and services. Moreover, separate taxation of goods and services requires splitting of transactions involving the supply of both goods and services, which further increases the cost of compliance.

Multiple taxes make India a fragmented market and impede the free flow of goods within the country and increase logistics costs. Cascading taxes discourage efficient production and lower India's competitiveness, particularly in manufacturing. The lack of a simple tax structure with one or two uniform tax rates increases the cost of compliance by businesses and is a further drag on efficiency.

Proposed Goods and Services Tax

A decision in principle has been taken to introduce a national-level goods and services tax (GST) to replace the existing multiple tax structure at both the central and state levels, but its introduction requires an amendment of the Constitution. After much delay, the Constitution (122nd Amendment) GST Bill, 2014, has been passed by the lower house of parliament (Lok Sabha) and is now under consideration in the upper house (Rajya Sabha). A point of criticism in the present bill is that a key provision proposes to empower the central government to impose an additional tax of up to 1 per cent, on the inter-state supply of goods for 2 years or longer, and such a tax is likely to have a cascading effect.

Until the GST is introduced, India's competitiveness as an FDI destination in manufacturing will continue to be weighed down by its complex internal taxation system. A summary of the relative position in internal taxes amongst comparator countries is given in Box 9.5.

Box 9.5 Internal Taxes Regimes in India and Comparator Countries

- Thailand has already implemented an integrated taxation system in goods and services wherein full set off is available for taxes on goods and services used in the earlier stages of production (Price waterhouse Coopers [PWC] 2013a). While the People's Republic of China (PRC) has not implemented such a system fully, and there are a number of services still subject to a business tax instead of VAT, the national expansion of value added tax (VAT) is planned for 2015 (KPMG 2013). Until recently, Malaysia was behind India as it had not introduced VAT (PKF 2013). However, on 1 April 2015, it introduced a goods and services tax (GST) regime, with the rate set at 6 per cent, the lowest in the Association of Southeast Asian Nations (ASEAN) (Ernst & Young [EY] 2015).
- In no country other than India is VAT levied and collected by more than one authority.
- No comparator country levies duties on goods crossing interstate borders or entering into the territory of a municipality, which is a major criticism of the Indian taxation regime figuring in investor feedback.

Land

During interviews, business and industry associations articulated the general complaint that buying land at suitable locations is a herculean task for new investors in India. Verification of titles is complex and procedures for purchasing land take time, sometimes more than a year. Developed land is also very expensive.

Population pressure has already been driving up land prices in the country, but the situation is aggravated by high stamp duties for registration of changes in ownership and large fees demanded by state governments for permission to change the use of agricultural land. Lack of updated records of title imposes an additional cost on the entrepreneurs as they have to carry out extensive research to establish title of land to be acquired by them.

The Land Acquisition, Rehabilitation and Resettlement (LARR) Act, 2013, which has been recently approved by the Indian parliament, is likely to make it even more problematic as well as expensive for industrial units to acquire land, whether through land acquisition by government or voluntarily agreed purchases. The act envisages that if land has to be acquired compulsorily, it should have the consent of 70 per cent of the landholders in public private partnership projects and 80 per cent of the landholders in the case of private companies. Before acquisition, a social impact assessment has to be carried out.[5] Compensation will

[5] In an attempt to reduce the adverse effect of LARR Act 2013 on development projects, the government had promulgated The Right to Fair Compensation and Transparency in Land Acquisition, Rehabilitation and Resettlement (Amendment) Ordinance, 2015. The Ordinance enabled the government to exempt projects related to infrastructure, industrial corridors, affordable housing, etc., from the requirements of social impact assessment and consent of affected families. However, under the Indian Constitution an Ordinance has temporary validity and needs to be replaced by a law, duly passed by the Parliament. With such a law in mind, on 11 May 2015, the government introduced the Right to Fair Compensation and Transparency in Land Acquisition, Rehabilitation and Resettlement (Second Amendment) Bill, 2015 in the Lok Sabha. Due to a logjam in Parliamentary proceedings, arising from a political dispute between the government and the opposition parties, its consideration has been delayed. In the meantime, with elections imminent in some states, the government has allowed the Ordinance to lapse. At the time of writing, the prospect of the Bill being eventually passed looks uncertain as there is intense opposition to changes in the LARR Act, 2013.

be payable at twice the market value for urban land and four times the market value for rural land.

In addition, there is a substantial rehabilitation and resettlement (R&R) package for project-affected families (landowners and the families whose livelihood is primarily dependent on the land acquired) to be arranged by the investor. The R&R package is also applicable to voluntarily acquired land for industry, if the area is 100 acres or more in rural areas and 50 acres or more in urban areas.

Population pressure has made availability of land for industry problematic in all Asian countries, and all governments are keen to ensure that farmers and others who get dispossessed by the diversion of their land to industry are guaranteed a standard of living at least equal to the level that existed before the acquisition. However, in India, acquisition of land for industry has been more difficult than in comparator countries, and has become considerably more burdensome after the enactment of the LARR Act, 2013, as shown in Box 9.6.

Box 9.6 Land for Industry in India and Comparator Countries

- The PRC and Malaysia have provision not only for adequate compensation but also resettlement of farmers and others whose land is acquired. However, in Malaysia the compensation is related to the market value of land and in the People's Republic of China (PRC) to the annual value of production (Land Acquisition Act, 1960, Malaysia and Land Administration Law, 1986, the PRC). In India alone the compensation for landowners has to be in multiples of the market value (four times for rural land and two times for urban), and separate payment is to be made to people other than landowners if their livelihood is dependent on the acquired land.
- In the PRC, if the acquisition involves more than 35 hectares of farmland, the approval of the state council is needed. There are procedures to resolve disputes on the amount of compensation, and if all efforts fail at the level of local government, the government that approves the compensation is obliged to take recourse to arbitration. In Malaysia, public hearings are held not on the purpose of land acquisition but on the compensation. Thailand's Constitution recognizes the concept of eminent domain, under which the state has the right to

(Contd.)

Box 9.6 (*Contd.*)

take over private immoveable property compulsorily for public utilities, town and country planning agricultural and industrial development, amongst others, subject to fair compensation. In comparator countries, the emphasis is on ensuring adequate compensation while in India, landholders have the right to object to the acquisition itself, irrespective of compensation. The Land Acquisition, Rehabilitation and Resettlement (LARR) Act, 2013 has introduced a new hurdle by requiring that before acquisition, a social impact assessment should be carried out. This is over and above the requirement that 80 per cent of the landholders must voluntarily agree to the land acquisition for private companies, and 70 per cent in respect of public private partnership projects.

- In India, even after land has been acquired by industry, it is sometimes a problem to actually take possession of the land. This type of governance problem is unknown in comparator countries.

Source: Authors' elaboration based on the text of the statutes referred to in the box.

Special Economic Zones and Other Industrial Clusters

Special Economic Zones in India

In the pre-reform era, the Export Processing Zones (EPZ) policy and the Export Oriented Units (EOUs) scheme in India achieved very little of significance. Infrastructural deficiencies and high logistics costs affected the international competitiveness of the units and tight customs control hobbled their functioning.

In the post-liberalization period, the Government of India announced an SEZ policy in 2000 and moved on to a comprehensive policy by enacting the Special Economic Zones Act, 2005. The new regime envisages a single window for all clearances, exemption from nearly all internal taxes as well as income tax concessions for developers and the units. In the first 5 years, the new policy was a great success in terms of the investment attracted, employment created, and exports generated. The share of SEZs in total exports rose from 6 per cent in 2006–07 to

28 per cent in 2010–11. However, since then, the momentum for expansion of SEZs activity has been on a decline (Aggarwal 2012; Department of Commerce 2011).The immediate causes for this are changes in taxation laws in the 2011–12 budget and the build up of public opposition during the 2011 state elections against acquisition of agricultural land for industrial and infrastructural purposes. As mentioned earlier, the exemption for SEZ units and developers from MAT was withdrawn and the exemption for developers from DDT was terminated with effect from 2011–12. Predictability in taxation policies is a sine qua non for making the environment conducive for investment, whether foreign or domestic, and the withdrawal of direct tax benefits has been a setback for the SEZ programme and has affected its future prospects.

Another major reason for the SEZs languishing is the absence of external infrastructure support. The SEZs have to be connected with ports and airports with world-class roads and rail; ports and airports too have to be world class, with customs authorities adopting international best practices in trade facilitation. This is not the case at present. Deficiencies in the availability and quality of power are an equally important constraint, particularly for medium and small enterprises, which cannot set up cost-efficient captive power units. The SEZs need other utility services as well, including water and drainage connections, which have not been provided for adequately. Investor feedback placed great emphasis on the creation of industrial complexes with basic infrastructural amenities.

Alleviating the shortcomings in external infrastructure will undoubtedly require sustained effort by the government over a long period, but the central government has taken a conscious decision not to restore the benefits relating to MAT and DDT for SEZs. Instead, in the new Foreign Trade Policy (2015–20) it has extended the benefit of the Merchandise Export from India Scheme, which entitles the units in SEZs to receive different kinds of duty scrips admissible for exports. While the export subsidies that the scheme entails will no doubt be to the advantage of the SEZ units, it must be observed that on account of its rising per capita income, India is likely to lose very soon the status of a developing country under Annex VII of the WTO Agreement on Subsidies and Countervailing Measures, which entitles it to use export subsidies on manufactured products.

Industrial Area Development Schemes in India

Of the area development schemes undertaken in the country, the Delhi Mumbai Industrial Corridor (DMIC) announced by the Government of India in 2007 has received the maximum attention. Eight investment regions/industrial areas have been identified in the first phase. Master planning has been completed for these eight regions and land procurement is underway (Department of Industrial Policy and Promotion [DIPP] 2013). The idea is to develop the physical infrastructure over the investment regions with a minimum area of 200 sq. km and industrial areas with a minimum area of 100 square kilometre. Government funding will be provided for trunk infrastructure and private participation will be invited for infrastructure projects that are commercially viable.

In order to disperse industrial activity more widely in the country, four more economic/industrial corridors have been proposed and are in various stages of development. These are Bengaluru-Mumbai, Amritsar-Kolkata, Chennai-Bengaluru, and Visakhapatnam-Chennai.

A related development is the idea of the National Investment and Manufacturing Zones (NIMZs), which was put forward as the most important instrumentality of the new national manufacturing policy announced in 2011. The NIMZs will function as self-governing and autonomous bodies and to make this possible, they would be declared as Industrial Townships under Article 243(c) of the Constitution. State governments will have to provide full assurance of infrastructural linkages and, on its part, the central government has undertaken to provide rail, road, ports, airports, and telecom connectivity. To start with, eight investment regions of the DMIC and three others have been notified as NIMZs (DIPP 2013).

Conceptually, the NIMZs scheme has all the ingredients of success and its early implementation will constitute a big step in attracting FDI and domestic investment in manufacturing and boost India's participation in regional production networks.

The SEZs and industrial area developments in India have not achieved the level of success of the comparator countries because of shortcomings in external physical infrastructure, absence of full involvement of the state government machinery in the implementation of projects, and lack of stability in the tax incentives. Details are given in Box 9.7.

Box 9.7 Special Economic Zones and Industrial Area Development Schemes in India and Comparator Countries

- The contribution of Special Economic Zones (SEZs) and other area development schemes to the development of manufacturing in India has been hampered by inadequacies in the external infrastructure (comprising the transport infrastructure, logistics parks, power, water, and drainage). The extraordinary success of SEZs and similar programmes in the People's Republic of China (PRC) and other comparator countries was due to the fact that they benefitted from world-class external physical infrastructure, modern expressways, and transport networks linking them with the hinterland and high-class port and airports and transport services with the markets abroad. PRC established SEZs over large swathes of territory enabling the development of industry clusters and fostering individual plants that sometimes accounted for a large share of world production.
- In India, SEZs and industrial area development schemes and industrial units within them are victims of apathy from state government officials when they seek connectivity with networks or clearance under various regulations. Lack of coordination between the state and central authorities on matters related to SEZs is a big hurdle. The situation is compounded by the fact that there is multiplicity of authorities at the state level and they are preoccupied with manifold duties. Due to the lack of interest at the state level, the authorities are not proactive in assisting entrepreneurs in securing regulatory clearances or obtaining connectivity. In Penang (Malaysia), one of the main reasons for the remarkable success in developing the electronics industry was the proactive involvement of government officials, right up to the level of chief minister (Athukorala 2011).
- Policy stability has been another critical factor. The initial momentum in the SEZs programme in India was thwarted by an abrupt retrospective change in the direct tax incentives. In PRC, tax incentives were maintained over long periods and changed only prospectively after advance notice.

Source: Author's elaboration largely based in widely known general information. In case of specific information, source is provided in the box text.

Entry and Exit Barriers

Entry Barriers in India

Entry barriers for industry were a big issue in the pre-reform era, prior to 1991–92, as industrial licensing applied comprehensively. Foreign equity in industrial ventures also could not be above 40 per cent, except with the express permission of the central government, which was given only in limited cases involving transfer of technology, and that too with strict conditions.

The situation has completely changed after the introduction of economic reforms. Licenses have been replaced by registration in a vast majority of cases now. Entry barriers for industry now are not substantive but procedural (Federation of Indian Micro and Small & Medium Enterprises [FISME] 2013), in obtaining power, water, and drainage connectivity, particularly if the unit is situated outside a designated industrial area.

The FDI is permitted automatically over virtually the entire manufacturing sector. It is prohibited only for cigarettes and other manufactures of tobacco, and sectoral caps and conditions apply in respect of defence industries (49 per cent) and products reserved for Ministry of Micro, Small and Medium Enterprises (24 per cent). Conditions may also be imposed on brown field investments in the pharmaceutical sector (DIPP 2013a).

Exit Barriers in India

Ease of exit is as important for investors as ease of entry and businesses take these into consideration while choosing between alternative destinations. Two aspects of the law and the judicial system have given India a bad name in connection with the problems of exit. First, as we noted in the section on labour laws, permission is needed by industrial units employing more than 100 workers before laying off or retrenching workers or before closure. Second, until recently, the Companies Act, 1956 provided for the process of liquidation to be initiated by a court order if the company concerned was unable to pay its debt. Since the judicial system was clogged with a large backlog, the cases of liquidation of companies were badly delayed. Fortunately, the situation changed in August 2013 with the enactment of the Companies

Act, 2013, which has established the National Company Law Tribunal (NCLT) and the National Company Law Appellate Tribunal (NCLAT) with exclusive jurisdiction on all matters, proceedings, or cases under the Companies Act, 2013 (as well as the previous act), including winding up of companies.

While on the subject of exit barriers, it is necessary to mention the related issue of the long time taken in contract enforcement and dispute settlement because of delays in legal procedures are endemic in the country. An alternative mechanism was introduced in India in 1998 in the form of the Arbitration and Conciliation Act, which replaced the 1940 legislation. However, this too has proved to be a non-starter because of the large fees charged by the retired judges acting as arbitrators (FISME 2013).

India suffers in comparison with PRC, Malaysia, and Thailand in the ease of entry as well as of exit of industrial enterprises as evaluated by the World Bank in its Doing Business Report, 2013. The comparative picture is given in Box 9.8.

Box 9.8 Entry and Exit Barriers in India and Comparator Countries

- If we take the time taken in days (shown in brackets) for starting business as a proxy for entry barriers, prima facie there is not much difference between India (27), the People's Republic of China (33), and Thailand (29) but clearly Malaysia (6) outshines the bigger players. However, what is not captured by the data is the facility to establish manufacturing enterprises provided by not only the Special Economic Zones (SEZs) but also the industrial zones in the PRC, which provide at the outset the full infrastructure, including shell factories (on plug-and-play basis), regulatory clearances, and connectivity with external infrastructure.
- In terms of the facility for closing a business, clearly the time taken in years, shown in brackets is a good indicator of the ease of exit: India (4.3), the PRC (1.7), Malaysia (1.5), and Thailand (2.7). Although the situation has improved in India with the enactment of the Companies Act, 2013, it is still well behind the comparator countries. No other country has a requirement for companies to seek government permission to close a business.
- In so far as enforcement of contract is concerned, India is a laggard by a big margin, in terms of the time taken, shown in days in brackets: India (1,420), the PRC (406), Malaysia (425), and Thailand (440).

Recommendations

If India wishes to achieve quick growth in manufacturing, as it must, to quicken the pace of economic growth and provide regular and decent employment opportunities to millions of job seekers, encouraging international production sharing by stimulating FDI inflows seems to be an attractive strategy.

Top Priority Measures for Stimulating International Production Sharing

Taxation Incentives

To improve the environment for FDI inflows, it is imperative as a first step to eliminate discriminatory taxation of foreign enterprises. The next step should be to bring down corporate tax levels progressively to the ASEAN level of 25 per cent, which is also the level in PRC. It would be important that the plan for reduction of basic corporate tax for domestic companies from 30 to 25 per cent over 4 years beginning 2016–17 is implemented. In addition, high-technology industries should be granted incentives by way of reduced corporate taxes to provide for a level playing field between India, PRC, and ASEAN countries.

It is also imperative for the government to renounce enactment of tax laws with retrospective effect. In order to improve investor sentiment, which suffered a severe setback when the government amended the law retrospectively in 2012, it is necessary to amend the law to provide that the change shall apply prospectively only. In fact, it would be best to introduce a provision in the Income Tax Act, 1961 that no change in future shall apply retrospectively.

Tariff Barriers, Inverted Tariff Structure, and Other Tariff Anomalies

There is a case for India to cut duties on capital goods in order to improve its overall competitiveness in manufacturing. More importantly, India needs to eliminate the inverted duty structure in a number of consumer durables in which the establishment of manufacturing enterprises in India is being impeded by this anomaly. In the case of ITA-I products, the procedures need to be streamlined for duty-free import of materials on which the levy of customs duty results in an inverted duty structure. It is also necessary for India to gradually bring down its tariffs on automobiles so as to reduce the excessively high effective rate of protection on the product.

Gateway Infrastructure

The port infrastructure has to be improved by increasing the capacity of the 12 major ports substantially from the current level of about 1,000 to 2,500 million tonne entirely through public-private partnership. The government should fund programmes for carrying out capital dredging for deepening drafts in harbours and channels up to 14 metres wherever necessary. The rail and road connectivity of ports needs improvement on a war footing.

Customs Procedures

Equally important is the improvement of customs procedures. In particular, it is necessary to ensure that a single window is made effective for the processing of documents and that the application of electronic data interchange (EDI) enables a truly paperless process and eliminates face-to-face contact between the customs officials and agents of exporters and importers. For this, the customs need to stop the practice of seeking paper copies of documents and instead accept digital copies and digital signature. In risk management system (RMS), physical checking should be gradually brought down to the international level of 2–3 per cent. To widen the use of the accredited client programme (ACP), the eligibility criteria should be made less stringent and only those who have been found actually guilty of wrong-doing should be excluded.

Priority Measures to Improve Domestic Environment for Investment in Manufacturing

Physical Infrastructure

Power: Power shortages have a crippling effect on the international competitiveness of manufacturing in India and deter foreign investors from setting up manufacturing establishments in the country. Since adequacy of fuel supplies for generation is the critical factor responsible for the gap between the availability and requirement of power from time to time, the main action needed is to augment domestic coal supplies on a sustained basis. For this, it is necessary to build political consensus within the country for the denationalization of coal mines.

Dedicated freight corridors: In railways, the North-South and East-West dedicated freight corridors should be completed speedily and work should be taken up in four other identified stretches in which the traffic has reached saturation levels to improve the reliability of container delivery through the railways.

Roadways: While the existing programme of building national highways needs to be implemented with greater speed, an important gap that needs to be filled is the construction of access-controlled expressways with good connectivity with metropolitan areas and major ports. Without such expressways, India will not have world-class roadway infrastructure. In addition, the process of repair and maintenance of highways already built needs to be streamlined.

Land

The LARR Act, 2013 has undeniably raised the price of land steeply and also put formidable procedural hurdles in the way of land acquisition for industrial purposes. These hurdles, such as the need to have consent of 80 per cent landholders for private companies and 70 per cent in case of public private partnership projects, and the requirement for social impact assessment, are particularly worrisome. While the outlook for changes in the LARR Act, 2013 at the national level appears dim, it is still possible for individual states to propose changes valid for that state only and obtain the assent of the president on them, as envisaged in Article 254 of the Constitution of India. Such a line of action seems to have the tacit support of the current leadership at the centre and deserves to be encouraged.

One other line of action can be envisaged to alleviate the difficulty in finding land for industry. The Government of India should move quickly towards establishing industrial/economic corridors and or NIMZs in accordance with ambitious plans that have been undertaken. Providing developed land to industry is even better than facilitating access to land for them.

Labour Laws

Chapter VB of the Industrial Disputes Act, 1947, which is out of tune with the current economic policies of government and acts as a psychological barrier against large investments in manufacturing, needs to be removed from the statute books. As a balancing act, it would be necessary to raise the compensation for workers, in the event of retrenchment or closure, from the current level of 15 days' average pay to 30 days' average pay for every completed year of continuous service. We have seen that contract labour is being widely used in the country even for mainline production activities and a fallout of this practice has been the development of a wide gap in wage levels and conditions of service between contract and regular workers in the same enterprise and that this has become a new source of industrial unrest. What is needed is effective enforcement of the law as intended in the central act and for this a prerequisite will be for each state to clearly define the non-core activities which are prohibited.

Additionally, as in comparator countries, specific provision has to be made in the law to allow employment on fixed-term contracts.

Trade union laws need to be revamped in order to improve the process of collective bargaining and promote harmony in industrial relations. For efficiency of collective bargaining, it is necessary to introduce a provision for recognition of bargaining agent. Either a single union with a membership of 51 per cent or more or two or more unions, whose joint membership comes to that level should be recognized as the bargaining agent. The agenda should include granting industrial relations rights only to recognized unions, providing for election of office bearers, and requiring endorsement of a majority for taking industrial action. To limit the role of outsiders, it should be provided that out of the two key posts of president and general secretary, at least one should be held by workers, as suggested by FICCI and All India Organisation of Employers (AIOE) (2014).

Other Measures to Boost Domestic Investment Environment

Internal Taxes

Abolition of central sales tax, which is an indirect tax on interstate transactions, and the introduction of the goods and services tax (GST), which are already at an advanced stage of legislative consideration, need to be accomplished at the earliest.

Special Economic Zones

The most important action that needs to be taken is to strengthen the physical infrastructure around the SEZs so that individual units get power, water, and connectivity to drainage automatically once they decide to establish units in SEZs. The governance structure of the SEZs or the nodes in the industrial corridors must have the involvement of state chief ministers so that there are no problems for the SEZ units in getting connectivity and regulatory clearances. Lastly, and importantly, the fiscal benefits announced in the past for developers and units of SEZs should be restored for existing beneficiaries. Changes, if any, made in the future should apply prospectively.

Entry and Exit Barriers

The foremost action needed in India is the upgradation of external infrastructure needed by industry—power supply, water supply, drainage, and roads (both trunk routes and roads leading to industrial areas)—so that once land is allocated to industrial units in SEZs or national manufacturing zones, there is no hassle in power, water, drainage, and road connectivity. These are the new entry barriers with which entrepreneurs are confronted.

The repeal of Chapter VB of the Industrial Disputes Act, 1947 as recommended earlier will also improve the situation regarding exit barriers in India. In addition, it is necessary to address the practical problem that has made the Arbitration and Conciliation Act, 1998 a non-starter, so that the enforcement of contracts in India is not delayed by congestion in courts.

★ ★ ★

The measures suggested here will stimulate FDI inflows into manufacturing in India and also improve the environment for domestic investment in manufacturing. As has been noted earlier, foreign enterprises participate in international production sharing not only by undertaking manufacturing by affiliates established in different countries, but also by outsourcing manufacturing of P&C to purely domestic enterprises.

The measures suggested here will not only facilitate foreign investment into India but also strengthen the MSMEs in India and make it possible for multinational firms to outsource to these enterprises. Such outsourcing has already taken place substantially in the automobile sector in India and has resulted in the MSMEs growing up into highly competitive units and exporting large volumes to the OEMs unconnected with the multinational firms that first outsourced P&C to them. Technology-cooperation agreements rather than FDI have helped these enterprises to grow into world-class suppliers of P&C. A replication of the experience in the automobile sector will bear rich dividend for the Indian manufacturing sector.

Annexure 9A: List of Companies, Associations, and Institutions Interviewed/Consulted during the Field Survey

TABLE 9A.1 Names of the Companies Interviewed/Consulted during the Fieldwork

No.	Name	Economy
1	Hitachi Ltd	Japan
2	Suzuki Motor Corporation	Japan
3	Sony Corporation	Japan
4	Mitsubishi Heavy Industries	Japan
5	Toyo Denki	Japan
6	MIKUNI Corporation	Japan
7	Toyota Motor Corporation	Japan
8	Toshiba Corporation	Japan
9	Acer Incorporated	Taipei,China
10	Volktek Corporation	Taipei,China
11	Giga-Byte Technology Co. Ltd	Taipei,China
12	Youyang Airport Lighting Equipment Inc.	Korea, Republic of
13	YG-1 Co., Ltd	Korea, Republic of

14	C.S. Wind Corporation	Korea, Republic of
15	Hyo Seong Electric Co. Ltd	Korea, Republic of
16	ACE Technology	Korea, Republic of
17	SPCO Ltd	Korea, Republic of
18	Woongjin Chemical Co. Ltd	Korea, Republic of
19	ILJIN Electric Co., Ltd	Korea, Republic of
20	Neo Technical Systems	Korea, Republic of
21	ALSTOM India	India
22	HP	India
23	Moser Baer	India
24	TVS Electronics Limited	India
25	Renault-Nissan	India
26	Videocon Industries Ltd	India

TABLE 9A.2 Names of the Industry Associations Interviewed/Consulted during the Fieldwork

No.	Name	Economy
1	Keidanren	Japan
2	Japan Machinery Center for Trade and investment (JMC)	Japan
3	TCA	Taipei,China
4	TEEMA	Taipei,China

TABLE 9A.3 Names of the Freight Forwarders/Express Carriers Interviewed/Consulted during the Fieldwork

No.	Name	Country
1	Beijing Harmony Shipping and Forwarding Agent Co. Ltd	PRC
2	DHL, Beijing	PRC
3	Shanghai Asian Development International Transportation Pudong Co. Ltd	PRC
4	JJB Link Logistics Company Ltd, Shanghai	PRC
5	Shanghai Sijin International Transport Co. Ltd	PRC
6	Hellmann Worldwide Logistics (Shanghai) Ltd	PRC
7	Gati Cargo Express (Shanghai) Co. Ltd	PRC
8	HKI Worldwide Movers Co. Ltd	Thailand
9	Freight Express International Co. Ltd	Thailand
10	Union Freight Forwarder Co. Ltd	Thailand
11	JVK International Movers Co. Ltd	Thailand
12	Century Logistics Holdings Berhad	Malaysia
13	Felix Relocations	Malaysia
14	VPC Freight Forwarders Pvt. Ltd Chennai	India
15	International Clearing and Shipping Agency (India) Pvt. Ltd Chennai	India
16	S. Natsea Iyer & Co. Chennai	India
17	Jupiter Sea and Air Services Pvt Ltd Chennai	India
18	DHL Logistics Pvt. Ltd Mumbai	India
19	Shaan Marine Services Pvt. Ltd, Mumbai	India
20	Seahorse Ship Agencies Pvt. Ltd, Mumbai	India
21	Activair Airfreight India Pvt. Ltd New Delhi	India
22	Dachser India Pvt. Ltd New Delhi	India
23	Agility Logistics Pvt. Ltd New Delhi	India
24	TNT Express, New Delhi	India

TABLE 9A.4 Names of the Freight Forwarders/Express Carriers Associations Interviewed/Consulted during the Fieldwork

No.	Name	Country
1	Thai International Freight Forwarders Association	Thailand
2	Federation of Malaysian Freight Forwarders	Malaysia
3	Selangor Freight Forwarders and Logistics Association	Malaysia
4	The Bombay Customs House Agents Association, Mumbai	India

TABLE 9A.5 Names of the Port Authorities Interviewed/Consulted during the Fieldwork

No.	Name	Country
1	Port Klang Authority	Malaysia
2	Jawaharlal Nehru Port Trust, Mumbai	India

References

Aggarwal, Aradhna. 2012. *Social and Economic Impact of SEZs in India*. Oxford University Press, New Delhi.

Athukorala, Prema-chandra. 2010. 'Production Networks and Trade Patterns in East Asia: Regionalization or Globalization?', ADB Working Paper Series on Regional Economic Integration No. 56, August.

———. 2011. 'Growing with Global Production Sharing: The Tale of Penang Export Hub', Working Paper No. 2011/13, Australia National University.

Athukorala, Prema-chandra and Jayant Menon. 2010. 'Global Production Sharing, Trade Patterns and Determinants of Trade Flows', Working Papers in Trade and Development No. 2010/06, July, Australian National University.

Athukorala, Prema-chandra and Nobuyuki Yamashita. 2007. 'Production Fragmentation in Manufacturing Trade: The Role of East Asia in Cross-border Production Networks', Working Paper Series, CCAS No. 003, Center for China and Asian Studies, College of Economics, Nihon University, June.

Bhalla, Surjit. 2014. 'No More Bandaid Tax Policy', *Indian Express*, 7 June.

Department of Commerce. 2011. 'Discussion Paper to Facilitate Stakeholder Consultation on Potential Reform of the SEZ Policy and Operating Framework', Discussion Paper on Potential Reform of the SEZ Policy and Operating Framework, SEZ Division, Ministry of Commerce and Industry, Government of India. Available at http://sezindia.nic.in/writereaddata/updates/SEZ_REVIEW.pdf (accessed on 30 October 2013).

Department of Electronics and Information Technology. 2012. 'Modified Special Incentive Package Scheme (M-SIPS) to Offset Disability and Attract Investment in Electronics Systems Design and Manufacturing (ESDM) Industries', Notification No. 24(10)/2010-IPHW, 27 July, Ministry of Communication and Information Technology, Government of India. Available at http://deity.gov.in/sites/upload_files/dit/files/MSIPS%20 Notification.pdf (accessed on 28 October 2013).

DIPP. *Fact Sheet on Foreign Direct Investment (FDI) (from April 2000 to June 2013)*. Ministry of Commerce and Industry, Government of India.

———. 2013. *Annual Report 2012-13*. Ministry of Commerce and Industry. Government of India.

———. 2013a. 'Consolidated FDI Policy: Effective from April 5, 2013', Circular 1 of 2013, Ministry of Commerce and Industry, Government of India.

Electricity Generation Authority of Thailand. *Various Annual Reports*. Available at http://www.egat.co.th/en/index.php?option=com_content&view=article&id=165&Itemid=146 (accessed 25 October 2013).

Energy Commission of Malaysia. 2012. *Electricity Supply Industry in Malaysia: Performance and Statistical Information 2010*. Putrajaya: Department of Energy Management and Industry Development. Available at http://meih.st.gov.my/documents/10620/e92bbc28-ff35-4e80-8981-a849b2fce14b (accessed on 30 October 2013).

EY. 2015. *Worldwide VAT, GST and Sales Tax Guide- Malaysia*. Available at http://www.ey.com/GL/en/Services/Tax/Worldwide-VAT--GST-and-Sales-Tax-Guide---XMLQS?preview&XmlUrl=/ec1mages/taxguides/VAT-2015/VAT-MY.xml (accessed on 30 July 2015).

FICCI. 2012. *Lack of Affordable & Quality Power: Shackling India's Growth Story*. Available at http://www.irgamag.com/images/pdf/Power%20Report.pdf (accessed on 25 October 2013).

FICCI and All India Organisation of Employers (AIOE). 2014. *Suggested Labour Policy Reforms*. New Delhi.

FISME. 2013. *Suggestions for Inter-Ministerial Committee (IMC) for Accelerating Manufacturing in the Micro, Small and Medium Enterprises (MSME) Sector*. Available at http://www.fisme.org.in/document/IMC_FISME_Suggestions_26042013.pdf (accessed 30 October 2013).

Gaulier, Guillaume, Françoise Lemoine, and Deniz Ünal-Kesenci. 2005. 'China's Integration in East Asia: Production Sharing, FDI & High-Tech Trade', Working Paper No. 2005-09, CEPII.

Hollweg, Claire and Marn-Heong Wong. 2009. 'Measuring Regulatory Restrictions in Logistics Services', ERIA Discussion Paper Series, ERIA-DP-2009-14. Available at http://www.eria.org/ERIA-DP-2009-14.pdf (accessed on 18 May 2015).

Jade & Fountain: PRC Lawyers. N.d. 'Impact of the New Enterprise Income Tax Law on Foreign Investment in China', China Legal Update. Available at *http://www.iln.com/articles/pub_1312.pdf* (accessed on 29 September 2016).

Kimura, Fukunari and Ayako Obashi. 2010. 'International Production Networks in Machinery Industries: Structure and Its Evolution', ERIA Discussion Paper Series, ERIA-DP-2010-09, Economic Research Institute for ASEAN and East Asia (ERIA), Jakarta, Indonesia.

———. 2011. Production Networks in East Asia: What We Know So Far, ADBI Working Paper Series, No. 320, Asian Development Bank Institute, Tokyo.

KPMG. 2013. 'New Regulations to Implement Nationwide Expansion of China's VAT Pilot Programme on August 1, 2013', *China Tax Alert*, 13, June.

———. 2015. *Corporate Tax Rates Table*. Available at http://www.kpmg.com/global/en/services/tax/tax-tools-and-resources/pages/corporate-tax-rates-table.aspx (accessed on 21 May 2015).

Metropolitan Electricity Authority, Thailand. 2013. *Statistic Data-Statistical Knowledge*, Reliability Indices. Available at http://www.mea.or.th/profile/index.php?l=en&tid=2&mid=96&pid=91 (accessed 11 November 2013).

Ministry of Commerce, PRC. 2007. *Trade Union Law of the People's Republic of China*, 20 March. Available at http://English.mofcom.gov.cn/aarticle/policyrelease/international policy/20070304475394.html (accessed on 3 November 2013).

Ministry of Power. 2012. *Annual Report 2012–12*. New Delhi: Government of India. Available at http://powermin.nic.in/sites/default/files/uploads/Annual_Report_2011-12_English.pdf (accessed on 29 September 2016).

Nath, Surendra. 2005. 'Labour Policy and Economic Reform in India', in Bibek Debroy and P D Kaushik (eds), *Reforming the Labour Market*, pp. 173–233. Academic Foundation, New Delhi.

PKF. 2013. *Malaysia Tax Guide 2013*. Available at http://www.pkf.com/media/1960332/malaysia%20pkf%20tax%20guide%202013.pdf (accessed on 10 November 2013).

PWC. 2013a. *Thai Tax 2013 Booklet*. Available at http://www.pwc.com/en_TH/th/publications/2013/thai-tax-2013-booklet.pdf(accessed on 9 November 2013).

———. 2013b. *Navigating Growth amidst Challenges: Union Budget 2013*. Available at http://spain-india.org/files/documentos/38_india-union-budget-2013-pwc-analysis-booklet.pdf (accessed on 10 November 2013).

Rajan, S. Ramkishen. 2003. 'Production-Sharing in East Asia: Implications for India', *Economic and Political Weekly*, XXXVIII(36): 3770–72.

RBI. 2012. *Master Circular- Priority Sector Lending—UCBs*, RBI/2012-13/57, 2 July. Available at http://rbi.org.in/scripts/BS_CircularIndexDisplay.aspx?Id=7334 (accessed on 5 November 2013).

Sen, Rahul and Sadhana Srivastava. 2011. 'Integrating into Asia's International Production Networks: Challenges and Prospects for India', in Witada Anukoonwattaka and Mia Mikic (eds), *India: A New Player in Asian Production Networks?*, *Studies in Trade and Investment 75*, pp. 78–119. Thailand: UNESCAP.

Small Industries Development Bank of India (SIDBI). 2012. *Annual Report 2011-12: Adressing Gaps in MSME Eco-system*. Available at http://www.sidbi.in/sites/default/files/financials/SIDBI%20ANNUAL%20REPORT%20%20 2011-12(ENGLISH)-Final.pdf (accessed on 14 November 2013).

SME Bank of Malaysia. 2013. Available at http://www.smebank.com.my/ (accessed on 3 November 2013).

SME Bank of Thailand. 2013. Available at http://www.smebank.co.th/en/about.php (accessed on 3 November 2013).

'Speech of Arun Jaitley, Minister of Finance'. 2015. Budget 2016–17. Available at http://indiabudget.nic.in/ub2015-16/bs/bs.pdf (accessed on 21 May 2015).

The New York Times. 2011. 'Outsourcing Giant Finds It Must Be Client, Too', 30 November. Available at http://www.nytimes.com/2011/12/01/world/asia/for-india-outsourcing-does-the-job-at-home-too.html?_r=0 (accessed on 2 November 2013).

UNCTAD. 2011. 'UNCTAD Liner Shipping Connectivity Index', in *Review of Maritime Transport 2011*, Report by the UNCTAD Secretariat, United Nations Conference on Trade and Development, New York and Geneva. Available at http://unctad.org/en/docs/rmt2011_en.pdf (accessed on 3 November 2013).

———. 2013. *World Investment Report 2013: Global Value Chains- Investment and Trade for Development*. United Nations, New York and Geneva.

World Bank. 2005. 'Linkages between Foreign Direct Investment and Trade Flows', in *From Disintegration to Reintegration: Eastern Europe and the Former Soviet Union in International Trade.* Washington, D.C. Available at http://siteresources.worldbank.org/INTECA/Resources/tradereport-complete.pdf (accessed on 5 November 2013).

———. 2008. 'Thailand Investment Climate Assessment Update', Report No. 44248-TH, June. Available at http://siteresources.worldbank.org/THAILANDEXTN/Resources/333295-1249970320257/TH_ICA_Update08_fullreport.pdf (accessed on 1 November 2013).

———. 2009. 'Air Freight: A Market Study with Implications for Landlocked Countries', Transport Papers, No. TP-26, August, Washington, D.C. Available at http://siteresources.worldbank.org/EXTAIRTRANSPORT/Resources/515180-1262792532589/6683177-1268747346047/air_cargo_study.pdf (accessed on 6 May 2015).

———. 2011. 'The Air Connectivity Index: Measuring Integration in the Global Air Transport Network', Policy Research Working Paper 5722, World Bank.

World Bank. 2012. 'Connecting to Compete 2012: Trade Logistics in global Economy- The Logistics Performance Index and Its Indicators', available at http://siteresources.worldbank.org/TRADE Resources/239070-1336654966193/LPI_2012_final.pdf (accessed on 10 November 2013).

———. 2013. *Doing Business 2013—Smarter Regulations for Small and Medium Size Enterprizes*. Washington, D.C.: World Bank and International Finance Corporation.

WTO. n.d. Tariff Profiles, available at http://stat.wto.org/TariffProfile/WSDBTariffPFHome.aspx?Language=E (accessed on 29 September 2016).

Yeats, Alexander J. 1998. 'Just How Big Is Global Production Sharing?', Policy Research Working Paper No. 1871, World Bank.

10

ARPITA MUKHERJEE
TANU M. GOYAL

Integrating South and Southeast Asia through Services Value Chain

The Case of India and Thailand*

Traditionally, production of goods was divided in two stages—raw materials and finished goods (Ohlin 1933). With technological developments and the liberalization of world economies, production is being

* Views expressed in this chapter are authors' own. This chapter is part of a project funded by the Asian Development Bank (ADB). We are grateful to Rajat Kathuria, Director and Chief Executive, Indian Council for Research on International Economic Relations (ICRIER), for giving us the opportunity to work in this area. Earlier versions of this chapter were presented at the joint workshop of the ADB–Korea Institute for International Economic Policy in Seoul, Republic of Korea on 22–23 October 2012, and at the ADB workshop in Manila, Philippines on 4 September 2013. The authors are grateful to the workshop participants for their valuable inputs. The chapter was also presented at the ICRIER–Confederation of Indian Industry (CII) Industry Consultation organized by the CII on 6 February 2013. We would like to thank the conference participants for their comments. T.N. Srinivasan, Anwarul Hoda, and Rupa Chanda reviewed the chapter and we are grateful for their valuable inputs.

fragmented and the concept of global value chains has emerged (De Backer and Miroudot 2013). This has led to the development of distinct services activities within the global value chain of goods (Brockman and Stephenson 2012; López, Niembro, and Ramos 2011).

The composition of services in the value of tradable has been increasing over time. According to the World Trade Organization (WTO) International Trade Statistics (2014), 'trade in value added show that services take a more pronounced role in international trade. This is because services are increasingly embodied in the production of manufactures; they play a key role in defining the competitiveness of a country's exports. Additionally, services can be instrumental in helping countries to upgrade to higher value-added tasks in global value chains.'[1] Services such as logistics services help to increase the global competitiveness of manufacturing through faster end-to-end reliable transportation of goods. In addition, with increasing use of information technology (IT), the rise in outsourcing of services, and the development of new business models, the services value chain has evolved to complement the global production networks (Rubalcaba, Gallego, and Hipp 2011; World Economic Forum 2012).

One facilitator of production networks and global value chains is the regulatory policies that affect cross-border trade and investment. Realizing the importance of these, liberalization of the entire value chain is now being addressed through trade agreements for efficient cross-country delivery of both goods and services. The most recent trade agreements are comprehensive, covering goods, services, investments, e-commerce and trade facilitation, amongst others, to ensure easier movement of goods and services and to facilitate the creation of a value chain. In the past two decades, South and Southeast Asian

---

The authors would also like to thank all survey participants in India and Thailand. Thanks are due to Sumanta Chaudhuri, Sudhanshu Panday (Department of Commerce and Industry, Government of India), and Saikat Sen Sharma (Ministry of External Affairs, Government of India), and their respective teams for input and for their help in coordinating the survey. We are also grateful to Ramneet Goswami who helped us with the data analysis. Renu Gupta helped us with copyediting and Anu Mohandas helped us in coordinating the meetings and interviews.

[1] For details, see WTO (2014, p. 3).

countries have signed several comprehensive free trade agreements (FTAs) and they are in the process of negotiating regional trade agreements such as the Regional Comprehensive Economic Partnership (RCEP) Agreement. The services sector is a key component of these agreements and it is expected that this will lead to the integration of the services market and the creation of a services value chain in the region.

Studies have highlighted that fostering connectivity between India and countries in Southeast Asia will not only reduce the service-linked cost of trading goods but also accelerate the development of manufacturing, production networks, and value chains. There are broadly three types of connectivity—institutional connectivity, people-to-people connectivity, and physical connectivity (Kimura, Kudo, and Umezaki 2011). Studies have also highlighted that cross-country connectivity can be fostered through liberalization of services trade, either autonomously or through trade agreements (United Nations 2014).

Given this background, the objective of this chapter is to understand the prospects of enhancing services trade, investment, and cooperation between South and Southeast Asia, taking the example of one country from each region—India and Thailand. It also focuses on development of services value chains through services sector liberalization. This chapter introduces the scope of services in the creation of global value chains and production networks in the region. India and Thailand have been selected because the two countries are members of the WTO and have concluded or are currently engaged in negotiations of multiple trade agreements that include liberalisation of services. They are also negotiating a comprehensive economic cooperation agreement with each other and have several similarities and complementarities in terms of the services sector.

Bilateral data on trade in services is not readily available for most countries, including India and Thailand. The study is, therefore, based on a primary survey and an analysis of the literature. The primary survey was conducted in 2012–13 and covered 180 stakeholders in India and Thailand. These included Indian companies that have operations or are interested in operating in Thailand; Thai companies operating in India or those trying to establish a presence in India; and government officials, sector regulators, associations, professional bodies, and sector experts in both India and Thailand. The companies were selected through information provided by the Indian and Thai embassies and industry associations and an Internet search. The survey was based on a semi-structured questionnaire, with some open-ended questions to gather more information. Detailed questions were included to understand the services value chain, prospects for export of new services, the extent of integration of services in the two markets, barriers to services exports and market integration, and expectations of the two governments and trade agreements.

Overview, Composition, and Trends in Trade in Services—India and Thailand

Trade in services is a growing component of global trade. World trade in commercial services has increased manifold—from $2,905 billion in 2001 to $9,025 billion in 2013 (WTO 2012, 2014). The share of trade in services in world trade was around 33 per cent in 2013. Both India and Thailand are key exporters and importers of trade in services. In 2013, India was ranked the 6th largest exporter of services with a share of 3.2 per cent in world export of commercial services and the 9th largest importer with a share of 2.8 per cent. In the same year, Thailand was ranked 23rd in terms of both export and import with a share of 1.3 per cent in each. In 2014, both India and Thailand had a positive trade balance in trade in services; however, the balance for India was higher than for Thailand (Table 10.1).

To evaluate the global competitiveness of India and Thailand in specific services sectors, their revealed comparative advantage (RCA) was calculated.[2] The RCAs for three different years as given in Table 10.2 show that in 2012, India had a comparative advantage in computer services and other business services vis-à-vis the rest of the world, whereas

[2] The RCA is used to examine and assess the pattern and specialisation of a country and therefore its global competitiveness in a particular sector vis-à-vis the rest of the world. To analyse the export competitiveness of different services of India and Thailand vis-à-vis the rest of the world, we used the Balassa index. The formula is:

$$RCA_{ij}^{2} = (x_{ij}/X_{it}) \;/\; (x_{wj}/X_{wt})$$

where x_{ij} and x_{wj} are the values of a country's exports of services sector j and the world's exports of services sector j, and X_{it} and X_{wt} refer to the country's total exports and world total exports.

TABLE 10.1 India and Thailand Global Trade in Service in 2014 ($ million)

Sector	India		Thailand	
	Exports	Imports	Exports	Imports
Services	154,643.6	–124,971.7	55,360.0	–53,286.7
Goods-related services	320.3	–285.5	–	–
Manufacturing services on physical inputs owned by others	142.8	–15.6	–	–
Maintenance and repair services not included elsewhere	177.5	–269.9	–	–
Transport	17,955.2	–56,032.0	5,757.3	–26,716.6
Travel	18,602.3	–12,679.3	38,447.4	–6,951.9
Other services	115,401.8	–48,626.0	11,155.3	–19,618.2
Construction	1,524.6	–1,171.5	613.1	–761.5
Insurance and pension services	2,181.9	–5,695.0	81.7	–2,708.2
Financial services	6,530.1	–4,833.6	178.4	–170.0
Charges for the use of intellectual property not included elsewhere	697.8	–4,278.5	212.1	–3,971.4
Telecommunications, computer, and information services	55,398.0	–3,911.9	531.6	–707.9
Other business services	47,269.1	–26,824.1	9,125.2	–10,967.4
Personal, cultural, and recreational services	1,291.4	–996.9	61.2	–19.3
Government goods and services not included elsewhere	509.0	–914.5	351.9	–312.7
Services not allocated	2,364.1	–7,348.9	–	–
Memo item: Commercial services	154,134.7	–124,057.2	55,008.1	–52,974.1
Memo item: Other commercial services	114,892.8	–47,711.5	10,803.5	–19,305.6

Source: Extracted from UNCTAD statistics, available at http://unctad.org/en/Pages/Statistics.aspx (last accessed on May 20, 2015).

TABLE 10.2 Revealed Comparative Advantages of India and Thailand in Exports of Services

Service Sectors	India					Thailand				
	2001	2005	2010	2011	2012	2001	2005	2010	2011	2012
Communications	2.79	1.27	0.51	0.50	0.51	0.37	0.40	0.55	0.51	0.41
Computers and information technology	9.72	6.88	5.81	5.52	5.38	0.00	0.02	0.01	0.01	0.02
Construction	0.18	0.38	0.17	0.25	0.24	1.10	0.59	0.54	0.43	0.36
Financial	0.29	0.44	0.65	0.63	0.58	0.00	0.04	0.04	0.06	0.08
Government services	1.46	0.18	0.23	0.25	0.20	0.33	0.35	0.41	0.41	0.39
Insurance	0.85	0.76	0.58	0.84	0.78	0.35	0.00	0.08	0.17	0.35
Other business services	0.61	1.51	1.10	1.11	1.25	0.79	0.82	0.75	0.61	0.59
Personal, cultural, and recreational	0.00	0.53	0.33	0.30	0.47	0.00	0.29	0.29	0.36	0.22
Royalties and licence fees	0.04	0.01	0.02	0.03	0.03	0.01	0.03	0.07	0.06	0.07
Transportation	0.60	0.47	0.47	0.52	0.50	1.05	1.00	0.84	0.70	0.60
Travel	0.60	0.47	0.47	0.52	0.50	1.77	2.09	2.41	2.67	2.72

Note: NA= data is not available.

Source: Calculated by the authors from various tables extracted from 'International Trade: Services', UNCTADSTAT available at http://unctadstat.unctad.org/ReportFolders/reportFolders.aspx (last accessed on 8 October 2013).

Thailand had a comparative advantage in travel services. Since the two countries have comparative advantages in different services sectors, there is scope for enhancing bilateral trade.

Bilateral Trade in Services: India and Thailand

India does not have disaggregated data on India–Thailand bilateral trade on services. The data provided by the Bank of Thailand was only for 2 years (2009 and 2010) and is outdated. Nevertheless, it shows that bilateral trade is declining. In 2009, bilateral services trade was valued at $692 million, but in 2010 it declined to $520 million. However, Thai services imports from India have increased—from $127 million in 2009 to $132 million in 2010. Over the years, the trend in bilateral trade in services between India and Thailand has changed. In 1990 and in 2000, Thailand had a negative trade balance with India, but this was reversed in 2010. The bilateral trade data for only 2 years does not allow us to draw conclusions. The Indian government has recently started a survey for bilateral trade data collection and is trying to design a regulatory framework for collecting bilateral trade data.

Investment Flows

Over the years, the foreign direct investment (FDI) inflows and outflows of India and Thailand have increased. In 2012, FDI contributed around 2.4 per cent to the GDP of both countries (World Bank 2013). In India, the services sector has a large share in FDI inflows (64 per cent between 2000 and 2012), while in Thailand the manufacturing sector is a large recipient of FDI. In Thailand, the percentage of services in FDI inflows in services was 20.4 per cent in December 2000 and it increased to 31.2 per cent in June 2011.[3]

The major investors in India are Mauritius, Singapore, the US, the UK, and Japan. Between April 2000 and July 2013, FDI inflows from these five countries was valued at $141 billon and contributed 70.4 per cent to India's total FDI inflows (Department of Industrial Policy and

[3] Calculated by the authors from Table EC_XT_027: Net Flow of Foreign Direct Investment Classified by Sectors 1/2/3 (From 2010 to 2011), Bank of Thailand, available at *http://www2.bot.or.th/statistics/BOTWEBSTAT.aspx?reportID=77&language=ENG* (accessed on 9 October 2013).

Promotion [DIPP] 2013). Japan, the Netherlands, the US, Hong Kong, China and Singapore are the major investing economies in Thailand. In June 2011, these economies contributed 56.6 per cent to Thailand's net FDI inflows.[4]

In July 2000, India and Thailand signed the Bilateral Investment Promotion and Protection Agreement (BIPA),[5] which came into force on 13 July 2011. Its objective is to promote and protect the interests of investors and to create conditions that foster greater investment by investors of one country in the territory of the other country. The two countries also signed a Double Taxation Avoidance Agreement (DTAA)[6] on 22 March 1985, which came into force on 27 June 1986.

Despite these agreements, both India and Thailand do not have major investments in each other's market. From April 2000 to July 2013, the cumulative FDI inflow from Thailand was $128.62 million. During this period, Thailand was the 38th country in terms of investment inflows into India, accounting for 0.06 per cent of the total FDI inflows (DIPP 2013). The services sector (including construction, telecommunications, information, trading, and hotel and tourism) accounted for the major share of FDI inflows.

In recent years, India's FDI outflow to Thailand has increased. India is now amongst the top-20 investors in Thailand. From 1970 to 2010, the total investment from India to Thailand was $702 million[7] (22,443 million Baht) (Board of Investment [BOI] 2010). In 2010, India invested $60 million (1,906 million Baht), which accounted for 0.66 per cent of total FDI inflows into Thailand.[8] Since 1970, cumulative approved

[4] Calculated by the authors from Table EC-XT_25: Net Flow of Foreign Direct Investment by Country 1/2/3, Bank of Thailand, *http://www2.bot.or.th/statistics/ReportPage.aspx?reportID=74&language=eng* (accessed on 9 October 2013).

[5] For details, see http://finmin.nic.in/bipa/bipa_index.asp (accessed on 8 December 2011).

[6] The agreement covers taxes on income proposed on behalf of each contracting state. It also provides reduced tax rates on dividends, interest, royalties, technical service fees, etc. received by residents of one country from those in the other.

[7] Exchange rate for 2010, 1 Thai Baht =$0.313 (average), as seen on http://www.oanda.com/currency/historical-rates/ (accessed 1 October 2016)

[8] As in BOI (2010) and information provided by the Indian Embassy in Thailand.

FDI from India to Thailand was over \$1.5 billion.[9] Most of the Indian investment in Thailand has been concentrated in the manufacturing sector, and since 2007 the services sector has accounted for only around 9 per cent of the total FDI from India to Thailand.

Overall, the analysis of the secondary data shows that bilateral trade and investment in services between India and Thailand is small but growing and there are trade complementarities.

Reforms in the Services Sector and Creation of Value Chains

The services sector has the major share in the value added to the GDP in both India and Thailand. In the case of India, with a share of 51.3 per cent in 2013, services accounted for more than 50 per cent of the value added in GDP. Compared to this, in Thailand services accounted for 45 per cent of the value added in GDP in the same year (World Bank 2013). The growth of the services sector in the two countries is linked to reforms and liberalization that the countries initiated in the 1990s. In India service sector reforms have been part of the overall economic reform process that began in the early 1990s due to the balance of payments crisis. India took assistance from the International Monetary Fund (IMF) and, as part of the conditions, it embarked on an ambitious reform process. The core features of the reform were dismantling public monopoly in sectors such as air transport, telecommunications, and financial services and allowing private and foreign investment. Most services have been liberalized in a phased manner. Except for a few services sectors such as multi-brand retail, legal, postal, banking, insurance, and railways where there are full or partial FDI restrictions, almost all the other services sectors have been opened up for foreign investment. Public-private partnerships have been encouraged in several sectors, especially infrastructure services, to improve efficiency, productivity, quality of services, and global competitiveness. The government is in the process of streamlining rules and regulations in the services sector to facilitate foreign and domestic investment. Despite the liberalization, services continue to face FDI and other regulatory restrictions in India.

[9] Information provided by the Indian Embassy in Thailand.

Thailand also started liberalizing its services sector in the 1990s when it faced the Asian financial crisis in 1997. To tackle the crisis, the Thai government implemented a comprehensive economic reform programme that was part of its IMF loan conditions and focused on macro-economic stabilization and structural reforms in the corporate and financial sectors. As part of the IMF package requisites, the government opened up the financial sector (with full ownership of 100 per cent) to foreign nationals for 10 years. The retail sector was also opened up for foreign investment. Several laws such as the Bankruptcy Law (1940) and the Foreign Business Act, B.E. 2542 (A.D. 1999) were amended or passed in 1999. The government also started deregulation of state-owned enterprises in state-dominated utilities such as telecommunications, transportation, water, and energy.

Even after a decade of reforms and autonomous liberalization, both India and Thailand have restrictive FDI regimes in services. Compared to India, Thailand has a more restrictive regime for foreign investment in services (Sally 2005). Foreign investment is governed by the Foreign Business Act, B.E. 2542 (A.D. 1999), which gives a negative list of sectors for investment and allows up to 49 per cent foreign ownership.

Services sector reforms in both countries have enhanced the role of services in their global value chain and production networks. The OECD gives data on value added[10] by other countries in the exports of a particular country. In 2009, countries in East and Southeast Asia contributed to about 4.6 per cent of the value added embodied in India's exports. Amongst Association of Southeast Asian Nations (ASEAN) countries, Thailand is the third largest in terms of value addition, with

[10] Trade in value-added is a statistical approach used to estimate the source(s) of value (by country and industry) that is added in producing goods and services for export (and import). It recognises that growing global value chains mean that a country's exports increasingly rely on significant intermediate imports (and, so, value added by industries in upstream countries). For example, a motor vehicle exported by country A may require significant parts, such as engines and seats, produced in other countries. In turn, these countries will use intermediate inputs imported from other countries, such as steel and rubber, to produce the parts exported to A. The Trade in Value-Added (TiVA) approach traces the value added by each industry and country in the production chain and allocates the value added to these source industries and countries.

about $24.41 million or 20 per cent of the value added by ASEAN member states (Table 10.3).

TABLE 10.3 Value Added Embodied in Exports of India by Select Countries in 2009

Source Country/Region	Value Added ($ million)
Europe	689.429
United States	239.672
East and Southeast Asia	433.315
East Asia	310.427
ASEAN	122.888
Singapore	38.748
Indonesia	25.215
Thailand	24.414
Malaysia	21.59
Viet Nam	4.975
Philippines	4.861
Brunei Darussalam	2.795
Cambodia	0.291
Total	9,387.274

Source: Extracted from OECD Database on Global Value Chain Indicators available at http://stats.oecd.org/Index.aspx?DataSetCode=TIVAORIGINVA# (last accessed on 19 May 2015).

Thailand's value added in India's exports has been the highest in wholesale and retail trade, hotels and restaurant services, and the manufacturing sector (Table 10.4). This suggests the possibilities of creating a global value chain in certain services sectors between India and Thailand such as hotel and restaurant services.

Within ASEAN, Singapore is one of the largest contributors to the value added in India's exports, and India already has a comprehensive agreement with the country. India is now negotiating trade agreements with Thailand, which is also a key contributor to global value added in India's exports. It is likely that bilateral agreement can facilitate trade and investment in both intermediate and finished goods and services between the two countries and help in creation of value chain. This helps in the creation of global value chains.

TABLE 10.4 Sector-wise Value Added by Thailand in India's Exports in 2009

Sector	Value Added ($ million)
Wholesale and retail trade; hotels and restaurants	8.457
Manufacturing not elsewhere classified; recycling	4.678
Basic metals and fabricated metal products	2.611
Chemicals and non-metallic mineral products	2.023
Transport and storage, post and telecommunication	1.41
Electrical and optical equipment	1.307
Agriculture, hunting, forestry and fishing	0.745
Electricity, gas, and water supply	0.509
Textiles, textile products, leather, and footwear	0.481
Wood, paper, paper products, printing, and publishing	0.431
Mining and quarrying	0.406
Financial intermediation	0.358
Transport equipment	0.345
Business services	0.26
Food products, beverages, and tobacco	0.223
Machinery and equipment, not elsewhere classified	0.135
Other services	0.026
Construction	0.01
Total	24.415

Source: Extracted from OECD Database on Global Value Chain Indicators available at http://stats.oecd.org/Index.aspx?DataSetCode=TIVAORIGINVA# (last accessed on 19 May 2015).

Since data on bilateral trade in services is not available for the two countries, a primary survey was conducted to understand the trade patterns and barriers to integrating the services sectors in the two countries. The findings are discussed in the following section.

Primary Survey: Key Findings

A primary survey was conducted in both India and Thailand to understand the trends and potential for enhancing bilateral trade and investment. Participants were asked detailed questions on their modes of entry and operation in each other's market, the market potential they visualize, and the barriers they face. Participants were also asked for their views on market integration and the role of trade agreements in achieving it.

The survey found that Indian companies have a greater presence in Thailand in the services sector than Thai companies in India. In general, Thai companies operating in the services sector are less globalized than Indian companies and they prefer to operate within the ASEAN region. Indian companies in Thailand largely concentrate on services sectors such as construction services, while Thai companies in India are in sectors such as hotels and restaurants.

Broad Survey Findings

In terms of the nature of enterprise, of the 59 Indian companies interviewed, about 51 per cent operates in Thailand through agents and distributors, 34 per cent has wholly-owned subsidiaries and the remainder have joint ventures. Only 10 Thai companies responded to the survey, of which 8 have wholly owned subsidiaries.

When asked about the factors determining their decision to invest, Indian companies emphasized stable political and social conditions and market growth potential (Figure 10.1). Investment incentives/FDI regime is ranked lower, since there are no major investment incentives in services and there are FDI restrictions in Thailand. It is difficult for expatriates to own land and get citizenship, amongst other factors, in Thailand and this is reflected in the survey rankings. The Thai companies in India also gave preference to stable political and social conditions as very important factors in determining investment decisions in India. India's large domestic market, growing consumer base, and high-quality staff are other important factors.

Of the 59 Indian companies, about 48 per cent get projects in Thailand through agents, 14 per cent through international competitive bidding, 10 per cent through their joint venture partner, 7 per cent through advertisements, and the remaining companies through their networks. About 51 per cent of Indian companies pointed out that registration from the government of Thailand has been the most important requirement for entering/operating in Thailand. About 17 per cent of the companies said that other licences such as export licences and

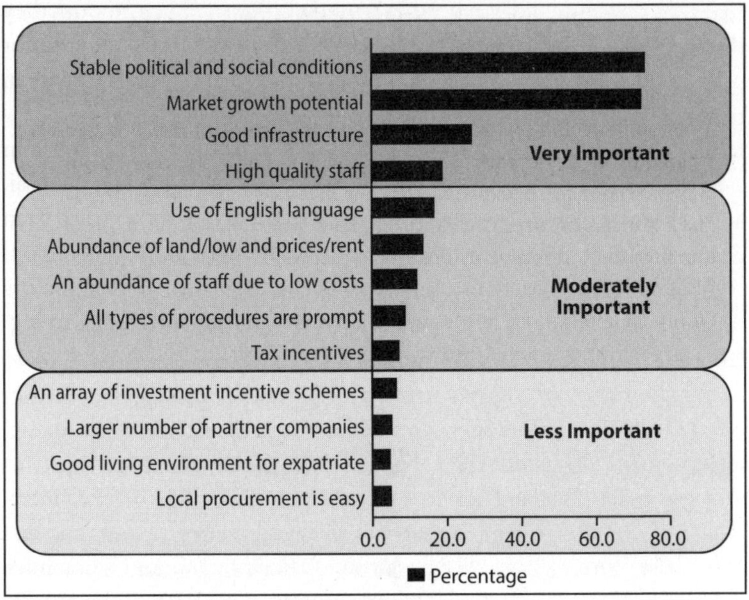

Figure 10.1 Factors Determining Investment Decisions for Indian Companies in Thailand

Source: Compiled by the authors from information collected during the primary survey.

sector-specific licences for sectors such as banking, freight forwarding, health, and construction services are required to operate in Thailand. These are key supporting services for production networks.

A large percentage of Indian companies (82 per cent) that operate in Thailand have a presence in other ASEAN countries. Of these, about 33 per cent (19) have operations only in Singapore, 17 per cent (10 companies) have operations in two ASEAN countries—Singapore and Malaysia—and 9 per cent (5 companies) have operations in three other ASEAN countries—Singapore, Malaysia and the Philippines. Thus, entry and presence in Thailand is part of the companies' overall strategy to expand in the ASEAN region.

When asked about the workforce and employees, the majority of the Indian and Thai companies were satisfied with the each other's skilled workforce. Around 68 per cent of Indian companies said they were fully satisfied with the skill level of Thai workers, 18 companies said that they face difficulties due to their lack of knowledge of English, and the rest did not comment. More than 70 per cent of Indian companies send employees to Thailand, and the majority of them apply for work permits.[11] All the Thai companies interviewed were fully satisfied with Indian workers and their skills.

When asked about the scope for collaboration in third-country markets, about 30 per cent pointed out that there is scope for India–Thai collaboration in European countries, the US, Australia, Canada, and ASEAN countries, such as Singapore, Malaysia and the Philippines, through joint ventures. Companies agreed that joint ventures and collaboration could lead to wider market integration and enable companies to complement each other's strengths. The survey participants further pointed out that India's services trade agreement with ASEAN (signed in September 2014) and ASEAN market integration in 2015 are likely to increase India–Thailand services trade and India's trade with ASEAN. However, for this to happen barriers to market entry, operations, and regulatory hurdles have to be addressed. Both Indian and Thai companies felt that the present agreement in services between India and ASEAN is not very comprehensive and therefore the India–Thailand Comprehensive Economic Cooperation Agreement (CECA) will be beneficial only if it has substantial services sector coverage and can go beyond the autonomous level of liberalization. This is a key input, as it will support the development of the value chain within ASEAN and in other markets where both Thai and Indian companies have a presence.

In-Depth Survey of Select Services Sectors

This section focuses on services sectors where there is scope for enhanced trade, investment, and collaboration. These are infrastructure services such as transport and logistics, telecommunications, banking, and IT and information technology enabled services (ITeS) (where India has emerged as a global leader); movement of professionals; and specialized skills such as spa workers.

[11] According to statistics shared by Thailand, few Indian professionals received Thai work permits in 2010: 176 in engineering; 13 for medical services (doctors, nurses, physiotherapists); 2–3 for architects; and 2–3 for accountants/auditors/tax specialists, amongst others.

To enhance trade in services and investment flows and to encourage market integration and the development of value chains, there are three types of connectivity—physical connectivity, people-to-people connectivity, and institutional connectivity (Kimura, Kudo, and Umezaki 2011).

Physical Connectivity

This is crucial for integrating the South and Southeast Asian markets and developing production networks and service value chains. In the specific case of India and Thailand, there has been a significant amount of research and policy papers on transport and logistics connectivity, the establishment of communications networks and financial linkages (Asian Development Bank [ADB] 2008, 2009; De 2011; Kimura, Kudo, and Umezaki 2011). At the 11th India–ASEAN Summit in Brunei Darussalam on 10 October 2013, the Indian prime minister pointed out that *transport connectivity* is a strategic priority for the India–ASEAN relationship. The land route from India to ASEAN is through Thailand where Myanmar plays an important role. The two main links connecting India and Thailand are:

1. India–Myanmar–Thailand Trilateral Highway (IMTTH): India can be connected to Thailand by road from the northeast of India through Myanmar. The IMTTH is a cross-border transportation network being financed by the governments of India, Myanmar and Thailand. It links Moreh (in Manipur, India) with Mae Sot (in Tak, Thailand) through Bagan (in Mandalay, Myanmar).
2. Mekong–India Economic Corridor (MIEC): The corridor will link Chennai (India) with Bangkok (Thailand) through Dawei port (Myanmar) (Figure 10.2). The MIEC will be an extension of the Southern Economic Corridor from Myanmar and Thailand to other ASEAN countries such as Cambodia and Viet Nam.

The survey found that India and Thailand have to develop their domestic transport and logistics infrastructure to benefit from these two projects. Specifically, for the trilateral highway, there is a need for greater connectivity between the northeast regions in India with the rest of the country. At present, northeast India is connected with the

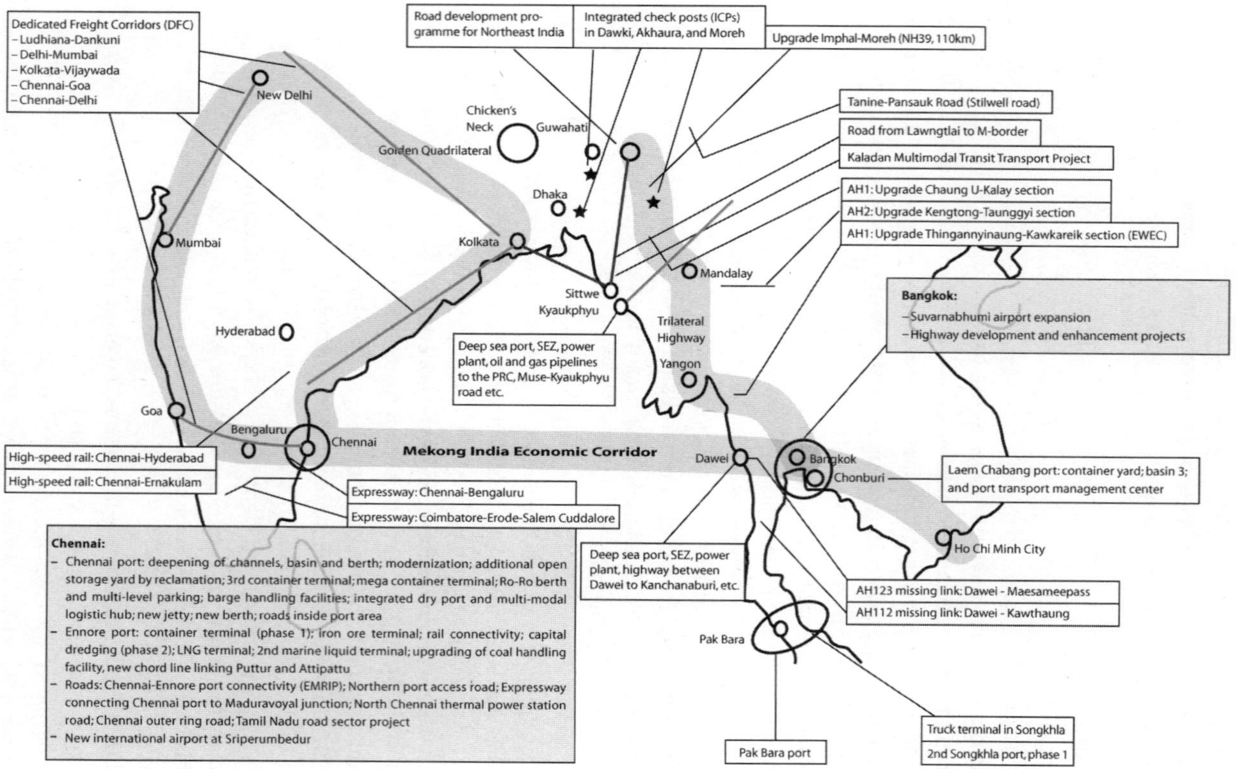

FIGURE 10.2 Select Infrastructure Projects for ASEAN–India Connectivity

Source: Adapted from Kimura, Kudo, and Umezaki (2011), Figure 5, p. 52; with inputs from the survey conducted by the authors.

rest of India through a 26-kilometre road from Siliguri, called Chicken's Neck (Figure 10.2). Development of this highway faces problems such as land acquisition and state government clearances. If India has to integrate with the ASEAN market, it should develop dedicated freight corridors, especially the Chennai–Kolkata corridor. The Delhi–Mumbai Industrial Corridor is under construction and the proposed Chennai–Bengaluru–Mumbai corridor will provide seamless connectivity. Survey participants said that India should focus on developing two hub ports—one on the west coast and the other on the east coast—and link them through dedicated freight corridors if the country wants to be part of the global production network. The Chennai port is one of the most active ports in India and is the gateway to ASEAN countries. Therefore, there is a need to develop the infrastructure of this port. However, the capacity of the Chennai port is limited, which may constrain future development. Similarly, the Thai ports have to be developed and connected to industrial corridors.

The survey found that there is potential for India–Thai joint ventures in transport and logistics projects through a public-private partnership (PPP) model. Thailand is strategically located to become a transshipment hub between South Asia, Southeast Asia, and East Asia. If the country can be connected with Myanmar through the land route, it can become an important channel of transportation between PRC, India, and the CLMV countries (Cambodia, Lao PDR, Myanmar, and Viet Nam) as well as with Malaysia and Singapore. The survey found that there is strong support from both the Indian and Thai governments for transport and logistics development. The first meeting between India and the ASEAN Connectivity Co-ordinating Committee was held in December 2012. The numerous bottlenecks to transport connectivity are discussed in the third section.

Telecommunications

This is another key sector for market integration. India and ASEAN are already cooperating in several communication projects including satellite tracking and broadband connectivity. The survey found that the telecommunications sectors in India and Thailand are at different levels of development. In both countries, telecommunications used to be a government monopoly, but the privatization process has been much faster in India. Unlike India, a telecommunications regulator has only recently been constituted in Thailand. In both countries, the role of the regulator is limited—it can give recommendations but such recommendations need not be implemented. In Thailand, the majority of the infrastructure is still owned and controlled by the government and the telecommunications sector works on a build-transfer-operate (BTO) model where the infrastructure is created by the private sector and then transferred to the government. In India, mobile telecommunications has a strong private presence and, compared to Thailand, the foreign investment and regulatory regime is more open.

At present, there is limited presence of Thai and Indian companies in each other's market. Indian companies such as Matrix Cellular International Service Private Limited and Idea Cellular Limited are investing in telecommunications infrastructure in Thailand through joint ventures. Bharti Enterprises has a wholly owned subsidiary in Thailand that provides data services. The Thai telecommunications market is quite saturated and Indian companies feel that investment opportunities are limited. There are no Thai companies in India in the telecommunications sector.

Survey participants pointed out that call rates between India and Thailand are high, Internet penetration in the two markets is low, broadband connectivity is poor, and both countries have not subscribed fully to the WTO Reference Paper on Telecommunications that aims to establish a sound regulatory regime. They felt that there is scope for developing telecommunications infrastructure connecting the two markets. Specifically, they referred to the scope for broadband connectivity through Myanmar or an undersea cable from India connecting the Andaman and Nicobar Islands to the southern Islands in Thailand, such as Phuket and Krabi. It was also pointed out that Indian companies have potential in software development and could jointly work with Thai telecommunications companies in telecommunications-related R&D software programming and maintenance.

Banking and Financial Services

The banking and financial services value chain is closely linked to the production value chain (Brockman and Stephenson 2012). The survey showed that with the growing commercial integration between the two markets, there is a need for greater financial integration for easier flow of funds.

Thailand is undergoing financial sector reforms. In 2002, after the Asian financial crisis, the Bank of Thailand (BoT) and the Ministry of Finance structured the Financial Sector Master Plan (FSMP), which was divided into three phases. In the first phase, foreign banks were allowed to open two branches; subsidiaries established between 2004 and 2008 under the first phase are entitled to open up to five bank branches, including a headquarter office. At present, Thailand is in the second phase of the FSMP (2010–14). In 2010, the BoT allowed foreign banks to open 20 more branches in Thailand, and in 2012 it allowed foreign banks to go through the subsidiary route and open 20 branches with a minimum capital requirement of 10 billion Baht. Up to 49 per cent foreign participation is allowed in the Thai banking sector.

The Indian banking sector is more open than in Thailand. The aggregate foreign investment from all sources in a private bank is a maximum of 74 per cent of the paid-up capital of the bank. In public sector banks, the overall statutory limit on FDI and portfolio investment is 20 per cent through the Foreign Investment Promotion Board (FIPB) route. A foreign bank is allowed to operate in India through one of the three channels: (i) branches, (ii) a wholly owned subsidiary and (iii) a subsidiary with aggregate foreign investment up to a maximum of 74 per cent in a private bank.

Indian Overseas Bank has a branch in Thailand, while ICICI Bank and the Bank of Baroda have representative offices there. The Bank of Baroda has been trying (since August 2005) to get a licence for a subsidiary office but has not been successful. Only one Thai bank—Krung Thai Bank—is present in India.[12]

According to the rules of the Reserve Bank of India (RBI), Indian banks have to maintain a ratio between national and foreign branches. An Indian bank can allow five countries to open joint ventures and subsidiaries and, therefore, Indian banks have to carefully select their foreign destinations. The return on investment in Thailand is low and therefore, several Indian banks are not keen on establishing operations in Thailand.

With growing inter-Asia trade, the idea of a common Asian currency has been mooted. However, survey participants felt that a common

[12] As on 30 September 2013 as per the RBI list available at http://rbidocs.rbi.org.in/rdocs/Content/pdfs/71207.pdf (accessed on 28 May 2015)

currency would not be feasible in the near future. Financial market integration happens in a phased manner and in the first phase there is a need to share information about the banking and financial systems and regulatory cooperation between the Indian and Thai central banks. They pointed out that the ASEAN Financial Integration Plan for 2015 is likely to lead to greater integration in the ASEAN region.

Information Technology and Information Technology Enabled Services

This is the most important component of India's services sector growth and accounted for over 33 per cent of services exports and around 18.5 per cent of India's total trade in services in 2012.[13] Indian companies are moving up the value chain and are focusing on market diversification and expansion of their products and services. After India signed the CECA with Singapore, several Indian IT companies have established their base in Singapore to cater to ASEAN countries, including Thailand on a project basis. Thailand is not a major IT / ITeS exporter, but the domestic market is large and less saturated than other ASEAN countries.

In both India and Thailand, the IT / ITeS sector is projected to grow at a rapid pace. In India it is projected to grow at a compound annual growth rate of 13–15 per cent during 2014 and the projection for Thailand is 13 per cent for 2010–2014 (National Association of Software and Services Companies [NASSCOM] 2014). Thai companies use international products such as Microsoft and Oracle and the associated software is imported from developed countries such as the US. Often, an Indian company's entry in Thailand is due to the presence of its global client in Thailand.

In India, 100 per cent FDI is allowed in the IT / ITeS sector, while Thailand allows only 49 per cent FDI. Due to the FDI restrictions and language issues, the survey found that only a few Indian companies operate in Thailand. Some companies operate through agents and provide services to sectors such as banking and telecommunications. Indian companies mainly do software project implementation, training, and maintenance. They pointed out that there is scope for Indian companies to diversify their industry and services base and provide IT / ITeS services in Thailand in sectors such as logistics and supply chain

[13] Calculated from UNCTAD Statistics.

management and content for telecommunications. A large number of second or third generation Thai of Indian descent provide low-end IT/ITeS services.

Participants pointed out that since the Thai government plays a major role in the IT sector, an inter-government agreement between India and Thailand in areas such as e-governance could benefit Indian companies. In 2009, Thailand's government outlined several projects to help close the digital divide. For software development, the Thai government has announced a series of measures to support the local software industry. The Software Industry Promotion Agency (SIPA) has led 'Buy Thai First' campaigns to persuade local small and medium-sized enterprises (SMEs) to buy Thai-developed software and has lobbied with the government to give tax incentives to local developers. Similarly, the Indian government has initiated a policy of 30 per cent local content for the hardware and electronics sector. This will link services delivery with local manufacturing and, thereby, impact trade patterns. However, survey participants were not sure whether such impacts would be positive or negative for service providers.

People-to-People Connectivity

People-to-people connectivity in terms of easier movement of professionals and workers facilitates bilateral trade and market integration. The movement of professionals is a key component of India's trade agreements, while Thailand seeks market access for certain specialized skills under its trade agreements. These two types of movements are examined as follows.

Professional Services

This has become an important component of India's services exports and it has the second largest share in India's export basket after IT/ITeS. The country has a large educated workforce that can provide services at competitive rates. The supply of professionals in Thailand is much lower. Both India and Thailand are defensive about opening up their respective domestic markets to foreign professionals and have imposed several restrictions, such as nationality and residency requirements and requirements to register with professional bodies. The domestic market is virtually closed to foreign professionals in India and Thailand in sectors such as legal and accountancy services.

The survey found that the movement of professionals between the two countries is limited. Survey participants pointed out that although the skill levels in professions such as engineering and management consultancy are higher in India and there is a demand in Thailand for these skills, bilateral trade will not increase unless market access and regulatory barriers to trade are addressed. In the past 8 years, citizenship has not been given to any Indian applicant in Thailand. Thai professional bodies fear that a large inflow of professionals from India may adversely impact the employment prospects of the local workforce. Some Indian professional bodies such as the Bar Council of India and the Council of Architecture have expressed a similar fear. Thus, professional bodies in both countries lobby against the removal of entry barriers for foreign professionals. Participants also pointed out that since the qualification requirements and standards in the two countries differ and they have limited knowledge about each other's market, there is a need for greater interaction and sharing of knowledge amongst professional bodies. For instance, the Institute Chartered Accountants of India can share information with the Institute of Certified Accountants and Auditors of Thailand. There is a shortage of management professionals in Thailand and the Institute of Management Consultants of India has expressed an interest in collaborating with the Institute of Management Consultants, Thailand for easier movement of professionals. The Dental Council of India also pointed out that there is scope for mutual recognition agreements (MRAs) between the professional bodies of the two countries for recognition of each other's qualifications in the areas of dentistry and nursing.

Workers with specialized skills such as cooks, spa workers, and yoga instructors are covered under 'other categories' in services trade agreements. India and Thailand have developed competence in alternative medicine (for example, Ayurveda) and beauty treatments. In Thailand, traditional spa and massage are an important contributor to revenue and employment, while India is globally recognized for yoga. The two countries share complementary skills and are keen to export such specialized skills to foreign markets. These skills are closely linked to the cultural, tourism, and healthcare services sectors.

Thailand is known as the 'Spa Capital of Asia' and after establishing their presence in the ASEAN region, the Middle East and developed country markets, Thai companies and spa workers are keen to explore the Indian market. There is significant scope for collaboration in this sector. For example, yoga instructors can combine with spa service providers to set up integrated wellness centres not only in India and Thailand but also in third countries. Companies from the two countries can jointly offer medical treatment packages linking the two markets.

The survey found that there is a demand for Thai spa specialists in India. Indian companies pointed out that Thai products are of good quality and Thai therapists have a good customer interface. There is also a shortage of spa therapists and experts in India due to which Indian companies such as Kaya Skin Clinic and VLCC get trainers from Thailand to train their staff. However, due to the minimum salary requirements of $2,500 in India, it is not profitable to employ spa specialists from Thailand on work permits, so they usually come on tourist visas for 6 months, which impacts the continuity of their services. It is also a misuse of market entry regulations. The survey participants pointed out that to enhance bilateral trade there should be collaboration between the Indian Spa and Wellness Association and the Thai Spa Association and between the Association of Beauty Therapy and Cosmetology, India (which has around 82 Thai members) and the Siamese Association of Beauty Therapy, Thailand.

Institutional Connectivity

Institutional connectivity through sharing of knowledge and regulatory synergies is key to the success of a trade agreement. Such connectivity can be at different levels—government-to-government, between professional bodies of the two countries, between industry associations, between government and businesses, and between businesses and businesses. It can be bilateral—between India and Thailand—and regional—between South Asia and ASEAN or India and ASEAN. The Indian and Thai governments share some common policies. Both are proponents of multilateral liberalization and have now focused on bilateral trade agreements since the Doha Round of WTO negotiations has not progressed. India's Look East policy complements Thailand's Look West policy. The governments of the two countries are engaged in trade negotiations in different forums and signed an Early Harvest Scheme in goods in 2004 that covered 82 product categories, aiming to reduce tariffs. The two countries have engaged in the India ASEAN services agreement, which was signed in September 2014. The two countries are engaged in the Bay of Bengal Initiative for Multi-Sectoral Technical and

Economic Co-operation (BIMSTEC) and are currently negotiating the India–Thailand CECA. While there is strong intent amongst the policy-makers of the two countries to enhance bilateral trade and investment flows, there are several barriers to trade and investment in services, which are discussed in the next section.

Barriers to Bilateral Trade and Investments

The survey found several barriers to bilateral trade and investment; most of them are common to both countries and can be addressed at the *institutional* level. First, both India and Thailand have a restrictive FDI regime in services. While the two countries have liberalized the manufacturing sector, the lack of liberalization in allied services such as logistics and banking is limiting the establishment of global value chains that can support production networks and efficient product deliveries. Second, the reform process in the two countries is slow and their regulatory frameworks are still weak. There is lack of inter-ministerial coordination. In several cases (such as the case of telecommunications in Thailand) foreigners are granted approvals on a case-by-case basis, making the procedure non-transparent. Multiple documents are required, which creates delays and causes operational uncertainty. Third, there is limited knowledge about each other's market—at the government, industry association, and company levels. Fourth, there is limited involvement by different stakeholders, industry bodies, and sector experts in the reform process and trade negotiations. Fifth, both India and Thailand have similar interests in gaining greater market access for service providers or Mode 4 in their respective trade negotiations. However, within Mode 4, Thailand wants greater market access for specialized skills, while Indian seeks easier entry for professionals. However, with respect to opening up of their domestic markets, both countries have a defensive approach towards liberalizing the movement of people.

Barriers Related to Investment and Movement of People in Thailand

On market-specific barriers, the Indian companies were asked to rank the barriers faced while investing in the Thai market on a 5-point scale, with 1 representing 'unimportant' and 5 for 'very important'.[14] For each factor, the percentage of respondents that rated it as 'very important' or 'important' was calculated and the factors were then ranked. The key barriers faced by Indian companies in Thailand are presented in Figure 10.3. This figure shows that Indian companies are facing multiple barriers in Thailand.

Indian companies were also asked about the barriers that they face with respect to the movement of people. In Thailand, a large number of professions such as engineering, accounting, legal, and architectural services are reserved for Thai nationals. In occupations where foreign nationals are permitted to work, a foreign national requires both a work permit and the correct work visa. However, different authorities issue these documents; the work permit is issued by the Ministry of Labour, whereas visas are given by the Ministry of Interior.

Thailand has been restrictive in giving work permits. Applicants must have a job offer with a person or company in Thailand that will pay a salary that meets the requirements in the Ministry of Labour's foreign labour regulations. In addition, the job should not fall under the category of jobs restricted for citizens of Thailand under the Thai Foreign Business Act, B.E. 2542 (A.D.1999),[15] the Thailand Ministry of Labour Ministerial Regulations, or any other applicable laws. In addition, there is some form of an Economic Needs Test (ENT) or a Labour Market Test, since work permits are not granted to foreigners for jobs for which a Thai national is available to join. To avoid these ENTs, it becomes necessary to draft a job description that will avoid undue scrutiny by the Thai official reviewing the application. To do this, a legal expert is hired to draft the application, which is expensive.

The Thai work permit allows the applicant to work at the company location listed in the work permit. This is a major barrier to IT companies that send workers on projects; at the end of a project, the worker cannot be transferred to another project within the country.

[14] This was a multiple-choice question and respondents marked more than one option. Several barriers received a very high rank, indicating the presence of a large number of restrictions in Thailand.

[15] For details of the professions restricted under the Thai Foreign Business Act, B.E. 2542 (A.D.1999).

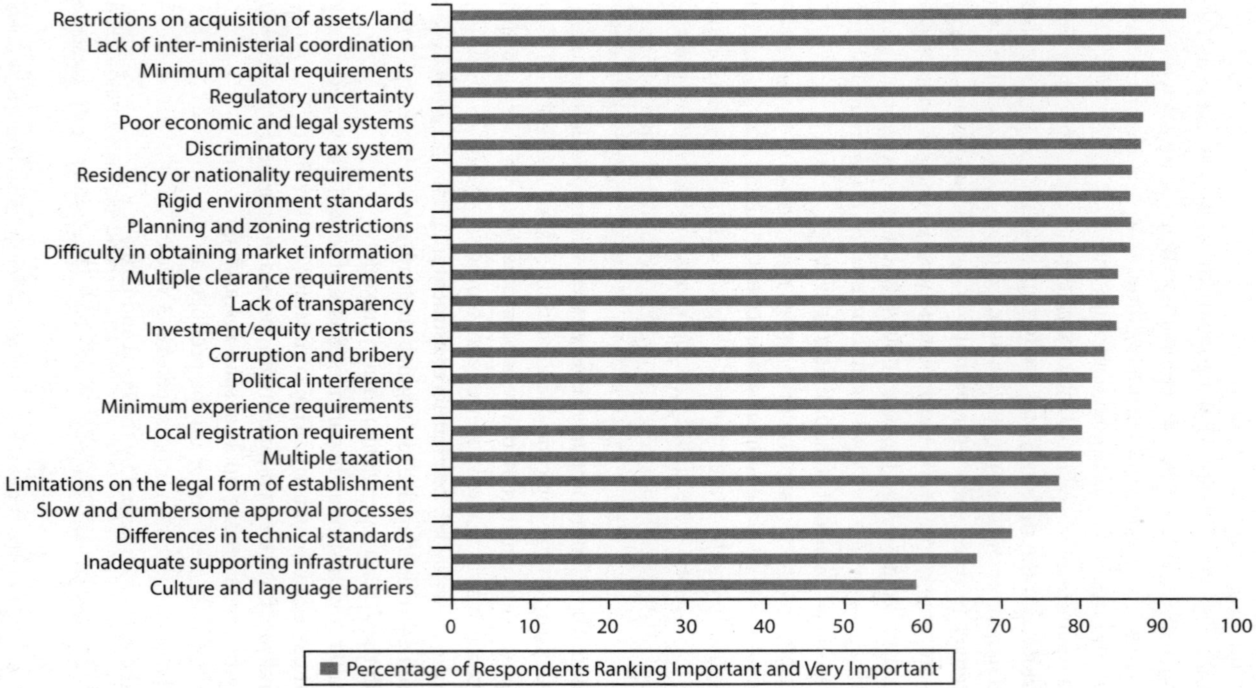

FIGURE 10.3 Ranks of Barriers Faced by Indian Companies in Thailand

Source: Authors' compilation from survey.

The company applying for the work permit is required to hold a minimum amount of registered capital per work permit; if the applicant is married to a Thai national, the required amount is 1 million Baht ($29,555).[16] If the company is registered with the BOI, it can obtain multiple work permits without increasing the registered capital, depending on the agreement with the BOI, but they need to hold a minimum of 1 million Baht in registered capital. If the company does not have BOI approval and the foreign employee is not married to a Thai national, the company requires 2 million Baht ($59,110) of registered capital for each work permit.

About 50 per cent of the Indian companies pointed out that it takes 55–60 days to get a visa for longer stays (a business visa is given on arrival). Also, the visa and work permit are usually issued for only 1 year and can be extended only for another year. Thus, there is a restriction on the length of stay. Moreover, in the past 6 years, the Thai government has not issued any citizenship or residence permits.

Barriers Related to Investment and Movement of People in India

The number of Thai companies interviewed was fewer and, therefore, it is difficult to rank their views on barriers. Thai companies referred to high land prices, difficulties in land acquisition, lack of regulatory transparency, lack of inter-government coordination, and high and multiple taxes as some key barriers to investment in India. They specifically referred to the differences in regulations and taxes across states that prohibit pan-India operations. Thai companies and individuals find it difficult to identify the right partners. Some of them have been cheated, which has led to scepticism. Thai companies also pointed out that it is generally difficult to do business with Indians, because there are delays in payments. In setting up Thai spas, spa and medicinal products have to be imported, but duties on spa products are as high as 30 per cent and the documentation process takes 2–3 weeks. India does not recognize the certificate issued by the Food and Drug Administration (FDA), Thailand, which acts as a barrier to bringing in products for the services.

[16] Converted using www.oanda.com; as on 29 May 2015.

One of the most important barriers to the movement of Thai specialist workers is the minimum salary condition of $25,000 per annum imposed on foreign nationals in India.[17] This barrier is particularly restrictive for Thai nationals in specialized services, such as spa and massage services. The survey participants pointed out that $25,000 per annum is a managerial-level salary and not that of a therapist or a masseuse. Around 50 spa projects in India had to close down due to this salary restriction.

Liberalization in International Trade Agreements

The previous sections show that trade agreements facilitate bilateral trade and enhance market integration. The survey identified some the trends and barriers to enhancing the role of services between India and Thailand. This section assesses the present status of liberalization in India and Thailand and scope for addressing these barriers through negotiations.

Multilateral Liberalization

Both India and Thailand are founder members of the WTO and are actively participating in the ongoing Doha Round of WTO negotiations. Thailand has a more restrictive regime for foreign investment than India and this is reflected in their Revised Offers submitted to the WTO in August 2005 and November 2005.[18] Both countries tend to offer below the level of their autonomous liberalization in the WTO.

There are differences in how India and Thailand define certain categories of service providers (for example, managers and specialists), but in general India's definitions are broader and the offers are better

[17] According to the visa regime in India, a foreigner seeking an employment visa should draw a salary of more than $25,000 per annum. However, this condition of an annual floor limit on income does not apply to: (a) ethnic cooks, (b) language teachers (other than English language teachers)/translators, and (c) staff working for the concerned Embassy/High Commission in India.

[18] For Thailand's Revised Offer to the WTO, see http://www.esf.be/pdfs/GATS%20Revised%20Offers/Thailand%20Revised%20Offer.pdf (accessed on 1 October 2016) and for India's revised offer to the WTO, see http://commerce.nic.in/trade/revised_offer1.pdf (accessed on 1 October 2016).

than those of Thailand for high-skilled workers or professionals. The schedule of sector-specific market access commitments of the two countries in the WTO Revised Offer shows that while the two countries have shown an interest in improving upon their Uruguay Round commitments, India's Revised Offers are much better. Following the MTN. GNS/W/120 classification that is used in the WTO negotiations on services, India offered to undertake commitments in 11 broad services sectors, while Thailand offered to take commitments in 10 broad services sectors. Both countries covered a limited number of sub-sectors within each of these broad categories. Some of the sensitive sectors for Thailand are integrated engineering services, medical and dental services, services provided by midwives, nurses, physiotherapists, and para-medical personnel, R&D services in social sciences and humanities, services related to management consulting, services incidental to energy distribution, placement and supply services of personnel, and tourist guide services. The sensitive sectors for India are education services, legal services, postal and courier services, and retail trade.

In the WTO, both India and Thailand have taken most favoured nation (MFN) exemptions to accord preferential treatment to select trading partners. In the WTO, both India and Thailand are demandeurs of Mode 1 and Mode 4. However, while India demands easier market access for high-skilled people, Thailand focuses on easier movement of specialized skills. Amongst ASEAN countries, Thailand is less offensive on services negotiations compared to countries such as Singapore, but more offensive than countries such as Malaysia, Indonesia, and the Philippines (Sally 2005). Along with other ASEAN countries (except Singapore), it is campaigning for an emergency safeguard mechanism in GATS to protect against a surge of imports in exceptional situations (Sally 2005).

Bilateral and Regional Liberalization

The bilateral and regional trade agreements of India and Thailand play a key role in the integration the South and Southeast Asian markets. India and Thailand have been engaged in multiple bilateral and regional agreements involving services, and are negotiating with each other in multiple international forums. The list of trade agreements of India and Thailand that include services is given in Appendix 10A.

Thailand has a special strategic and bilateral engagement with the US known as the Treaty of Amity and Economic Relations. Under this agreement, the US is allowed to have majority ownership of investment in most sectors, despite it being prohibited in the Thai Foreign Business Act, B.E. 2542 (A.D. 1999). The Treaty was signed in 1966 and ratified in 1968. This treaty gives similar treatment to an American majority-owned company as a Thai majority-owned company. Since Thailand has not taken major reform initiatives in the post-Uruguay Round period and the Treaty of Amity and Economic Relations covers several services sectors, US nationals have a distinct economic advantage vis-à-vis nationals from other countries such as India.

Regional Agreements

This section examines progress under Association of Southeast Asian Nations Agreement on Services (AFAS) and South Asian Association for Regional Cooperation Agreement on Trade in Services (SATIS), the two key regional agreements involving services, along with the ASEAN–India Comprehensive Economic Co-operation Agreement (CECA).

Association of Southeast Asian Nations Framework Agreement on Services

This agreement, signed on 15 December 2005, provides a legal framework for the broad parameters that enable ASEAN member states to progressively liberalize and integrate their services markets. It follows the structure and positive list approach of GATS for scheduling commitments, but it aims to expand the depth and scope of liberalization beyond GATS.[19] The AFAS also introduced the 'ASEAN Minus X' formula in the implementation of member states' services commitments.[20] Under this formula, countries that are ready to liberalize a certain service sector may proceed do so without having to extend the concessions to non-participating countries.

[19] Available at http://www.asean.org/6628.htm (accessed on 1 October 2016).

[20] Available at http://www.aseansec.org/8205.htm (accessed on 1 October 2016).

In 2007, ASEAN adopted the ASEAN Economic Community (AEC) Blueprint[21] to strengthen the institutional framework and have a unified legal identity by putting in place rule-based systems so that the AEC could be established by 2015.[22] In the area of trade in services, the Blueprint focuses on removing barriers to foreign investment, integrating markets in sectors such as air transport, health, tourism, and logistics services and MRAs in professions such as engineering, architectural services, and nursing to facilitate easier movement of people within ASEAN. As a member of ASEAN, Thailand is in the process of initiating domestic reforms to meet the regulatory requirements of this agreement.

South Asian Association for Regional Cooperation Agreement on Trade in Services

The SAARC Agreement on Trade in Services (SATIS) was signed between the SAARC countries (Afghanistan, Bangladesh, Bhutan, India, Maldives, Nepal, Pakistan, and Sri Lanka) at the 16th SAARC Summit held in Thimphu in April 2010 and came into force on 29 November 2012 after ratification by all SAARC member states. At present, negotiations on the Schedule of Specific Commitments of individual SAARC countries are ongoing.[23]

Association of Southeast Asian Nations–India Comprehensive Economic Co-operation Agreement

The Framework Agreement on the CECA between ASEAN and India was signed at the second ASEAN–India Summit in 2003 at Bali, Indonesia. This is India's only agreement where goods negotiations preceded services negotiations under a comprehensive agreement. After 6 years of negotiations, the ASEAN–India Trade in Goods (TIG) Agreement was signed in August 2009 and came into force on

[21] Available at http://www.asean.org/21083.pdf (pp. 8–11, accessed on 1 October 2016).

[22] Available at http://www.asean.org/21082.htm (accessed on 1 October 2016).

[23] Available at http://saarc-sec.org/areaofcooperation/detail.php?activity_id=46 (accessed on 23 October 2013).

1 January 2010. At the 10th ASEAN–India Summit in New Delhi on 20 December 2012, India and ASEAN concluded negotiations for FTAs in services and investment. In the 11th ASEAN–India Summit in Brunei Darussalam on 10 October 2013, it was announced that the ASEAN–India Trade in Services and Investment Agreement would be signed by the end of the year 2013 and become operational by July 2014.[24] The agreement was signed in September 2014.

According to information given by the Press Information Bureau of the Government of India,[25] the Trade in Services Agreement with ASEAN contains all features of a modern and comprehensive agreement on services and is in line with the other bilateral agreements that India has signed so far. Some important articles contained in the agreement are the ones on transparency, domestic regulations, recognition, joint committee on services and review, amongst others. Both India and ASEAN member states have taken GATS plus commitments in various services and modes of supply. While each ASEAN member state has tabled an individual schedule of commitments, India has tabled three schedules of commitments—one for the Philippines, one for Indonesia and one for the remaining eight ASEAN member states. India also agreed that in order to increase the participation of least developed countries, no additional requests would be tabled to the CLMV countries. All three schedules tabled by India are well within the existing autonomous regime of India. A brief annex on movement of natural persons (one of the key areas of interest for India) has been included in the agreement, which defines all categories of service suppliers, except independent professionals.

Bilateral Agreements

This section examines four bilateral agreements by India and Thailand, namely, Thailand–Australia Free Trade Agreement, Thailand–Japan Economic Partnership Agreement, India–Japan Comprehensive Economic Partnership Agreement, and India–Republic of Korea

[24] For details, see Ministry of External Affairs (2013).

[25] Available at http://pib.nic.in/newsite/PrintRelease.aspx?relid=109489 (last accessed on 21 May 2015.)

Comprehensive Economic Partnership Agreement in terms of their structure, coverage, and depth of commitments.

India and Thailand have different approaches in designing their FTAs. While India follows a fixed pattern, Thailand has customized its agreements to the requirements of its trading partner. This is reflected in the architecture of their respective agreements, which are compared in Table 10.4.

In terms of their commitments, under Mode 3 Thailand has gone beyond its autonomous regime in its bilateral agreements. For instance, in the agreement with Japan, in sectors such as wholesale trade and retail services that are under List 3 of the Foreign Business Act, B.E. 2543 (1999),[26] Thailand has allowed foreign participation. Moreover, in sectors such as travel and tourism services, foreign investment has increased from 49 per cent to 60 per cent. Compared to the WTO, Thailand has improved its commitment in sectors such as professional services, distribution services, education services, and hotel and restaurant services. In the agreement with Australia, Thailand allows 100 per cent Australian ownership in general management consulting services. For education services, Thailand permits Australian equity participation up to 60 per cent in some specialized tertiary education services. In its autonomous regime, Thailand permits 49 per cent foreign ownership in these sectors. India has not gone beyond its autonomous regime in bilateral agreements; however, it has improved its commitments compared to the WTO Revised Offer in sectors such as professional services, R&D services, telecommunications services, audiovisual services, and construction- and engineering-related services.

In movement of natural persons, while India made commitments under all four categories of service suppliers, Thailand has not covered independent professionals. Thailand seems to give preferential treatment to its bilateral trading partners in terms of temporary entry of people. For example, in the Thailand–Australia Free Trade Agreement, Australian business visitors do not require a work permit and can attend or conduct business meetings in Thailand for up to 15 days; this condition does not apply to business visitors from other countries, who require both a visa and a work permit. Thailand also has the

[26] In sectors listed in List 3, foreigners are prohibited from operating unless permitted by the Director-General.

provision of an Asia-Pacific Economic Cooperation (APEC) Australian Business Travel Card (ABTC) under the Thailand–Australia Free Trade Agreement. The ABTC cardholders are permitted to attend business meetings/seminars or conduct business contracts without engaging in making direct sales of goods to the general public, and they can supply services or can acquire remuneration in Thailand for up to 90 days. Thailand also permits spouses of service suppliers to work as managers, executives, or specialists for Thai companies. In its trade agreement, Thailand requests easier movement in specialized skills such as Thai chefs and spa workers.

In its bilateral agreements, India has given commitments in a wide range of professions across four categories of movements, namely, business visitors (BV),[27] intra-corporate transferees (ICT),[28] independent professionals (IP)[29] and contractual service suppliers (CSS).[30] It seeks market access for professionals. However, Indian commitments do not go beyond the domestic regime or the request that India makes is not beyond the work permit and visa regimes of its trading partners. None of India's trade agreements has provisions for specialized visas or free movements as under North American Free Trade Agreement (NAFTA), nor do India's trade agreements focus on liberalization of the entire value chain within each professional category. The professional categories that India seeks to liberalize under trade agreements do not match the ILO (International Labour Organization) classifications or any other internationally recognized labour classifications (for details, see Mukherjee and Goyal 2013).

Overall, in its bilateral agreements, India wants liberalization commitments in knowledge-based services, such as computer-related services, and Modes 4 and 1, while Thailand pushes for movement of specialized skills. Table 10.4 highlights that in their respective trade

[27] A person who visits another country for a short duration specifically for business negotiations and/or for preparatory work to establish a presence.

[28] Employee of a company who transferred from the originating country's office to an office of the same company in another country.

[29] A self-employed person who entered another country to perform a service on contract basis.

[30] Employee of a foreign company who enters another country temporarily in order to perform a service pursuant to a contract.

TABLE 10.5 Design and Coverage of India and Thailand's Bilateral Agreements

Parameters	India–Republic of Korea CEPA	India–Japan CEPA	Thailand–Japan EPA	Thailand–Australia FTA
Sectors covered	India has taken commitments in all 11 broad services sectors covered under the W/120 of the WTO (that is, MTN.GNS/W/120)	India has taken commitments in all 11 broad services sectors covered under the W/120 of the WTO	Thailand has taken commitments in 10 broad sectors. The excluded sector is health and social services.	Thailand has undertaken commitments in 8 broad sectors identified in W/120.[a] The three excluded sectors are environmental, financial, and health and social services.
Scheduling	GATS-style hybrid approach: positive listing of sectors and negative listing of barriers	GATS-style hybrid	GATS-style hybrid	Negative list
Sectoral carve-outs	Air transport services	Air transport services and cabotage in maritime transport services	Air transport services and cabotage in maritime transport services	–
Coverage	Dual coverage for investments (under investment chapter and under Mode 3 in trade in services chapter) and movement of people	Dual coverage for investments and movement of people	Dual coverage for investments and movement of people	Single schedule
Separate chapters on	Telecommunication, movement of natural persons and investments	Movement of natural persons and investments	Movement of natural persons and investments	Movement of natural persons, investments and e-commerce

(Contd.)

Table 10.5 (*Contd.*)

Parameters	India–Republic of Korea CEPA	India–Japan CEPA	Thailand–Japan EPA	Thailand–Australia FTA
Types of service suppliers covered	BV, CSS, ICT, IP	BV, CSS, ICT, IP	BV, CSS, ICT	BV, CSS, ICT
The Agreement has provision for bilateral co-operation in areas such as:	Energy; ICT; science and technology; SMEs; infrastructure and transportation; audiovisual; tourism; healthcare; government procurement; renewable energy resources	Environment; trade and investment promotion; infrastructure; ICT; science and technology; energy; tourism; SMEs; health; entertainment and information	Education and human resource development; enhancement of business environment; financial services; ICT; science, technology, energy and environment; SMEs; tourism; trade and investment promotion	Research and development; human resource and professional development and apprenticeship; trade in services data management; SMEs capacity enhancement; education; healthcare; tourism; promoting the facilitation of temporary entry of business people, in particular through developing the capacity to grant applications offshore for business entry; e-commerce
Government procurement	Co-operation	Separate chapter on government procurement. Proposes establishment of comprehensive chapter on government procurement.	Separate chapter on government procurement. Proposes establishment of sub-committee on government procurement.	Separate chapter on government procurement. Proposes establishment of working group.

Mutual Recognition Agreements	After the date of entry into force of this Agreement, upon request being made in writing by a Party to the other Party in any regulated service sector, the Parties shall encourage their respective professional bodies to negotiate and conclude, within 12 months of the date of entry into force of this agreement, in that service sector for mutual recognition of education, or experience obtained, requirements met, or licences or certifications granted in that service sector.	Parties should encourage their respective professional bodies to negotiate and conclude within 12 months any arrangement for mutual recognition of education, experience, licences or certification with a view to early outcomes.	Recognise the education or experience obtained, requirements met, or licenses or certifications granted, in whole or in part (compared to no indication of such scope in GATS), in the other Party. Recognition may be achieved through harmonisation or based on an agreement or arrangement between the Parties or may be accorded 'unilaterally'.	Parties lay down the possibility to recognise the education, experience obtained, requirements met, or licences or certifications granted in the other party and to conclude agreements in this respect. In addition, the parties are called upon to encourage their relevant bodies to enter into negotiations in this regard.

Note: [a] This document includes a 12th category: other services not included elsewhere; available on the WTO website at http://www.wto.org/english/tratop_e/serv_e/mtn_gns_w_120_e.doc (accessed on 15 September 2016).

BV = Business Visitors, CSS = Contractual Service Supplier, ICT = Intra-corporate Transferees, IP = Independent Professionals, CEPA = Comprehensive Economic Partnership Agreement, EPA = Economic Partnership Agreement, FTA = Free Trade Agreement, GATS = General Agreement on Trade in Services, SME = Small and Medium Enterprises, WTO = World Trade Organization.

Source: Compiled by the authors from the four trade agreements of the two countries.

agreements, India and Thailand have provisions for cooperation in several services sectors. Both India and Thailand seem to have a weak government procurement chapter in trade agreements where they propose to cooperate rather than take commitments. Similarly, they leave it to their respective professional bodies to enter into MRAs.

The Way Forward

The services sector contributes significantly to the GDP and employment of South and Southeast Asian countries. With globalization, liberalization, and increase in trade, the services sector has become a key component of market integration and global production networks through their role in the value chain. Services such as logistics and communications facilitate trade and enhance the global competitiveness of other services, manufacturing, and agriculture sectors. Countries in South and Southeast Asia have complementarities in services but they also compete with one another. In the past, trade agreements in this region focused only on trade in goods, but services is increasingly becoming an important component of trade agreements because it helps develop production networks and value chains. To understand how services can be traded within the region and how it can lead to improved efficiency, market integration, and the creation of value chains, this chapter discussed the case of bilateral trade in services between India and Thailand.

The study found that these two countries have certain commonalities in their approach to services trade. Both have a fairly restrictive FDI regime in services and the regulations in this sector are evolving. This creates a non-transparent operating environment for foreign service providers. The two countries are proponents of liberalizing the movement of people or Mode 4 in their WTO and bilateral/regional trade agreements. While India focuses on the movement of professionals, Thailand focuses on the movement of specialized skills. On their part, the two countries are sceptical about opening up the domestic market to the entry of foreign service providers (movement of people). There are some noticeable differences between the two countries. India is a much larger exporter of services than Thailand, but its exports are concentrated largely in the IT/ITeS sector and to developed countries. Thailand, on the other hand, has tried to develop competence in exports of some services such as tourism and alternative healthcare, and has focused on improving the competence of delivery of goods through improvements in services such as logistics. Thus, Thailand's export basket in services is more diversified than that of India.

There has been an increase in investment flows between India and Thailand in services. While Thai companies prefer to operate in India in sectors such as hotels and restaurants, Indian companies operate in Thailand in sectors such as construction services. However, the number of companies in each other's market is limited and the governments of the two countries do not regularly monitor and collect bilateral trade data. Therefore, this chapter is based on both secondary data and a primary survey. The chapter showed that Thai companies, unlike Indian companies, prefer to operate in the domestic market and within the ASEAN member states. Indian companies are more global than Thai companies and they prefer English-speaking, developed countries. It is only recently, after the global slowdown, that Indian companies have started to focus on Southeast Asia and, within Southeast Asia, on Singapore as their preferred destination. In Thailand, Indian companies have shown investment interest in sectors such as IT / ITeS and telecommunications. In banking, Indian banks are keen to have a presence, despite the fact that they have a small share in the Thai market. Thai companies and associations are interested in establishing a foothold in spa services in India.

This survey-based study found that integration in physical infrastructure and ease of movement of people are key to facilitating bilateral trade and investment and for integrating markets. The major barriers to physical connectivity and seamless supply chains are FDI restrictions, regulatory barriers, and procedural delays. There are other barriers to investment such as problems related to land acquisition, multiple clearance requirements, and lack of coordination between different government bodies. Business-facilitating instruments such as banks have a limited presence in each other's market and, despite their close proximity, transport connectivity between India and Thailand is poor. The survey also showed that most of the barriers to physical connectivity could be addressed through domestic reforms in the two countries. While for Thailand the key driver of domestic reforms is the ASEAN market integration of 2015, in India it is the slowdown in growth rate and FDI inflows. The pace of reforms in the two markets is relatively slow especially compared with other Southeast Asian countries and there is an urgent need to prioritize and implement reforms especially those related to the removal of FDI restrictions and regulatory hurdles. The two countries have to develop a sound institutional framework and there is a need for greater cooperation at three levels—government to government, amongst industry associations, and amongst businesses. Cooperation and sharing of information and knowledge will facilitate market integration.

The movement of people between the two countries is limited by the restrictive work permit and visa regimes of the two countries. While Thailand grants visas on arrival to Indian citizens, which enables them to travel for business, India does not have a 'visa on arrival' facility for Thai nationals. India should reciprocate. Some initiatives can be taken under the India–Thailand CECA, which will facilitate the movement of people. For example, India can relax or reduce the minimum salary condition for services that are of interest to Thailand and which the domestic market will benefit from without adversely affecting local labour. For instance, the Indian government can remove/reduce the $25,000 per annum salary condition for spa professionals, whereas for beauty services the restriction could remain. On a reciprocal basis, India can ask for easier work permit and visa conditions for its IT/ITeS professionals. Thus, the two countries can select certain categories of professionals and specialized skills as a first step to facilitate easier cross-country movements. The professional bodies of the two countries hardly interact and they prefer a closed domestic market. The professional bodies should start interacting and should share information on curriculum and registration processes, amongst others. Since the professional market in ASEAN is likely to become integrated through MRAs, a carefully designed chapter on movement of people under the India–Thailand CECA will benefit both countries. There are some issues such as language and cultural differences, low productivity of the workforce in the Indian services sector, and the lack of a social security agreement between India and Thailand, but these are not major impediments to trade if the work permit and visa barriers, barriers due to lack of recognition of each other's qualifications, nationality, and registration requirements are addressed. On the movement of people, this study found that unless there is cooperation at the institutional level, it is difficult to have market integration or sign agreements such as MRAs for professional cooperation.

India and ASEAN signed a services agreement in the year 2014. India and Thailand are also negotiating an India–Thailand CECA and services is a key component of this agreement. India's CECA negotiation with Thailand is part of its larger ASEAN integration strategy. This chapter found that India's commitments in different services sectors in the bilateral agreements are either equal to or lower than the level of autonomous liberalization. However, Thailand is willing to go beyond its domestic regime in trade agreements. Ideally, a bilateral trade agreement should go beyond the domestic regime to facilitate market integration. Nevertheless, if it even binds the existing regime, it provides operational certainty to businesses, since both countries will find it difficult to roll back the existing regime. Such operational certainty is important in countries such as India and Thailand that frequently change their regulatory regime. Since both India and Thailand continue to negotiate trade agreements such as the RECP market, integration will enable them to leverage each other's strengths. Collaboration in areas such as spa and Ayurveda will enable them to jointly access third-country markets. It will also enhance their joint bargaining power in RCEP vis-à-vis countries such as PRC.

Overall, the chapter found that for services market integration and the development of services value chains, countries in this region have to speed up their domestic reforms process, remove market access barriers, and implement a sound regulatory framework that enables foreign companies to operate in a transparent and non-discriminatory environment. The trade agreements of countries such as India and Thailand are weaker agreements, since they focus on cooperation rather than on commitments. Commitments under trade agreements may help speed up the domestic reform process in the region and integrate the services markets in South and Southeast Asia.

Appendix 10A

TABLE 10A.1 List of India's Free Trade Agreements and Preferential Trade Agreements That Include Services (as on October 2013)

FTAs/PTAs	Date of Signing	Date of Enforcement
Concluded		
India–Singapore CECA	June 2005	August 2005
India–Republic of Korea CEPA	August 2009	January 2010
India–Japan CEPA	16 February 2011	April 2011
India–Malaysia CECA	18 February 2011	July 2011
SATIS	April 2010	November 2012[a]
ASEAN–India CECA	December 2012	20 December 2012[b]
India–ASEAN Trade in Services and Trade in Investment Agreement	September 2014	–
Under Negotiation	**Launch of Negotiations**	
India–Thailand CECA	October 2003	
India–Mauritius CECPA	August 2005	
India–New Zealand CECA	April 2007	
India–Canada CEPA	November 2010	
India–Australia CECA	July 2011	
India–Indonesia CECA	October 2011	
India–EU BTIA	June 2007	
India–EFTA BTIA	October 2008	
RCEP Agreement between ASEAN + six (PRC, Japan, Republic of Korea, Australia, New Zealand, and India) or ASEAN+6 FTA	May 2013	
Under Consideration	**Date of Proposal**	
India–Russia CECA	February 2006	
India–Turkey FTA	September 2009	
CEPEA/ASEAN+6	December 2005	

Note: CECA = Comprehensive Economic Cooperation Agreement, CEPA = Comprehensive Economic Partnership Agreement, SATIS = SAARC Agreement on Trade in Services, CECPA = Comprehensive Economic Co-operation and Partnership Agreement, BTIA = Broad-based Trade and Investment Agreement, EFTA = European Free Trade Association, RCEP = Regional Comprehensive Economic Partnership.

Partnership, CEPEA = Comprehensive Economic Partnership for East Asia
[a] Available at http://saarc-sec.org/areaofcooperation/detail.php?activity_id=46 (accessed on 1 October 2016). The Agreement entered into force on 29 November 2012, and at present negotiations on the Schedule of Specific Commitments of individual SAARC countries are ongoing.
[b] At the 10th ASEAN-India Summit in New Delhi on 20 December 2012, India and ASEAN concluded negotiations for FTAs in services and investments. In the 11th ASEAN–India Summit in Brunei Darussalam on 10 October 2013, it was announced that the ASEAN-India Trade in Services and Investment Agreement would be signed by the end of the year 2013 and become operational by July 2014.
Source: Compiled from the Asia Regional Integration Centre (ARIC), Asian Development Bank accessible at https://aric.adb.org/india (accessed on 20 September 2016).

TABLE **10A.2** List of Thailand's Free Trade Agreements and Preferential Trade Agreements That Include Services (as on October 2013)

FTAs/PTAs	Date of Signing	Date of Enforcement
Concluded		
Japan–Thailand Economic Partnership Agreement	3 April 2007	1 November 2007
Thailand–Australia FTA	5 July 2004	1 January 2005
Thailand–New Zealand Closer Economic Partnership Agreement	19 April 2005	1 July 2005
AFAS	15 December 1995	2015
ASEAN–Australia–New Zealand Free Trade Agreement	27 February 2009	1 January 2010
ASEAN–Japan CEPA	14 April 2008	1 December 2008
ASEAN–Republic of Korea Agreement on Trade in Services	21 November 2007	1 May 2009
ASEAN–PRC CECA	29 November 2004	1 July 2005
ASEAN–India CECA	December 2012	2015
India–ASEAN Trade in Services and Trade in Investment Agreement	September 2014	–

(*Contd.*)

Table 10A.2 (*Contd.*)

FTAs/PTAs	Date of Signing	Date of Enforcement
Under Negotiations	**Launch of Negotiations**	
India–Thailand CECA	October 2003	
TUSFTA	June 2004	
Thailand–Chile Comprehensive FTA	1 April 2011	
TEFTA	October 2005	
ASEAN–EU FTA	May 2007	
ASEAN–Pakistan FTA	August 2009	
RCEP Agreement between ASEAN + six (PRC, Japan, Republic of Korea, Australia, New Zealand, and India) or ASEAN+6FTA	May 2013	
Under Consideration		
Republic of Korea–Thailand FTA	August 2003	
Pakistan–Thailand FTA	April 2004	
East Asia Free Trade Area (ASEAN+3) (PRC, Japan, and Republic of Korea)	November 2004	

Note: FTA = Free Trade Agreement, PTA = Preferential Trade Agreement, AFAS = ASEAN Framework Agreement on Services, CEPA = Comprehensive Economic Partnership Agreement, CECA = Comprehensive Economic Co-operation Agreement, TUSFTA = Thailand–US Free Trade Agreement, TEFTA = Thailand–European Free Trade Agreement.

Source: Compiled from Asia Regional Integration Centre (ARIC), ADB.

References

ADB. 2008. 'Transport and Trade Facilitation in the Greater Mekong Subregion—Time to Shift Gears', Evaluation Study, Operations Evaluation Department, Asian Development Bank, Manila, December.

———. 2009. 'Designing and Implementing Trade Facilitation in Asia and the Pacific', ADB and UNESCAP, Manila, November.

Board of Investment (BOI). 2010. '2010 Foreign Investor Confidence Survey Report—Summary Report', Thailand.

Brockman, Jane Drake and Sherry Stephenson. 2012. 'Implications for 21st Century Trade and Development of the Emergence of Services Value Chain', International Centre for Trade and Sustainable Development, Geneva, October.

De Backer, K. and S. Miroudot. 2013. 'Mapping Global Value Chains', OECD Trade Policy Papers, No. 159, OECD Publishing. Available at http://dx.doi.org/10.1787/5k3v1trgnbr4-en (accessed 15 September 2-16).

De, Prabir. 2011. 'Trade Facilitation in India: An Analysis of Trade Processes and Procedures', Working Paper Series No. 95, Asia-Pacific Research and Training Network on Trade.

DIPP. 2013. *Factsheet on Foreign Direct Investment* FDI Factsheet. Available at http://dipp.nic.in/English/Publications/FDI_Statistics/2013/india_FDI_July2013.pdf (accessed on 1 October 2016).

Kimura, F., T. Kudo, and S. Umezaki. 2011. 'ASEAN-India Connectivity: A Regional Framework and Key Infrastructure Projects', in F. Kimura and S. Umezaki (eds), *ASEAN-India Connectivity: The Comprehensive Asia Development Plan, Phase II*, pp. 1–56. Jakarta: ERIA Research Project Report 2010-7, ERIA.

López, A., Andrés Niembro, and Daniela Ramos. 2011. 'Global Value Chains, Services Offshoring and the Role of Human Resources: Lessons from Argentina', Universidad Nacional de General Sarmiento, Argentina.

Ministry of External Affairs. 2013. *Chairman's Statement of the 11th India-ASEAN Summit, Bandar Seri Begawan*. Government of India. Available at http://www.mea.gov.in/in-focus-article.htm?22311/Chairmans+Statement+of+the+11th+IndiaASEAN+Summit+Bandar+Seri+Begawan (accessed on 23 October 2013).

Mukherjee, Arpita and Tanu M. Goyal. 2013. 'Examining Mode 4 Commitments in India and the EU's Agreements: Implication for the India-EU BTIA', CARIM-India Research Report, Migration Policy Centre, European University Institute.

NASSCOM. 2014. 'NASSCOM Strategic Review', New Delhi.

Ohlin, B. 1933. *Interregional and International Trade*. Cambridge: Harvard University Press.

Rubalcaba, L., J. Gallego, and C. Hipp. 2011. 'Organisational Innovation, Service Innovation, and the Value Chain: New Trends and Policy Implications', Input Paper for the Workshop on January 25—Task 5, Europe INNOVA Sectoral Innovation Watch, European Commission, January.

Sally, 2005. 'Thailand's New FTAs and its Trade Policies Post Asian Crisis: An Assessment', mimeo. Available at www.bilaterals.org/IMG/doc/Razeen_Sally_2005.doc (accessed on 20 September 2016).

———. 2007. 'Thai Trade Policy: From Non-discriminatory Liberalisation to FTAs', *World Economy*, 30(10): 1594–620.

UN. 2014. 'Enhancing Regional Connectivity: Towards a Regional Agreement for the Facilitation of Cross-border Paperless Trade', Studies in Trade and Investment, United Nations, Thailand.

World Bank. 2013. *World Development Indicators—2013*. Washington D.C.: World Bank. Available at http://databank.worldbank.org/data/download/WDI-2013-ebook.pdf (accessed on 15 September 2016).

World Economic Forum. 2012. *The Shifting Geography of Global Value Chains: Implications for Developing Countries and Trade Policy.* Global Agenda Council on the Global Trading System.

WTO (World Trade Organization). 2012. *International Trade Statistics*. Available at https://www.wto.org/english/res_e/statis_e/its2002_e/its2002_e.pdf (accessed on 18 May 2015).

———. 2014. *International Trade Statistics*. Available at https://www.wto.org/english/res_e/statis_e/its2014_e/its2014_e.pdf (accessed on 20 May 2015).

Index

About the Editors and Contributors

Editors

Jayant Menon is Lead Economist at the Asian Development Bank (ADB), in Manila, Philippines, where he works on trade, international investment, and development issues. He holds adjunct appointments with the Australian National University of Canberra, Australia, University of Nottingham, England, UK, and Cambodian Institute for Cooperation and Peace, Cambodia. He has served on the Advisory Boards of the University of Nottingham, England Campus in Malaysia and the Cambodia Development Research Institute. Prior to joining ADB, he worked as an academic in Australia for more than a decade, mainly at the Center of Policy Studies at Monash University in Melbourne, Australia. He has authored and co-authored more than a hundred academic publications, mostly on trade and development, and particularly related to Asia.

T.N. Srinivasan is Samuel C. Park, Jr Professor of Economics Emeritus and Professor Emeritus in International and Area Studies at Yale University, New Haven, Connecticut, USA. Srinivasan is Distinguished Professor (2014–19) at the Indian Institute of Technology Madras, Tamil Nadu, India. He was elected Fellow of the Econometric Society, USA in 1970, Fellow of the American Association of Arts and Sciences in 1982, Fellow of the American Philosophical Society in 1999, and Foreign Associate of the National Academy of Sciences in 2000. He was named Distinguished Fellow of the American Economic Association, Tennessee, USA, in 2003 and was awarded the Padma Bhushan—the third highest civilian award of the Government of India—in 2007. In 1975, he was awarded the Mahalanobis Memorial Medal (International Award) of the Indian Econometric Society, India.

Contributors

Prema-chandra Athukorala is a professor of economics in the Arndt-Corden Department of Economics at the Australian National University, Canberra, Australia; Fellow of the Academy of the Social Sciences in Australia; and Honorary Professorial Research Fellow in the School of Environment and Development at the University of Manchester, UK. He has been a consultant to the World Bank, Washington, D.C., USA; Asian Development Bank, Manila, Philippines; Asian Development Bank Institute, Tokyo, Japan; World Trade Organization, Geneva, Switzerland; International Labour Organisation, Geneva, Switzerland; United Nations Industrial Development Organization, Vienna, Austria; International Trade Centre, Geneva, Switzerland; and the Australian Agency for International Development, Canberra, Australia.

Uttara Balakrishnan is currently a PhD student in the Agricultural and Resource Economics Department at the University of Maryland, College Park, USA. Her areas of research are development economics and sustainable agricultural policy. She has worked on the impact of agricultural pricing and procurement policies in South Asia and Sub-Saharan Africa. Her current research interests include identifying the future of high value manufacturing in India as well as the causal impact of the Mahatma Gandhi National Rural Employment Guarantee Act on child outcomes in India. She holds a master's degree in development economics from Yale University, New Haven, Connecticut, USA.

Choongjae Cho is a research fellow and head of South Asia team at Korea Institute for International Economic Policy, Sejong City, Republic of Korea. He teaches Indian economy at the Graduate School of International Studies at Sogang University in the Republic of Korea. He is currently a member of the board at the Korean Association of Indian Social Science Research and the Institute of Indian Studies, both in the Republic of Korea. He was an adviser to the National Economic Advisory Council, Republic of Korea and the National Intelligence Service, a consultative body for the president, in the Republic of Korea.

Alisa DiCaprio is a Research Economist at the Asian Development Bank Institute in Tokyo, Japan. She is on secondment from the Asian Development Bank (ADB) where she is a Regional Cooperation Specialist in the Economic Research and Regional Cooperation Department. Prior to joining ADB, she worked for the United Nations University, New York University, and the US Department of Commerce. Her current research explores ways to optimize the development impact of trade. Specific workstreams in this area include the digitization of trade, trade finance gaps, e-commerce, and issues specific to fragile and landlocked states.

Raveen Ekanayake is a research officer at the Institute of Policy Studies, Colombo, Sri Lanka. He was previously engaged as a credit analyst at a state sector development bank. He holds a bachelor's degree in Science Accounting and Finance from the University of London, UK, and a master's degree in public policy, specializing in economic policy from the Australian National University in Canberra. His research interests are in the areas of foreign direct investment, trade policy reforms, and export-oriented industrialization.

Tanu M. Goyal is a consultant at the Indian Council for Research on International Economic Relations (ICRIER), New Delhi, India. She has been working at ICRIER since 2008 and her research interests include trade in services, retail sector, food supply chain, international trade agreements, and policy and regulatory issues. Most of her work concerns trade, openness, and restructuring of the Indian economy in the global landscape. Goyal holds a master's degree in economics, with specialization in world economy, from Centre of Trade and Development, Jawaharlal Nehru University, New Delhi, India.

Anwarul Hoda, a former civil servant, is Chair Professor, Trade Policy at the Indian Council for Research on International Economic Relations, New Delhi, India. He has held senior positions in the Ministry of Commerce and Industry, Government of India, where his responsibility was trade negotiations under the auspices of the General Agreement on Tariffs and Trade. He was the Chief Policy Coordinator in the Government of India during the Uruguay Round. From 1994–99, he worked as Deputy Director General at the World Trade Organization, Geneva, Switzerland. During 2004–09, he was a member of the Planning Commission, Government of India.

Rajat Kathuria is Director and Chief Executive at the Indian Council for Research on International Economic Relations, New Delhi, India. He has over 20 years' experience in teaching and 15 years' experience in economic policymaking besides research interests in a range of issues relating to markets, regulation, and competition policy. He has worked with the World Bank, Washington, D.C. as a consultant and carried out project assignments for a number of international organizations, including the International Labour Organization, Geneva, Switzerland; United Nations Conference on Trade and Development, Geneva, Switzerland; LirneAsia, Colombo, Sri Lanka; World Bank, Washington, D.C., USA; and Asian Development Bank, Manila, Philippines.

Mansi Kedia is a consultant at the Indian Council for Research on International Economic Relations, New Delhi, India. She has close to 6 years of policy experience in telecom regulation and competition issues in India. Her other research interests include industrial policy, foreign direct investments, high value manufacturing, and compliance cost of taxation. She has published work in the aforementioned areas of policy research. She also has a background in management consulting and financial services. She has worked for about 4 years in the industry, across functions at different levels.

Arpita Mukherjee is a professor at the Indian Council for Research on International Economic Relations, New Delhi, India. She has several years of experience in policy-oriented research, working closely with the government in India as well as policymakers in the European Commission and its member states, the US, Association of Southeast Asian Nations, and East Asian countries. She has conducted studies for different international organizations, Indian industry associations, and international foundations. Her research is a key contributor to India's negotiating strategies in the World Trade Organization and bilateral trade agreements.

Ramesh Paudel is a consultant with the World Bank. He recently finished his consulting role at the Ministry of Finance, Government of Nepal, where he worked as a development policy expert. Previously, he was a visiting fellow at the Australian National University, Canberra, Australia. Paudel has extensive research and teaching experience in Nepal and Australia. His research interests include international trade liberalization and reforms, foreign direct investment, landlocked economies, development economics, and macroeconomics. Paudel has published several academic papers in peer-reviewed journals as well as working papers. He has also authored a book, *Financial Liberalization in*

Sri Lanka: An Analysis (2010), and co-authored *Rural Economics* (2002), and *Government Accounting System of Nepal* (2001).

Durgesh Kumar Rai is a research associate at the Indian Council for Research on International Economic Relations, New Delhi, India. His areas of research include international trade, regional/bilateral economic integration and cooperation, human capital and economic development, and migration. He has done MPhil in economics from Jawaharlal Nehru University, New Delhi, India. He has worked in the areas of India's international trade and policy, trade in services, regional and bilateral economic and trade agreements, manufacturing growth and labour regulations in India, international and regional productions networks, and human capital and development of information technology–business process outsourcing industry in India.

Manjeeta Singh teaches economics at the Bhavan's Usha and Lakshmi Mittal Institute of Management, in New Delhi, India. Prior to that, she worked as a research associate at the Indian Council for Research on International Economic Relations, New Delhi, India. Her research interests include policy-oriented research on international trade and economic development. She is particularly interested in firm-level trade dynamics. She has worked on issues related to international trade, regional bilateral trade agreements, and global value chains. She has a PhD in economics from Jawaharlal Nehru University, New Delhi, India.

Sithanonxay Suvannaphakdy is Trade Facilitation Specialist in the Department of Import and Export, Ministry of Industry and Commerce of the Lao People's Democratic Republic (Lao PDR). Prior to this, he worked as a research associate for the Asian Development Bank, Manila, Philippines, and the National Economic Research Institute in Lao PDR. His current research interests focus on the integration of small- and medium-sized enterprises into the global value chains, trade facilitation in fragile and landlocked states, and dynamic panel-data modelling.

Meenu Tewari teaches Economic and International Development at the University of North Carolina at Chapel Hill, USA. Her research focuses on the political economy of development, industrialization, and institutional reform in the public and urban sectors. This includes the changing nature of work in rapidly urbanizing low-income economies and the challenge of skill formation and upgrading within regional and global production networks. Her work has been published in several journals including *World Development*, *Competition and Change*, *Environment and Planning A*, *Oxford Development Studies*, and *Global Economy Journal*.

C. Veeramani is an associate professor at the Indira Gandhi Institute of Development Research (IGIDR) Mumbai, India. He got his PhD in economics from Jawaharlal Nehru University, New Delhi, India, in 2003. Prior to joining IGIDR, he worked at Indian Council for Research on International Economic Relations, New Delhi, India, and Indian Institute of Technology Bombay, Maharashtra, India. He is the recipient of the EXIM Bank International Economic Development Research Award 2003 for the best doctoral dissertation in International Economics. He is the Joint Managing Editor of the *Journal of Quantitative Economics* (Springer) and Economics Area Editor of the *Journal of Indian Business Research* (Emerald).

Swarnim Waglé is a member of the National Planning Commission in the Government of Nepal, ranked at par with an assistant minister. He served earlier in the same position between May 2014 and November 2015, and advised on the formulation of growth strategies. Waglé worked as an international development professional for more than 15 years on policy assignments in over 20 countries, most recently as a senior economist at the World Bank in Washington, D.C. He holds a PhD in economics from the Australian National University and an MPA in International Development (MPA/ID) from Harvard University, Cambridge, Massachusetts, USA.

Ganeshan Wignaraja is a Senior Research Associate at the Overseas Development Institute, UK, and was formerly an advisor in the Economic Research and Regional Cooperation Department of the Asian Development Bank in Manila, Philippines. During 2012–15, he was the Director of Research at the Asian Development Bank Institute in Tokyo, Japan. He has published 16 books on trade, regional integration, infrastructure and development strategies including *Pan-Asian Integration: Linking East and South Asia* (2009), *Production Networks and Enterprises in East Asia* (2016), and *Connecting Asia: Infrastructure for Integrating South Asia and Southeast Asia* (2016).